# Ownership, Financial Accountability and the

There is something visceral about ownership. This is mine; you can't have it. This is mine; you can share it. This is ours. Try to find it.

Contemporary literature and investigative journalism are showing that the scale of the problem of tax evasion, money laundering, organised crime, terrorism, bribery, corruption and gross human rights abuses is vast.

Ownership – specifically, the quest to identify beneficial owners – has been chosen by national and international regulators as the touchstone, the litmus test in the fight back. An owner by definition must possess something for which they are financially accountable. But what is meant by "ownership"? This book explains why ownership is pivotal to accountability and what ownership means in common law, civil law and Shariah law terms. It looks in detail at state, regional and international transparency strategies and at an equally powerful global private counter-initiative to promote beneficial ownership avoidance through the use of so-called "orphan structures". Where there is no owner, there is no accountability. The distinction between privacy and legitimate confidentiality on the one hand and concealment on the other is explained with reference to commercial and trade law and practice, principles of corporate governance and applicable business human rights. This book introduces one further counter-initiative: the phenomenon of transient ownership made possible through the use of cryptocurrency and the blockchain. The study concludes with a blueprint for action with recommendations addressed to states, international organisations, practitioners and other stakeholders.

**Paul Beckett** has forty years' experience as a lawyer, practising offshore as a commercial and trust specialist and a human rights defender. He graduated from Worcester College, Oxford, in 1978 with First Class honours in Jurisprudence. He also completed a Master of Studies in International Human Rights Law at New College, Oxford, in 2014. He is a member of the Solicitor Judges Division, Law Society of England and Wales, the Chartered Institute of Arbitrators and the Society of Legal Scholars. He has written extensively on finance, banking, taxation and human rights law.

# The Law of Financial Crime
Series Editor: Nicholas Ryder

Available titles in this series include:

For more information about this series, please visit: www.routledge.com/
The-Law-of-Financial-Crime/book-series/FINCRIME.

# Ownership, Financial Accountability and the Law

## Transparency Strategies and Counter-Initiatives

Paul Beckett

Routledge
Taylor & Francis Group

LONDON AND NEW YORK

First published 2019
by Routledge
2 Park Square, Milton Park, Abingdon, Oxon OX14 4RN

and by Routledge
605 Third Avenue, New York, NY 10017

First issued in paperback 2020

*Routledge is an imprint of the Taylor & Francis Group, an informa business*

*British Library Cataloguing-in-Publication Data*
A catalogue record for this book is available from the British Library

*Library of Congress Cataloging-in-Publication Data*
Names: Beckett, Paul, 1956–
Title: Ownership, financial accountability and the law: transparency strategies and counter-initiatives / Paul Beckett.
Description: Abingdon, Oxon ; New York, NY : Routledge, 2019. | Series: The law of financial crime
Identifiers: LCCN 2019002255 | ISBN 9781138359888 (hardback) | ISBN 9780429433443 (ebook)
Subjects: LCSH: Finance—Law and legislation. | Property—Law and legislation. | Commercial crimes—Law and legislation.
Classification: LCC K1066 .B43 2019 | DDC 343/.02—dc23
LC record available at https://lccn.loc.gov/2019002255

ISBN 13: 978-0-367-72915-8 (pbk)
ISBN 13: 978-1-138-35988-8 (hbk)

Typeset in Galliard
by Apex CoVantage, LLC

This book is dedicated to my wife, Dr Lesley M. Stone

# Contents

# Acknowledgements

I practise offshore as a commercial and trust specialist and a human rights defender, with many years of experience in dealing with the rich and powerful and with the hard pressed and powerless. *Ownership* has been generated out of this contradiction.

*Ownership* follows on from where *Tax Havens and International Human Rights* (which was published by Routledge in October 2017) left off. I have acknowledged in that earlier book those to whom I am indebted for supporting the writing of it. My thanks to them extend to the writing of *Ownership*, which serves as a companion volume to it.

In the course of writing *Tax Havens and International Human Rights*, I became increasingly aware of the worldwide industry in beneficial ownership avoidance structures and felt that this deserved a more extensive piece of research and commentary in its own right. Accountability avoidance strategies have a generic adverse impact on international human rights but have a far wider footprint. They underpin tax evasion, money laundering, organised crime, terrorism, bribery and corruption. Transparency initiatives have not yet come to terms with beneficial ownership avoidance and yet are particularly susceptible to it, having elected to use "ownership" as the litmus test for both registration and accountability.

*Ownership* is the result.

My wife Dr Lesley Stone has accommodated my passion for human rights for decades, and her support during the writing of *Ownership* has meant the world to me. *Tax Havens and International Human Rights* first appeared on the booksellers' shelves on the day of our 30th wedding anniversary. There have been times this past year when we both felt married to *Ownership* as well.

Thanks are also due to our elder son Dr Christopher Beckett of Edinburgh University for his guidance on presentational methodology – it takes a civil engineer to help a lawyer draw up his structural plans.

Blue-sky thinking with my colleague at MannBenham, Advocate Carly Stratton, set many a thought train in motion regarding cryptocurrencies and the blockchain.

Written by a middle-aged lawyer, this book has the faults of all legal writings (and of middle-aged lawyers) and may at times lapse into the arcane. For this, your author apologises.

Paul Beckett
Union Mills, Isle of Man
1 January 2019

# 1 Introduction

## Why ownership matters

There is something visceral about ownership.

This is mine; you can't have it. This is mine; you can share it. This is ours. Try to find it.

Contemporary literature and investigative journalism show that the scale of the problem of tax evasion, money laundering, organised crime, terrorism, bribery, corruption and gross human rights abuses is vast.[1]

Ownership has been chosen by national and international regulators as the touchstone, the litmus test in the fight back. An owner by definition must possess something for which they are financially accountable. But what is meant by "ownership"?

The theme is why and, more importantly, how a super elite manages to own nothing yet benefit from so much. The why is easily understood: wealth, power and influence are addictive. The how is more difficult to unknot: legions of lawyers, accountants, tax and financial advisers are busying away combining elements, plotting charts and formulating strategies. In the opposing ranks, far fewer in number, compliance professionals attempt to match or thwart them,

---

1 Many of the issues considered in this book are evolving rapidly, and wherever possible, I have selected research materials which can be accessed easily on the web. The economic impact analysis, the investigative journalism and the naming of names I leave to others. See the work of the International Consortium of Investigative Journalists – the *Panama Papers* <www.icij. org/investigations/panama-papers/> accessed 25 November 2018 and the *Paradise Papers* <www.icij.org/investigations/paradise-papers/> accessed 25 November 2018. Nicholas Shaxson's work is a leader in the field – *Treasure Islands: Tax Havens and the Men Who Stole the World* (The Bodley Head, London, 2011) and *The Finance Curse: How Global Finance Is Making Us All Poorer* (The Bodley Head, London, 2018). See also Oliver Bullough *Moneyland: Why Thieves and Crooks Now Rule the World and How to Take It Back* (Profile Books Ltd., 2018). A statistical and economic analysis is provided by Gabriel Zucman (Teresa Lavender Fagan tr), *The Hidden Wealth of Nations: The Scourge of Tax Havens* (The University of Chicago Press, 2015). On a commercial level, investor confidence in financial markets depends in large part on the existence of an accurate disclosure regime that provides transparency of beneficial ownership and control structures: Erik P M Vermeulen, *Beneficial Ownership and Control* (OECD Corporate Governance Working Papers, 18 January 2013) <https://doi. org/10.1787/5k4dkhwckbzv-en> accessed 25 November 2018. Useful websites for further study (all of which are referred to in this book) are listed in the Appendix to this chapter.

move for move. Somewhere in between stand the lawmakers and regulators and, to one side, the politicians.

The separation of ownership and accountability on the one hand from benefit on the other is not esoteric financial wizardry. The anonymisation of a super elite removes them from the day-to-day grind of society and can dull their social conscience. If you are a member of such a super elite, perhaps this book will be a whetstone. The rest of us have to care, because the manipulation of ownership and the avoidance of accountability are the means by which our well-being and sustainability are imperilled.

Long familiar structures, state sanctioned and created to meet the developing needs of commerce and society – trusts, charities, Wakf, foundations, corporations, partnerships – have not ceased to evolve, if for no other reason than that the needs of commerce and society have themselves not ceased to develop. Having existed for centuries, their very existence predicated on the desire to separate ownership from benefit, the legal DNA of these structures is being altered to serve darker purposes. The rise of cryptocurrencies and the blockchain have added to the complexity.

This book is arranged sequentially and best read as such, but each chapter is complete in itself and can be studied without first having had to study the others.

## Chapter 2: What is meant by ownership?

Ownership is key to the transparency strategies – it is what those strategies aim to discover, in order to attach accountability to an owner. Yet from a philosophical and legal perspective, it is an enigma. The international, regional and national transparency initiatives all have the search for the owner at their core but do not appreciate the fluidity of the concept.

This chapter looks at what is meant by ownership in three legal systems: common law and equity, civil law and Shariah law. It poses the question whether "ownership" and "beneficial ownership" are capable of definition and, if so, whether that definition can be fixed and universal or must perforce be fluid and fragmentary. Applying theory to practice, what it means to be an "owner" of generic corporations, generic trusts, the Wakf and Foundations is explored.

## Chapter 3: Disclosure and registration initiatives

This chapter is divided into nine parts, which, like the chapters of this book themselves, can be read independently of any of the other parts but which are best understood when read sequentially. Transparency strategies are international, regional and national, but all have in common the use of ownership as a defining marker – either built into them as working definitions or tacitly underpinning them as necessary investigative steps in a reporting process.

The pioneering, fundamental transparency strategies pioneered by the World Bank and the G20 appear at first sight to be comprehensive. Yet they fall far short of evidencing a working understanding of the issues.

Held up as the gold standard, the work and methodology of the Financial Action Task Force is on close textual and contextual analysis unfit for purpose. This is of crucial importance, as it is the FATF standards on what constitutes "ownership" which have been adopted uncritically by the OECD, the European Union and the Council of Europe MONEYVAL.

The work and strategies put forward by each of those three organisations is examined in detail. This includes the OECD initiatives on bribery and responsible business conduct, the exchange of information on request, automatic information exchange and Base Erosion Profit Shifting (BEPS) together with the Fifth Anti-Money Laundering Directive of the European Union. The Council of Europe MONEYVAL is a smaller scale version of the FATF, regulating jurisdictions which either did not make the cut for FATF membership or which volunteered to be regulated in this secondary market.

Three national jurisdictions are sampled.

The Foreign Account Tax Compliance Act 2010 (FATCA) of the United States of America is boldly extraterritorial, an extraterritoriality enabled by the practice of the United States of taxing its citizens on their worldwide income regardless of where they live. This is a one-way valve when it comes to information flow but is not as comprehensive as it makes out. Content to identify "US Persons" without providing any guidance as to how these "US Persons" are deemed connected to a structure, it simply ducks the question of ownership and throws the burden of identifying owners on reporting institutions according to the laws of whichever jurisdiction they are located.

In introducing Unexplained Wealth Orders, which deem who is an owner and place the burden of proof squarely on the person on whom a UWO is served to prove otherwise, the United Kingdom is giving way to pragmatism. The United Kingdom follows the extraterritorial lead of the United States when it makes demands of the British Overseas Territories to disclose the beneficial owners of structures in their jurisdictions. It offers no guidance on how to define or discover "beneficial owners". The storm of anti-colonial protest against this "shades of Empire" initiative is deepening.

As a case study of how workable (or not) beneficial ownership legislation can be when drafted to meet the FATF standard, the Beneficial Ownership Act 2017 of the Isle of Man is analysed.

Question marks hang over the transparency strategies. Is there a genuine political will to eradicate beneficial ownership avoidance? Do the inherent flaws in the strategies – flaws of which those framing the strategies may not be wholly unaware – point to a reluctance to resolve the problem?

## Chapter 4: Confidentiality versus concealment

In this chapter, the distinction between privacy and legitimate confidentiality on the one hand and concealment on the other and their legitimacy or abuse is explained with reference to commercial and trade law and practice, principles of corporate governance and applicable business human rights. There is a real difference between the rights of contracting parties to keep the details of their negotiations and agreements confidential between them and the claimed right of business organisations to conceal their true ownership and control. This chapter looks at the legitimate limits of commercial confidentiality.

Opening with what is meant by "privacy", the chapter then examines to what extent privacy is a principle of commercial confidentiality under English Common Law and the law of the European Union.

To what extent must privacy rights be set aside in the interests of good corporate governance? This is explored on an international, regional and national level: the United Nations Global Compact (2000) and the United Nations Convention Against Corruption (2004), the United Nations Guiding Principles on Business and Human Rights 2011, IGCN Global Governance Principles and IGCN Stewardship Principles, Guiding Principles issued by the Islamic Financial Services Board, the UK Corporate Governance Code (July 2018) and a century-old American perspective.

The relationship between privacy and business human rights, including the human rights of companies, is analysed.

## Chapter 5: "Orphan Structures"

This chapter reviews the burgeoning global fiduciary services promotion of ownerless entities, sold expressly to those wanting to be held wholly unaccountable. So-called "orphan structures" render any beneficial ownership registration or disclosure system toothless. Yet none of the transparency strategies analysed in this book pays any heed to them or even acknowledges the existence of this worldwide industry in accountability avoidance.

What are "orphan structures", where are they and how do they wholly avoid there being a beneficial owner?

The chapter sets "orphan structures" in their jurisdictional context and examines how they are further privileged in terms of immunity from lawsuit, absence of public registration, impunity concerning fraudulent transfers of property and protection against "whistle-blowers".

The "orphan structures" reviewed are: Seychelles IBC; Bahamas Executive Entities; Cayman STAR Trusts; BVI VISTA Trusts; non-charitable purpose trusts (with a case study on the Isle of Man Purpose Trusts Act 1996); foundations as a generic concept, and specifically the Liechtenstein private-benefit foundation, Panama Private Foundation and Nevis Multiform Foundation.

## Chapter 6: Cryptocurrency and the blockchain

This chapter introduces one further counter-initiative. This is the phenomenon of *transient ownership* made possible through the use of cryptocurrency and the blockchain. The nature of both cryptocurrency and blockchain transactions is analysed and how regulations and legal analysis are capable of adapting to the new technology.

The technical definition of cryptocurrency is followed by its review from an ownership perspective. Due diligence and regulation initiatives on the part of the European Union and the Financial Action Task Force are analysed. There is a case study in the regulation of cryptocurrency by the Isle of Man.

Blockchain is set in the context of the Fourth Industrial Revolution. How the blockchain facilitates an absence of ownership transparency through anonymity and pseudoanonymity and its role in "outlaw" or "anational" transactions are reviewed. As an example of the exploitation of these possibilities, the introduction by Delaware, United States, of the blockchain maintenance of corporate records serves as a case study.

The challenges posed by cryptocurrency in the identification of owners have become massively more fragmented and numerous with the rise of Initial Coin Offerings (ICOs). The nature of an ICO and its associated risks are explained. The concept of an ICO in the context of ownership transparency is reviewed. Ownership as a regulatory criterion is examined, using Switzerland, the United States, Bermuda and a Shariah law analysis as examples.

## Chapter 7: Recommendations

This chapter sets out my recommendations for legislative and regulatory initiatives and for further study in this field.

This book has been written for policy makers and regulators; for legal, accountancy and tax practitioners; and for academics and students active in the fields of financial crime and regulation, banking and finance law. The areas it covers are rapidly evolving, and therefore wherever possible I have prioritised online sources as research materials and as suggestions for further study.

The law is as stated at 1 January 2019.

# Appendix

## Useful websites[2] (in alphabetical order of organisation)

| Organisation | Website |
|---|---|
| Accounting and Auditing Organization for Islamic Financial Institutions (AAOFI) | http://aaoifi.com |
| Ahlul Bayt Digital Islamic Library Project | www.al-islam.org |
| Alternative Investment Management Association Ltd, The | www.aima.org |
| American Bar Association | www.americanbar.org |
| Amnesty International – Corporate Accountability | www.amnesty.org/en/what-we-do/corporate-accountability/ |
| Anti-Corruption Digest | www.anticorruptiondigest.com |
| Bahamas Investor, The | www.thebahamasinvestor.com |
| Business & Human Rights Resource Centre | www.business-humanrights.org |
| Business and Industry Advisory Committee to the OECD | www.biac.org |
| Center for Public Integrity, The | www.publicintegrity.org |
| Charity Commission for England and Wales | www.gov.uk/government/organisations/charity-commission |
| Council of Europe | www.coe.int; www.coe.int/en/web/moneyval |
| Council of Europe MONEYVAL | |
| Council on Foreign Relations | www.cfr.org |
| CORE (The Corporate responsibility Coalition) | www.corporate-responsibility.org |
| CryptoUK | www.cryptocurrenciesuk.info |
| Delaware Division of Corporations (US) | *https://corp.delaware.gov* |
| Egmont Group | www.egmontgroup.org |
| Etherium Blockchain App Platform | www.ethereum.org |
| European Banking Authority | *https://eba.europa.eu* |
| European Business Network for Corporate Social Responsibility, The | www.csreurope.org |

2 Accessed 12 January 2019.

| Organisation | Website |
|---|---|
| European Securities and Markets Authority | www.esma.europa.eu |
| FATF – Financial Action Task Force | www.fatf-gafi.org |
| FCPA Blog, The | www.fcpablog.com |
| Financial Reporting Council | www.frc.org.uk |
| Financial Stability Board | www.fsb.org |
| Financial Transparency Coalition, The | www.FinancialTransparency.org |
| FINMA (Swiss Financial Market Supervisory Authority) | www.finma.ch |
| G20 Information Centre | www.g20.utoronto.ca |
| Global Human Rights Group | www.globalhumanrightsgroup.org |
| Global Reporting Initiative | www.globalreporting.org |
| Global Risk Affairs, Berlin Risk | www.globalriskaffairs.com |
| Human Rights Watch | www.hrw.org |
| ICAR – International Corporate Accountability Roundtable | www.icar.ngo |
| ICIJ – International Consortium of Investigative Journalists | www.icij.org |
| IHRB – Institute for Human Rights and Business | www.ihrb.org |
| International Institute of Advanced Islamic Studies, Malaysia | www.iais.org.my |
| International Labour Organisation | www.ilo.org |
| IOSCO – International Organization of Securities Commissions | www.iosco.org |
| Islamic Financial Services Board | www.ifsb.org |
| Isle of Man Financial Services Authority | www.iomfsa.im |
| IWPX – International Wealth Planning X-change | www.iwpx.net |
| Journal of Islamic Studies | www.aljamiah.or.id |
| OECD – Organisation for Economic Co-operation and Development | www.oecd.org |
| openDemocracy | www.opendemocracy.net |
| OpenGlobalRights | www.openglobalrights.org |
| Organized Crime and Corruption Reporting Project | www.occrp.org |
| Panama Papers | www.icij.org/investigations/panama-papers/ |
| Paradise Papers | www.icij.org/investigations/paradise-papers/ |
| Society of Trust and Estate Practitioners | www.step.org |
| South Centre | www.southcentre.int |
| State Secretariat for International Finance SIF (Switzerland) | www.sif.admin.ch/sif/en/home.html |

(*Continued*)

*Appendix:* (Continued)

| Organisation | Website |
| --- | --- |
| SwissBanking – Swiss Bankers Association | www.swissbanking.org/en/home?set_language=en |
| Tax Advisors Europe | *https://taxadviserseurope.org/* |
| Tax Justice Network | www.taxjustice.net |
| Tax Justice Network Financial Secrecy Index | www.financialsecrecyindex.com |
| Transparency International | www.transparency.org |
| UN Global Compact | www.unglobalcompact.org |
| UN Human Rights – Office of the High Commissioner | www.ohchr.org |
| UN Principles for Responsible Investment | www.unpri.org |
| Universal Rights Group, Geneva | www.universal-rights.org |
| US Department of the Treasury – Financial Crimes Enforcement Network | www.fincen.gov |
| US Helsinki Commission – The Commission on Security and Co-operation in Europe | www.csce.gov |
| US Securities and Exchange Commission (SEC) | www.sec.gov |
| WAQF Academy | www.waqfacademy.org |
| Wolfsberg Group, The | www.wolfsberg-principles.com |
| World Bank, The | www.worldbank.org |
| World Economic Forum Centre for the Fourth Industrial Revolution | www.weforum.org/centre-for-the-fourth-industrial-revolution/ |

## Bibliography

Bullough, Oliver *Moneyland: Why Thieves and Crooks Now Rule the World and How to Take It Back* (Profile Books Ltd, London, 2018)

*International Consortium of Investigative Journalists – Panama Papers* <www.icij.org/investigations/panama-papers/> accessed 25 November 2018

——— *Paradise Papers* <www.icij.org/investigations/paradise-papers/> accessed 25 November 2018

Shaxson, Nicholas *Treasure Islands: Tax Havens and the Men Who Stole the World* (The Bodley Head, London, 2011)

——— *The Finance Curse: How Global Finance Is Making Us All Poorer* (The Bodley Head, London, 2018)

Vermeulen, Erik P M *Beneficial Ownership and Control* (OECD Corporate Governance Working Papers, 18 January 2013) <https://doi.org/10.1787/5k4dkhwckbzv-en> accessed 25 November 2018

Zucman, Gabriel (Teresa Lavender Fagan tr) *The Hidden Wealth of Nations: The Scourge of Tax Havens* (The University of Chicago Press, Chicago, 2015)

# 2  What is meant by "ownership"?

## Introduction

Searching for the holy grail of ultimate beneficial ownership has become the defining characteristic of so many regulatory and enforcement strategies that the very word "ownership" has taken on an elemental meaning. Ownership is simply what you enjoy when you own something, or so the thinking goes. Everyone knows an owner when they see one. But ownership is a complex, multi-layered concept, and basing a regulatory system on such a simplistic approach to ownership (indeed, using ownership as the marker in the first place) is to build on sand. The sociological sense of "ownership" is largely at odds with the clusters of "ownership" structures being aggressively marketed worldwide.

This chapter gives the grounding on ownership concepts which is necessary for an understanding of how and why many international, state and regulatory disclosure and regulation initiatives fall short of the mark,[1] and why chimeric orphan structures[2] exert such an allure.

What "ownership" means in the context of common law, civil and Islamic legal systems is examined.

Trusts, charities and the wakf gradually developed in response to social needs, to protect and support the vulnerable. Corporations, partnerships and foundations were the state's regulatory response to growing commercial complexity. The separation of the individual from the ownership of property and from the financial accountability inherent in ownership of that property has been fundamental to each.

## The philosophy: Kelsen and Wittgenstein

In looking for a meaning of "ownership", it is tempting to start from a common point – the hub of a wheel, say – and then to radiate out to different legal forms

---

1 See ch 3.
2 See ch 5.

of ownership, each spoke distinct but all the forms aligned on a rim. This assumes that ownership is an elemental concept which, though applied in different legal systems, remains in essence unchanged. It also assumes connectivity between the forms. Yet legal systems have developed independently of each other, and what constitutes "ownership" in one does not derive its meaning from any other or from a common hub.

Nevertheless, it is the elemental approach which is currently taken by regulators and enforcement agencies, who look for the "owner" or the "ultimate beneficial owner". When they are unable to find one, they are forced to employ convenient fictions, flying in the face of legal and equitable principles, maintaining that directors, trustees, nominees or fiduciaries are the "owners". Does this approach result in a legal norm on which transparency strategies can be built?

Hans Kelsen defined "law" as a series of norms in the canonical form: "If x *is*, then y *ought* to happen". We begin with a fact and then determine what consequence ought to result (always "ought" rather than "will", because to argue for the certainty of a consequence would be naïve). "The difference between is and ought cannot be explained further. We are immediately aware of the difference [. . .]".[3] Transparency strategies, in *deeming* who the owner should be, are not grounded in law in the sense postulated by Kelsen. Instead of beginning with a fact, they begin with an assumption – someone *ought* to be the owner, and so will be treated as such. It is a circular argument to assert that "if x *ought* to be, then y *ought* to happen". The result is that such transparency strategies are purely self-referring and largely out of sync with legal concepts of ownership.

Wittgenstein's theory of family resemblances can be applied to show how using "ownership" as a one-size-fits-all marker is both flawed and unnecessary in light of a far better working alternative. Wittgenstein's concern was language, but his theory of family resemblances can be adapted to the problem of defining "ownership". He suggests that concepts may not share a common characteristic (a hub) but instead draw upon common characteristics – "a complicated network of similarities overlapping and criss-crossing: sometimes overall similarities, sometimes similarities of detail".[4] Once this is accepted, it can be understood that "ownership" cannot be elemental. In a family, children may have the features of a parent and may share features with each other but may not all resemble each other: nevertheless, they bear a resemblance to each other. "Once one sees

---

3  Hans Kelsen, *Pure Theory of Law* (Max Knight tr, University of California Press, 1967) 6.
4  "Wir sehen ein kompliziertes Netz von Ähnlichkeiten, die einander übergreifen und kreuzen. Ähnlichkeiten im Großen und Kleinen". Ludwig Wittgenstein *Philosophical Investigations* (G E M Anscombe, P M S Hacker and Joachim Schulte tr, Wiley-Blackwell, Revised 4th Edition, Oxford, 2009) para 66, and see the general discussion on family resemblances in paras 67 to 77

the variety of cases and the family resemblances between them, the attempt to establish an *a priori* generalisation is thwarted. There is no one answer, but a variety of answers depending on a variety of factors. The moral is: Look to the circumstances!"[5]

To regard "ownership" as a universal descriptive, self-defining and rigidly bound is to play into the hands of tax-planners and offshore alchemists for whom "ownership" is not a stable element but a mutable categorisation: "The empirical evidence [. . .] presents a picture of categorization as an imaginative and dynamic process that is flexible in application and elastic in scope".[6]

## "Ownership" and "Beneficial Ownership"

The separation of "ownership" and "beneficial ownership", in the sense that a person whose name is on the asset is not the person who enjoys that asset is self-evident; but the technique of separating out the holder from the enjoyer by using *ownership* as the key indicator – instead of focussing on control or simply on enjoyment itself – has its origins in trust law.[7]

The transfer of beneficial ownership under English law (and the common law in general) takes three forms: outright transfer of both legal and equitable title by conveyance, sale or assignment; transfer to a third-party trustee or a declaration by the legal owner that they hold the property on trust.

This familiarity with the principles of ownership and beneficial ownership has channelled law enforcement agencies, taxation authorities and financial regulators into hunting the *owner* and finding ever more elaborate ways in which to define an *owner*, even when in many cases no owner in the sense they have applied to the term actually exists. This is compounded by the dissimilarities in approach between the common law jurisdictions which gave rise to trusts and the civil law jurisdictions whose jurisprudence, rooted in classical Roman law, evolved quite separately and distinctly. The quest for a global definition of *beneficial owner* falls at the first hurdle.

For every transparency strategy which assumes that in order to benefit one must own, there is a counter-initiative under which benefit stands apart from ownership of any kind.

---

5 Judith Genova, *Wittgenstein: A Way of Seeing* (Routledge, London, 1995) 44.
6 Steven L Winter, *A Clearing in the Forest: Law, Life, and Mind* (The University of Chicago Press, Chicago, 2001) 69.
7 For example, Lord Diplock's remarks in *Ayerst v C & K (Construction) Ltd* [1976] AC 167 at 177: "[. . .] the full ownership in the trust property was split into two constituent elements which became vested in different persons: the 'legal ownership' in the trustee, the 'beneficial ownership' in the *cestui que trust* [beneficiary]". On the constitution of trusts generally see J Glister and J Lee, *Hanbury & Martin: Modern Equity* (20th Edition, Sweet & Maxwell, London, 2015) ch 5.

## The Common Law and equity: legal and equitable title

The distinction between legal and equitable title underlies the distinction between "ownership" and "beneficial ownership".

In any legal system one set of rules will work well for the majority of cases, but no system can foresee and make provision for all circumstances. That can lead to unfairness. The English solution was to establish a parallel system of justice known as "equity" – notoriously difficult to encapsulate in a single definition, though many have attempted to do so:

> "Equity is no part of the law, but a moral virtue, which qualifies, moderates and reforms the rigour, hardness and edge of the law, and is a universal truth [. . .] and defends the law from crafty evasions, delusions, and new subtleties, invented and contrived to delude the common law [. . .]".[8]

Sir Nathan Wright L.K. from whose 1705 judgment this is taken could not possibly have foreseen how many subtleties have been invented and contrived in our century but derived instead from equitable principles, precisely to delude and defeat statute and the common law, the whole field of beneficial ownership avoidance being paramount amongst them.

In England the rigidity of approach of the common law courts was modified by the work of the Courts of Chancery, "a gloss or appendage to the common law and not a rival or competing system"[9] until the two branches fused in 1875, with equitable principles to take precedence.[10]

The concept has since spread throughout common law jurisdictions worldwide, operating to provide equitable relief when there is a recognisable right but no remedy under the common law.[11]

---

8  *Lord Dudley and Ward v Lady Dudley* (1705) Prec.Ch 241 at 244, quoted in J McGhee (ed), *Snell's Equity* (31st Edition, Sweet & Maxwell, 2005) para 1–03.

9  J McGhee (ed), *Snell's Equity* (n 8) para 1–23.

10  The Supreme Court of Judicature Acts 1873 and 1875, repealed and ultimately replaced by the Supreme Court Act 1981, now re-titled Senior Courts Act 1981 s 49(1) which provides: "Subject to the provisions of this or any other Act, every court exercising jurisdiction in England or Wales in any civil cause or matter shall continue to administer law and equity on the basis that, wherever there is any conflict or variance between the rules of equity and the rules of the common law with reference to the same matter, the rules of equity shall prevail". <www.legislation.gov.uk/ukpga/1981/54/section/49> accessed 10 December 2018. For a discussion on how far English law and equity have fused and whether in the alternative the only "fusion" is that both systems are now pleaded in the same courts but retain their separate character – as for example the law of trusts, which distinguishes between legal and equitable rights – see J Glister and J Lee, *Hanbury & Martin* (n 8) paras 1–020 to 1–023.

11  Canada: Connie L Mah, *Equitable Doctrines and Maxims* (Law Now, 1 May 2008) <www.lawnow.org/equitable-doctrines-and-maxims/> accessed 10 December 2018); Singapore: Singapore Academy of Law, *Equity and Trusts* <www.singaporelaw.sg/sglaw/laws-of-singapore/commercial-law/chapter-18> accessed 10 December 2018.

# Ownership in civil law: Usufruct, Fiducie and Treuhand

"The greatest and the most distinctive achievement performed by Englishmen in the field of jurisprudence [. . .] [is] the development from century to century of the trust idea".[12] It is indeed the case that neither a trust nor the duties and powers of a trustee is the equivalent of usufruct or of a fidéicommissaire or Treuhänder. *Lewin* cites three essential differences: the control and management of the trust property is not in any agency capacity; beneficiaries have a proprietary interest in the trust property, at least in so far as their interest prevails over those of the trustee; and the trust property is capable of being liquidated and reinvested in other assets subject to the trust.[13]

However, the genius of the trust is not unique, and in terms of ownership structures – and the open doors to beneficial ownership avoidance – civil law has principles and devices which owe nothing to that common law tradition.[14] Usufruct in particular "[. . .] with the conception of ownership which it implies, is a fundamental feature of a Civil law system. It could indeed serve as the identifying mark of such a system, just as the doctrine of estates is the mark of a Common law system".[15]

## *Usufruct*

The usufruct is a device for fragmenting ownership or, more precisely, for making a distinction between the ownership of property and its enjoyment. The usufructuary has the right to use the property and, figuratively, to take its fruits ('usufruct') for a particular period – usually for life. The 'bare owner' remains out of possession or enjoyment of that property until the usufruct ends. The arrangement binds the successors of the original bare owner (including good-faith purchasers for value without notice), but the usufructuary at no time has a share in the ownership of the property. The usufructuary is not an "ultimate beneficial owner" simply because the transfer or displacement of ownership never comes into the equation.

12 Frederic William Maitland, "The Unincorporate Body" in *The Collected Papers of Frederic William Maitland*, vol. 3 (H A L Fisher ed) (Cambridge University Press, 1911) 271, 272.
13 See L Tucker and others, *Lewin on Trusts* (19th Edition, Sweet & Maxwell, 2014) para 1–027.
14 For a concise, comparative overview of the common law and civil law see *The Common Law and Civil Law Traditions* (The Robbins Collection, School of Law (Boalt Hall), University of California at Berkeley) <www.law.berkeley.edu/library/robbins/pdf/CommonLaw CivilLawTraditions.pdf> accessed 10 December 2018. See also Michele Graziadei, Ugo Mattei and Lionel Smith (eds), *Commercial Trusts in European Private Law* (Cambridge University Press, 2005).
15 For a discussion on the Roman law origins of the usufruct see Barry Nichols, *An Introduction to Roman Law* (Clarendon Law Series, 1972) 145–148, from which this quotation is taken.

## *Fiducie and Treuhand*

The fiduciary contract is best known in French, Belgian and Luxembourg law as the fiducie, in Italian law as fiducia, in Spanish law as fideicomiso and in German law as the Treuhand.[16] In each case the owner of an asset transfers ownership to another person, who holds the property not for a third-party beneficiary, but for the benefit of the original owner. If to ascertain "ultimate beneficial owner" the key is ownership, then the Fiducie and the Treuhand in facilitating the divestment of ownership block any such initiative. Were the focus to be changed – letting go of the need to find an "owner" and looking instead for the person who has the benefit irrespective of ownership – then arguable that blockage would be removed.

## Ownership in Islam

All property belongs to God, who created it, but is held on trust (*amanah*) from God. Man is a viceregent (*khalifa*) of God on Earth. The needs of destitute and poor ought always to be borne in mind, but this apart property may be dealt with freely.[17]

Ownership (*milkiyah*) and the mere right of possession (*qabd*) are distinguished. The defining characteristic of ownership is that the owner has control over his or her property to the exclusion of others. Title to an asset may be obtained by purchase, inheritance or as a gift or donation.

Private and public property are distinguished, and private property includes both moveables and immoveables. The ownership of businesses comes within the private sphere, as do the assets held by such privately owned businesses.

It would therefore seem that the ascertaining of ownership of an asset could easily be determined, ownership being absolute. This has not proved to be the case, and Shariah law through contact with other legal systems has been augmented.

It is in the law relating to sale that a divergence between ownership and beneficial ownership manifests itself. Shariah recognises only a 'true sale' under which

---

16  All these terms are the modern equivalents of the Roman law fiducia. See Barry Nichols, *An Introduction to Roman Law* (n 15) 268ff.

17  "The delicate point to remember here, is that Islam and the current jurisprudence have assigned watertight compartments to violation of religious and moral obligations on one hand, and 'legal and canonical' violations on the other hand". Ali Reza Afghani, *Ownership in Islam* (Sayyid Muhammad Husayni Beheshti trs, Islamic Thought Foundation) available via Ahlul Bayt Digital Islamic Library Project <www.al-islam.org/ownership-islam-sayyid-muhammad-husayni-beheshti> accessed 10 December 2018. For a discussion on the social function of ownership in Islam, with specific reference to *Zakat* (one of the five pillars of Islam – a religious obligation or tax which requires wealthy Muslims to share part of their wealth with the needy) see Euis Nurlaelawati, 'Zakat and the Concept of Ownership in Islam: Yusuf Qaradawi's Perspective on Islamic Economics' 48 *Al-Jami'ah* 2 (2010 M/1431 H 365) <www.aljamiah.or.id/index.php/AJIS/article/view/115/136> accessed 10 December 2018.

all rights to an asset are transferred by the seller to the buyer, including the right of onward sale. However, taking a principle from the common law, there is in practice a second form of sale known as 'a sale that falls short of a true sale', which gives rise merely to beneficial ownership. In particular the use of a *sukuk* otherwise conventionally (but not entirely accurately) known as an Islamic bond exploits this difference. An asset-based (as distinct from an asset-backed) *sukuk* certificate describes ownership or an interest in one or more assets; and gives the holder the proportionate beneficial ownership of that asset together with the associated risk and potential return of cash flow.[18]

The Islamic Financial Services Board (IFSB)[19] defines *sukuk* as "Certificates that represent a proportional undivided ownership right in tangible assets, or a pool of tangible assets and other types of assets. These assets could be in a specific project or specific investment activity that is Shariah compliant" and *sukuk* securitisation as "The process of issuing *sukuk* or investment certificates which

---

18 See *Guiding Principles on Disclosure Requirements for Islamic Capital Market Products (Sukuk and Islamic Collective Investment Schemes)* (IFSB-19, April 2017) 14 FN 18: As mentioned in footnote 115 in IFSB-15, the IDBG Sharī'ah Board is of the following view:

Ṣukūk assets must be undividedly owned by the ṣukūk holders either directly or through their agent (SPV). This ownership should be valid from both the legal and Sharī'ah perspectives, in the sense that the ṣukūk holders (whether as individuals or through their agent – that is, an SPV) have the ownership of the underlying assets. The ownership of the underlying assets should be transferred to the ṣukūk holders and registered in their names with legal authorities. (These ṣukūk may be known, rather incongruously, in the market as "asset-backed".) However, in jurisdictions where there is a prohibition on transferring legal titles to such assets, only the beneficial ownership is permitted to be transferred to the ṣukūk holders (such ṣukūk may be known, rather incongruously, in the market as "asset-based") based on the following conditions:

(a) The definition of beneficial ownership must be stated clearly in the ṣukūk documentation. The beneficial ownership of ṣukūk assets refers to valid ownership with all the rights and obligations, but excluding the right of registration with the legal authorities.
(b) There must be a statement by the SPV (included in the trust certificate) confirming that valid ownership has been transferred to the ṣukūk holders along with associated rights and obligations. The SPV may only utilise the assets in accordance with terms permitted by the ṣukūk holders, as the assets have been registered under the SPV's name as a fiduciary only.
(c) The trust certificate can be enforced through legal mechanisms in legal systems which prohibit the legal transfer of the underlying assets to the ṣukūk holders. In the view of the IDBG Sharī'ah Board, "asset-based" ṣukūk may only be issued in a Sharī'ah-compliant manner by the observance of the above conditions'.

All publications of the IFSB are available online in Arabic and in English at <www.ifsb.org/published.php> accessed 10 December 2018.

19 The IFSB is based in Kuala Lumpur, was inaugurated on 3 November 2002 and started operations on 10 March 2003. It serves as an international standard-setting body of regulatory and supervisory agencies that have a vested interest in ensuring the soundness and stability of the Islamic financial services industry – banking, capital markets and insurance. It formulates and promotes the adoption of Shariah compliant standards <www.ifsb.org/background.php> accessed 10 December 2018.

represent a common share of certain assets; these *sukuk*, or certificates, can be issued by the owners of such assets or another body (a special purpose entity) as trustee acting as a fiduciary".[20]

The special-purpose entity – known variously as a special-purpose vehicle, special-purpose entity and special-purpose company – stands between the obligator (the government or corporation which stands to benefit from the *sukuk*) and the investors. The entity is not a subsidiary of nor is it owned by the obligator (and hence ring-fenced from any risks to which the obligator may be prone). Legal title to the assets is in that entity, and the investors receive periodic profit distributions, derived from the obligator's trading activities (which are then shared between the obligator and the entity, which holds the investors' portion in a trustee capacity).

Commenting on the dichotomy of ownership and beneficial ownership, Abdul Karim Abdullah writes: "The common law and the Shariah, while overlapping in some respects, nonetheless constitute disparate legal systems. In order for Islamic securitisation to remain Shariah compliant, maintain its credibility, and ensure investor protection, it is advisable to utilise Shariah notions of sale and ownership rather than those 'imported' from other legal systems, such as the common law. Otherwise, there is a risk that Islamic securitisation may produce instruments that reflect those of the common law more fully than that of the Shariah".[21]

In December 2018 the IFSB issued its Core Principles for Islamic Finance Regulation (IFSB-21) ("Core Principles")[22] which set out 38 high-level core principles and their associated assessment methodology providing a broad general framework for the regulation of Islamic capital markets. The Core Principles take into consideration the specificities of Islamic finance and closely reflect the Objectives and Principles of Securities Regulation of the International Organization of Securities Commissions[23] (IOSCO) and the IOSCO Methodology For Assessing Implementation of the IOSCO Objectives and Principles of Securities Regulation,[24] both issued in May 2017.

In providing guidance on beneficial ownership, the Core Principles adopt the IOSCO Principles on Client Identification and Beneficial Ownership for the Securities Industry issued in May 2004 ("IOSCO Principles").[25] The IOSCO

20 <www.ifsb.org/terminologies.php> accessed 10 December 2018 and see Guiding Principles on Disclosure Requirements for Islamic Capital Market Products (n 18) section 2.2. All publications of the IFSB are available online in Arabic and in English at <www.ifsb.org/published.php> accessed 10 December 2018.
21 <www.iais.org.my/e/index.php/component/k2/item/137-legal-vs-beneficial-ownership-in-islamic-finance.html> accessed 10 December 2018. See also Aini Aryani, *Ownership in Islamic Perspective* (3 June 2008) <http://ainiaryani.blogspot.com/2008/06/ownership-in-islamic-perspective.html> accessed 10 December 2018 and Ali Reza Afghani, *Ownership in Islam* (n 17).
22 See n 20 concerning soft copy availability.
23 <www.iosco.org/library/pubdocs/pdf/IOSCOPD561.pdf> accessed 10 December 2018.
24 <www.iosco.org/library/pubdocs/pdf/IOSCOPD562.pdf> accessed 10 December 2018.
25 <ttp://www.iosco.org/library/pubdocs/pdf/IOSCOPD167.pdf> accessed 10 December 2018.

Principles refer to standards set by the Financial Action Task Force ("FATF") in the FATF Forty Recommendations, which were published in October 2004[26] (and subsequently revised) and so find themselves a decade behind current FATF guidance. In spite of this time lag, the effect of the Core Principles is to introduce into IFSB standards the methodology of the FATF in relation to the identification of beneficial owners and what substantively constitutes a beneficial owner.[27]

## Charity

Charity is a characteristic which colours the structures to which it applies. It is not a structure in itself, though the delivery mechanism of charity is often a trust or a corporation.[28]

The essence of charity is that it is for the benefit of the public, or a section of the public, whose individual identities need to be ascertained. The concept of charity is notoriously difficult to define, though there is a current trend towards sampling charitable purposes in the form of siloed lists, which merely exacerbates the problem – where there's a list, there's a litigant.[29]

A charity must be exclusively charitable in nature and for the public benefit.[30] Examples of charitable objects under English law were famously given by Lord Macnaghten in *Commissioners of Income Tax v Pemsel*[31]

> *'Charity' in its legal sense comprises four principal divisions: trusts for the relief of poverty; trusts for the advancement of education; trusts for the advancement of religion; and trusts for other purposes beneficial to the community, not falling under any of the preceding heads.*

In England, a pragmatic approach has been adopted, and the responsibility for determining whether institutions are charities or not has been given to the

---

26 <www.fatf-gafi.org/publications/fatfrecommendations/documents/the40recommenda tionspublishedoctober2004.html> accessed 10 December 2018.

27 Financial Action Task Force, *FATF Guidance on Transparency and Beneficial Ownership* (Financial Action Task Force, October 2014) <www.fatf-gafi.org/media/fatf/documents/ reports/Guidance-transparency-beneficial-ownership.pdf> accessed 10 December 2018. See ch 3, Part Two for a discussion on the shortcomings of the FATF's transparency strategy with regard to beneficial ownership.

28 For a concise overview of express public/charitable trusts see J McGhee (ed), *Snell's Equity* (n 8) ch 21.

29 For example, in the United Kingdom the Charities Act 2011 <www.legislation.gov.uk/ ukpga/2011/25/contents> accessed 10 December 2018. Charities Act 2011 s 1 begins bravely by giving a meaning of "charity", which simply self-defines it as a structure "for charitable purposes only" which must be for "public benefit" and goes on to define "charitable purpose" in ss 3(1) and 5 in terms of a list of examples and general guidelines. This sampling approach was first encountered in England in the Preamble to the Statute of Elizabeth (43 Eliz.1, c.4, 1601), which was subsequently used by the English courts as a guideline.

30 Something which for what amounts to little more than marketing and finance sector promotion purposes offshore has been sidelined: see the discussion of the hybridisation of charities and non-charitable purposes within a Cayman STAR trust in ch 5.

31 [1891] A.C. 531 at 583.

Charity Commission for England and Wales, with an evolutionary element – "In performing its functions, the Commission must, in appropriate cases, have regard to the desirability of facilitating innovation [. . .]".[32]

In the United States of America, the definition of charity at federal and state levels, overlaid by the Internal Revenue Code, and their innovative interaction, creates a state of flux:

> *Due to the fact that the purposes of charities are permitted to change over time, the law of charity is not like other areas of the law where basic definitions tend to remain fixed. And this is possibly the distinguishing factor of this body of law – its built-in processes that permit change.*[33]

Some jurisdictions, however, have steered away from even attempting to pin down what is meant by "charity". For example, the technical and artificial meaning attached under English law to the words 'charity' and 'charitable' do not apply under Isle of Man law, which is more liberal 'and in any event not narrower' than that of England:[34] nevertheless, a clear charitable intention is necessary, and in this regard English, Scottish and Irish cases are treated by Isle of Man courts as guides to those courts in deciding what is charitable.[35] Even the rigidity of English law, which would not regard composite descriptions such as "charitable *or* philanthropic", "charitable *or* benevolent" as being sufficiently exclusively charitable in intent to bring them within the ambit of charity[36] has not been followed in the Isle of Man, which in the Charities Act 1962 expressly extends the meaning of charitable purposes: "Trusts expressed to be for the purpose of benevolence, philanthropy or social welfare which are for the public benefit shall be charitable trusts".[37]

The compulsory registration of charities is one of the earliest examples of public availability of what would otherwise be information confidential to benefactors. The Isle of Man serves as an illustration. Charitable status may be obtained by trusts, companies and foundations. However, regard must be had to the provisions of the Charities Registration Act 1989[38] which provides that any institution which in the Isle of Man takes or uses any name, style, title or description implying

---

32  Charities Act 2011 s 15(1) <www.legislation.gov.uk/ukpga/2011/25/section/15> accessed 10 December 2018 and s 16 <www.legislation.gov.uk/ukpga/2011/25/section/16> accessed 10 December 2018. And see the Charity Commission for England and Wales <www.gov.uk/government/organisations/charity-commission> accessed 10 December 2018.

33  M R Freemont-Smith, *The Legal Meaning of Charity* (The Urban Institute, April 2013) 15 <www.urban.org/sites/default/files/the-legal-meaning-of-charity.pdf> accessed 10 December 2018.

34  *Costain, Re* (1961) 1961–71 MLR 1, 7 (Deemster Kneale).

35  *Ring, Re* (1962) 1961–71 MLR 60, 66 (Deemster Kneale).

36  J McGhee (ed), *Snell's Equity* (n 8) para 21–18.

37  Charities Act 1962 (Isle of Man) s 2(1) <https://legislation.gov.im/cms/images/LEGISLATION/PRINCIPAL/1962/1962-0001/CharitiesAct1962_1.pdf> accessed 10 December 2018.

38  <www.legislation.gov.im/cms/images/LEGISLATION/PRINCIPAL/1989/1989-0011/CharitiesRegistrationAct1989_1.pdf> accessed 10 December 2018. For the somewhat more elaborate position in England see s 30 and Schedule 3 Charities Act 2011 <www.legislation.gov.uk/ukpga/2011/25/section/30> accessed 10 December 2018 and <www.legislation.gov.uk/ukpga/2011/25/schedule/3> accessed 10 December 2018.

or otherwise pretending that it is a charity, or which holds itself out as a charity, is guilty of an offence unless it files a statement in the prescribed form at the General Registry in the Isle of Man.[39] The Chief Registrar has the power to refuse the filing if he is of the opinion that the institution is not established for charitable purposes, does not have a substantial connection with the Isle of Man or has a name which is undesirable or misleading.[40]

Charities everywhere are open to abuse. Should the donor of the charitable trust choose at the outset that the trust is to be revocable,[41] the property in the trust is alienated only for its duration. The unscrupulous may make merely token distributions, in order to maintain a semblance of public benefit, whilst preserving the bulk of the charitable trust fund for ultimate return to the donor upon its being revoked. The potential to 'warehouse' assets in plain sight within a socially worthy medium, only later to have them 'returned to sender', represents ownership accountability avoidance in its purest form.

As Marion R Freemont-Smith writes:

> *There are also critics who find the law of charity too messy, too rigid, or not sufficiently in tune with modern life. Attempts to correct these shortcomings, however, are likely to lead to such fundamental changes in the nature of charities that their benefits to society might be totally lost.*[42]

For those wanting to create beneficial ownership avoidance strategies, the exploitation of the flexibility of the concept of charity, and their ability to exploit its weakness and need for further reform for their own and not the public benefit, is irresistible.

## The structures

### *Generic corporations*[43]

Corporations in their modern form owe their existence to the state and have to secure "a franchise from society".[44] A corporation is a separate legal entity, which divorces ownership from control.

---

39  Charities Registration Act 1989 (Isle of Man) s 1.

40  Ibid. s 3(1).

41  In the absence of any requirement as to irrevocability in relevant registration legislation.

42  M R Freemont-Smith, *The Legal Meaning of Charity* (n 33).

43  For a detailed discussion on why and how generic corporations in the form in which they now exist (and proliferate) came into being, see J Micklethwait and A Wooldridge, *The Company, A Short History of a Revolutionary Idea* (Modern Library, New York, 2005) and A Berle and G C Means, *The Modern Corporation and Private Property*, original published in 1932 by Harcourt, Brace & World, Inc. (reprinted with an Introduction by M L Weidenbaum and M Jensen, Transaction Publishers, New Brunswick (USA) and London, 1991, tenth printing 2009).

44  This fact alone has in the context of international human rights spawned a vast literature and body of soft law on what standards of corporate governance must be applied in order

> *Companies sprang from the loins of the state. Even when they were set free in the mid-nineteenth century, they still had to secure what might be called a 'franchise from society'. [. . .] To keep doing business, the modern company still needs a franchise from society, and the terms of that franchise still matter enormously.*[45]

Shareholders enjoy limited liability, which affords them the prospect, at worst, of losing a fixed investment and, at best, of gaining a substantial share of the profit. Though a company's stakeholders are arguably far more wide-ranging than just its shareholders – the interests of lenders, suppliers, employees and customers should also be borne in mind – attention has focussed on the shareholders as the legal owners of the company. Is undisclosed ownership compatible with seeking society's franchise? Is anonymity a natural concomitant of limited liability? Limited liability is a privilege and is not immune to constraint.

A corporation can take a number of forms – public or private, limited by shares or by guarantee (or by both), with directors or (in the case of a limited liability company – LLC) without. The key in all cases is that the corporation has a legal personality which is separate from its members. Also key, in general terms, is that the property held by a corporation is owned by that corporation and is not held directly by the members of the corporation – it is the simplest of concepts: the

---

that a corporation, bound by proxy as it were to observe the human rights obligations of the state which has enacted the legislation which creates it and which by not repealing that legislation sustains it, is not used as a vehicle of abuse. See the *Guiding Principles on Business and Human Rights: Implementing the United Nations "Protect, Respect and Remedy" Framework ("the Ruggie Principles")* A/HRC/17/31 / 21 March 2011. <www.ohchr.org/Docum ents/Issues/Business/A-HRC-17-31_AEV.pdf> accessed 10 December 2018; United Nations Economic and Social Council, *Statement on the Obligations of States Parties Regarding the Corporate Sector and Economic, Social and Cultural Rights* (12 July 2011) UN Doc E/C.12/2011/1 <https://tbinternet.ohchr.org/_layouts/treatybodyexternal/Download. aspx?symbolno=E%2FC.12%2F2011%2F1&Lang=en> accessed 10 December 2018; UNC-ESCR, *General Comment: Business Activities* (10 August 2017) UN Doc E/C.12/GC/24 <https://tbinternet.ohchr.org/_layouts/treatybodyexternal/Download.aspx?symbolno=E %2FC.12%2fGC%2f24&Lang=en> accessed 10 December 2018; Nadia Bernaz, *Business and Human Rights: History, Law and Policy – Bridging the Accountability Gap* (Routledge 2017), ch 7, 'International Soft Law Initiatives on Business and Human Rights'; Paul Beckett, *Tax Havens and International Human Rights* (Routledge 2017) ch 2 'Offshore Structures'. Whether little more than lip service is paid to the promotion of corporate social responsibility is a moot point: see for example the European Union's IMPACT project (*Impact Measurement and Performance Analysis of CSR*) launched in 2010 which made minimal impact and the results of which were substantially suppressed – David Sogge, *The corporate wax nose* (Transformation, 16 November 2016) <www.opendemocracy.net/transformation/david-sogge/corporate-wax-nose?> accessed 10 December 2018.
45 J Micklethwait and A Wooldridge, *The Company* (n 43) 182, 186. The phrase "a franchise from society" is attributed by the authors to Professor Leslie Hannah <https://en.wikipedia. org/wiki/Leslie_Hannah> accessed 10 December 2018. And see Stefan J Padfield 'In Search of a Higher Standard: Rethinking Fiduciary Duties of Directors of Wholly-owned Subsidiaries' 10 *Fordham Journal of Corporate & Financial Law* 1, 79 (2004) which includes (at 86) a history and analysis of the American evolution of the corporation, "from State-dominated, to Manager-dominated, to Market-dominated".

members own the company; the company owns the assets. In the classic statement of Lord Buckmaster, analysing the relationship between a shareholder and the assets held in the name of the company:

> *Turning now to his position as shareholder, this must be independent of the extent of his share interest. If he were entitled to insure holding all the shares in the company, each shareholder would be equally entitled, if the shares were all in separate hands. Now, no shareholder has any right to any item of property owned by the company, for he has no legal or equitable interest therein. He is entitled to a share in the profits while the company continues to carry on business and a share in the distribution of the surplus assets when the company is wound up.*[46]

## Piercing the corporate veil

To what extent a company may be "looked through" to its shareholders – known as "piercing the corporate veil" – has been controversial. Yet this is central to the question of ownership and financial accountability. In the words of Lord Sumption, sitting in the Supreme Court of the United Kingdom:

> *I conclude that there is a limited principle of English law which applies when a person is under an existing legal obligation or liability or subject to an existing legal restriction which he deliberately evades or whose enforcement he deliberately frustrates by interposing a company under his control. The court may then pierce the corporate veil for the purpose, and only for the purpose, of depriving the company or its controller of the advantage that they would otherwise have obtained by the company's separate legal personality. The principle is properly described as a limited one, because in almost every case where the test is satisfied, the facts will in practice disclose a legal relationship between the company and its controller which will make it unnecessary to pierce the corporate veil.*[47]

---

46 *Macaura v Northern Assurance Company Limited* [1925] A.C. 619, at 626,627 (House of Lords).

47 Lord Sumption, *Prest v Petrodel Resources Ltd* [2013] UKSC 34, at para 35. At para 28 he ruled: "References to a 'facade' or 'sham' beg too many questions to provide a satisfactory answer. It seems to me that two distinct principles lie behind these protean terms, and that much confusion has been caused by failing to distinguish between them. They can conveniently be called the concealment principle and the evasion principle. The concealment principle is legally banal and does not involve piercing the corporate veil at all. It is that the interposition of a company or perhaps several companies so as to conceal the identity of the real actors will not deter the courts from identifying them, assuming that their identity is legally relevant. In these cases the court is not disregarding the 'facade', but only looking behind it to discover the facts which the corporate structure is concealing. The evasion principle is different. It is that the court may disregard the corporate veil if there is a legal right against the person in control of it which exists independently of the company's involvement, and a company is interposed so that the separate legal personality of the company will defeat

*Tax haven corporations*

Tax havens manipulate the generic corporate structure to promote concealment.[48] The dangers are compounded by the sheer volume of companies formed
within or formed elsewhere but managed and controlled within, the tax havens.
Motivated by a combination of the need for low taxation, for privacy (or concealment), for local legitimacy of the structures, thousands upon thousands seek to
use corporate structures in and from the tax havens.[49]

*Nominee directors, nominee shareholders*

The simplest form of concealment is to employ nominee shareholders and nominee directors of corporations.[50] It is a strategy widely used and, until recent years

---

the right or frustrate its enforcement. Many cases will fall into both categories, but in some
circumstances the difference between them may be critical".

48  It must however not be overlooked that unaccountability and a lack of oversight in the matter of company formation is by no means exclusive to the tax havens. See Tom Bergin and
Stephen Grey, *Insight – How UK Company Formation Agents Fuel Fraud* (Reuters, United
Kingdom, 18 March 2016) <http://uk.reuters.com/article/uk-regulations-agents-insight-
idUKKCN0WK17W> accessed 10 December 2018. This has ostensibly been addressed in
the UK with effect from 30 June 2016 by the introduction of the Register of People with
Significant Control. United Kingdom Government, Department for Business, Innovation &
Skills, "*People with Significant Control" Companies House Register Goes Live (gov.uk,* 30
June 2016) <www.gov.uk/government/news/people-with-significant-control-companies-
house-register-goes-live> accessed 10 December 2018; United Kingdom Government,
Companies House, *Summary Guide for Companies – Register of People with Significant
Control (gov.uk,* 27 January 2016) <www.gov.uk/government/publications/guidance-
to-the-people-with-significant-control-requirements-for-companies-and-limited-liability-
partnerships> accessed 10 December 2018. The full statutory guidance takes no account of
the tax haven technique of separating ownership and control or of avoiding beneficial ownership altogether: United Kingdom Government, Department for Business, Innovation &
Skills, *Statutory Guidance on the Meaning of "Significant Influence or Control" over Companies in the Context of the Register of People with Significant Control (gov.uk,* 14 April 2016)
<www.gov.uk/government/uploads/system/uploads/attachment_data/file/523120/
PSC_statutory_guidance_companies.pdf> accessed 10 December 2018.
49  Though the tide may be turning (e.g. the British Virgin Islands). On 19 January 2017,
bvinews.com reported that company incorporation dropped 35% in the third quarter of
2016 compared to the corresponding quarter in 2015. In his budget speech on 16 January 2017, BVI Premier and Finance Minister Dr D Orlando Smith said: "We are currently
facing some headwinds in our financial services sector, and we need to retool", blaming
"global regulatory challenges, new restrictive banking practices, negative media and percep-
tions". Aspects of internationally acknowledged standards of corporate governance did not
feature in the debate. BVI News Online, 'More Bad News for Financial Services: 35% Drop'
(*bvinews.com,* 19 January 2017) <http://bvinews.com/new/more-bad-news-for-financial-
services-35-drop/> accessed 10 December 2018.
50  David Leigh, Harold Frayman and James Ball, 'How the Nominee Trick Works' *ICIJ*
(Washington, DC, 25 November 2012) <www.icij.org/offshore/how-nominee-trick-done>
accessed 10 December 2018. An indication of the potential scale of the nominee business
was shown in a joint investigation by the ICIJ, the BBC and *The Guardian* newspaper (UK)

with the growing awareness of drug trafficking and international terrorism, had not aroused significant interest.[51]

A simple company limited by shares is controlled by its directors who are answerable to the shareholders. The shareholders as such do not take part in the day-to-day management and control of the company. They have the right to vote in general meetings of the company, and the extent to which their consent is required, if at all, to proposed management decisions, will be set out in the company's constitutional documents. The issue is not therefore one of undue empowerment of shareholders through the use of nominees, but of the inability of any third party accurately to position the company within a wider framework. If, in addition to there being nominee shareholders in place, the directors are themselves de facto (when not de juris) nominees, the problem is compounded. Those truly pulling the strings are invisible and seemingly inviolable. Corporate responsibility becomes opaque, and the cross-border activities of such companies as potential members of a network of similar institutions under common ownership cannot be successfully investigated: 'Currently, we regulate the birth certificates of people far more closely than the birth certificates of companies'.[52]

Statutory checks on money laundering, drug trafficking and anti-terrorism[53] are fine and necessary in themselves, but the inability of those who in practical terms only nominally manage and control trading companies to influence in any meaningful way the activities of those companies is an open door to abuse. Financial services regulators may try to stem the tide, but in practice there are not enough hours in the day – in a lifetime – for those holding multiple directorships to be made and kept fully aware of each company's trading activities.

---

in 2012, which unmasked 28 nominee directors who between them held more than 21,500 directorships: David Leigh, Harold Frayman and James Ball, 'Front Men Disguise the Offshore Game's Real Players' *ICIJ* (Washington, DC) <www.icij.org/front-men-disguise-offshore-players> accessed 16 April 2017 (since removed from the ICIJ website). See also Gerard Ryle and Stefan Candea, 'Faux Corporate Directors Stand in for Fraudsters, Despots and Spies' *ICIJ* (Washington, DC, 4 July 2013) <www.icij.org/offshore/faux-corporate-directors-stand-fraudsters-despots-and-spies> accessed 10 December 2018.

51 See ch 3 for the critique by the G20 of this planning in its High-Level Principles on Beneficial Ownership Transparency.

52 Paul Collier, 'In Pursuit of the $21 Trillion' *Prospect Magazine* (2013) <www.prospectmagazine.co.uk> (article no longer available online).

53 For example, see the Anti-Money Laundering and Countering the Financing of Terrorism Requirements Guidance issued by the Isle of Man Government Financial Services Authority 'AML/CFT Requirements and Guidance' (*The Isle of Man Financial Services Authority*) <www.iomfsa.im/amlcft/amlcft-requirements-and-guidance/> accessed 10 December 2018 and Cayman Islands Monetary Authority, 'Guidance Notes on the Prevention and Detection of Money Laundering and Terrorist Financing in the Cayman Islands' (13 December 2017) (*Cayman Islands Monetary Authority*) <www.cima.ky/upimages/commonfiles/151318 4321GuidanceNotesonthePreventionandDetectionofMoneyLaunderingandTerroistFinanc inghintheCaymanIslands_1513184322.pdf> accessed 10 December 2018.

*De facto ownership*

The most straightforward ownership escape mechanism is to encumber the thing which is held in one's name. The owner has legal title and may legitimately be regarded as the owner.[54] However, that person has charged or in some other way encumbered the asset to a third party to the extent that no element of benefit generated by the asset accrues to the owner. Examples of encumbrances are a mortgage, charge (fixed or floating), pledge, lien, option, hypothecation, restriction, right to acquire, right of pre-emption or interest (legal or equitable) including any assignment by way of security, reservation of title, guarantee, trust, right of set off or other third party right or any other security interest having a similar effect, under whatever circumstances this may have occurred.

A common example of a right to acquire property is a put option or a call option (or both) under which at a given time or on the occurrence of a triggering event, the owner may require a third party to assume ownership by *putting* it to them or a third party may be entitled to *call* for the asset to be transferred into their name. In each case the original owner ceases to have any ownership interest (legal or beneficial) in the asset.[55]

### Generic trusts

Trusts are a long-established vehicle in those common-law jurisdictions which include the principles of equity.[56] A trust is a relationship, and like all relationships, it is very difficult to describe just how it works. Trusts are a means whereby funds can be alienated by a donor, held by persons whom the donor trusts to deal with them fairly and responsibly, for the benefit of named individuals (or for charitable purposes). A simple discretionary trust is a triangular structure, the three points being the donor (or 'settlor/grantor'), the trustees themselves, and the beneficiaries for whom the trustees hold the assets.

---

54 For example, most company legislation does not require – or actively prohibits – a company from looking through the name of the shareholder on its register of members to an ultimate beneficial owner. See for example Companies Act 2006 (United Kingdom) ss 112 and 126, which together provide that every person who agrees to become a member of a company, and whose name is entered in its register of members, is a member of the company; no notice of any trust, expressed or constructive, is capable of being entered on the register of members <www.legislation.gov.uk/ukpga/2006/46/contents> accessed 10 December 2018.
55 Though an artful drafter may include a provision for the re-transfer of an asset in given circumstances, which has the effect of "parking" it, legally owned but newly encumbered, this time in the hands of the third party.
56 The definitive works on trusts under English law are L Tucker and others, *Lewin on Trusts* (n 13) (Third Supplement, 2018) and D Hayton and others, *Underhill and Hayton Law of Trusts and Trustees* (19th Edition, LexisNexis, 2016). On principles of equity, see J McGhee (ed), *Snell's Equity* (33rd Edition, Sweet & Maxwell, 2014) and J Glister and J Lee, *Hanbury & Martin* (n 7).

## The Hague Convention

Under Article 2 of the Convention on the Law Applicable to Trusts and on their Recognition (1 July 1985, which entered into force on 1 January 1992, usually referred to as "the Hague Convention" in trust circles, as if there were no other)[57] proposes a universal definition:

*Article 2*

> *For the purposes of this Convention, the term "trust" refers to the legal relationships created – inter vivos or on death – by a person, the settlor, when assets have been placed under the control*[58] *of a trustee for the benefit of a beneficiary or for a specified purpose. A trust has the following characteristics – a) the assets constitute a separate fund and are not a part of the trustee's own estate; b) title to the trust assets stands in the name of the trustee or in the name of another person on behalf of the trustee; c) the trustee has the power and the duty, in respect of which he is accountable, to manage, employ or dispose of the assets in accordance with the terms of the trust and the special duties imposed upon him by law.*
>
> *The reservation by the settlor of certain rights and powers, and the fact that the trustee may himself have rights as a beneficiary, are not necessarily inconsistent with the existence of a trust.*

The Convention covers far more than the common law trust, as it was drafted to include civil law institutions having core features mirroring trusts. It is not necessary that the concept of equitable ownership be known in a legal system for it to have a "trust" within the meaning of the Convention.[59]

---

57 www.hcch.net/en/instruments/conventions/full-text/?cid=59 accessed 10 December 2018. For a comprehensive and concise analysis of the Convention see D Hayton and others, *Underhill and Hayton Law of Trusts and Trustees* (n 56) ch 25 'Conflicts of laws issues and the Hague Trusts Convention' and Donovan Waters, 'The Hague Trusts Convention Twenty Years On' in Michele Graziadei, Ugo Mattei and Lionel Smith (eds), *Commercial Trusts in European Private Law* (Cambridge University Press, Cambridge, 2005) 56–97. For details of the Contracting Parties as at 1 January 2019 see Appendix Two.

58 This was a compromise definition which was intended to cover situations where a trustee employed the use of custodians to hold trust assets. The word "control" does not imply that agency or bailment arrangements come within the definition of a trust. See D Hayton and others, *Underhill and Hayton Law of Trusts and Trustees* (n 56) paras 1.9 and 100.57. And see Donovan Waters, 'The Hague Trusts Convention Twenty Years On' in Michele Graziadei, Ugo Mattei and Lionel Smith (eds) (n 57) 56, at 72–73: "The natural instinct of those civilians who framed their thoughts in terms of contract was to see 'trust' as originating a continuing relationship between the settlor and the trustee, to which the beneficiary in some manner is a party. [. . .] Moreover, in an attempt to reach out to civilian fiduciary property-holding and administrative notions, diverse and numerous though they are, the Hague 'trust' describes the trustee as having mere 'control' of the trust property. What for a civilian should 'control' be taken to mean? The verdict is that the Hague 'trust' is 'shapeless'".

59 "Structurally similar institutions to the common law trust, such as exist in States such as Argentina, Egypt, Ethiopia, Israel, Japan, Liechtenstein, Louisiana, Mexico, Panama, Peru, Quebec and Venezuela may very well be 'trusts' for the purposes of the Convention".

It is important however not to over-estimate the significance of the Convention. The number of Contracting Parties who have both signed and ratified the Convention more than a quarter of a century after the Convention entered into force remains low and does not, for example, include the vast majority of the members of the European Union or any jurisdiction within Africa.[60]

### *The Hague Convention – offshore counter-initiatives*

Offshore jurisdictions compete between themselves to offer services attractive to foreign investors, and this competitiveness has emboldened some to set their own standards for what is and is not a fully constituted, impregnable trust. This marketing by one state of its trusts amongst the residents of another state was, at the time of drafting of the Hague Convention, not apparent to the drafters.[61]

The approach of the Isle of Man, a Crown Dependency of the United Kingdom, to recognition serves as an example of a global offshore counter-initiative driven by market forces. Under the Recognition of Trusts Act 1988 the provisions of the Hague Convention on the Law Applicable to Trusts and on their Recognition has the force of law in the Isle of Man.[62] However, under the Trusts Act 1995[63] s 2 "*A term of a trust selecting the law of the Island to govern the trust is valid, effective and conclusive regardless of any other circumstances*". Upon this a fortress is built, s 5 of the Act excluding foreign law. The exclusion is so comprehensive that the section is worth quoting in full:

## *5 Exclusion of foreign law*

1   *[. . .] no trust governed by the law of the Island and no disposition of property to be held upon the trusts of such a trust is **void, voidable, liable to be set aside or defective in any fashion**, nor is the capacity of a settlor, trustee, protector or*

---

D Hayton and others, *Underhill and Hayton Law of Trusts and Trustees* (n 56) paras 100.51 and 100.58.

60  See Appendix Two.

61  Donovan Waters, 'The Hague Trusts Convention Twenty Years On' in Michele Graziadei, Ugo Mattei and Lionel Smith (eds) (n 57) 56, at 87. Donovan Waters comments that the ramifications of the offshore trusts industry had "not yet burst upon the consciousness of the mainland states" but in the author's professional experience at that time, the industry was already widespread and aggressively promoted by and substantially profitable in the hands of what are in the current decade referred to as "trust service providers". This is not an isolated example of Conventions and other international regulatory initiatives lagging behind and failing to grasp commercial reality in such matters – see the discussion of the G20 High-Level Principles in ch 3, Part Two.

62  Recognition of Trusts Act 1988 s 1(1) <https://legislation.gov.im/cms/images/LEGIS-LATION/PRINCIPAL/1988/1988-0008/RecognitionofTrustsAct1988_1.pdf> accessed 10 December 2018.

63  <https://legislation.gov.im/cms/images/LEGISLATION/PRINCIPAL/1995/1995-0018/TrustsAct1995_2.pdf> accessed 10 December 2018.

*beneficiary to be questioned, nor is any person to be subjected to an obligation or liability or deprived of a right, claim or interest, by reason that –*

(a) *the law of any foreign jurisdiction prohibits or does not recognise the concept of a trust; or*

(b) *the trust or disposition – (i)* **avoids or defeats any right, claim or interest conferred by foreign law upon any person by reason of a personal relationship to a settlor or beneficiary or by way of heirship rights;** *or (ii)* **contravenes any rule of foreign law or any foreign judicial or administrative order or action intended to recognise, protect, enforce or give effect to such a right, claim or interest.**

2 **No judgment or order of a court outside the Island is to be recognised or enforced or give rise to any right, obligation or liability or raise any estoppel if and to the extent that –**

(a) **it is inconsistent with this Act;** *or*

(b) *the High Court so orders – (i) for the purpose of protecting the interests of the beneficiaries of the trust; or (ii) in the interests of the proper administration of the trust.*

3 **Subsection (2) has effect despite any other statutory provision or rule of law in relation to the recognition or enforcement of judgments.**

4 *This section applies – (a)* **whenever** *the trust or disposition arose or was made; and (b) despite any other statutory provision.*

*(Emphasis added)*

It is therefore immaterial that the jurisdiction in which a settlor is domiciled itself does or does not recognise trusts or whether forced heirship/droit de réserve/ Pflichtanteil provisions apply for the benefit of the settlor's heirs – all will be ignored, and no statute of or ruling by a court in that foreign jurisdiction will be enforceable against the settlor, the trustee, the beneficiaries or the trust property.

Equally apparent is that any concept of ownership under the law of that foreign jurisdiction is also, as far as the property held under the trust is concerned, rendered a nullity.

## Trustees

The trustees do not themselves benefit from the funds placed in the trust by the donor (though they may be reasonably remunerated). The trustee merely has legal title to the trust fund. A trustee is neither an agent nor a bailee of the settlor – the trustee acts as principal.[64]

---

64 See L Tucker and others, *Lewin on Trusts* (n 13) paras 1–021 to 1–023 and D Hayton and others *Underhill and Hayton Law of Trusts and Trustees* (n 56). para 1.1(2).

*Trusteeship is ownership-management, not agency-management on a princi-
pal's behalf or bailee management of property deposited by the owner into his
custody or 'attorney-management' of property by a person holding a power of
attorney granted by the owner [. . .].*[65]

The trust fund is immune from claims of the trustee's private creditors. As a
trust, unlike a company or a foundation, has no legal personality, it is the trustee
as principal who assumes liability (for example for contractual breaches or torts),
a liability which because it is personal does not pass to successor trustees after his
resignation, retirement or death.[66]

BENEFICIARIES

If a beneficiary is the only beneficiary (amongst a group of beneficiaries) interested in a specific asset (usually in the form of a life interest), he will have an
equitable proprietary interest in that asset, but the vast majority of trusts are in
discretionary form. Where a beneficiary is just one of a class of undifferentiated
beneficiaries, they do not individually 'own' the trust funds in any sense of the
word (though collectively their equitable proprietary interest prevails over the
trustee) and merely have a right to be considered as and when the trustees exercise their discretion whether or not to make payments from the trust fund to any
one of them.[67]

Trusts are not required to be publicly registered, and all details remain confidential.[68] Taking advantage of the division in common law jurisdictions between

65  D Hayton and others, *Underhill and Hayton Law of Trusts and Trustees* (n 56) para 1.3.
66  Ibid. paras 1.1(3) and 1.14 to 1.16. It is this personal liability of a trustee, combined with
    their holding of legal title to the trust fund, which may, albeit mistakenly, lie behind the
    current registration initiative of treating trustees as owners for the purposes of beneficial
    ownership registration. See the discussion in ch 4.
67  An English authority on the rights of beneficiaries to be considered is *Gartside v I.R.C.*
    [1968] A.C. 533, HL. Alternative approaches are noted by J Glister and J Lee, *Hanbury &
    Martin Modern Equity* (n 7) para 1–019: "The trustee is the owner of at law; and the benefi-
    ciary is the owner in equity" or "[T]he interest of the beneficiary is negative, or 'exclusion-
    ary': it is a positive right to exclude non-beneficiaries from the assets as opposed to a positive
    right trustee duties on them". An absence of any proprietary interest – even if merely equi-
    table and not legal – has profound implications for the registration of beneficial owners – see
    the discussion in ch 3.
68  A further refinement common in tax haven trusts is that the name of the settlor/grantor
    does not appear in the trust deed itself. The trust takes the form of a 'declaration' whereby
    the trustees state that they hold and have held the trust fund since a given date. The identity
    of the settlor remains confidential to them. In the hands of less scrupulous trust practition-
    ers, a sham settlor may be used – truly the settlor of a trust having on its face trust funds of,
    say, $100, but not the source of the bulk of the after-settled trust fund. This device is also
    common in the case of foundations where the founder is in many cases a service provider
    acting as a man of straw. As to the debate currently raging on whether or not, and if so by
    what means, trusts should be registered, see the discussion in ch 3.

legal ownership (in simple terms, the name on the property) and equitable ownership (those entitled to benefit from the property), individuals using trusts can alienate property rights and distance themselves from creditors[69] and transfer responsibility for the management of the property to the trustees.

*Offshore trusts*

Offshore jurisdictions have exploited the inherent flexibility (or vagueness) of the definition in equity to produce something far wider.

> *[S]tatutory developments in the offshore jurisdictions [. . .] have shifted the conceptual axis of the trust in private client property management and disposition work. It has shifted away from the fiduciary relationship between a trustee and a beneficiary with property rights, to another relationship. The emphasis is now upon the creator of the trust (the settlor) and the trustee. [. . .] The beneficiary is one who may or may not benefit as the result of the way in which the ongoing settlor/trustee arrangement works out.[70]*

An example of this is found in The Trusts (Guernsey) Law, 2007 s 1:[71]

### Existence of a trust.

1   *A trust exists if a person (a "trustee") holds or has vested in him, or is deemed to hold or have vested in him, property which does not form or which has ceased to form part of his own estate –*

>    (a)  *for the benefit of another person (a "beneficiary"), whether or not yet ascertained or in existence, and/or*
>    (b)  *for any purpose, other than a purpose for the benefit only of the trustee.[72]*

---

69  A number of tax haven structures specifically exclude the rights of creditors who would otherwise be in a position to bring an action in respect of fraudulent transfers (e.g. the Nevis Multiform Foundation). In others, this right of action is not extinguished. In the Isle of Man, for example, the principle that a transfer made with the intention of defeating a just creditor (i.e. a current debtor or a debt falling due on a known future date) is void and of no effect became hard law under the Fraudulent Assignments Act 1736 <www.legislation. gov.im/cms/images/LEGISLATION/PRINCIPAL/1736/1736-0002/FraudulentAssignmentsAct1736_1.pdf> accessed 10 December 2018. (The Act remains in full force and effect today.)

70  Donovan Waters, 'The Hague Trusts Convention Twenty Years On', in Michele Graziadei, Ugo Mattei and Lionel Smith (eds) (n 57) 56, at 59.

71  <www.guernseylegalresources.gg/article/97620/Trusts-Guernsey-Law-2007-Consolidated-text> accessed 10 December 2018.

72  The reference to "any purpose" is expanded in The Trusts (Guernsey) Law, 2007 s 12 to include *trusts for non-charitable purposes.* See the discussion of this global phenomenon in ch 5.

In the tax havens, this long-established trust device has morphed into many artificial forms, some of which – for example, the non-charitable purpose trusts which have no beneficiaries of any kind – are wholly counter-intuitive. The driving force behind the populating of this legal freak show has, as with the re-engineering of corporate forms, been the desire for secrecy (more euphemistically characterised as an assertion of privacy rights) and the avoidance – or outright evasion – of taxation.[73]

It is easy to see why the identification and registration of beneficial ownership flounders so badly in the case of trusts:

> *The lack of rigid formal requirements for the creation and operation of trusts, unlike companies, the proprietary protection accorded to beneficiaries and the tremendous flexibility allowed in inserting clauses in trust instruments, concerning management powers and diverse beneficial interests, make the trust a very useful device for achieving any commercial purpose [. . .].*[74]

Not all commercial purposes are benign, and facilitating beneficial ownership avoidance through the use of trusts is moving inexorably towards centre stage. When civil law trust-like structures are added to the mix, the scale of the problem confronting those wishing to pin down ownership of the assets held within them becomes apparent.

## The Wakf[75]

A *wakf* is an endowment, which may be for private or public benefit. In the case of private endowments, the beneficiaries are a few individuals or a limited class such as the children or descendants of the founder (*wakf al-ahli*). Public, and hence charitable, endowments (far more common) are for the benefit of the public or a large class of society and become part of public property (*wakf al-khayri*).

---

73 See ch 5. In a fiscal context, see Andres Knobel (Nicholas Shaxson ed), 'Trusts: Weapons of Mass Injustice?' *Tax Justice Network* (13 February 2017) <www.taxjustice.net/wp-content/uploads/2017/02/Trusts-Weapons-of-Mass-Injustice-Final-12-FEB-2017.pdf> accessed 10 December 2018. For an example of mass marketing see Barry S Engel, *Protect Your Assets – Set Up a Trust* (2018): "These versatile legal structures can put your money beyond the reach of creditors, whether the claim ensues from a malpractice case, an accident on your property, or a divorce. They can save your heirs (or your heirs' heirs) hundreds of thousands of dollars in taxes. In all kinds of trusts, you arrange for a trustee to manage certain assets for a beneficiary. Some trusts are revocable, which means you can modify or cancel them at any time". <www.barryengel.com/protect-your-assets-set-up-a-trust> accessed 10 December 2018.

74 D Hayton and others, *Underhill and Hayton Law of Trusts and Trustees* (n 56) para 1.139.

75 See Abdul Qadir, *Wakf: Islamic Law of Charitable Trust* (Global Vision Publishing House, Dehli 2004). More generally, see Ayatullah Sayyid Abulqasim al-Khui, *Rationality of Islam* (Islamic Seminary Publication, available via Ahlul Bayt Digital Islamic Library Project <www.al-islam.org/rationality-islam-ayatullah-sayyid-abulqasim-al-khui/islamic-teachings#wakf-endowment>) accessed 10 December 2018.

Not mentioned in the Qur'an, the *wakf* is regarded as deriving its legitimacy principally from a number of *hadiths*.[76] The founder of a *wakf* need not be a Muslim but must be of full legal capacity and not under interdiction for prodigality or bankruptcy. Property transferred to a *wakf* must be something over which the founder has control and which is freely alienable by the founder. The property must be in a form which is transferable and not of a nature which would be unlawful under Sharia. The purpose of the *wakf* must itself not be unlawful under Sharia. *Wakfs* must be perpetual, and their foundation is an irrevocable and binding act. The founder usually appoints the administrator of the *wakf* (which role he may fulfil himself – it is generally held that he must be Muslim and male).

Islamic scholar Dr Hossein Esmaeili is of the opinion that the *wakf* in comparison to the trust has lacked dynamism: "*Waqf*, which was established as an innovative institution from the early stages of development of Islamic law has frozen in time and arguably failed to be an effective institution in addressing wealth management in the Muslim world".[77]

Perhaps this lack of evolutionary verve has prompted instances of its abuse. Undoubtedly firmly grounded in charitable intent, the *wakf* has on occasion, not unlike its cousin the trust, been employed a little less than altruistically. It became a means of safeguarding property against the risk of expropriation (whilst permitting the founder still to be able to control and maintain the property held in the *wakf* in his and his heirs assumed capacity as *mutawali* (trustees)). It has been used as a method to evade taxation.[78]

A point of disagreement amongst Islamic jurists is whether the assets held by a *wakf* are owned (albeit without right of disposal) by the beneficiaries, or in the

---

76  A *hadith* is a written record of speech, actions and commands of the Prophet Muhammad (pbuh).

77  Hossein Esmaeili, *The Relationship Between the Wakf Institution in Islamic Law and the Rule of Law in the Middle East* 1 <http://waqfacademy.org/wp-content/uploads/2013/03/Dr-Hossein-Esmaeili-HE.-Date.-Relationship-between-waqf-institution-in-islamic-law-rule-of-law.pdf> accessed 10 December 2018. However, the increasing popularity of the "*cash wakf*" which is by its nature moveable based (tracing its origin to the Ottoman empire in the 15th century CE) has the potential to solve the problem of unproductive and immobilised *wakf* properties: Mohammad Mahbubi Ali, 'Unleashing the Potential of Cash *Waqf New Straits Times* (9 June 2017) <www.nst.com.my/opinion/columnists/2017/06/247185/unleashing-potential-cash-waqf> accessed 10 December 2018.

78  Hossein Esmaeili, *The Relationship Between the Wakf Institution* (n 77) 6. Corruption on the part of administrators of *wakfs* holding real estate in India has become a point of public debate: Saba Naqvi, 'Allah's Left the Building' *Outlook Magazine* (21 September 2009) <www.outlookindia.com/magazine/story/allahs-left-the-building/261789> accessed 10 December 2018. For a growing awareness of the need for transparency and accountability in the administration of *wakfs* see Hidayatul Ihsan and Muhammad Akhyar Adnan, *Waqf Accounting and the Construction of Accountability* <http://waqfacademy.org/wp-content/uploads/2013/02/Hidayatul-Ihsan-Muhammad-Akhyar-Adnan-HI-MAA.-Date.-Waqf-Accounting-The-Construction-of-Accountability.-Place.-Pub.pdf> accessed 10 December 2018.

alternative whether – because a *wakf* is irrevocable and perpetual – that ownership, immediately upon the declaration, is transferred to God.[79]

A structure in which the assets are owned in perpetuity by God is one which current thinking on beneficial ownership – let alone the registration and disclosure of beneficial ownership – has yet to embrace. Whilst it would be impious to claim that a *wakf* was on a par with ownerless "orphan structures",[80] the absence of a human (or other legal person) as owner of the underlying assets will surely not go unnoticed amongst the more creative designers of chimeric offshore structures.

### *Foundations*[81]

Foundations, once in offshore terms the preserve of Liechtenstein (Stiftungen), are now available globally, and what was originally the preserve of civil law is now a form recognised by and promoted within common law jurisdictions.[82]

Unlike a trust, which has no legal personality of its own (a trust exists in the relationship between the settlor, trustees and beneficiaries), a foundation is a legal entity, with the capacity – like a corporation – to govern itself.[83] Unlike a corporation, it has no shareholders or other form of participation, but, in common with a trust, it has beneficiaries. Unlike beneficiaries under a trust, they have no proprietary interests and are perforce passive. It is an 'orphan' structure.[84]

The more common uses of foundations (and the motivations for using foundations) relevant to human rights abuse include tax and estate planning, asset protection planning, maintenance of corporate control, assistance to charities, separation of voting and economic benefits in investment holding companies, ownership of private trust companies, operation of employee share option schemes and holding assets off balance sheet.

As a state creation, a foundation registers its creation with that state, though in many cases the register is not available for public inspection or merely to the extent that the name of the foundation is accessible.

As with a trust, a foundation exists in order to hold a fund, which can comprise any form of property. A foundation itself does not trade, but by holding shares in trading entities this limitation is of no practical effect. The assets transferred to a foundation may come from any person and not merely the founder identified in

---

79  See Abdul Qadir, *Wakf* (n 75) 13.
80  See ch 5.
81  See ch 5 for a wider discussion on foundations in Liechtenstein, Panama and Nevis.
82  See Paolo Panico, *Private Foundations, Law and Practice* (Oxford University Press, 2014) and Appendix One.
83  In civil law systems, as a special-purpose fund, a foundation comes into existence as a legal person in order to fulfil its purpose; in common law systems its existence as a legal person is a matter of statute. See generally Paolo Panico, *Private Foundations, Law and Practice* (n 82) paras 6.11 to 6.34.
84  See ch 5.

the constitutional documents of the foundation itself. This is reflected in the fact that it is very common for the founder to be a professional fiduciary.

The purpose of the foundation is contained in its constitution. It is common for the founder to have powers reserved under which the founder can amend the purpose and amend the identity (or percentage entitlement) of the beneficiaries, in much the same way as the objects of a company and the rights attaching to its shares can be mutated over time. Entitlement to benefit can therefore pass from group to group, each supplanting its predecessor, and prominence may be given to a particular individual, wholly secretly.

Unlike a trust, which is open to attack as a sham – on the basis that the settlor did not have a true intent to create it, that those intended to benefit and the funds to be settled are insufficiently identified (the 'three certainties'), the existence and validity of a foundation once registered is beyond challenge. Even the requirement that a foundation in order to be constituted has to hold property has been abandoned in some offshore jurisdictions, and the foundation – wholly unlike a trust or a corporation – is born naked and unadorned.[85] Paolo Panico regards this abandonment as radical, providing "operational flexibility" but "although it may look like a small step for practical purposes, is in fact a major conceptual leap that involves a dramatic departure from the very notion of a foundation".[86]

Because the founder has in many jurisdictions wide powers in relation to the administration of the foundation and of disposition, the difficulty often encountered by over-zealous and possessive settlors of trusts, who whilst acquiescing in the transfer of assets to trustees nevertheless seek still to control those assets (which eliminates one of the three certainties and fatally wounds the trust) is entirely absent.

From an ownership perspective, there is a vacuum. In the modern, offshore forms, no property will have passed from a founder to the foundation, and as the beneficiaries of the foundation have no proprietary rights to the foundation assets,[87] the only "owner" is the foundation itself; yet the foundation cannot itself benefit from the assets which it holds.

---

85  For example, Foundations (Jersey) Law 2009 Art 7(1) and Foundations Act 2011 s 15 (Isle of Man) provide that a foundation need not have "an initial endowment" (Jersey) or "an initial dedication of assets" (Isle of Man). Initial minimum capital requirements are however found in Liechtenstein, Austria, Panama, Malta and Luxembourg, though in each case the amount is modest (the highest being €70,000 in Austria – Privatstiftungsgesetz, s 4; the lowest, US$1 in the Seychelles – Foundations Act 2009 s 8).

86  Paolo Panico, *Private Foundations, Law and Practice* (n 82) para 6.34.

87  For example, both Foundations Act 2011 s 30(1) (Isle of Man) and Foundations Act 2012 s 29(1) (Cook Islands) provide: "A beneficiary under a foundation has no interest in the foundation's assets".

## Conclusions

Ownership is not an elemental concept, and the very word "ownership" has to be applied with great caution. To regard "ownership" as a universal descriptive, self-defining and rigidly bound, is to play into the hands of tax-planners and offshore alchemists for whom "ownership" is not a stable element but a mutable categorisation.

To speak of an "owner" and to search for the "beneficial owner" (outright, ultimate, intermediary or immediate) across a whole range of different legal structures which have their origins in widely different legal systems is to seek the holy grail. Hordes of diligent legislators, regulators, law enforcement officers and assorted bureaucrats are engaged in such a quest.

No one can "own" the property held in a trust, foundation or charity in the sense in which "ownership" is commonly understood. In Muslim scholarship, the ultimate owner of property held in a waqf is God Himself. An apparent owner may be a person of straw, their asset encumbered to the hilt. There may even be no owner at all.[88]

This has self-evidently serious consequences for transparency strategies which are based on the disclosure of "ownership".

88 See the discussion of so-called "orphan structures" in ch 5.

# Appendix one

## Foundation jurisdictions

| Jurisdiction | Statute |
| --- | --- |
| Anguilla | Anguilla Foundation Act 2008 |
| Antigua and Barbuda | International Foundations Act 2007 |
| Austria | Privatstiftungsgesetz 1993 |
| Bahamas | Foundations Act 2004 (amended 2005, 2007, 2011) |
| Barbados | Foundations Act 2013–2 |
| Belize | International Foundations Act 2010 |
| Cook Islands | Cook Islands Foundations Act 2012 |
| Denmark | Danish Foundation Act (Fondsloven) |
| Guernsey | Foundations (Guernsey) Law 2012 |
| Isle of Man | Foundations Act 2011 |
| Jersey | Foundations (Jersey) Law 2009 |
| Liechtenstein | Personen und Gesellschaftsrecht 1926; Stiftungsrechtsverordnung 2009 |
| Malta | Act XIII of 2007 |
| Mauritius | Foundations Act 2012 |
| Netherlands Antilles | National Ordinance Regarding Foundations 1998; Civil Code, Book 2 2004 ("Stichting Particulier Fonds") |
| Nevis | Multiform Foundation Ordinance 2004 |
| Panama | La Ley de Fundaciones de Panamá 1995 |
| Seychelles | Foundations Act 2009 |
| St Kitts | Foundations Act 2003 |
| Vanuatu | Foundations Act 2009 |

# Appendix two

## Convention on the law applicable to trusts and on their recognition 1 July 1985

## Contracting parties (as at 1 July 2018)[89]

| Contracting Party | Signature | Ratification/ Accession | Entry into Force |
|---|---|---|---|
| Australia | 17.10.1991 | R 17.10.1991 | 01.01.1992 |
| Canada | 11.10.1988 | R 20.10.1992 | 01.01.1993 |
| Cyprus | 11.03.1998 | R 15.03.2017 | 01.06.2017 |
| France | 26.11.1991 | | |
| Italy | 01.07.1985 | R 21.02.1990 | 01.01.1992 |
| Liechtenstein | | A 13.12.2004 | 01.04.2006 |
| Luxembourg | 01.07.1985 | R 16.10.2003 | 01.01.2004 |
| Malta | | A 07.12.1994 | 01.03.1996 |
| Monaco | | A 01.06.2007 | 01.09.2008 |
| Netherlands | 01.07.1985 | R 28.11.1995 | 01.02.1996 |
| Panama | | A 30.08.2017 | 01.12.2018 |
| San Marino | | A 28.04.2005 | 01.08.2006 |
| Switzerland | 03.04.2007 | R 26.04.2007 | 01.07.2007 |
| United Kingdom of Great Britain and Northern Ireland | 10.01.1986 | R 17.11.1989 | 01.01.1992 |
| United States of America | 13.06.1988 | | |

89 <www.hcch.net/en/instruments/conventions/status-table/?cid=59> accessed 1 January 2019.

# Bibliography

## Cases

*Ayerst v C & K (Construction) Ltd* [1976] AC 167
*Commissioners of Income Tax v Pemsel* [1891] A.C. 531 at 583
*Costain, Re* (1961) 1961–71 MLR 1
*Gartside v I.R.C.* [1968] A.C. 533, HL
*Lord Dudley and Ward v Lady Dudley* (1705) Prec.Ch 241
*Macaura v Northern Assurance Company Limited* [1925] A.C. 619
*Prest v Petrodel Resources Ltd* [2013] UKSC 34
*Ring, Re* (1962) 1961–71 MLR 60

## Legislation and regulations

Cayman Islands Monetary Authority 'Guidance Notes on the Prevention and Detection of Money Laundering and Terrorist Financing in the Cayman Islands' (13 December 2017) (*Cayman Islands Monetary Authority*) <www.cima.ky/upimages/commonfiles/1513184321GuidanceNotesonthePreventionandDetectionofMoneyLaunderingandTerroistFinancinghhintheCaymanIslands_1513184322.pdf> accessed 10 December 2018

Charities Act 1962 <https://legislation.gov.im/cms/images/LEGISLATION/PRINCIPAL/1962/1962-0001/CharitiesAct1962_1.pdf> accessed 10 December 2018 (Isle of Man)

Charities Act 2011 <www.legislation.gov.uk/ukpga/2011/25/contents> accessed 10 December 2018 (UK)

Charities Registration Act 1989 <www.legislation.gov.im/cms/images/LEGISLATION/PRINCIPAL/1989/1989-0011/CharitiesRegistrationAct1989_1.pdf> accessed 10 December 2018 (Isle of Man)

Companies Act 2006 <www.legislation.gov.uk/ukpga/2006/46/contents> accessed 10 December 2018 (UK)

Convention on the Law Applicable to Trusts and on their Recognition (1 July 1985) *The Hague Convention* <www.hcch.net/en/instruments/conventions/fulltext/?cid=59> accessed 10 December 2018

Foundations Act 2009 <https://seylii.org/sc/legislation/act/32-2> accessed 10 December 2018 (Seychelles)

Foundations Act 2011 <https://legislation.gov.im/cms/images/LEGISLATION/PRINCIPAL/2011/2011-0017/FoundationsAct2011_6.pdf> accessed 10 December 2018(Isle of Man)

Foundations Act 2012 <www.fsc.gov.ck/cookIslandsFscApp/content/assets/d419dd8deb9aa1057b6033ac7faa6979/Foundations%20Act%202012%20No11.PDF> accessed 10 December 2018 (Cook Islands)

Foundations (Jersey) Law 2009 <www.jerseylaw.je/laws/revised/Pages/13.265.aspx> accessed 10 December 2018 (Jersey)

Fraudulent Assignments Act 1736 <www.legislation.gov.im/cms/images/LEGISLATION/PRINCIPAL/1736/1736-0002/FraudulentAssignmentsAct1736_1.pdf> accessed 10 December 2018 (Isle of Man)

Isle of Man Government Financial Services Authority, 'AML/CFT Requirements and Guidance' (*The Isle of Man Financial Services Authority*) <www.iomfsa.im/amlcft/amlcft-requirements-and-guidance/> accessed 10 December 2018

Recognition of Trusts Act 1988 <https://legislation.gov.im/cms/images/LEGIS
    LATION/PRINCIPAL/1988/1988-0008/RecognitionofTrustsAct1988_1.pdf>
    accessed 10 December 2018 (Isle of Man)
Senior Courts Act 1981 <www.legislation.gov.uk/ukpga/1981/54/> accessed 10
    December 2018 (UK)
Statute of Elizabeth (43 Eliz.1, c.4, 1601) (England)
Trusts Act 1995 *<https://legislation.gov.im/cms/images/LEGISLATION/PRINCIPAL/
    1995/1995-0018/TrustsAct1995_2.pdf>* accessed 10 December 2018 (Isle of Man)
The Trusts (Guernsey) Law, 2007 <www.guernseylegalresources.gg/article/97620/
    Trusts-Guernsey-Law-2007-Consolidated-text> accessed 10 December 2018
    (Guernsey)

## International documents

Convention of 1 July 1985 on the Law Applicable to Trusts and on their Recog-
    nition (*Hague Convention*) <www.hcch.net/en/instruments/conventions/full-
    text/?cid=59> accessed 12 December 2018

## United Nations documents

*Guiding Principles on Business and Human Rights: Implementing the United
    Nations "Protect, Respect and Remedy" Framework ("The Ruggie Principles")* A/
    HRC/17/31 / 21 March 2011. <www.ohchr.org/Documents/Issues/Business/
    A-HRC-17-31_AEV.pdf> accessed 10 December 2018
UNCESCR, *General Comment: Business Activities* (10 August 2017) UN Doc E/C.12/
    GC/24 <https://tbinternet.ohchr.org/_layouts/treatybodyexternal/Download.
    aspx?symbolno=E%2fC.12%2fGC%2f24&Lang=en> accessed 10 December 2018
United Nations Economic and Social Council, *Statement on the Obligations of States
    Parties Regarding the Corporate Sector and Economic, Social and Cultural Rights*
    (12 July 2011) UN Doc E/C.12/2011/1 <https://tbinternet.ohchr.org/_lay-
    outs/treatybodyexternal/Download.aspx?symbolno=E%2FC.12%2F2011%2F1&
    Lang=en> accessed 10 December 2018

## Secondary sources

Afghani, Ali Reza *Ownership in Islam (Sayyid Muhammad Husayni Beheshti trs,
    Islamic Thought Foundation) available via Ahlul Bayt Digital Islamic Library Pro-
    ject* <www.al-islam.org/ownership-islam-sayyid-muhammad-husayni-beheshti>
    accessed 10 December 2018
Ali, Mohammad Mahbubi 'Unleashing the Potential of Cash Waqf' *New Straits Times*
    (9 June 2017) <www.nst.com.my/opinion/columnists/2017/06/247185/
    unleashing-potential-cash-waqf> accessed 10 December 2018
Aryani, Aini *Ownership in Islamic Perspective 3 June 2008* <http://ainiaryani.
    blogspot.com/2008/06/ownership-in-islamic-perspective.html> accessed 10
    December 2018
Ayatullah Sayyid Abulqasim al-Khui *Rationality of Islam* (Islamic Seminary Pub-
    lication, *available via Ahlul Bayt Digital Islamic Library Project* <www.al-islam.

org/rationality-islam-ayatullah-sayyid-abulqasim-al-khui/islamic-teachings#wakf-endowment>) accessed 10 December 2018

Beckett, Paul *Tax Havens and International Human Rights* (Routledge, Abingdon. 2017)

Bergin, Tom and Grey, Stephen *Insight – How UK Company Formation Agents Fuel Fraud* (Reuters, United Kingdom, 18 March 2016) <http://uk.reuters.com/article/uk-regulations-agents-insight-idUKKCN0WK17W> accessed 10 December 2018

Berle, A and Means, G C *The Modern Corporation and Private Property*, original published in 1932 by Harcourt, Brace & World, Inc (reprinted with an Introduction by M L Weidenbaum and M Jensen, Transaction Publishers, New Brunswick (USA) and London, 1991, tenth printing 2009)

Bernaz, Nadia *Business and Human Rights: History, Law and Policy – Bridging the Accountability Gap* (Routledge, Abingdon 2017)

BVI News Online 'More Bad News for Financial Services: 35% Drop' (*bvinews.com*, 19 January 2017) <http://bvinews.com/new/more-bad-news-for-financial-services-35-drop/> accessed 10 December 2018

Collier, Paul 'In Pursuit of the $21 Trillion' *Prospect Magazine* (2013) <www.prospectmagazine.co.uk> (article no longer available online)

*The Common Law and Civil Law Traditions* (The Robbins Collection, School of Law (Boalt Hall), University of California at Berkeley) <www.law.berkeley.edu/library/robbins/pdf/CommonLawCivilLawTraditions.pdf> accessed 10 December 2018

Engel, Barry S *Protect Your Assets – Set up a Trust* (2018) <www.barryengel.com/protect-your-assets-set-up-a-trust> accessed 10 December 2018

Esmaeili, Hossein *The Relationship Between the Wakf Institution in Islamic Law and the Rule of Law in the Middle East* 1 <http://waqfacademy.org/wp-content/uploads/2013/03/Dr-Hossein-Esmaeili-HE.-Date.-Relationship-between-waqf-institution-in-islamic-law-rule-of-law.pdf> accessed 10 December 2018

Financial Action Task Force, Forty Recommendations (October 2004) <www.fatf-gafi.org/publications/fatfrecommendations/documents/the40recommendationspublishedoctober2004.html> accessed 10 December 2018

——— *FATF Guidance on Transparency and Beneficial Ownership* (Financial Action Task Force, October 2014) <www.fatf-gafi.org/media/fatf/documents/reports/Guidance-transparency-beneficial-ownership.pdf> accessed 10 December 2018

Freemont-Smith, M R *The Legal Meaning of Charity* (The Urban Institute, April 2013) 15 <www.urban.org/sites/default/files/the-legal-meaning-of-charity.pdf> accessed 10 December 2018

Genova, Judith *Wittgenstein: A Way of Seeing* (Routledge, Abingdon, 1995)

Glister, J and Lee, J *Hanbury & Martin: Modern Equity* (20th Edition, Sweet & Maxwell, London, 2015)

Graziadei, Michele, Mattei, Ugo and Smith, Lionel (eds), *Commercial Trusts in European Private Law* (Cambridge University Press, Cambridge, 2005)

*Guiding Principles on Disclosure Requirements for Islamic Capital Market Products (Sukuk and Islamic Collective Investment Schemes)* (IFSB-19, April 2017)

Hayton, D and others *Underhill and Hayton Law of Trusts and Trustees* (19th Edition, LexisNexis, London, 2016)

Ihsan, Hidayatul and Adnan, Muhammad Akhyar, *Waqf Accounting and The Construction of Accountability* <http://waqfacademy.org/wp-content/uploads/2013/02/

Hidayatul-Ihsan-Muhammad-Akhyar-Adnan-HI-MAA.-Date.-Waqf-Accounting-The-Construction-of-Accountability.-Place.-Pub.pdf> accessed 10 December 2018

*IOSCO Objectives and Principles of Securities Regulation of the International Organization of Securities Commissions* (May 2017) <www.iosco.org/library/pubdocs/pdf/IOSCOPD561.pdf> accessed 10 December 2018

────── *Methodology for Assessing Implementation of the IOSCO Objectives and Principles of Securities Regulation* (May 2017) <www.iosco.org/library/pubdocs/pdf/IOSCOPD562.pdf> accessed 10 December 2018

────── *Principles on Client Identification and Beneficial Ownership for the Securities Industry* (May 2004) <www.iosco.org/library/pubdocs/pdf/IOSCOPD167.pdf> accessed 10 December 2018

Islamic Financial Services Board Core Principles for Islamic Finance Regulation (IFSB-21)

Kelsen, Hans *Pure Theory of Law* (Max Knight tr, University of California Press, Berkeley, CA, 1967)

Knobel, Andres (Shaxson, Nicholas ed), 'Trusts: Weapons of Mass Injustice?' *Tax Justice Network* (13 February 2017) <www.taxjustice.net/wp-content/uploads/2017/02/Trusts-Weapons-of-Mass-Injustice-Final-12-FEB-2017.pdf> accessed 10 December 2018

Leigh, David, Frayman, Harold and Ball, James 'How the Nominee Trick Works' *ICIJ* (Washington, DC, 25 November 2012) <www.icij.org/offshore/how-nominee-trick-done> accessed 10 December 2018

────── 'Front Men Disguise the Offshore Game's Real Players' *ICIJ* (Washington, DC) <www.icij.org/front-men-disguise-offshore-players> accessed 16 April 2017 (since removed from the ICIJ website)

Mah, Connie L *Equitable Doctrines and Maxims* (Law Now, 1 May 2008) <www.lawnow.org/equitable-doctrines-and-maxims/> accessed 10 December 2018

Maitland, Frederic William *The Unincorporate Body in, the Collected Papers of Frederic William Maitland, vol. 3* (H A L Fisher ed, Cambridge University Press, Cambridge, 1911)

McGhee, J (ed), *Snell's Equity* (31st Edition, Sweet & Maxwell, London, 2005)

Micklethwait, J and Wooldridge, A *The Company, a Short History of a Revolutionary Idea* (Modern Library, New York, 2005)

Naqvi, Saba 'Allah's Left the Building' *Outlook Magazine* (21 September 2009) <www.outlookindia.com/magazine/story/allahs-left-the-building/261789> accessed 10 December 2018

Nichols, Barry *An Introduction to Roman Law* (Clarendon Law Series, London, 1972)

Nurlaelawati, Euis 'Zakat and the Concept of Ownership in Islam: Yusuf Qaradawi's Perspective on Islamic Economics' 48 *Al-Jami'ah* 2 (2010 M/1431 H 365) <www.aljamiah.or.id/index.php/AJIS/article/view/115/136> accessed 10 December 2018

Padfield, Stefan J 'In Search of a Higher Standard: Rethinking Fiduciary Duties of Directors of Wholly-owned Subsidiaries' 10 *Fordham Journal of Corporate & Financial Law* 1, 79 (2004)

Panico, Paolo *Private Foundations, Law and Practice* (Oxford University Press, Oxford, 2014)

Qadir, Abdul *Wakf: Islamic Law of Charitable Trust* (Global Vision Publishing House, Delhi, 2004)

Ryle, Gerard and Candea, Stefan 'Faux Corporate Directors Stand in for Fraudsters, Despots and Spies' *ICIJ* (Washington, DC, 4 July 2013) <www.icij.org/offshore/faux-corporate-directors-stand-fraudsters-despots-and-spies> accessed 10 December 2018

Singapore Academy of Law, *Equity and Trusts* <www.singaporelaw.sg/sglaw/laws-of-singapore/commercial-law/chapter-18> accessed 10 December 2018

Sogge, David *The corporate wax nose* (Transformation, 16 November 2016) <www.opendemocracy.net/transformation/david-sogge/corporate-wax-nose?> accessed 10 December 2018

Tucker, L and others *Lewin on Trusts* (19th Edition, Sweet & Maxwell, London, 2014)

United Kingdom Government, Department for Business, Innovation & Skills *People with Significant Control" Companies House Register Goes Live (gov.uk,* 30 June 2016) <www.gov.uk/government/news/people-with-significant-control-companies-house-register-goes-live> accessed 10 December 2018

———— Companies House, *Summary Guide for Companies – Register of People with Significant Control (gov.uk,* 27 January 2016) <www.gov.uk/government/publications/guidance-to-the-people-with-significant-control-requirements-for-companies-and-limited-liability-partnerships> accessed 10 December 2018

———— Department for Business, Innovation & Skills, *Statutory Guidance on the Meaning of "Significant Influence or Control" over Companies in the Context of the Register of People with Significant Control (gov.uk,* 14 April 2016) <www.gov.uk/government/uploads/system/uploads/attachment_data/file/523120/PSC_statutory_guidance_companies.pdf> accessed 10 December 2018

Waters, Donovan 'The Hague Trusts Convention Twenty Years On' in Michele Graziadei, Ugo Mattei and Lionel Smith (eds), *Commercial Trusts in European Private Law* (Cambridge University Press, Cambridge, 2005)

Winter, Steven L *A Clearing in the Forest: Law, Life, and Mind* (The University of Chicago Press, Chicago, 2001)

Wittgenstein, Ludwig *Philosophical Investigations* (G E M Anscombe, P M S Hacker and Joachim Schulte tr, Wiley-Blackwell, Revised 4th Edition, Oxford, 2009)

# 3 Disclosure and registration initiatives

## Part one: Introduction

This chapter is a review and comparative analysis of disclosure and registration initiatives taken globally, regionally and nationally. The primary objective in this chapter is to determine to what extent all transparency strategies share a common methodology and whether that methodology is fit for purpose. Specifically, to what extent is each based on beneficial ownership disclosure, and how does such reliance weaken those initiatives?

When from the mid-nineteenth century onwards ever more elaborate corporate structures were evolving, the underlying principle was to promote trade through the limitation of liability of those beneficially interested who would otherwise have been financially exposed. In our own time, the greatly evolved and morphed successors to such structures are increasingly used to conceal the identity of those beneficial owners, and this concealment is, in the hands of the unscrupulous, a cloak of invisibility thrown over tax evasion, bribery and corruption, fraud, the financing of terrorism and the abuse of internationally recognised human rights norms.

The thesis is simple, but potent. Worldwide, efforts are being made to implement enforcement mechanisms for identifying beneficial owners and thereby rendering them accountable. Yet the very meaning of "ownership" is far from clear.[1] In most cases, transparency strategies based on registration are self-referring, in that they *deem* what is meant by "ownership" and base their conclusions as to what is to happen in consequence upon mere assumptions. Furthermore, there now exists a worldwide industry in beneficial ownership avoidance using orphan structures.[2] This uncertain definition coupled with such robust counter-initiatives calls the reliance on an ownership-disclosure-based registration and transparency strategy into question.

That those framing and seeking to implement the transparency initiatives cannot fail to be aware of these triple impediments suggests that the political will – at

---

1 Ch 2.
2 Ch 5.

a national level as well as internationally – behind beneficial ownership disclosure measures may not be what it appears.[3] There is no compelling political reason why it ought not to be:

> BOT [beneficial ownership transparency] remains low-hanging fruit in the fight to protect the transatlantic region against the threat of authoritarian finance. The democratic rule of law systems of the United States and Europe should work together to build a resilient financial sphere and, ultimately, a fair and just international financial system that is difficult for autocrats to abuse. These countries should learn from one another's successes and missteps to implement the most effective BOT standards possible.[4]

The reality is not as polarised or as confrontational as this book's sub-title "Transparency Strategies and Counter-Initiatives" would suggest. There are indeed winners and losers but by no means always because the one defeats the other. There are own goals, in the sense that the transparency strategies themselves are flawed.

## Part two: Fundamental transparency strategies

### *The World Bank's StAR initiative*

On 24 March 2011, the Stolen Asset Recovery (StAR) Initiative of the World Bank and the United Nations Office on Drugs and Crime issued their report, *The*

---

3　This apparent lack of political will, at least as regards cross-border solutions, has already manifested itself in the context of anti-money-laundering initiatives: "Despite the transnational nature of most money-laundering schemes that allow kleptocrats, tax dodgers and organised crime barons to enjoy the proceeds of their crimes with impunity, the global response remains trenchantly national, hindered by complex cross-border mutual legal assistance treaties and a lack of information sharing. The adage 'follow the money' is often impossible to implement". Tom Keatinge, 'We Cannot Fight Cross-border Money Laundering with Local Tools' *Financial Times* (9 September 2018) <www.ft.com/content/0397fc40-b281-11e8-87e0-d84e0d934341> accessed 20 December 2018. For an overview of international beneficial ownership strategies see Yunhong Liu, *How Compliance Practices Should Adapt to Increased Beneficial Ownership Scrutiny* (Dun & Bradstreet, 2016) <www.dnb.co.uk/content/dam/english/dnb-solutions/supply-management/beneficial-ownership-white-paper.pdf> accessed 20 December 2018.

4　Helsinki Commission Report, *Incorporation Transparency: The First Line of Financial Defense* (4 October 2018) <www.csce.gov/sites/helsinkicommission.house.gov/files/BOT%20Final.pdf> accessed 20 December 2018. (The Commission on Security and Cooperation in Europe, also known as the US Helsinki Commission, is an independent agency of the United States federal government charged with monitoring compliance with the Helsinki Accords and advancing comprehensive security through promotion of human rights, democracy, and economic, environmental and military cooperation in 57 countries. The Commission consists of nine members from the US Senate, nine from the House of Representatives, and one member each from the Departments of State, Defense, and Commerce. <www.csce.gov> accessed 20 December 2018).

*Puppet Masters: How the Corrupt Use Legal Structures to Hide Stolen Assets and What to Do About It*[5] *commenting*:[6]

> '*We need to put corporate transparency back on the national and international agenda*,' said Emile van der Does de Willebois, World Bank Senior Financial Sector Specialist who led the StAR research team. '*It is important for governments to increase the transparency of their legal entities and arrangements and at the same time improve the capacity of law enforcement.*'
>
> The report . . . examines how bribes, embezzled state assets and other criminal proceeds are being hidden via legal structures – shell companies, foundations, trusts and others. The study also provides policy makers with practical recommendations on how to step up ongoing international efforts to uncover flows of criminal funds and prevent criminals from misusing shell companies and other legal entities.
>
> The study explains how corrupt public officials and their associates conceal their connection to ill-gotten funds by exploiting legal and institutional loopholes that allow opacity in companies, foundations, and trust-like structures. It also lists obstacles to investigating and establishing the origin and ownership of stolen assets: the difficulty of identifying where legal entities operate and have business relationships, lack of access to information on beneficial ownership, and the use of complex and multi-jurisdictional corporate structures.

The introduction to *The Puppet Masters* makes clear the extent of the problems of establishing transparency and the urgent social need to do so:

> Corruption is estimated to be at least a $40 billion a year business. Every day, funds destined for schools, healthcare, and infrastructure in the world's most fragile economies are siphoned off and stashed away in the world's financial centers and tax havens. Corruption, like a disease, is eating away at the foundation of people's faith in government. It undermines the stability and security of nations. So it is a development challenge in more ways than one: it directly affects development assistance, but it also undermines the preconditions for growth and equity. We need mobilization at the highest level so that corruption is tackled effectively. This report, *The Puppet Masters*, deals with the corporate and financial structures that form the building blocks of hidden money trails. In particular, it focuses on the ease with which

---

5  Emile van der Does de Willebois and others, *The Puppet Masters* (World Bank Publications, 2011). The report examines over 150 cases of large-scale corruption, finding that most such cases involve the use of one or more corporate vehicles to conceal beneficial ownership.
6  The World Bank, 'Corrupt Money Concealed in Shell Companies and Other Opaque Legal Entities, Finds New StAR Study' *The World Bank* (24 October 2011) <www.worldbank.org/en/news/press-release/2011/10/24/corrupt-money-concealed-in-shell-companies-and-other-opaque-legal-entities-finds-new-star-study> accessed 20 December 2018.

corrupt actors hide their interests behind a corporate veil and the difficulties investigators face in trying to lift that veil.

## G20

*Brisbane November 2014, Washington DC April 2016, Hangzhou September 2016, Hamburg July 2017*

The 2014 G20 Brisbane Summit endorsed the initiative by the Financial Action Task Force ('FATF') in 2012 to set the benchmarks for the determination of beneficial ownership.[7]

Following the November 2014 G20 Brisbane Summit, the leaders issued their communiqué under which they adopted the High-Level Principles:

> 14. We endorse the 2015–16 G20 Anti-Corruption Action Plan that will support growth and resilience. Our actions are building cooperation and networks, including to enhance mutual legal assistance, recovery of the proceeds of corruption and denial of safe haven to corrupt officials. We commit to improve the transparency of the public and private sectors, and of beneficial ownership by implementing the G20 High Level Principles on Beneficial Ownership Transparency.[8]

In the communiqué[9] issued on 27 April 2016 following the meeting of G20 Finance Ministers and Central Bank Governors in Washington, DC, that month, beneficial ownership and the need for transparency featured prominently:

> 8. The G20 reiterates the high priority it attaches to financial transparency and effective implementation of the standards on transparency by all, in particular with regard to the beneficial ownership of legal persons and legal arrangements. Improving the transparency of the beneficial ownership of legal persons and legal arrangements is vital to protect the integrity of the international financial system, and to prevent misuse of these entities and

---

7 Now central in the context of taxation also to the exchange of information on request (EIOR) and to the automatic exchange of information (AEOI) embodied in the Common Reporting Standard (CRS) – see the discussion on this in the Organisation for Economic Co-operation and Development (OECD 'OECD Secretary-General's Report to G20 Finance Ministers, April 2016' (*OECD*, April 2016) <www.oecd.org/tax/oecd-secretary-general-tax-report-g20-finance-ministers-april-2016.pdf> accessed 20 December 2018.

8 'G20 High-Level Principles on Beneficial Ownership Transparency' (*Australian Government, Attorney General's Department*, 2014) <www.ag.gov.au/CrimeAndCorruption/AntiCorruption/Documents/G20High-LevelPrinciplesOnBeneficialOwnershipTransparency.pdf> accessed 20 December 2018. See also G20 High-Level Principles on Private Sector Transparency and Integrity 2015 <www.g20.org/sites/default/files/media/g20_high_level_principles_on_private_sector_transparency_and_integrity.pdf> accessed 20 December 2018.

9 <www.g20.utoronto.ca/2016/160415-finance.html> accessed 20 December 2018.

arrangements for corruption, tax evasion, terrorist financing and money laundering. The G20 reiterates that it is essential that all countries and jurisdictions fully implement the FATF standards on transparency and beneficial ownership of legal persons and legal arrangements and we express our determination to lead by example in this regard. We particularly stress the importance of countries and jurisdictions improving the availability of beneficial ownership information to, and its international exchange between, competent authorities **for the purposes of tackling tax evasion, terrorist financing and money laundering**. We ask the FATF and the Global Forum on Transparency and Exchange of Information for Tax Purposes to make initial proposals by our October meeting on ways to improve the implementation of the international standards on transparency, including on the availability of beneficial ownership information, and its international exchange.

The G20 leaders in repeating themselves in their communiqué issued on 5 September 2016 following the Hangzhou Summit state:

20. Financial transparency and effective implementation of the standards on transparency by all, in particular with regard to the beneficial ownership of legal persons and legal arrangements, is vital to protecting **the integrity of the international financial system, and to preventing misuse of these entities and arrangements for corruption, tax evasion, terrorist financing and money laundering.**[10]

Distilling their approach in the form of the G20 Anti-Corruption Action Plan 2017–2018, they state:

Beneficial ownership: Transparency over beneficial ownership is critical to preventing and exposing **corruption and illicit finance**. We will fully implement the FATF Recommendations on Transparency and Beneficial Ownership of Legal Persons[11] and our Action Plans to implement the G20 High Level Principles on Beneficial Ownership Transparency. The G20 will further promote the identification of the true beneficial ownership and control of companies and legal arrangements, including trusts, wherever they are located. We will encourage and support other countries to implement beneficial ownership standards and best practice. We will promote the utilization of beneficial ownership information **to tackle corruption and related money laundering.**[12]

---

10 'G20 Leaders' Communiqué: Hangzhou Summit, Hangzhou' (University of Toronto, 5 September 2016) <www.g20.utoronto.ca/2016/160905-communique.html> accessed 20 December 2018 (Hangzhou Communiqué).
11 FATF Guidance on Transparency and Beneficial Ownership (n 29) makes no mention of beneficial ownership avoidance mechanisms.
12 'G20 Anti-Corruption Action Plan 2017–2018: 2016 Hangzhou Summit: Hangzhou, 5 September 2016' (University of Toronto, 2016) <www.g20.utoronto.ca/2016/160905-anticorruption.html> accessed 20 December 2018.

They propose to combat corruption and illicit finance flows 'while fully respecting international law, human rights and the rule of law as well as the sovereignty of each country'.[13]

Transparency and beneficial ownership get only a passing mention in the G20 Leaders' Declaration "Shaping an interconnected world" issued following the G20 Summit in Hamburg 7/8 July 2017:

> As an important tool in our fight against corruption, tax evasion, terrorist financing and money laundering, we will advance the effective implementation of the international standards on transparency and beneficial ownership of legal persons and legal arrangements, including the availability of information in the domestic and crossborder context.[14]

The Hamburg G20 2017 Leaders' Statement on Countering Terrorism is even briefer:

> We will advance the effective implementation of the international standards on transparency and beneficial ownership of legal persons and legal arrangements for the purposes of countering financing terrorism.[15]

This is amplified slightly in the G20 Hamburg Action Plan issued on 8 July 2017:

> As an important tool in our fight against corruption, tax evasion, terrorist financing and money laundering, we will advance the effective implementation of the international standards on transparency and beneficial ownership of legal persons and legal arrangements, including the availability of information in the domestic and cross-border context. In this regard, we welcome the work by the Financial Action Task Force (FATF) and the Global Forum on Transparency and Exchange of Information for Tax Purposes. We welcome the OECD's progress report on its work in complementary tax areas relating to beneficial ownership.[16] We ask the FATF and the OECD to

---

13 Hangzhou Communiqué (n 10) para 22. The scale of the problem of illicit fund flows is addressed by the World Customs Organization, *Illicit Financial Flows via Trade Mis-invoicing Study Report 2018* <www.wcoomd.org/-/media/wco/public/global/pdf/media/newsroom/reports/2018/wco-study-report-on-iffs_tm.pdf?db=web> accessed 20 December 2018 prepared in response to the G20 Hangzhou Communiqué.

14 G20 Leaders' Declaration: Hamburg Summit, Hamburg (University of Toronto, 2017) <www.g20.utoronto.ca/2017/2017-G20-leaders-declaration.pdf> accessed 20 December 2018.

15 G20 Leaders' Statement on Countering Terrorism: Hamburg Summit, Hamburg (University of Toronto, 2017) <www.g20.utoronto.ca/2017/2017-g20-statement-antiterror-en.pdf> accessed 20 December 2018.

16 Global Forum on Transparency and Exchange of Information for Tax Purposes: Tax Transparency 2017, Report on Progress <www.oecd.org/tax/transparency/global-forum-annual-report-2017.pdf> accessed 20 December 2018.

report back to our Finance Ministers and Central Bank Governors on further progress by early 2018.[17]

The absence of any suggested implementation mechanism does tend to imply that they have not quite thought this through.[18]

### *The 2014 G20 High-Level Principles on Beneficial Ownership Transparency*[19]

From the outset, the High-Level Principles make the assumption that legal structures and arrangements have a beneficial owner. It seems beyond their grasp that beneficial ownership may indeed be absent. The agenda, however, is apparently limited to the role of ultimate beneficial owner as ultimate taxpayer, the exchange of beneficial ownership information being characterised as desirable for the purposes of protecting 'the integrity and transparency of the global financial system' as if for no other.[20]

In its introduction to the principles issued following the 2014 Brisbane summit the G20 states:

> The G20 considers **financial transparency**, in particular the transparency of beneficial ownership of legal persons and arrangements, is a high priority. The G20 Leaders' Declaration from St Petersburg states, 'We encourage all countries to tackle the risks raised by the opacity of legal persons and legal

---

17  G20 Hamburg Action Plan para 6 (University of Toronto, 2017) <www.g20.utoronto.ca/2017/2017-g20-hamburg-action-plan-en.pdf> accessed 20 December 2018.

18  For example, the G20 High-Level Principles on the Liability of Legal Persons for Corruption, issued at the G20 Hamburg Summit, make no mention of beneficial ownership at all: (University of Toronto, 2017) <www.g20.utoronto.ca/2017/2017-g20-acwg-liberty-legal-persons-en.pdf> accessed 20 December 2018.

19  All G20 Australia 2014 materials are available from the 'G20 Information Centre' (University of Toronto, Munk School of Global Affairs) <www.g20.utoronto.ca/> accessed 20 December 2018.

20  Reflected at each G20 summit in the OECD Secretary General's Report to G20 Leaders November 2014 (Brisbane) <www.oecd.org/g20/topics/taxation/OECD-secretary-general-report-tax-matters-brisbane-november-2014.pdf> accessed 20 December 2018 and to the G20 Finance Ministers in April 2016 (Washington, DC). OECD, 'OECD Secretary-General's Report to G20 Finance Ministers, April 2016' (n 7) (as updated in OECD, 'OECD Secretary-General Report to G20 Finance Ministers: Chengdu People's Republic of China 23–24 July 2016' (*OECD*, 2016) <www.oecd.org/ctp/oecd-secretary-general-tax-report-g20-finance-ministers-july-2016.pdf> accessed 20 December 2018. And see OECD, 'G20/OECD Principles of Corporate Governance' (University of Toronto, September 2015) <www.g20.utoronto.ca/2015/G20-OECD-Principles-of-Corporate-Governance.pdf> accessed 20 December 2018 and the discussion of the application of the principles to publicly listed, regulated financial institutions in *Thematic Review on Corporate Governance* issued on 28 April 2017 by the Financial Stability Board <www.fsb.org/2017/04/thematic-review-on-corporate-governance/> accessed 20 December 2018.

arrangements'. In order to maintain the momentum, Leaders called upon Finance Ministers to update them by the 2014 G20 Leaders' Summit on the steps taken by G20 countries 'to meet FATF standards regarding the beneficial ownership of companies and other legal arrangements such as trusts by G20 countries leading by example.' At their meeting in Sydney in 2014, Finance Ministers and Central Bank Governors requested the ACWG provide them with an update before their April meeting on concrete actions the G20 could take to lead by example on beneficial ownership transparency and the implementation of relevant FATF standards. Following the G20 ACWG meeting in Sydney, ACWG co-chairs reported to Finance Ministers and Central Bank Governors that the ACWG agreed that G20 countries will lead by example by developing G20 High-Level Principles on Beneficial Ownership Transparency that will set out concrete measures G20 countries will take to prevent the misuse of and ensure transparency of legal persons and legal arrangements. **Improving the transparency of legal persons and arrangements is important to protect the integrity and transparency of the global financial system.** Preventing the misuse of these entities for illicit purposes such as corruption, tax evasion and money laundering supports the G20 objectives of increasing growth through private sector investment.

The G20 is committed to leading by example by endorsing a set of core principles on the transparency of beneficial ownership of legal persons and arrangements that are applicable across G20 work streams. These principles build on existing international instruments and standards, and allow sufficient flexibility to for our different constitutional and legal frameworks.

There are ten principles, recommendations in which range from the specific to the merely aspirational. Indeed, they are not so much "high level" as stratospheric:

1   Countries should have a definition of 'beneficial owner' that captures the natural person(s) who ultimately owns or controls the legal person or legal arrangement. [*Addressing the need for a definition, whilst at the same time making no attempt to structure that definition, is ultimately fruitless.*]

2   Countries should assess the existing and emerging risks associated with different types of legal persons and arrangements, [. . .] from a domestic and international perspective [*Self evidently*].

    a.   Appropriate information on the results of the risk assessments should be shared with competent authorities, financial institutions and designated non-financial businesses and professions (DNFBPs) and, as appropriate, other jurisdictions. [*Cross-border information flows undoubtedly aid detection, but the wording of this principle offers no guidance as to any implementation strategy and fatally assumes that in calling for an international approach there will in all cases be pre-existing international co-operation mechanisms.*]

b. Effective and proportionate measures should be taken to mitigate the risks identified. [*Self evidently, but what does the G20 have in mind, if anything?*]

c. Countries should identify high-risk sectors, and enhanced due diligence [. . .] [*Self evidently*].

3   Countries should ensure that legal persons maintain beneficial ownership information onshore and that information is adequate, accurate, and current. [*This largely overlaps with principle 4.*]

4   Countries should ensure that competent authorities (including law enforcement and prosecutorial authorities, supervisory authorities, tax authorities and financial intelligence units) have timely access to adequate, accurate and current information regarding the beneficial ownership of legal persons. [. . .] [*Limiting access to "competent authorities" is at odds with growing calls for unrestricted public access to such information and clashes with principle 7a itself.*]

5   Countries should ensure that trustees of express trusts maintain adequate, accurate and current beneficial ownership information, including information of settlors, the protector (if any) trustees and beneficiaries. [. . .] [*This is merely a specific example otherwise covered by principle 3. The idea that a trust has a beneficial owner is nonsense.*][21]

6   Countries should ensure that competent authorities [. . .] have timely access to adequate, accurate and current information regarding the beneficial ownership of legal arrangements. [*A mere restatement of principle 4.*]

7   Countries should require financial institutions and DNFBPs, including trust and company service providers, to identify and take reasonable measures, including taking into account country risks, to verify the beneficial ownership of their customers.

a. Countries should consider facilitating access to beneficial ownership information by financial institutions and DNFBPs. [*This is at odds with principle 4.*]

b. [. . .]

8   Countries should ensure that their national authorities cooperate effectively domestically and internationally [and] ensure that their competent authorities participate in information exchange on beneficial ownership with international counterparts in a timely and effective manner. [*This duplicates principle 2a.*]

9   Countries should support G20 efforts to combat tax evasion by ensuring that beneficial ownership information is accessible to their tax authorities and can be exchanged with relevant international counterparts in a timely and effective manner. [*This duplicates principles 2a, 4 and 8.*]

21 See ch 2.

10 Countries should address the misuse of legal persons and legal arrangements which may obstruct transparency, including:

    a.   prohibiting the ongoing use of bearer shares and the creation of new bearer shares, or taking other effective measures to ensure that bearer shares and bearer share warrants are not misused; and

    b.   taking effective measures to ensure that legal persons which allow nominee shareholders or nominee directors are not misused. [*The use of bearer shares, nominee shareholders and nominee directors harks back to antediluvian tax haven strategies of the 1970s and 1980s.*]

The ten principles appear to resonate with an almost Biblical authority, as if carried down the mountain on stone tablets, but on closer examination are less than they seem – though are almost certainly what the G20 intended them to be.

The principles suffer from a degree of abstraction, stemming from the use of the term 'beneficial ownership' without any attempt to define this. There is no proposal for a formula – merely the exhortation that '[c]ountries should have a definition of 'beneficial owner' that captures the natural person(s) who ultimately owns or controls the legal person or legal arrangement'.

The principles overlap and repeat each other. The ten principles, when edited to remove these overlaps and repetitions, amount to no more than a call for risk assessment, registration (access to this being restricted to state-designated taxation and law enforcement authorities) and information exchanges between states.

Reference to the curbing of the use of bearer shares and controls on nominee shareholders and nominee directors, which have been for the past fifty years the most obvious, most easily identifiable and least sophisticated of beneficial ownership avoidance structures, indicates how superficial an understanding the G20 has of the subtleties and complexities of the modern approach to avoidance.

Without addressing these weaknesses, the G20 in July 2016 issued its 'Progress Report on the Implementation of the G20/OECD High-Level Principles of Corporate Governance'.[22] Unaware that ownership may be entirely absent, the report states:

> Disclosure of ownership should be provided once certain thresholds of ownership are passed. Such disclosure might include data on major shareholders and others that, directly or indirectly, significantly influence or control or may significantly influence or control the company through, for example, special voting rights, shareholder agreements, the ownership of controlling or large blocks of shares, significant cross shareholding relationships and cross guarantees.[23]

---

22 OECD (University of Toronto, July 2016) <www.g20.utoronto.ca/2016/g20-oecd-progress-report-corporate-governance.pdf> accessed 20 December 2018.
23 s 5.2.1.3 para 222.

The report does, however, concede that 'empirical work indicates that in a number of jurisdictions, a large number of firms fail to report ownership data and in particular share ownership by management and members of the board. Moreover, enforcement can be weak and regulations unclear'.[24]

The G20 High-Level Principles on the beneficial ownership of companies are not fit for purpose. They are a paper tiger. They lack specificity as to how to define beneficial ownership, how effectively to gather data and how to disseminate data broadly. They take no account of beneficial ownership avoidance structures, which simply stop the principles dead in their tracks.

Lip service is being paid to these flawed principles in the form of legislation itself hesitant and incomplete. At the same time, seemingly unobserved by the G20 but by no means underutilised, legislation promoting beneficial ownership avoidance is advancing apace, not merely in the tax haven micro nations, unchallenged.

## *Financial Action Task Force*[25]

### *FATF's origin and mission*

The Financial Action Task Force (FATF) is an independent intergovernmental body that develops and promotes policies to protect the global financial system against money laundering, terrorist financing and the financing of proliferation of weapons of mass destruction. The FATF Recommendations[26] are recognised as the global anti-money laundering (AML) and counter-terrorist financing (CFT) standard.

The huge significance of the FATF in the context of ownership and transparency is that when reference is made in transparency initiatives to "accepted international beneficial ownership standards" (or words to that effect), it is to FATF guidance.

It is over a decade since the FATF in 'The Misuse of Corporate Vehicles Including Trust and Company Service Providers' (13 October 2006)[27] identified the concealment of true beneficial ownership as that which fuelled the engine of abuse:

---

24  s 5.2.1.3 para 223. For the full text of s 5.2.1.3 dealing with major share ownership, including beneficial owners and voting rights, see Appendix 3.

25  (*Financial Action Task Force*) <www.fatf-gafi.org/about> accessed 20 December 2018.

26  Financial Action Task Force, 'FATF Recommendations 2012' (updated to October 2018) (*Financial Action Task Force*, 16 February 2012) <www.fatf-gafi.org/publications/fatfrecommendations/documents/fatf-recommendations.html> and <www.fatf-gafi.org/publications/fatfrecommendations/documents/fatf-recommendations.html#UPDATES> accessed 20 December 2018.

27  (*Financial Action Task Force*) <www.fatf-gafi.org/media/fatf/documents/reports/Misuse%20of%20Corporate%20Vehicles%20including%20Trusts%20and%20Company%20Services%20Providers.pdf> accessed 20 December 2018, Executive Summary.

Despite the important and legitimate roles corporate entities, including corporations, trusts, foundations and partnerships with limited liability, play in the global economy, they may, under certain conditions, be used for illicit purposes. The present study's prime aim has been to seek to identify in respect of corporate vehicles areas of vulnerability for money laundering and terrorist financing, along with evidence of their misuse. Faced with the vast scope of a general project on corporate vehicle misuse the study focuses on what is considered to be the most significant feature of their misuse – the hiding of the true beneficial owner.

The flywheel turns only slowly. In October 2014, the FATF in its Guidance on Transparency and Beneficial Ownership was again intoning:

1. Corporate vehicles[28] – such as companies, trusts, foundations, partnerships and other types of legal persons and arrangements – conduct a wide variety of commercial and entrepreneurial activities. However, despite the essential and legitimate role that corporate vehicles play in the global economy, under certain conditions, they have been misused for illicit purposes, including money laundering (ML), bribery and corruption, insider dealings, tax fraud, terrorist financing (TF) and other illegal activities. This is because, for criminals trying to circumvent anti-money laundering (AML) and counter-terrorist financing (CTF) measures, corporate vehicles are an attractive way to disguise and convert the proceeds of crime before introducing them into the financial system.

2. The misuse of corporate vehicles could be significantly reduced if information regarding both the legal owner and the beneficial owner, the source of the corporate vehicle's assets, and its activities were readily available to the authorities. Legal and beneficial ownership information can assist law enforcement and other competent authorities by identifying those natural persons who may be responsible for the underlying activity of concern or who may have relevant information to further an investigation. This allows the authorities to 'follow the money' in financial investigations involving suspect accounts/assets held by corporate vehicles. In particular, beneficial ownership information can also help locate a given person's assets within a jurisdiction. However, countries face significant challenges when implementing measures to ensure the timely availability of accurate beneficial owner information. This is particularly challenging when it involves legal persons and legal arrangements spread across multiple jurisdictions [. . .]

88. . . [C]orporate vehicles are increasingly attractive to criminals for the purpose of disguising their identity and distancing themselves from their

---

28 The FATF in this paper uses the term "corporate vehicles" to mean *legal persons* and *legal arrangements*, as defined in the glossary of the FATF Recommendations 2012 (updated to October 2018).

illicit assets. Increasing the transparency of corporate vehicles is an effective way to prevent their misuse for criminal purposes, including for the commission of offenses such as money laundering or terrorism financing, corruption, tax fraud, trafficking and other organized crime related offences.[29]

Though the focus is on corporate vehicles, the FATF expresses the hope that its guidance may have far wider application:

> The purpose of the FATF standards on transparency and beneficial ownership is to prevent the misuse of corporate vehicles for money laundering or terrorist financing. However, it is recognised that these FATF standards support the efforts to prevent and detect other designated categories of offences such as tax crimes and corruption. In this respect, the measures that countries implement to enhance transparency in line with the FATF Recommendations may provide a platform to more effectively address serious concerns such as corruption, as well as to meet other international standards.[30]

### Beneficial ownership

The FATF gives examples of how beneficial ownership information can be obscured:[31]

a)   shell companies [i.e. companies having no significant operations or related assets] (which can be established with various forms of ownership structure), especially in cases where there is foreign ownership which is spread across jurisdictions.

b)   complex ownership and control structures involving many layers of shares registered in the name of other legal persons

c)   bearer shares and bearer share warrants [*The significance of this is that a bearer share or bearer share warrant is, unlike a share certificate, an entitlement to a share without the need for any holder's name to be on it – whoever holds it owns the share to which it refers. Ownership therefore can pass from moment to moment, just on a handover, without any other registration requirements. Ownership is untraceable.[32]*]

29  Financial Action Task Force, 'FATF Guidance on Transparency and Beneficial Ownership' (*Financial Action Task Force*, October 2014) <www.fatf-gafi.org/media/fatf/documents/reports/Guidance-transparency-beneficial-ownership.pdf> accessed 20 December 2018 paras 1, 2, 88.
30  Ibid. para 5.
31  Ibid. para 9.
32  Placing bearer shares and bearer share warrants ahead of shares held in the blockchain which though capable of being passed electronically in an instant are "imprinted" with details both

d)   unrestricted use of legal persons as directors [ *that is, the use of corporate direc-tors, which may in turn be subsidiaries of other corporations, usually corporate service providers.* ]

e)   formal nominee shareholders and directors where the identity of the nomi-nator is undisclosed [*for "nominee", read "puppet"*]

f)   informal nominee shareholders and directors, such as close associates and family [*This is a high-risk strategy for any owner, but does ensure anonymity and a lack of accountability. It may however take more than a degree of gentle persuasion on the part of the "true" owner to recover the assets into his or her hands.* ]

g)   trusts and other legal arrangements which enable a separation of legal owner-ship and beneficial ownership of assets [ *Trusts are a legitimate form of wealth and inheritance planning. The problem is that many jurisdictions now offer structures which are described as trusts but which in fact have as their sole pur-pose accountability avoidance.* ][33]

h)   use of intermediaries in forming legal persons, including professional inter-mediaries [ *This is a curious inclusion in the list, dealing as it does with profes-sional relationships rather than with structural elements, and appears to be a coded reference to lawyers and accountants who have gone over to the dark side.* ]

All these devices are commonly found, particularly in the offshore jurisdictions, in corporate and trust structuring. There is however something else, something very powerful, which this list does not address. The FATF appears to be unaware of the global industry in orphan structures which have no beneficial owner of any kind.[34] For example, in focussing[35] on the misuse of bearer shares and bearer share warrants and of nominee shares and nominee directors, the FATF reveals just how out of touch it has become. There are undoubtedly some bottom-feeder jurisdictions which still promote pre-Eighties strategies like these (and the G20 High-Level Principles[36] themselves refer to them as if they are in common use), but this is not an adequate contemporary response on the part of the FATF to a burgeoning international ownership avoidance counter-initiative.

This is compounded by the FATF having of necessity to adopt an overly prag-matic approach to the definition of "beneficial owner" and "beneficiary", which is fundamental to the FATF's transparency strategy. The concept of ownership is itself multi-faceted.[37] No single definition can be made to fit all structures and

---

of their point of origin and of each subsequent holder and can (in theory, if not in practice) be made to reveal their history.

33   For example, non-charitable purpose trusts, discussed in ch 5.

34   See the discussion of orphan structures in ch 5.

35   As it does also in its interpretive note to Recommendation 24, the "Obstacles to Trans-parency" <www.fatf-gafi.org/media/fatf/documents/recommendations/pdfs/FATF%20 Recommendations%202012.pdf> paras 14 and 16 at 86, 87 accessed 20 December 2018.

36   G20 High-Level Principles on Beneficial Ownership Transparency (n 8).

37   See ch 2.

situations, but nevertheless the FATF has tasked itself with formulating a universal standard, across all structures and all jurisdictions.

The FATF's definition of "beneficial owner" is found in the Glossary to the FATF Recommendations[38]

> Beneficial owner refers to the natural person(s) who ultimately owns or controls a customer and/or the natural person on whose behalf a transaction is being conducted. It also includes those persons who exercise ultimate effective control over a legal person or arrangement.
>
> Reference to "ultimately owns or controls" and "ultimate effective control" refer to situations in which ownership/control is exercised through a chain of ownership or by means of control other than direct control. This definition [customer] should also apply to beneficial owner or a beneficiary under a life or other investment linked insurance policy. [*The introduction of "customer" adds a further hook from which to suspend endless definitional argument*]

The limitation of such a definition soon becomes clear. The FATF tacitly acknowledges that in the context of *trusts* – including non-charitable purpose trusts[39] – the definition of "beneficiary" is necessarily fluid:

The meaning of the term "beneficiary" in the FATF Recommendations depends on the context:

> In trust law, a beneficiary is the person or persons who are entitled to the benefit of any trust arrangement. A beneficiary can be a natural or legal person or arrangement. All trusts (other than charitable or statutory permitted non-charitable trusts) are required to have ascertainable beneficiaries. While trusts must always have some ultimately ascertainable beneficiary, trusts may have no defined existing beneficiaries but only objects of a power until some person becomes entitled as beneficiary to income or capital on the expiry of a defined period, known as the accumulation period. This period is normally coextensive with the trust perpetuity period which is usually referred to in the trust deed as the trust period.[40]

---

38  <www.fatf-gafi.org/media/fatf/documents/recommendations/pdfs/FATF%20Recom mendations%202012.pdf> 111 accessed 20 December 2018.

39  See ch 2 and 5. A charitable trust does have beneficiaries, but they need not be specifically identified as individuals – a class definition ("the poor of the Parish") suffices. A non-charitable purpose trust has no beneficiaries.

40  G20 High-Level Principles on Beneficial Ownership Transparency (n 38) *111* The immediately evident breach in the wall is the reference to the absence of beneficiaries under a non-charitable purpose trust (a vehicle designed to avoid beneficial ownership). See ch 2.

*Legal persons*

The heart of the matter is contained in FATF Recommendations 24 and 25:

### 24. Transparency and beneficial ownership of legal persons

Countries should take measures to prevent the misuse of legal persons for money laundering or terrorist financing. Countries should ensure that there is adequate, accurate and timely information on the beneficial ownership and control of legal persons that can be obtained or accessed in a timely fashion by competent authorities. In particular, countries that have legal persons that are able to issue bearer shares or bearer share warrants, or which allow nominee shareholders or nominee directors, should take effective measures to ensure that they are not misused for money laundering or terrorist financing. Countries should consider measures to facilitate access to beneficial ownership and control information by financial institutions and DNFBPs [*Designated Non-Financial Business or Profession*] undertaking the requirements set out in Recommendations 10 [*customer due diligence*] and 22 [*DNFBP customer due diligence*].

### 25. Transparency and beneficial ownership of legal arrangements

Countries should take measures to prevent the misuse of legal arrangements for money laundering or terrorist financing. In particular, countries should ensure that there is adequate, accurate and timely information on express trusts, including information on the settlor, trustee and beneficiaries, that can be obtained or accessed in a timely fashion by competent authorities. Countries should consider measures to facilitate access to beneficial ownership and control information by financial institutions and DNFBPs undertaking the requirements set out in Recommendations 10 and 22.

In its Interpretive Note to Recommendation 24[41] the FATF states (in paragraph 1):

Competent authorities should be able to obtain, or have access in a timely fashion to, adequate, accurate and current information on the beneficial ownership and control of companies and other legal persons (beneficial ownership information) that are created in the country.

"Beneficial ownership information" for *legal persons* is the information referred to in the interpretive note to FATF Recommendation 10, paragraph 5(b)(i), which makes a brave stab at the problem but, as with the FATF's recognition

---

41  Ibid. 84.

of inherent difficulties in determining the ownership of a trust, openly acknowledges serious impediments:

> (i.i) The identity of the natural persons (if any – as ownership interests can be so diversified that there are no natural persons (whether acting alone or together) exercising control of the legal person or arrangement through ownership) who ultimately have a controlling ownership interest in a legal person; and
>
> (i.ii) to the extent that there is doubt under (i.i) as to whether the person(s) with the controlling ownership interest are the beneficial owner(s) or where no natural person exerts control through ownership interests, the identity of the natural persons (if any) exercising control of the legal person or arrangement through other means.
>
> (i.iii) Where no natural person is identified under (i.i) or (i.ii) above, financial institutions should identify and take reasonable measures to verify the identity of the relevant natural person who holds the position of senior managing official.[42]

FATF Recommendation 10 makes no mention of percentages of ownership, but this is slipped in by the FATF in its Interpretive Note to Recommendation 24, as a seemingly innocuous suggestion in a footnote:

> Beneficial ownership information for legal persons is the information referred to in the interpretive note to Recommendation 10, paragraph 5(b)(i). Controlling shareholders as referred to in, paragraph 5(b)(i) of the interpretive note to Recommendation 10 may be based on a threshold, e.g. any persons owning more than a certain percentage of the company (e.g. 25%).[43]

This illustrative example of a 25% threshold has taken on a life of its own. The FATF Guidance on Transparency and Beneficial Ownership (October 2014)[44] in paragraph 33 gives examples of "natural persons who could be considered as beneficial owners on the basis that they are the ultimate owners/controllers of the legal person, either through their ownership interests, through positions held within the legal person or through other means". This is a vitally important, though often misinterpreted, intervention by the FATF. Its importance lies in the fact that it has almost by default become the gold standard when transparency initiatives are in need of a definition of beneficial ownership. Paragraph 33a repeats the reference to a 25% threshold, and even though the FATF is at pains

---

42  Ibid. 59, 60.
43  Ibid. 84 (n 39).
44  Financial Action Task Force 'FATF Guidance on Transparency and Beneficial Ownership' (n 29).

to stress that this is tentative, it is this threshold which has found purchase in implementation strategies.[45]

> The natural person(s) who directly or indirectly holds a minimum percentage of ownership interest in the legal person (the threshold approach). For example, Recommendation 24 allows the determination of the controlling shareholders of a company based on a threshold (for example, any persons owning more than a certain percentage of the company, such as 25%). **The FATF Recommendations do not specify what threshold may be appropriate. In determining an appropriate minimum threshold, countries should consider the level of ML/TF risk identified for the various types of legal persons or minimum ownership thresholds established for particular legal persons pursuant to commercial or administrative law.** The ownership interest approach suggests that it is likely that there could be more than one beneficial owner (for example, with a threshold of more than 25%, there could be a maximum of three beneficial owners). In any case, a percentage shareholding or ownership interest should be considered as a key evidential factor among others to be taken into account. It is also important to highlight that this approach includes the notion of indirect control which may extend beyond formal ownership or could be through a chain of corporate vehicles. Ultimately, countries should implement the concept of ownership interest that is sufficiently clear, practical, workable and enforceable for the full range of legal persons administered in a country.
>
> *[emphasis added]*

Should any *legal person* be owned (in the limited sense used by the FATF) by more than four persons, there is no "controlling shareholder" (or equivalent) and so on this test no controlling ownership interest. The power of five becomes irresistible. At a time when the availability of ownerless structures – the so-called "orphan structures"[46] – is increasing exponentially, it is disturbing to see that at the heart of the FATF's own strategy is an implementation strategy in the form of the threshold approach which is so very easy to side-line when (innocently or disingenuously) taken on face value by legislators.

The 25% threshold approach is a quick fix and overshadows the more nuanced guidance of the FATF found in the remainder of paragraph 33.

---

45 See The Law Library of Congress, Global Legal Research Center *Disclosure of Beneficial Ownership in Selected Countries* (July 2017) <www.loc.gov/law/help/beneficial-owner ship/disclosure-beneficial-ownership.pdf> accessed 20 December 2018 and Andres Knobel, Moran Harari and Marku Meinzer, 'The State of Play of Beneficial Ownership Registration: A Visual Overview' *Tax Justice Network* (27 June 2018) <www.taxjustice.net/wp-content/ uploads/2018/06/TJN2018-BeneficialOwnershipRegistration-StateOfPlay-FSI.pdf> accessed 20 December 2018. See the case study of the Beneficial Ownership Act 2017 of the Isle of Man below.

46 Ch 5.

Addressing the question of natural persons who may by *other means* control a *legal person* through ownership interests, the FATF stresses that:

> It is also important to highlight that this approach includes the notion of indirect control which may extend beyond legal (direct) ownership or could be through a chain of corporate vehicles and through nominees. This indirect control could be identified through various means, as shareholder's agreement, exercise of dominant influence or power to appoint senior management. Shareholders may thus collaborate to increase the level of control by a person through formal or informal agreements, or through the use of nominee shareholders.[47]

Control may also be exercised by natural persons through "personal connections" to controlling shareholders, by "financing of the enterprise" or "because of close and intimate family relationships, historical or contractual associations, or if a company defaults on certain payments"; "Furthermore, control may be presumed even if control is never actually exercised, such as using, enjoying or benefiting from the assets owned by the legal person".[48]

Nuanced though this guidance is, the acid test is whether or not it could be successfully litigated:[49]

- *Shareholders' agreements* are by their nature confidential and not in the public domain – nor, in the absence of a dispute between shareholders necessitating the disclosure of their agreement before a court, or a criminal or regulatory investigation (which would presuppose suspicion on the part of those investigators) will they ever see the light of day.
- Defining and proving *exercise of dominant influence* would be extremely difficult: what constitutes *exercise* – action or inaction?; what test is used to

---

47 Financial Action Task Force, 'FATF Guidance on Transparency and Beneficial Ownership' (n 29) para 33b).
48 Ibid. paras 33c and d.
49 Matters which are subject to client-attorney privilege (also known as legal privilege) are not disclosable. The FATF however has legal privilege in its sights. The FATF recognises that principles of international human rights dictate that "the right of a client to obtain legal representation and advice, be candid with his legal adviser and not fear later disclosure of those discussions to his prejudice is an important feature of the legal profession". However, investigators have found that a frequent obstacle to accessing information about corporate vehicles is the use of client privilege to refuse to divulge information relevant to the ownership and control of a corporate vehicle. [. . .] To help address these issues, competent authorities and professional bodies should work to ensure that there is a clear and shared understanding of the scope of legal professional privilege and legal professional secrecy in their own country. In particular, countries should ensure that there is a clear understanding of what is, and what is not covered to ensure that investigations involving suspected corporate vehicles are not inappropriately impeded". Ibid paras 79 and 80. And see the FATF Risk Based Approach Guidance for Legal Professionals (October 2008) <www.fatf-gafi.org/publications/fatfrecommendations/documents/riskbasedapproachguidanceforlegalprofessionals.html> accessed 20 December 2018.

establish *dominance?*; how is *influence* characterised and what causality test would be applied?

- A *personal connection* defies definition: a friend, a colleague, a supplier, a tennis partner?
- The distinction between *close* and *intimate* family relationships would presumably exclude warring cousins who haven't spoken in years, but how could this be evidenced?
- How far back does one look for *historical* associations, and what historiographic test is to be applied?
- *Contractual associations* are not in the public domain and are not disclosable other than in judicial or regulatory proceedings.
- Defaulting on certain payments seems to have been included on the list under a misapprehension. What relevance to ownership and control could be demonstrated? There are myriad reasons for default, even if a duty to pay can be established evidentially in the first place.

The concluding guidance in paragraph 33 in addressing "natural persons who may exercise control through positions held within a legal person" smack of desperation. What possible use from the point of view of establishing a connection between control and ownership (and therefore of accountability) is it to focus on "the natural person(s) responsible for strategic decisions that fundamentally affect the business practices or general direction of legal persons" or "natural persons(s) who exercises executive control over the daily or regular affairs of the legal persons through a senior management position"?[50] In observing that "identification of the directors may still provide useful information", the FATF does not sound wholly convinced. What use in practice could be made of this information? What pressure could in practice be brought to bear on such people in the search for ultimate beneficial ownership, control and accountability – civil or criminal proceedings, regulatory investigations, political initiatives, old-fashioned brute force?

*Trusts*

The equivalent beneficial ownership information provisions for *trusts*, contained in the interpretive note to FATF Recommendation 10 paragraph 5(b)(ii) are an act of definitional desperation. There is in equity no "owner" or "controller" of a trust in the sense meant by the FATF, yet (morphing a trust into a civil law fiduciary contract) it sallies forth undaunted:

> (ii.i) Trusts – the identity of the settlor, the trustee(s), the protector (if any), the beneficiaries or class of beneficiaries, and any other natural person

---

50 Financial Action Task Force, 'FATF Guidance on Transparency and Beneficial Ownership' (n 29) paras 33e and f.

62    *Disclosure and registration initiatives*

exercising ultimate effective control over the trust (including through a chain of control/ownership);[51]

The interpretive note to FATF Recommendation 25 paragraph 1[52] merely compounds the delusion that those who administer a trust or who advise those administrators are themselves in some meta-jurisprudential way the "owners":

> Countries should require trustees of any express trust governed under their law to obtain and hold adequate, accurate, and current beneficial ownership information regarding the trust. This should include information on the identity of the settlor, the trustee(s), the protector (if any), the beneficiaries or class of beneficiaries, and any other natural person exercising ultimate effective control over the trust. Countries should also require trustees of any trust governed under their law to hold basic information on other regulated agents of, and service providers to, the trust, including investment advisors or managers, accountants, and tax advisors.[53] [*The significance of this and of the similar wording in Recommendation 10 paragraph 5(b)(ii) is that although trustees have legal title to trust assets – the assets are held in their name – they cannot in equity enjoy any beneficial interest in those assets. A protector has neither legal nor equitable title – nothing is held in his or her name. Beneficiaries have the right to be considered for a distribution, and are the only persons to whom a distribution can be made, but until the assets are in their hands, they* own *no part of them. Gathering information on trustees, protectors and beneficiaries therefore does not produce ownership data.*]

Notwithstanding this fundamental misreading of the relationship between trustees and beneficiaries, and the nature of a trust, the FATF suggests severe penalties be imposed on trustees for failure to comply with the FATF recommendations and guidance, even though neither corresponds to the duties and responsibilities of trustees in equity:

> Countries should hold trustees liable for failing to perform their obligations as outlined above, or make them subject to effective, proportionate and dissuasive

---

51 In the interpretive note to FATF Recommendation 24 paragraph 16 concerning "other legal persons", the guidance becomes abstract: "In relation to foundations, Anstalt, and limited liability partnerships, countries should take similar measures and impose similar requirements, as those required for companies, taking into account their different forms and structures". Grouping companies, foundations, Anstalt and limited liability partnerships together as if they are susceptible to a monolithic approach analogous to that used for companies betrays a woeful ignorance of their fundamental differences. See ch 2.
52 (n 38) 89.
53 Financial Action Task Force, 'FATF Guidance on Transparency and Beneficial Ownership' (n 29) para 60 reflects this misunderstanding: "It is important to ensure that the trustee identifies any person who owns or controls the trust in whatever capacity they may be in".

sanctions (whether criminal, civil or administrative) for failing to comply. Countries should also ensure that there are effective, proportionate and dissuasive sanctions, whether criminal, civil or administrative, for failing to grant to competent authorities timely access to information regarding the trust.[54]

## *Ownership vs. Control*

The FATF does however have a fall-back strategy, which if further developed may help it overcome the inherent weakness of an ownership-based transparency initiative. In its Guidelines on Transparency and Beneficial Ownership it comments:

> The FATF definition of beneficial owner in the context of legal persons must be distinguished from the concepts of legal ownership and control. [. . .] [A]n essential element of the FATF definition of beneficial owner is that it extends beyond legal ownership and control to consider the notion of ultimate (actual) ownership and control. In other words, the FATF definition focuses on the natural (not legal) persons who actually own and take advantage of capital or assets of the legal person; as well as on those who really exert effective control over it (whether or not they occupy formal positions within that legal person), rather than just the (natural or legal) persons who are legally (on paper) entitled to do so.

So far, so good, but the paragraph then continues, re-introducing an element of ownership as a necessary component of control, rather than use a stand-alone definition of controller as being a person having no ownership rights of any kind.

> For example, if a company is legally owned by a second company (according to its corporate registration information), the beneficial owners are actually the natural persons who are behind that second company or ultimate holding company in the chain of ownership and who are controlling it. Likewise, persons listed in the corporate registration information as holding controlling positions within the company, but who are actually acting on behalf of someone else, cannot be considered beneficial owners[55] because they are ultimately being used by someone else to exercise effective control over the company.[56]

---

54 Financial Action Task Force 'FATF Guidance on Transparency and Beneficial Ownership' (n 29) para 68, referencing the FATF Interpretive Note to Recommendation 25, paragraph 11 (n 38).

55 As a matter of corporate law, directors are not, in their capacity as such, beneficial owners of a company – they merely manage and control the company. The FATF seems reluctant to abandon its flawed "ownership" model even at this level.

56 Financial Action Task Force, 'FATF Guidance on Transparency and Beneficial Ownership' (n 29) para 15.

Everything in the FATF approach therefore depends on ownership or on control analogous to ownership. If the FATF wishes to provide the means to identify who ultimately benefits from a structure, and who therefore should be held ultimately accountable, then the FATF should acknowledge that ownership is not the key. It should embrace the concept of control pure and simple and focus on who actually *benefits*.[57]

### FATF and concealment of beneficial ownership

On 18 July 2018 the FATF in association with Egmont Group[58] issued its report Concealment of Beneficial Ownership.[59] It is vast, using 106 case studies provided by 34 different jurisdictions of the FATF Global Network, the experiences of law enforcement and other experts, private sector input as well as open-source research and intelligence reports to identify the methods that criminals use to hide beneficial ownership. Vulnerabilities associated with beneficial ownership are analysed, with a particular focus on the involvement of professional intermediaries.

Crucially, however, it makes no changes to the definitions of beneficial ownership previously put forward in the FATF Recommendations and is ignorant of any beneficial ownership avoidance initiative.[60] The overview of the report on the FATF webpage,[61] referring as it does to traditional structures and well-worn offshore structuring approaches, reveals this:

> The ease with which legal persons, primarily limited liability companies (or similar) can be formed, make them particularly vulnerable, and are seen to be used in building complex legal ownership structures, often involving shell companies.[. . .] The use of nominee directors and shareholders, both formal and informal, exacerbates the risks by creating barriers between the owner or individual and laundered proceeds, and often professional intermediaries play a role in helping create or operate the structures used to conceal beneficial ownership, either complicit or unwitting.

---

57  Ibid. para 16 points in this direction. The FATF clearly believes that its definition of beneficial owner will prove to be sufficiently comprehensive if it shifts the focus to "customer relationships and the occasional customer". "This element of the FATF definition of beneficial owner focuses on individuals that are central to a transaction being conducted even where the transaction has been deliberately structured to avoid control or ownership of the customer but to retain the benefit of the transaction". This proposition, however, is underdeveloped in the Guidelines and in adding yet another definitional term – "customer" – muddies the waters further.

58  <www.egmontgroup.org> accessed 20 December 2018.

59  <www.fatf-gafi.org/publications/methodsandtrends/documents/concealment-beneficial-ownership.html with the full text at www.fatf-gafi.org/media/fatf/documents/reports/FATF-Egmont-Concealment-beneficial-ownership.pdf> accessed 20 December 2018.

60  Ibid. paras 27 to 32.

61  (n 59).

The report highlights the importance of the effective implementation of the FATF Recommendations on beneficial ownership [. . .].

The value of this report is open to question, on its own admission:

38. Given the broad range of legal persons in existence across the globe, an analysis of the similarities and differences among forms of legal persons would have exceeded the scope of this project. Furthermore, most of the case studies did not provide specific insights into the types and legal peculiarities of the legal persons used in the money laundering schemes. As such, the report has focused on broader characteristics of legal persons, and has not endeavoured to assess all of the specific forms available.[62]

Furthermore, the case studies presented to the FATF concern almost exclusively companies, to the exclusion of other structures.[63]

Whilst trusts are referred to in the report, the FATF appears uncertain as to why they would be used, though offers a tentative explanation, sensing somehow that trusts may be complex:[64]

50. Apart from the intent to separate legal and beneficial ownership, it is not clear precisely why criminals exploit trusts in money laundering schemes. There may be a multiplicity of reasons which will vary on a case-by-case basis. Criminals may exploit the secrecy provisions inherent in certain legal arrangements to prevent competent authorities from exerting authority to unravel the true ownership structure. This is particularly likely when schemes involve a foreign trust.

77. Whereas the situation of criminals setting up a complex structure involving multiple trusts seems relatively rare [. . .], the combination of a trust interacting with at least one company appears more frequently in the case studies. [. . .] *This demonstrates that trusts and similar legal arrangement are rarely used in isolation to hold assets and obscure beneficial ownership,*[65] but generally form part of a wider scheme; it might also show that schemes that only involve a trust may be more difficult for authorities to identify. The interaction of the trust with other legal persons adds an additional layer of complexity and helps frustrate efforts to discover beneficial ownership.

[Emphasis added]

---

62 <www.fatf-gafi.org/media/fatf/documents/reports/FATF-Egmont-Concealment-benefi cial-ownership.pdf> accessed 20 December 2018 para 38.

63 Ibid. para 44.

64 Ibid. paras 50 and 77.

65 Not a true statement of law or practice. See the discussion on trusts, specifically non-chari table purpose trusts, in ch 5.

The authors of the report appear therefore to have only a superficial understanding of the case studies and, it appears, are unable to determine whether the case studies are representative of a global beneficial ownership concealment initiative or merely the examples which the institutions that provided them felt able to share. In the case of beneficial ownership avoidance, it is the *specific forms* of legal persons which are determinative, not their "broader characteristics" (whatever that phrase means in this context). Focussing almost exclusively on corporate structures, and characterising trusts as mere ancillary elements, gives a very distorted and unrepresentative view of planning – particularly of offshore planning.

The report focuses on "shell", "front" and "shelf" companies,[66] intermediaries and "straw man", the report assuming that (as the report's title confirms) mere *concealment* of ownership is the ultimate aim.

> 4. Individuals and groups seeking to conceal the ownership of assets are most likely to exercise control over those assets via a combination of direct and indirect control, rather than strictly one or the other. In a majority of cases, the beneficial owner used a combination of layering and direct ownership chains, as well as professional intermediaries[67] and third parties exercising control on their behalf. In a limited number of cases, the beneficial owner exercised *only* indirect control and rarely retained direct control through a complicated structure without involving an intermediary. This demonstrates that, in many cases, the beneficial owner will maintain some level of direct control in a scheme, but will rarely do so without also involving an intermediary or "straw man" (informal nominee shareholders and directors,

---

66 Defined as "*Shell company* – incorporated company with no independent operations, significant assets, ongoing business activities, or employees. *Front company* – fully functioning company with the characteristics of a legitimate business, serving to disguise and obscure illicit financial activity. *Shelf company* – incorporated company with inactive shareholders, directors, and secretary and is left dormant for a longer period even if a customer relationship has already been established". <www.fatf-gafi.org/publications/methodsandtrends/docu ments/concealment-beneficial-ownership.html> Text box 5. The report provides examples of the use of each in paras 61 to 72.

67 The report is shockingly naïve in its assessment of the role of some legal and accounting professionals, assuming that lawyers are "not sufficiently aware of their inherent money laundering and terrorism financing vulnerabilities" but that accountants, who feature far less in the case studies than lawyers, by virtue of their "financial acumen [. . .] and the ease with which accountants can identify suspicious financial activities, limit their vulnerability to being unwittingly exploited to facilitate the concealment of beneficial ownership" (paragraph 6). As is discussed in chapter 6, lawyers and accountants are at the forefront of product development and marketing in the field of beneficial ownership avoidance. It does however in paragraph 16 acknowledge the impact of the *Panama Papers* and the *Paradise Papers*: "The leak of confidential information from two large international law firms [*which the report identifies as Panama-based law firm Mossack Fonseca, in 2015, and Bermuda-based law firm, Appleby, in 2017*] responsible for the establishment of complex international corporate structures in 2015 and 2017 has increased public awareness of the way in which legal structures can be used to conceal wealth and illicit assets".

such as spouses, children, extended family, and other personal or business associates).[68]

This is very archaic, mass-market, bargain basement planning. The elephant in the room is the fact that all 106 case studies are of strategies which ultimately proved ineffective at concealment – they all got found out. The complete absence of any beneficial ownership avoidance structure amongst those case studies is silent witness to the efficacy of such counter-initiatives. Such structures are legal in the jurisdictions where incepted, amoral and often abusive to the point of criminality in their cross-border application, yet wholly immune to the tests and challenges proposed in the FATF Recommendations.

The issues which the report identifies "to help address the vulnerabilities associated with the concealment of beneficial ownership" are the following,[69] which are (perhaps predictably) basic, open-ended, lacking an implementation strategy or the means to compel one and largely aspirational, in a curious echo of the vapid G20 High-Level Principles:[70]

- Consideration of the role of nominees including measures that may limit their misuse.
- The need for regulation of professional intermediaries in line with the FATF Standards, and the importance of efforts to educate professionals on ML and TF vulnerabilities to enhance awareness and help mitigate the vulnerabilities associated with the concealment of beneficial ownership.
- Further work to identify possible solutions or measures to prevent the misuse of legal professional privilege (LPP) to conceal beneficial ownership information, including through the provision of enhanced training and guidance material for legal professionals.
- Ensuring financial intelligence units have access to the widest possible range of financial information.
- Increased sharing of relevant information and transaction records to support global efforts to improve the transparency of beneficial ownership.
- Further work to understand what can be done to improve the quality and timeliness of the cross-border sharing of information, including through mutual legal assistance.

---

68 <www.fatf-gafi.org/media/fatf/documents/reports/FATF-Egmont-Concealment-benefi cial-ownership.pdf> accessed 20 December 2018 para 4.
69 Ibid. para 13.
70 G20 High-Level Principles on Beneficial Ownership Transparency (n 8). The report does however at length review in Annex D Sources of Information and Techniques to Discover Beneficial Ownership, augmenting the earlier work of the FATF found in its 2014 guidance paper *Transparency and Beneficial Ownership* (n 29). <www.fatf-gafi.org/media/fatf/documents/reports/FATF-Egmont-Concealment-beneficial-ownership.pdf> accessed 20 December 2018 172 to 180.

- Ensuring, for countries that make use of registers of beneficial ownership, and for all countries' company registers, that there is sufficient resource and expertise associated with their maintenance. This is to ensure that the information recorded in the register is adequate, accurate and up-to-date, and can be accessed in a timely manner.
- The need for countries to consider and articulate the vulnerabilities and threats relating to domestic and foreign legal persons and arrangements, the domestic and foreign intermediaries involved in their establishment, and the means by which criminals may exploit them to facilitate ML and other criminality.

Nowhere in the report is there a reference to the most blatant contemporary structures marketed for the express purpose of beneficial ownership avoidance (which go far beyond mere concealment, as they eliminate beneficial ownership entirely) – the non-charitable purpose trust, the Bahamas Enterprise Entity, the Nevis Multiform Foundation, to name but three.[71] The Bahamas is mentioned only in passing, and Nevis is not mentioned at all.

### How effective is the FATF's transparency strategy?

The FATF is attempting to ensure transparency using at best an incomplete, at worst a fundamentally misconceived one-size-fits-all, criterion of beneficial ownership. The Conclusion to the FATF Guidance on Transparency and Beneficial Ownership does evidence some self-awareness, albeit limited:

> The FATF recognises that there are significant challenges to the implementation of measures to prevent the misuse of corporate vehicles [*other structures go unmentioned*] and provides this guidance to support countries in their efforts. While this guidance supports the implementation of Recommendations 24 and 25, other standards such as CDD [Client Due Diligence] requirements are also relevant in this area, and countries should take a holistic approach to ensure transparency of corporate vehicles.[72]

Guidance and recommendations such as this – together with the issues raised in the 2018 report on the Concealment of Beneficial Ownership – are written by common sense lay bureaucrats for common sense lay citizens. They are, for all

---

71 Case Study 13 in the report does refer to the setting up of a trust in the Cayman Islands, but describes it simply as "a Cayman Islands revocable trust" without attempting to classify it or examine its particular characteristics. Indeed, all the case studies are extremely brief and superficial – most little more than a short paragraph. <www.fatf-gafi.org/media/fatf/documents/reports/FATF-Egmont-Concealment-beneficial-ownership.pdf> accessed 20 December 2018 35, 118 and 119. See the discussion of beneficial ownership avoidance strategies and structures in ch 5.
72 Financial Action Task Force, 'FATF Guidance on Transparency and Beneficial Ownership' (n 29) para 89.

the breadth of the case studies they use, superficial in their understanding of the equitable and legal issues, politically neutered and in consequence lacking in any compelling (or compulsory) implementation strategy:

> The publication takes a macro-level, global view of inherent vulnerabilities and is designed to support further risk analysis by governments, financial institutions, and other professional service providers. In undertaking further risk analysis, countries and private sector professionals should consider how the geopolitical and economic environment, as well as their own risk mitigation strategies, will affect the vulnerabilities associated with legal structures and the intermediary sectors that facilitate their formation and management.[73]

The FATF Recommendations concerning beneficial ownership are vulnerable to imploding utterly on even the most basic legal analysis. Yet they currently go unchallenged. A typical case is that of the G7.[74] The G7 Bari Declaration on Fighting Tax Crimes and Other Illicit Financial Flows, issued on 13 May 2017, is unequivocal in its support of the FATF standards, declaring:

> 2. We will continue to work to ensure access to beneficial ownership information for tax authorities, financial intelligence units and law enforcement agencies, and welcome the work by the FATF and the Global Forum on Transparency and Exchange of Information for Tax Purposes on reinforcing inter-agency and international cooperation, in particular on beneficial ownership information. We also look forward progress [sic] on the work by the OECD in complementary tax areas relating to beneficial ownership;
> 7. We reiterate our commitment to fully and effectively implement the FATF standards, including on designated non-financial businesses and professions, and we welcome the ongoing work on global professional conduct and practice standards that reflect the role that professions like lawyers, accountants and auditors can play in the fight against tax and financial crime;

It is important not to lose sight of the bigger picture. Though the FATF portrays its definition of beneficial ownership as a global standard, and this definition is indeed woven into a number of transparency strategies, the FATF approach is not the whole story:

> One major difference among the countries surveyed was in the definition of "beneficial owner." The definition accepted by the EU and its Member States

---

73  <www.fatf-gafi.org/media/fatf/documents/reports/FATF-Egmont-Concealment-benefi cial-ownership.pdf> accessed 20 December 2018 para 18.
74  The Group of Seven – Canada, France, Germany, Italy, Japan, the United Kingdom and the United States – an informal bloc meeting annually. See the analysis of the Council on Foreign Relations, noting that Russia is currently excluded <www.cfr.org/backgrounder/ group-seven-g7> accessed 20 December 2018.

is based on FATF Guidance, which defines a beneficial owner as a "natural person who ultimately owns or controls the customer and/or the natural person on whose behalf a transaction or activity is being conducted." Other countries add to the definition individuals with a "relevant interest" (Australia) or a "person with significant control" (United Kingdom). These are individuals holding securities with the power to control the corporation and its transactions. In some cases, these individuals are defined based on specific percentages of shares they own (the lower threshold is usually between 20% and 30%). Japanese reporting requirements apply to all major shareholders. While previously enacted legislation often does not address the issue of bearer shareholders or nominees, and treats beneficial owners as regular shareholders, newly proposed laws distinguish between a beneficial interest in a share and significant beneficial ownership (India), and contain a broad definition of "controlling beneficiary," meaning an "individual or group of individuals who ultimately benefits from a good or service, or exercise(s) control over a company through ownership of securities, a pertinent contract or any other act, which allow them to impose, directly or indirectly, decisions on the shareholders or partners" (Mexico). The study shows that even when the laws of a country do not contain transparency or beneficial ownership provisions, some countries may introduce special rules intended to prevent the use of corporate entities for unlawful purposes. To remedy this situation in Lebanon, the Governor of the Lebanese Central Bank prohibited dealings with corporate entities whose stocks and shares are totally or partially issued in bearer form.[75]

It is if anything more important not to lose sight of the fact that for as long as the FATF standards are accepted as a golden rule and imported into global and regional transparency strategies, then regardless of the level of sophistication and effectiveness of counter-initiatives, the very transparency strategies themselves will be fatally flawed.

## Part three: The Organisation for Economic Co-operation and Development (OECD)

### *OECD's origins and mission*

The OECD was established in 1961. Its mission statement is to promote policies which will improve the social and economic well-being of peoples around the world: "The OECD provides a forum in which governments can work together to share experiences and seek solutions to common problems. We work with

---

75  The Law Library of Congress, Global Legal Research Center, *Disclosure of Beneficial Ownership in Selected Countries* (July 2017) Summary 1 <www.loc.gov/law/help/beneficial-own ership/disclosure-beneficial-ownership.pdf> accessed 20 December 2018.

governments to understand what drives economic, social and environmental change. [. . .] We also look at issues that directly affect everyone's daily life, like how much people pay in taxes and social security [. . .]". Its stated goal is to build "a stronger, cleaner and fairer world".[76]

The OECD Global Forum (formed in 2009) sets out its mission statement in its Report on Tax Transparency 2017:

> The Global Forum is the largest international platform which brings together nearly 150 jurisdictions, and the European Union, to achieve the widespread and effective implementation of the internationally agreed standards on transparency and exchange of information for tax purposes. It has adopted and promotes two standards, one of which facilitates cross-border exchange of tax-relevant information on request (the EOIR Standard) and another one enables an automatic exchange of information on the financial accounts of non-residents (the AEOI Standard). By facilitating global cooperation on the implementation of these two complementary forms of information sharing between tax authorities, the Global Forum assists jurisdictions around the world in tackling illicit financial flows and raising public confidence in the tax system.[77]

The OECD's track record in relation to the curtailing of tax avoidance and tax evasions, as well as to the oversight and reform of practices within tax havens, has not been particularly effective or inspiring. It should not be forgotten that organisations such as the OECD are staffed by committed enthusiasts whose world is taxation, but that this self-referencing enthusiasm is not necessarily shared by many, or by any, members of the communities whom their work is intended to benefit. In this, however, the OECD is not alone:

> The frequent portrayals of international organisations, who police many international financial standards, as omnipotent bodies with endless resources and tentacles capable of poking into the dimmest recesses of domestic policy-making are considerably at odds with reality. [. . .] [I]nternational organisations often have to undertake this work on shoestring budgets, with few staff, and they are overwhelmingly reliant on participating countries to supply them with the requisite information.[78]

76 <www.oecd.org/about/> accessed 20 December 2018. There are currently 36 members, plus the Commission of the European Union: <www.oecd.org/about/membersandpartners/> accessed 20 December 2018.

77 OECD Global Forum Report on Tax Transparency 2017 <www.oecd.org/tax/transparency/global-forum-annual-report-2017.pdf> 2 accessed 20 December 2018.

78 Richard Woodward, 'A Strange Revolution: Mock Compliance and the Failure of the OECD's International Tax Transparency Regime' in Peter Dietsch and Thomas Rixen (eds), *Global Tax Governance: What Is Wrong with It and How to Fix It* (ECPR Press, 2016) ch 5 108. See also David S Kerzner and David W Chodikoff, 'The OECD's War on Tax Evasion

### OECD and Multinational Enterprises

The OECD Guidelines for Multinational Enterprises (2011 Edition)[79] whilst making references to ownership, do not address this on the level of beneficial ownership or ultimate control. Part III of the guidelines dealing with disclosure simply states (Disclosure III.1):

1   Enterprises should ensure that timely and accurate information is disclosed on all material matters regarding their activities, structure, financial situation, performance, ownership and governance. This information should be disclosed for the enterprise as a whole, and, where appropriate, along business lines or geographic areas. Disclosure policies of enterprises should be tailored to the nature, size and location of the enterprise, with due regard taken of costs, business confidentiality and other competitive concerns.

This is amplified, though slightly (Disclosure III.2c)):

2   Disclosure policies of enterprises should include, but not be limited to, material information on:

   c)   major share ownership and voting rights, including the structure of a group of enterprises and intra-group relations, as well as control-enhancing mechanisms;

The guidelines, these two references apart, are wholly silent on the question of ownership and provide no assistance as to how "ownership" is to be determined above and beyond the disclosure of "major share ownership and voting rights".

### OECD Due Diligence Guidance for Responsible Business Conduct (2018)

The OECD Due Diligence Guidance for Responsible Business Conduct was issued on 31 May 2018 with the objective being to provide practical support to enterprises on the implementation of the OECD Guidelines for Multinational Enterprises:

This Guidance also seeks to promote a common understanding among governments and stakeholders on due diligence for responsible business conduct. The UN Guiding Principles on Business and Human Rights[80] as well as the ILO Tripartite Declaration of Principles Concerning Multinational

---

1996–2014' in *International Tax Evasion in the Global Information Age* (Palgrave Macmillan, Basingstoke, UK, 2016) ch 3.

79  <www.oecd.org/daf/inv/mne/48004323.pdf> accessed 20 December 2018.

80  <www.ohchr.org/Documents/Publications/GuidingPrinciplesBusinessHR_EN.pdf> accessed 20 December 2018.

Enterprises and Social Policy[81] also contain due diligence recommendations, and this Guidance can help enterprises implement them.[82]

The Guidance, as with the guidelines, focusses on due diligence in relation to what an enterprise undertakes,[83] and is silent on any form of due diligence as to who owns and controls that enterprise. Consideration of the possibility that a legitimate business, conducted in accordance with both guidelines and Guidance, may have owners or controllers implicated in or pursuing unethical or criminal goals is absent.

### OECD Convention on Combating Bribery of Foreign Public Officials in International Business Transactions ("Anti Bribery Convention")[84]

A detailed consideration of international anti-bribery laws is outside the scope of this book, but what role does *ownership* play in its strategy? The Anti Bribery Convention was adopted by the OECD on 21 November 1997.[85] It is entirely silent on the question of the beneficial ownership of any entity which may be involved in the bribery (by a natural or a legal person) of a foreign public official, as set out in Article 1 paragraphs 1 and 2:

*Article 1 The Offence of Bribery of Foreign Public Officials*

1. Each Party shall take such measures as may be necessary to establish that it is a criminal offence under its law for any person intentionally to offer, promise or give any undue pecuniary or other advantage, whether directly or through intermediaries, to a foreign public official, for that official or for a third party, in order that the official act or

---

81 <www.ilo.org/empent/areas/mne-declaration/lang--en/index.htm> accessed 20 December 2018.

82 <https://mneguidelines.oecd.org/due-diligence-guidance-for-responsible-business-conduct.htm> accessed 20 December 2018 3 Foreword. The full text is available at <https://mneguidelines.oecd.org/OECD-Due-Diligence-Guidance-for-Responsible-Business-Conduct.pdf> accessed 20 December 2018.

83 "The purpose of due diligence is first and foremost to avoid causing or contributing to adverse impacts on people, the environment and society, and to seek to prevent adverse impacts directly linked to operations, products or services through business relationships. When involvement in adverse impacts cannot be avoided, due diligence should enable enterprises to mitigate them, prevent their recurrence and, where relevant, remediate them". <https://mneguidelines.oecd.org/due-diligence-guidance-for-responsible-business-conduct.htm> accessed 20 December 2018 16 *Characteristics of Due Diligence – the Essentials.*

84 <www.oecd.org/corruption/oecdantibriberyconvention.htm> accessed 20 December 2018.

85 The full text is (in English) at <www.oecd.org/daf/anti-bribery/ConvCombatBribery_ENG.pdf> and (in French) at <www.oecd.org/fr/daf/anti-corruption/ConvCombatBribery_FR.pdf> accessed 20 December 2018. Ratification status May 2017 <www.oecd.org/daf/anti-bribery/WGBRatificationStatus.pdf> accessed 20 December 2018.

refrain from acting in relation to the performance of official duties, in order to obtain or retain business or other improper advantage in the conduct of international business.

2. Each Party shall take any measures necessary to establish that complicity in, including incitement, aiding and abetting, or authorisation of an act of bribery of a foreign public official shall be a criminal offence. Attempt and conspiracy to bribe a foreign public official shall be criminal offences to the same extent as attempt and conspiracy to bribe a public official of that Party.

In dealing with accounting abuses, the Anti Bribery Convention addresses off-the-books transactions, from the standpoint that such transactions ought by recognised accounting standards to be on the books.

*Article 8*

**Accounting**

1. In order to combat bribery of foreign public officials effectively, each Party shall take such measures as may be necessary, within the framework of its laws and regulations regarding the maintenance of books and records, financial statement disclosures, and accounting and auditing standards, to prohibit the establishment of off-the-books accounts, the making of off-the-books or inadequately identified transactions, the recording of non-existent expenditures, the entry of liabilities with incorrect identification of their object, as well as the use of false documents, by companies subject to those laws and regulations, for the purpose of bribing foreign public officials or of hiding such bribery.

2. Each Party shall provide effective, proportionate and dissuasive civil, administrative or criminal penalties for such omissions and falsifications in respect of the books, records, accounts and financial statements of such companies.

For an offshore strategist, it is relatively straightforward to ring fence any company from the effects of so conventional an approach. The get out of jail free strategy takes advantage of the failure of the Anti Bribery Convention to address ownership issues. In the two decades since the Anti Bribery Convention was adopted, the worldwide industry in so-called "orphan structures", which have no owners, and one of the principal uses of which is the creation of off-balance sheet activity, has burgeoned.[86]

86 Ch 5.

For example: Company A will have committed no offence under relevant national laws conforming to the Anti Bribery Convention; all the illegal activity will be undertaken by Company B. Company B will not be its subsidiary or in any way liable to be shown on the balance sheet of Company A. Company B is a single purpose vehicle, held under an orphan structure such as a non-charitable purpose trust, which therefore has no beneficial owner. Sanctions may be applied against Company B, but it will be little more than a shell, principally financed to channel bribes; and as such wholly expendable and unaccountable. Company B will not have been an associate of Company A.[87] Company A will have benefitted, seemingly by mere coincidence.

In its Recommendations for Further Combatting Bribery of Foreign Public Officials in International Business Transactions (2009)[88] the OECD in considering Article 8 again focussed on the internal controls, ethics and compliance programmes and measures for the purpose of preventing and detecting foreign bribery in place (in the above example) in Company A.

The manipulation of ownership and the use of mere coincidence has the potential seriously to undermine the OECD's anti-bribery transparency strategy. The counter-argument can of course be advanced that there must in practice be some discernible connection between Company A and Company B. Someone must have acted as founder or intermediary. The problem lies in discharging the burden of proof. Will there be a whistle-blower? Possibly someone will emerge in Company A, but from the perspective of Company B (if this is, say, a Bahamas Enterprise Entity or a Nevis Multiform Foundation[89]) the state-sanctioned penalties for whistle-blowing may be sufficiently severe to dissuade anyone from talking, and when this is coupled with a total absence of publicly available information on the entity there will be an insurmountable barrier to disclosure. Whatever the whistle-blower in Company A may reveal, there may be no or inadequate corroboration.

87 By way of illustration, section 8 Bribery Act 2010 of the United Kingdom defines associated persons but does not cover seemingly unrelated, coincidental activity achieved by off-balance-sheet ownership manipulation: *Meaning of associated person.*

(1) *For the purposes of section 7, a person ("A") is associated with C if (disregarding any bribe under consideration) A is a person who performs services for or on behalf of C.*
(2) *The capacity in which A performs services for or on behalf of C does not matter.*
(3) *Accordingly A may (for example) be C's employee, agent or subsidiary.*
(4) *Whether or not A is a person who performs services for or on behalf of C is to be determined by reference to all the relevant circumstances and not merely by reference to the nature of the relationship between A and C.*
(5) *But if A is an employee of C, it is to be presumed unless the contrary is shown that A is a person who performs services for or on behalf of C* <www.legislation.gov.uk/ukpga/2010/23/section/8> accessed 20 December 2018.

88 <www.oecd.org/daf/anti-bribery/oecdantibriberyrecommendation2009.htm> with the full text at <www.oecd.org/daf/anti-bribery/44176910.pdf> accessed 20 December 2018.
89 These are discussed in ch 5.

## OECD and Supply Chains

Though the OECD is most often associated in the public mind with fiscal issues, its outreach is wider. In 2016 the OECD issued its Due Diligence Guidance for Responsible Supply Chains of Minerals from Conflict-Affected and High-Risk Areas.[90] Its stated objective is "to help companies respect human rights and avoid contributing to conflict through their mineral sourcing practices".[91] This complex issue is outside the scope of this book, but one aspect of accountability does resonate. The need to identify beneficial owners within supply chains comes within the remit of the OECD. Crucial to the monitoring of such supply chains is being able to ascertain who ultimately owns what the OECD refers to as the "significant actors" in the supply chain, and this is repeatedly referred to in the Due Diligence Guidance. The OECD applies to all supply chain structures on which it provides its Guidance, the Recommendations of the FATF[92] on a risk-based approach, including know your counterparty. In doing so without questioning the methodology of the FATF, the OECD in-builds the flawed approach of the FATF to beneficial ownership identification and may unwittingly have provided supply-chain operators with an excuse not to pursue their investigations too assiduously.

## OECD and Tax Evasion: Information Exchange

The OECD has a twin strategy in relation to countering tax evasion by the exchange of information: on request, and automatic. The latter evolved to address weaknesses in the former. It is outside the scope of this book to examine in detail the effectiveness of the implementation of OECD's initiatives,[93] but identifying the inherent weaknesses in these twin approaches is necessary in order to set in context the fundamental flaw: the importation of and reliance upon the not-fit-for-purpose FATF definition of "ownership". Think of that definition as a universal widget or line of source code, routinely and without any critical examination built into any number of machines and control systems. No matter how innovative or artificially intelligent, all will suffer from the same defect and will fail under pressure.

90 <www.oecd.org/daf/inv/mne/OECD-Due-Diligence-Guidance-Minerals-Edition3.pdf> accessed 20 December 2018.
91 Ibid. Introduction 3.
92 (n 38).
93 For the historical background to the creation of the OECD Global Forum, and a criticism of its shortcomings based on the lip service of those participating, see Richard Woodward, 'A Strange Revolution: Mock Compliance and the Failure of the OECD's International Tax Transparency Regime' (n 78) ch 5.

*Exchange of Information on Request*

The OECD Global Forum 2016 Terms of Reference[94] in section II set out the background to the exchange of information on request initiative:

> II. *The standard of transparency and exchange of information on request for tax purposes*
>
> 4. The principles of transparency and effective information exchange on request for tax purposes are primarily reflected in the 2002 OECD's Model Agreement on Exchange of Information on Tax Matters (the OECD Model TIEA) and its commentary and in Article 26 of the OECD Model Tax Convention on Income and on Capital ("the OECD Model Tax Convention")[95] and its commentary as updated in 2012 (and approved by the OECD Council on 17 July 2012). The 2012 revision to Article 26 and its commentary aimed at reflecting the international developments in tax transparency since the previous revision in 2005.[96] The standard of EOIR is now virtually universally accepted. All Global Forum members have committed to implement the standard and undergo a peer review to assess its implementation.

Article 26 (Exchange of Information) of the OECD Model Tax Convention requires Contracting States "to exchange such information as is foreseeably relevant[97] for carrying out of the provisions of this Convention" (Article 26.1).

---

94 2016 Terms of Reference to Monitor and Review Progress Towards Transparency and Exchange of Information on Request for Tax Purposes <www.oecd.org/tax/trans parency/about-the-global-forum/publications/terms-of-reference.pdf> accessed 20 December 2018.

95 This has since been further revised. Model Tax Convention on Income and on Capital (Condensed Version, as it read on 21 November 2017) <https://read.oecd-ilibrary.org/ taxation/model-tax-convention-on-income-and-on-capital-condensed-version-2017_mtc_ cond-2017-en#page1> accessed 20 December 2018.

96 United Nations Model Double Taxation Convention Between Developed and Developing Countries continues to reflect the 2005 version of the OECD Model Tax Convention and its Commentary. The 2017 update of that Convention is at <www.un.org/esa/ffd/wp-content/uploads/2018/05/MDT_2017.pdf> accessed 20 December 2018.

97 The test of foreseeable relevance replaced the 2005 test of "necessary". 'Fishing expeditions are not authorised but all foreseeably relevant information must be provided, including bank information and information held by fiduciaries, regardless of the existence of a domestic tax interest or the application of a dual criminality standard. The 2012 revision to Article 26 further developed the interpretation of the standard of "foreseeable relevance", notably spelling out the circumstances in which "group requests" meet the standard of "foreseeable relevance" and when they do not, and adding new examples regarding foreseeable relevance'. (Terms of Reference Section II 5) (n 94). Where the line is drawn between what constitutes a "fishing expedition" and simply a request perforce made in general terms because of difficulties on the part of the requesting Contracting State in identifying "owner" or "beneficial

Information is to be treated as secret and "disclosed only to persons or authorities (including courts and administrative bodies) concerned with the assessment or collection of, the enforcement or prosecution in respect of, the determination of appeals in relation to taxes referred to in [Article 26.1] or the oversight of the above" (Article 26.2). There is no obligation on a Contracting State "to supply information which is not obtainable under the laws or in the normal course of the administration of that or of the other Contracting State" (Article 26.3b) but this is heavily caveated in Article 26.5: "In no case shall the provisions of paragraph 3 be construed to permit a Contracting State to decline to supply information solely because the information is held by a bank, other financial institution, ^^nominee or person in an agency or a fiduciary capacity **or because it relates to ownership interests in a person**" [Emphasis added].[98]

Section II A paragraphs 10 and 11 of the Terms of Reference examine the question of ownership. Frustratingly, the Terms of Reference adopt the FATF standard definitions of "owner" and "beneficial owner" yet at the same time distinguish them in the context of exchange of information for tax purposes without giving any guidance as to how such a distinction is to be made:

> 10. Effective exchange of information requires the availability of reliable information. In particular, it requires that adequate, accurate and up to date information on the identity of the legal and beneficial owners [. . .] of relevant entities and arrangements[99] is available to competent authorities in a timely manner, as well as accounting information for these entities and arrangements. In addition, it is crucial for effective exchange of information that banking information is available.

---

owner" is not made clear. The onus appears to be on the requesting Contracting State. "In order to stop overseas tax authorities embarking on speculative enquiries – so-called 'fishing expeditions' – TIEAs [Tax Information Exchange Agreements] require them to know almost everything about their prey, something that secrecy provisions will almost certainly preclude". Richard Woodward, *A Strange Revolution* (n 78) ch 5 115. The regime in effect requires the requesting Contracting State to provide substantial preliminary evidence, and the evidence they need in order to do so may well consist largely of the very information they are requesting and therefore cannot produce.

98 The OECD Model Tax Convention (n 95) includes at 487 to 507 a detailed Commentary on Article 26. The position of Canada and the United States of America in relation to Article 26 is considered in David S Kerzner and David W Chodikoff, 'Article 26 of the OECD Model Tax Convention on Income and on Capital' in *International Tax Evasion in the Global Information Age* (Palgrave Macmillan, Basingstoke, UK, 2016) ch 7.

99 Footnote 5 to the Terms of Reference offers a definition with a degree of optimistic breadth: "The term 'Relevant Entities and Arrangements' includes: (i) a company, foundation, Anstalt and any similar structure, (ii) a partnership or other body of persons, (iii) a trust or similar arrangement, (iv) a collective investment fund or scheme, (v) any person holding assets in a fiduciary capacity and (vi) any other entity or arrangement deemed relevant in the case of the specific jurisdiction assessed". Presumably, Islamic Financial Services instruments and structures, which are nowhere expressly referred to, are caught under (vi).

11. Regarding beneficial ownership information [. . .], it is recognised that the purposes for which the FATF standards have been developed (combatting money laundering and terrorist financing) are different from the purpose of the standard on EOIR (ensuring effective exchange of information for tax purposes). Hence, in applying and interpreting the FATF materials regarding "beneficial owner", care should be taken that such application and interpretation do not go beyond what is appropriate for the purposes of ensuring effective exchange of information for tax purposes.

The interpretation of the FATF principles of beneficial ownership is itself a complex matter. The Terms of Reference serve to wrap those principles in a fiscal enigma.

The OECD in its Global Forum Report on Tax Transparency 2017[100] addresses the introduction under the updated Terms of Reference of the requirement to provide beneficial ownership information:

The second round of peer reviews was launched in July 2016 under the reinforced 2016 Terms of Reference which now reflect the latest developments in international tax transparency. One of the most notable changes is the introduction of the requirement of the availability of beneficial ownership information – aligned with the FATF standard – as well as access to it by the tax authorities. Previously, the Global Forum standard only required the availability of legal ownership and identity information of legal entities and arrangements. The new element strengthens the fight against anonymous shell companies and the use of legal arrangements to conceal ownership identity.[101]

But does it really strengthen the fight? The report acknowledges that there is a long way to go, as the member states of the Global Forum appear uncertain how in practice to provide beneficial ownership information:

Following the call by the G20 Leaders on ways to improve the implementation of the internationally agreed standards on transparency,[102] including on the availability of beneficial ownership information of legal persons and legal arrangements, and its international exchange, the Global Forum developed several proposals and has been working to implement them. To this end, the 2016 Terms of Reference now include new emphasis on the availability of and access to beneficial ownership information. The first EOIR reviews demonstrated that this requirement will require substantial technical assistance.

---

100 OECD Global Forum Report on Tax Transparency 2017 <www.oecd.org/tax/transparency/global-forum-annual-report-2017.pdf> accessed 20 December 2018.
101 Ibid. 23.
102 Which supposed international standards are not identified in the report itself.

In order to address this new emerging challenge, the Global Forum will publish a manual on beneficial ownership, as well as generally enhancing its technical assistance in this complex area.[103]

According to the report, more than 20 jurisdictions benefitted from EOIR-related drafting assistance, including that on beneficial ownership in 2017.[104] By October 2017 a total of 16 peer review reports had been adopted by the Global Forum under the Second Round under the 2016 Terms of reference, of which only 4 (Ireland, Italy, Jersey and Qatar) were compliant. Of the remaining 12, all were largely compliant or partly compliant, with the exception of Jamaica which was non-compliant.[105] These are just 16 reviews, out of a total Global Forum membership (as at September 2018) of 153 jurisdictions (to which are added 17 observers).[106]

In importing the FATF standards on beneficial ownership identification, the Global Forum inevitably suffers from the weaknesses of the FATF approach.

It remains to be seen what practical use can be made of what the Global Forum refers to in the OECD Global Forum 2016 Report on Tax Transparency[107] as "a flood of new information [which] will start to be provided by financial institutions all over the world". Information uninformed by principles of analysis is of itself purely raw data, a tax evasion information bubble.

The Global Forum acknowledges this: "But EOI relationships are not enough on their own. They must be utilised. It is the combination of global transparency with domestic efforts to identify and punish taxpayers who break the rules which gives international cooperation its real potency. While we are now beginning to see some successes, the number of requests made by African countries is still tiny in a global context. Also many developing countries have yet to engage with the new AEOI standard although it offers enormous potential to detect tax evasion which might otherwise go undetected, particularly in countries jurisdictions [sic] where tax administrations lack the necessary investigative skills to uncover it otherwise".[108]

Even well-resourced Western countries may not be fully engaged with the process. This is true of the United States of America. On 16 July 2018 the Global Forum issued its Second Round Peer Review Report on the Exchange of Information Request. It summarised the situation:

---

103 OECD Global Forum Report on Tax Transparency 2017 <www.oecd.org/tax/transparency/global-forum-annual-report-2017.pdf> 43 accessed 20 December 2018.

104 Ibid. 43.

105 Ibid. 28.

106 <www.oecd.org/tax/transparency/about-the-global-forum/members/> accessed 20 December 2018.

107 <www.oecd.org/tax/transparency/GF-annual-report-2016.pdf> 25 accessed 20 December 2018.

108 Ibid. 32, 33.

The United States remains Largely Compliant with the EOIR standard. Although recommendations made in the first-round review have been addressed, the availability of beneficial ownership information poses a challenge. Despite recent positive steps which significantly strengthen the availability of beneficial ownership information in the United States, gaps have been identified in respect of legal requirements to obtain and maintain beneficial ownership information as well as in respect of their implementation in practice. The United States' access powers are broad and allow provision of quality information to its exchange of information partners as also confirmed by peers. The United States has in place a robust EOI Program and is heavily involved in exchange of information receiving more than 2,600 requests over the period 1 January 2014 to 31 December 2016. Accordingly, the United States is valued by its exchange of information partners as a very important and reliable partner. The review noted that since July 2010, the United States has not ratified any signed EOI agreement that requires US ratification including the 2010 Protocol to the Multilateral Convention which negatively impacts significant number of US partners and the United States is recommended to ratify these signed agreements expeditiously so that all its EOI relationships are in force and, in the meantime, expeditiously pursue any alternative means to ensure effective EOI arrangements that meet the standard are in force with affected jurisdictions.[109]

Gabriel Zucman adopts a more jaundiced, though pragmatic, view:

> The fundamental problem is that authorities have no means to verify that offshore bankers are respecting the spirit – or the letter – of international regulations. All the steps being taken today and the plans devised for the future are based on the idea that we can trust bankers to carry out their obligations. However, this belief is, to say the least, problematic.[110]

## *Automatic Information Exchange: OECD Common Reporting Standard 2014*

Not entirely unconnected to the entry into force in 2010 of the US Foreign Account Tax Compliance Act (more commonly referred to by its acronym FATCA), which obliges all foreign financial institutions doing business in the US financial market to report *automatically* (and not merely on request) capital income earned by US account holders, the OECD in 2014 launched its Common

109 <www.oecd.org/unitedstates/global-forum-on-transparency-and-exchange-of-infor mation-for-tax-purposes-united-states-2018-second-round-9789264302853-en.htm> accessed 20 December 2018.
110 Gabriel Zucman, *The Hidden Wealth of Nations: The Scourge of Tax Havens* (Teresa Lavender Fagan tr, The University of Chicago Press, Chicago and London, 2015) 67.

Reporting Standard ("CRS"), itself also predicated on automatic information exchange.[111] In the Introduction to the CRS the OECD sets out its case. It is entirely fiscally driven: "Countries have a shared interest in maintaining the integrity of their tax systems. Co-operation between tax administrations is critical in the fight against tax evasion and in protecting the integrity of tax systems. A key aspect of that co-operation is exchange of information" (Introduction I.A.1).

Pointing to globalisation, the OECD notes that it is easier for all taxpayers to make, hold and manage investments through financial institutions outside of their country of residence. Its focus is the transfer of taxable funds offshore: "Vast amounts of money are kept offshore and go untaxed to the extent that taxpayers fail to comply with tax obligations in their home jurisdiction. Offshore tax evasion is a serious problem for jurisdictions all over the world, OECD and non-OECD, small and large, developing and developed" (Introduction I.A.1).

The CRS does not have automatic application in those states which decide to adopt it – domestic legislation, both primary and secondary, has first to be put in place. In essence financial institutions report information to the tax administration in the jurisdiction in which they are located. The information consists of details of financial assets they hold on behalf of taxpayers from jurisdictions with which their tax administration exchanges information. The tax administrations then exchange that information.

In order to ensure consistency in reporting, the CRS contains the due diligence rules for financial institutions to follow to collect and then report the information that underpins the automatic exchange of financial information. The OECD has produced its Multilateral Competent Authority Agreement on Automatic Exchange of Financial Account Information ("MCAA")[112] (signed in Berlin on 29 October 2014) as a blueprint for the exchange of information between jurisdictions. The automatic exchange functions between jurisdictions which have either mutually entered into an MCAA or which have an information exchange agreement equivalent to this already in place. The legal basis for the MCAA is Article 6 of the Multilateral Convention on Mutual Administrative Assistance in Tax

---

111 Standard for Automatic Exchange of Financial Account Information in Tax Matters (Second Edition, 2017) <www.oecd-ilibrary.org/docserver/9789264267992-en.pdf?expires= 1537085651&id=id&accname=guest&checksum=F0474BCD55FBB8138E01DBA985F 0EBBC> accessed 20 December 2018. And see Standard for Automatic Exchange of Financial Account Information in Tax Matters Implementation Handbook (Second Edition, 2018) accessed 20 December 2018 <www.oecd.org/tax/exchange-of-tax-information/ implementation-handbook-standard-for-automatic-exchange-of-financial-information-in-tax-matters.pdf> accessed 20 December 2018. A useful overview is found in David S Kerzner and David W Chodikoff, *Automatic Exchange of Information in International Tax Evasion in the Global Information Age* (Palgrave Macmillan, Basingstoke, UK, 2016) ch 8.
112 <www.oecd.org/tax/transparency/technical-assistance/aeoi/whatisthemultilateralcom petentauthorityagreement.htm> and <www.oecd.org/tax/exchange-of-tax-information/ multilateral-competent-authority-agreement.htm> accessed 20 December 2018. The MCAA is valid in both its English and French originals.

Matters ("Convention")[113] As at 29 November 2018, 126 jurisdictions participate in the Convention.[114] The MCAA draws on the definitions and due diligence procedures contained in the CRS. The information to be exchanged includes:

> The information to be exchanged is, with respect to each Reportable Account of another Jurisdiction:
>
> > a) the name, address, TIN(s) and date and place of birth (in the case of an individual) of each Reportable Person that is an Account Holder of the account and, in the case of any Entity that is an Account Holder and that, after application of due diligence procedures consistent with the Common Reporting Standard, is identified as having one or more Controlling Persons that is a Reportable Person, the name, address, and TIN(s) of the Entity and the name, address, TIN(s) and date and place of birth of each Reportable Person; [. . .][115]

To the extent therefore that the due diligence requirements of the CRS "look through" an Account Holder to a Controlling Person, beneficial ownership may be identified, but neither the Convention nor the MCAA itself addresses the question of beneficial ownership directly.

THE CRS AND TRUSTS – A PROBLEMATIC AREA[116]

One crucially important defect in the CRS regime, and one which has a great significance for the tax havens, is its treatment of trusts. A trust will only be classified

113 <www.oecd.org/tax/exchange-of-tax-information/convention-on-mutual-adminstra tive-assistance-in-tax-matters.htm> and <https://read.oecd-ilibrary.org/taxation/the-multilateral-convention-on-mutual-administrative-assistance-in-tax-matters_ 9789264115606-en#page2> accessed 20 December 2018.
114 <www.oecd.org/ctp/exchange-of-tax-information/Status_of_convention.pdf> accessed 20 December 2018. Of these, a substantial number are offshore jurisdictions which would popularly be described (though not by those jurisdictions themselves) as tax havens, including some to which the Convention has been extended by the United Kingdom, the Netherlands, Denmark or China.
115 MCAA Section 2, paragraph 2a) "Les renseignements qui doivent être échangés, concernant chaque Compte déclarable d'une autre Juridiction, sont les suivants : a) les nom, adresse, NIF et date et lieu de naissance (dans le cas d'une personne physique) de chaque Personne devant faire l'objet d'une déclaration qui est un Titulaire de ce compte et, dans le cas d'une Entité qui est Titulaire de ce compte et pour laquelle, après application des procédures de diligence raisonnable définies dans la Norme commune de déclaration, il apparaît qu'une ou plusieurs Personnes qui en détiennent le contrôle sont des Personnes devant faire l'objet d'une déclaration, le nom, l'adresse et le NIF de cette Entité ainsi que les nom, adresse, NIF et date et lieu de naissance de chacune de ces Personnes devant faire l'objet d'une déclaration ; [. . .]"
116 CRS Implementation Handbook <www.oecd.org/tax/exchange-of-tax-information/ implementation-handbook-standard-for-automatic-exchange-of-financial-information-in-tax-matters.pdf> accessed 20 December 2018. Ch 6: Treatment of trusts in the CRS.

as a financial institution if carrying on business in a given jurisdiction where more than 50% of the trust's gross income is attributable to trading in money market instruments, portfolio management or the investment and management of funds, or alternatively more than 50% of the trust's income is attributable to investing, reinvesting or trading in financial assets. Absent these, the trust is classified as a Non-Financial Entity and does not need to register or report. It takes little design effort to attain NFE status.[117]

In addition, the CRS employs a convenient fiction in defining "Controlling Persons" (Section VIII.D.6): "In the case of a trust, such term means the settlor(s), the trustee(s), the protector(s) (if any), the beneficiary(ies) or class(es) of beneficiaries, and any other natural person(s) exercising ultimate effective control over the trust, and in the case of a legal arrangement other than a trust, such term means persons in equivalent or similar positions. The term 'Controlling Persons' must be interpreted in a manner consistent with the Financial Action Task Force Recommendations".[118]

The CRS Implementation Handbook makes no express reference to "orphan structure" trusts (non-charitable purpose trusts), which are by statute prevented from having beneficiaries.[119]

The guidance sets out the CRS strategy on how to identify beneficial owners, drawing heavily on the FATF approach – including a strategy of "last resort":

> 271. It is important to point out that the ownership threshold for legal persons of 25% that is specified in footnote 30 in the Interpretative Note to Recommendation 10 of the 2012 FATF Recommendations (as printed in March 2012) is only indicative. For the purposes of determining the Controlling Person of an Account Holder, the AML/KYC procedures pursuant to the anti-money laundering or similar requirements as implemented in the domestic law and to which the Reporting Financial Institution is subject, apply [. . .]. For New Entity Accounts such AML/KYC Procedures must be consistent with Recommendations 10 and 25 of the 2012 FATF Recommendations. [. . .]
>
> 274. The identity of beneficial owner of a legal person is defined as any natural person who ultimately has controlling ownership interest which is usually defined on the basis of a threshold. Footnote 30 to the Interpretative

---

117  CRS Implementation Handbook (n 116) ch 6.2: Determining whether the trust is a Reporting Financial Institution or a Non-Financial Entity.

118  As with the treatment of trusts by the FATF, this application misrepresents the nature of a trust – see ch 2. This chosen fiction is all the more surprising as the CRS Implementation Handbook (n 116) itself in ch 6.1 sets out accurately the basic features of a trust. See the useful flowchart produced by STEP (The Society of Trust and Estate Practitioners) <www.step.org/sites/default/files/Policy/Trusts_under_CRS_flowchart_Jurisdiction_X.pdf> accessed 20 December 2018.

119  Ch 5.

Note to Recommendation 10 of the 2012 FATF Recommendations (as printed in March 2012) gives an exemplary ownership threshold of 25%.

275. Should the ownership structure analysis result in doubt as to whether the person(s) with the controlling ownership interest are the beneficial owners or where no natural person exercises control through ownership interest the analysis shall proceed to identifying any other natural person(s) exercising control of the legal person through other means. As a last resort, if none of the previously mentioned tests result in identification of the beneficial owner(s), the senior managing official(s) will be treated as the beneficial owner(s).

It is difficult to see how any form of accountability beyond that artificially attributed to them under the CRS regime could attach to "the senior managing official(s)" of a trust – even if that phrase had any meaning in equity, which it does not.

The fictional nature ("fictional" in the sense of lacking any conformity with the principles of equity which support the existence of trusts) of the definition of "beneficiary" is further compounded by the treatment of what is referred to as "indirect distributions by a trust":

> Pursuant to Section VIII(C)(4), a Reportable Person will be treated as a beneficiary of a trust "if such Reportable Person [. . .] may receive, directly or indirectly, a discretionary distribution from the trust". Indirect distributions by a trust may arise when the trust makes payments to a third party for the benefit of another person. For example, instances where a trust pays the tuition fees or repays a loan taken up by another person are to be considered indirect distributions by the trust. Indirect distributions also include cases where the trust grants a loan free of interest or at an interest rate lower than the market interest rate or at other non-arm's length conditions. In addition, the write-off of a loan granted by a trust to its beneficiary constitutes an indirect distribution in the year the loan is written-off. In all of the above cases the Reportable Person will be person that is the beneficiary of the trust receiving the indirect distribution (i.e. in the above examples, the debtor of the tuition fees or the recipient of the favourable loan conditions).[120]

Loans made to beneficiaries, which loans are subsequently written off are, in equity, distributions to that beneficiary – but it is not the making of the loan or its writing off which constitutes that person a beneficiary: they are a beneficiary because they are designated as such under the trust deed. Third parties of the kind referred to in this Q&A are not beneficiaries as understood in equity. This broad definition sweeps up any service provider who receives payment from a

---

120 CRS-related Frequently Asked Questions (June 2018) <www.oecd.org/tax/exchange-of-tax-information/CRS-related-FAQs.pdf> accessed 20 December 2018 Part C.11.

trust. It will come as a surprise to many a private educational institution that it is to be regarded as a beneficiary of a private trust and reportable as such. Payments to a professional trust service provider also appear to come within the definition. That a trustee should be deemed to be a beneficiary flies in the face of reason and exposes a fundamental misunderstanding of trusts on the part of the CRS regime draftspersons.

In addition to (no doubt unintentionally) fudging the definition of beneficiaries, the CRS regime fails to address a number of fundamental issues with regard to the creation and administration of trusts. The classic triangular model – a settlor gives assets to a trustee for the benefit of beneficiaries – is not always employed. There are permutations.

In its Guidance Note on CRS and trusts, issued on 8 March 2017,[121] the Society of Trust and Estate Practitioners[122] identifies these and proposes solutions (whilst admitting that none of its guidance can be seen as endorsed by the OECD). Key areas of concern in the Guidance Note can be summarised as follows:

- A settlor may not be named in the trust instrument – it is common practice that a trust instrument is in the form of a Declaration of Trust, in which only the trustees are named. The person providing the assets will therefore be the true "underlying settlor".
- A settlor may under the terms of a settlement be wholly excluded from benefitting (a very common occurrence). Discretionary beneficiaries under a trust have no economic interest in the trust assets. The result is a CRS vacuum.
- In some cases, trusts are not established directly by transfer of assets from an individual, but instead by a transfer of assets from Trust A to Trust B. In terms of equity, the *trustee* of Trust A is the settlor of Trust B. However, the CRS regime will artificially regard the *settlor* of Trust A as being the settlor of Trust B – even though at the time of the transfer, the settlor of Trust A has no economic or ownership interest in the assets which are being transferred (by virtue of having parted with these attributes upon the creation of Trust A).
- A trust may be created by a "nominal" settlor – nominal in the sense that the settlement is established by him or her on behalf of another person, who him- or herself contributes the bulk of the assets. In this way, the name of the "true settlor" remains confidential – a fact which contravenes no principles of equity. It is the next level up in legitimate concealment from the simpler

---

121 <www.step.org/sites/default/files/Policy/Guidance_note_CRS_and_trusts.pdf> accessed 20 December 2018. See this Guidance Note for cross-references to the CRS Implementation Handbook.
122 <www.step.org> accessed 20 December 2018.

Declaration of Trust. Nevertheless, for CRS purposes, the focus is on the "true settlor".

- The settlor may be a legal person. It is not uncommon for a company or a foundation to act as settlor. Who then is the ultimate underlying settlor? Ownership of a company may – and often does – change over the years. No one owns a foundation. Are the shareholders at the time of the setting up of the trust fixed in their responsibility as true settlor, or does this torch pass from shareholder to shareholder on subsequent transfers? Is the founder of a foundation indelibly marked with the status of true settlor, even though he or she has no economic interest in that capacity in the foundation assets?

- A settlor may be dead, or in the case of a legal person, dissolved. The CRS is silent on both possibilities: another CRS vacuum.

- The trustee is often a corporation. It may also be a company established specifically for the purpose of acting as trustee of a particular settlement (and no other). Offshore structuring commonly places the shares in such a private trust company in a non-charitable purpose trust (which has no beneficiaries) and so the private trust company is owned by no one[123] and has no legal or equitable connection to the settlor or beneficiaries. The CRS provides no guidance as to where "ownership or control" lies – which, in the context of an ownerless structure, would in any event be quite a challenge.

- *Sub-trusts* may be created out of an original trust – for example, when the needs of beneficiaries require them to have their personalised trust structure. Alternatively, *sub-funds* may be set up as an accounting exercise within the trust fund, by which although the trust remains as a unity, a separately identified part of the trust fund is earmarked for each. The CRS is silent both on sub-trusts and on sub-funds.

- A settlement may have a protector. This is a quasi-fiduciary role,[124] generally consisting of the right to be consulted when the trustees wish, for example, to make a distribution and may also vest in the protector powers of veto over those decisions. It rarely involves any pro-active role, and never requires (or entitles) the protector to hold trust assets. Nevertheless, the CRS regime in the case of a trust which is a Reporting Financial Institution deems a protector to be an account holder irrespective of whether the protector has effective control over the trust. The difficulties are further compounded when a protector is not a single individual but several individuals, or (very commonly)

---

123 See the discussion in ch 5.

124 A comprehensive account of the powers and responsibilities of a protector is found in Mark Hubbard, *Protectors of Trusts* (Oxford University Press, Oxford, 2013). For an overview of the changing role of protectors see Andrew T Huber, 'Trust Protectors: The Role Continues to Evolve' *Probate and Property Magazine* (January/February 2017 Volume 31 No 1, Section of Real Property, Trust and Estate Law, American Bar Association) <www.americanbar.org/publications/probate_property_magazine_2012/2017/january_february_2017/2017_aba_rpte_pp_v31_1_article_huber_trust_protectors.html> accessed 20 December 2018.

a professional corporation established for the purpose of offering protectors globally. That corporate protector may be privately owned, but even then may simply be one element in a complex corporate and trust service provider group of companies. The corporate protector may be a public company, or its shareholders may be held by a private equity fund. Cui bono?

- The reporting requirements for charitable trusts (which by their nature have no identified individual beneficiaries and may have many natural and legal persons contributing assets to the trust fund) is unclear.

Shoehorning trusts, settlors, trustees, protectors and beneficiaries into an "ownership or control" framework has resulted in these CRS absurdities with regards to trusts. The CRS may be a good hammer, but not every problem is a nail.

HOW EFFECTIVE IS THE CRS AEOI REGIME?

The OECD itself identifies in the Introduction to the CRS the objective advantages to automatic, standardised exchange as being "simplification, higher effectiveness and lower costs for all stakeholders concerned" (Introduction I.B.6). There is an argument that avoiding a proliferation of competing information exchange models and the consequent fragmentation of data should be cost-effective.

The OECD is however once again travelling a road paved with good intentions to a less than triumphant destination. The CRS regime is immensely time-consuming, resource hungry and complex, and this sheer complexity may be its undoing. It places a huge burden on the reporting institutions. The quality of information exchanged can be no higher than the quality of information gathered. It presupposes that both the reporting and the receiving jurisdictions have an information infrastructure capable of processing the information – and for developing countries, this required level of resourcing is likely to prove highly problematic.[125] The complexity of the CRS regime can overwhelm the resources of the weaker countries whose economies it is intended to benefit, both in terms of the ability of those countries to introduce enforceable domestic implementation legislation and to create an infrastructure capable of processing whatever information they receive, and take-up by such countries is minimal. It is heavily weighted in favour of predominantly western economies whose support systems and data processing capacity hugely outstrip those of the developing world. A recent shift in the approach of the OECD in this regard is however apparent. The OECD Secretary-General Report to the G20 Finance Ministers and Central Bank Governors (Buenos Aires, Argentina, March 2018) comments:

---

125 See 'TJN Responds to New OECD Report on Automatic Information Exchange' *Tax Justice Network* (13 February 2014) <www.taxjustice.net/2014/02/13/press-release-tjn-responds-new-oecd-report-automatic-information-exchange/> accessed 20 December 2018.

As the evidence of the benefits delivered through AEOI continue to emerge, the interest of developing countries in this powerful anti-evasion instrument is growing. At its plenary meeting, which took place on 15–17 November 2017 in Yaoundé (Cameroon), the Global Forum adopted the Plan of Action for Developing Country Participation in AEOI which draws a pathway for developing countries by offering a structured step-by-step approach to implementing the standard. Recognising that significant resources are required to support developing countries' efforts through the provision of technical assistance, the Global Forum plenary called on international development agencies, governments and other potential donors to support this vital agenda. With more than a dozen developing countries already receiving assistance under the step-by-step approach, this call for support is now also addressed to the G20 countries. [. . .]

The demand for Global Forum's technical assistance has surged due to rapidly growing membership, increasing requests for support with respect to beneficial ownership and AEOI-related assistance. The Yaoundé Declaration (2017), which calls for further progress on tax transparency and exchange of information in Africa, has now been signed by 6 countries (i.e. Cameroon, Benin, Ghana, Liberia, Togo and Uganda) and endorsed by France and the United Kingdom. This creates a momentum for closer engagement with African countries and regional organisations.[126]

The CRS regime also presupposes a degree of uniformity in the nature of the information to be exchanged and in the obligation to do so, but a simple example illustrates the difficulty. In which jurisdiction is a company required to comply with CRS reporting standards? There is no globally accepted definition of corporate domicile – a company may be domiciled in its jurisdiction of incorporation or, alternatively, where its directors are most likely to convene their meetings or where the true management and control of the company lies. Such true management and control could be exercised in a tax haven.[127]

The success of the CRS is ultimately dependent on a common political will to implement its mechanisms, no matter how flawed and in need of refinement those mechanisms may be. Yet that uniformity of will cannot be presumed to exist. Switzerland is a prime example of a country cutting back on its CRS obligations. Switzerland's implementation of CRS on 16 June 2017 allows it to refuse to exchange confidential bank client information with countries "in regions such as South America or Africa where data protection standards can be weak". This reflects the concern expressed during the implementation process by the

---

126 <www.oecd.org/tax/OECD-Secretary-General-tax-report-G20-Finance-Ministers-Argentina-March-2018.pdf> accessed 20 December 2018 23, 24.
127 The loopholes in the CRS, including the use of tax havens, are discussed in Hilary Osborne, 'Offshore Wealth: Loopholes Found in EU Ant-tax Evasion Rules' *The Guardian* (15 October 2018) <www.theguardian.com/business/2018/oct/15/offshore-wealth-loopholes-found-eu-anti-tax-evasion-rules> accessed 20 December 2018.

Swiss Banking Association, which issued a statement on 2 February 2017[128] that it "expects Switzerland to insist on the OECD criteria and to ensure that the OECD will regularly monitor adherence to these criteria. Should any country not adhere to these rules, the Swiss government must exercise its right and immediately suspend the AEOI agreement with the country at fault". In essence therefore, Switzerland regards itself as setting a high data protection standard and will simply not activate an automatic exchange of information with any country which *in Switzerland's estimation* cannot match that standard. In the words of the chairman of the Association of Swiss Private Banks Yves Mirabeaud: "I'm referring to countries where we're not very sure that the democratic process is the same as ours, or where corruption is very high".[129]

A similar approach is becoming evident elsewhere. Law firm Mishcon de Reya (London and New York) on 1 August 2018 fired an opening salvo,[130] citing the EU's General Data Protection Regulation[131]

> However the rights to privacy and data protection are fundamental rights. They are the cornerstone of the General Data Protection Regulation (GDPR) – which came into force in May 2018 – and emanate directly from European Convention on Human Rights and the EU's Charter of Fundamental Rights. [. . .] In order to be justified, any interference with these rights needs to have a clear legal basis, pursue a legitimate public interest (such as the fight against crime); and be proportionate, i.e. *limited to what is strictly necessary* to achieve the objective pursued.

128 <accessed>www.swissbanking.org/en/media/positions-and-press-releases/statement-from-the-sba-regarding-the-federal-council-decision-in-favour-of-a-further-aeoi-country-list>accessed 20 December 2018.
129 Joshua Franklin and John O'Donnell, 'Swiss Banks Lobby for Get-out Clause as End of Bank Secrecy Nears' *Reuters* (15 June 2017) <https://uk.reuters.com/article/uk-swiss-banks-secrecy-idUKKBN19623I> accessed 20 December 2018. This is a somewhat sanctimonious or at least disingenuous observation in respect of the country which the Tax Justice Network ranks as the world's top tax haven: Tax Justice Network Financial Secrecy Index (30 January 2018) <www.financialsecrecyindex.com/> accessed 20 December 2018. The Swiss State Secretariat for International Finance maintains a list of those countries with which Switzerland has agreed automatically to exchange information: <www.sif.admin.ch/sif/en/home/multilateral/steuer_informationsaust/automatischer-informationsaustausch/automatischer-informationsaustausch1.html> accessed 20 December 2018.
130 <www.mishcon.com/news/firm_news/legal-challenge-to-common-reporting-standard-crs-and-beneficial-ownership-bo-registers> accessed 20 December 2018 and David Pegg, 'Mishcon de Reya Complains About Anti-tax Evasion Measures' *The Guardian* (2 August 2018) <accessed>www.theguardian.com/money/2018/aug/02/mishcon-de-reya-complains-about-anti-tax-evasion-measures>accessed 20 December 2018. See ch 4 for a detailed review of the issues regarding confidentiality and concealment.
131 Regulation (EU) 2016/679 on the protection of natural persons with regard to the processing of personal data and on the free movement of such data <https://eur-lex.europa.eu/legal-content/EN/TXT/?qid=1532348683434&uri=CELEX:02016R0679-20160504> accessed 20 December 2018.

Our contention is that the publication of sensitive data concerning the internal governance and ownership of private companies by the Beneficial Ownership Registers is not necessary to achieve the stated objectives. Similarly, we believe that the exchange of information under the CRS is excessive, as information is exchanged indiscriminately and affects all account holders regardless of the size of the account. The information exchanged under the CRS includes sensitive personal data (such as the name, date/place of birth and tax identification number of the account holder) as well as financial data about the financial account itself such as the account number and balance. This exposes compliant account holders to risk of hacking and data loss: it could lead to identity theft on a grand scale.

The issue of inequality of arms in matters of resourcing is of fundamental concern. The CRS regime creates an information mountain which few can mine, and fewer refine. Access to information is no guarantee of access to justice.[132] This has not gone unnoticed by the OECD itself. The OECD Secretary-General Report to the G20 Finance Ministers and Central Bank Governors (Buenos Aires, Argentina, March 2018) comments:

> We must, however, not allow success to breed complacency. The "Paradise Papers" leaks show that we need to remain vigilant and active in achieving the goal of full transparency for tax purposes. The Global Forum's reviews of beneficial ownership have already resulted in important recommendations for improvement. The full implementation of AEOI must still be achieved and its effectiveness assured. The digitalisation of the economy poses important challenges to the international tax architecture.[133]

## *Multilateral Convention to Implement Tax Treaty Related Measures to Prevent Base Erosion and Profit Shifting (2016) (BEPS)*[134]

The OECD/G20 BEPS project is targeting an enormous annual revenue loss, which can be simply put as the prevention of double non-taxation, which comes

---

132 See Andres Knobel, 'It's Time for Countries to Start Publishing the Data They're Collecting Under OECD's Common Reporting Standard' *Tax Justice Network* (11 July 2018) <www.taxjustice.net/2018/07/11/its-time-for-countries-to-start-publishing-the-data-theyre-collecting-under-oecds-common-reporting-standard/> accessed 20 December 2018.

133 <www.oecd.org/tax/OECD-Secretary-General-tax-report-G20-Finance-Ministers-Argentina-March-2018.pdf> accessed 23 September 2018 8.

134 <www.oecd.org/tax/treaties/multilateral-convention-to-implement-tax-treaty-related-measures-to-prevent-beps.htm> with the full text at <accessed>www.oecd.org/tax/treaties/multilateral-convention-to-implement-tax-treaty-related-measures-to-prevent-BEPS.pdf>accessed 20 December 2018. For an analysis of the role of the G20 in the inception and support of the BEPs initiative, and likely opposition to it both at government and at multinational corporation level, addressing political challenges and the normative debate

about when multinational corporations shift their profits away from the jurisdictions in which genuine economic activity takes place to low or no-tax jurisdictions:

> Base erosion and profit shifting (BEPS) refers to tax planning strategies that exploit gaps and mismatches in tax rules to artificially shift profits to low or no-tax locations where there is little or no economic activity, resulting in little or no overall corporate tax being paid. Conservative estimates indicate annual losses of anywhere from 4 to 10% of global corporate income tax revenues, i.e. USD 100–240 billion annually.[135]

The thinking behind the BEPS Convention is to minimise the substantial corporate tax revenue losses suffered by governments because of what the Convention refers to in its opening recitals as:

> aggressive international tax planning that has the effect of artificially shifting profits to locations where they are subject to non-taxation or reduced taxation [. . .] Noting the need to ensure that existing agreements for the avoidance of double taxation on income are interpreted to eliminate double taxation with respect to the taxes covered by those agreements without creating opportunities for non-taxation or reduced taxation through tax evasion or avoidance (including through treaty-shopping arrangements aimed at obtaining reliefs provided in those agreements for the indirect benefit of residents of third jurisdictions).[136]

The OECD/G20 do not underestimate the scale of the challenge facing them:

> The OECD/G20 BEPS Project is the most ambitious multilateral international tax policy initiative ever undertaken. Ensuring fairness, coherence, transparency and that taxation is aligned with where economic activity takes place in the vastly complex space of international tax provisions covering virtually all of the world's economic activity requires an enormous effort and commitment.[137]

---

about fiscal sovereignty and tax competition, see Richard Eccleston and Helen Smith, 'The G20, BEPS and the Future of International Tax Governance' in Peter Dietsch and Thomas Rixen (eds), *Global Tax Governance: What Is Wrong with It and How to Fix It* (ECPR Press, Colchester, UK, 2016).

135  Information Brochure <www.oecd.org/tax/treaties/multilateral-instrument-BEPS-tax-treaty-information-brochure.pdf> accessed 20 December 2018.

136  See the Explanatory Statement <www.oecd.org/tax/treaties/explanatory-statement-multilateral-convention-to-implement-tax-treaty-related-measures-to-prevent-BEPS.pdf> ("Explanatory Statement") accessed 20 December 2018.

137  OECD/G20 Inclusive Framework on BEPS Progress Report July 2017–June 2018 <www.oecd.org/ctp/inclusive-framework-on-beps-progress-report-june-2017-july-2018.htm> accessed 20 December 2018 3. A complete list of the 119 Members of the OECD/G20

Double taxation agreements in force on a bilateral basis between parties are "Covered Tax Agreements" (Article 2) for the purposes of the BEPS Convention. The BEPS Convention modifies all Covered Tax Agreements by the implementation of "agreed changes in a synchronised and efficient manner across the network of existing agreements for the avoidance of double taxation on income without the need to bilaterally renegotiate each such agreement" (Recitals).

Much use is made in the text of the BEPS Convention of the phrase "beneficial interests", though this is not defined. In contrast to other OECD initiatives referred to in this chapter, the BEPS Convention, by means of the Explanatory Statement, attempts to get to grips with how to interpret "holder" and "beneficial owner". Paragraph 121(ii) of the Explanatory Statement (in the context of Dividend Transfer Transactions under Article 8 of the BEPS Convention) refers:

> 121. In addition, given the variations of existing dividends provisions of Covered Tax Agreements, the following changes have been made [. . .]. The terms "own" and "control" have been added to address existing provisions that use those terms instead of "hold".
>
> (i)  [. . .]
> (ii) The term "recipient" has been added to address existing provisions that use that term instead of "beneficial owner". There may be a variety of examples other than "beneficial owner" or "recipient". Some existing provisions may use the terms "beneficiary", "owner" or "receiving company", and others may refer to dividends "beneficially owned by", "paid to", "distributed to" or "received by" a parent company, or a parent company "beneficially entitled" to dividends. In this regard, it is intended that all of these examples would be covered by "beneficial owner" or "recipient".

## *BEPS Project Action 12 – the disclosure of CRS avoidance arrangements and offshore structures*

This explanation of beneficial ownership itself is of little use, drawing as it does no firm conclusions and setting no markers, but this is far from the whole story: the OECD/G20 BEPS Project has identified 15 actions intended to equip governments with domestic and international instruments to address tax avoidance, to ensure that profits are taxed where economic activities are performed and where value is created.[138] Action 12, Disclosure of Aggressive Tax Planning, has a particular relevance in the context of ownership. It was in the context of Action 12

---

Inclusive Framework on BEPS as of October 2018 is available online at <www.oecd.org/tax/beps/inclusive-framework-on-beps-composition.pdf> accessed 20 December 2018.

138 All 15 Actions are available at <www.oecd.org/tax/beps/beps-actions.htm> accessed 20 December 2018.

that the OECD on 11 December 2017 sought input on new tax rules requiring the disclosure of CRS avoidance arrangements and offshore structures:[139]

> There have been dramatic improvements in tax transparency over the past decade. However, challenges still remain. High profile leaks, such as the release of the 'Panama' and the 'Paradise' papers by the International Consortium of Investigative Journalists (ICIJ), underscore the widespread use of offshore structures to hide beneficial ownership of assets and income.
>
> The rapid and widespread adoption of the Common Reporting Standard (CRS) for automatic exchange of financial account information is limiting taxpayers' ability to hide their income and assets offshore. However the experience of a number of tax administrations and the information disclosed through the OECD's CRS disclosure initiative show that a number of advisers and service providers are actively marketing schemes designed to circumvent the CRS reporting requirements.
>
> In light of these ongoing challenges, G7 Finance Ministers, in the Bari Declaration issued on 13 May 2017,[140] called on the OECD to start "discussing possible ways to address arrangements designed to circumvent reporting under the Common Reporting Standard or aimed at providing beneficial owners with the shelter of non-transparent structures." The Declaration states that these discussions should include consideration of "model mandatory disclosure rules inspired by the approach taken for avoidance arrangements outlined within the BEPS Action 12 Report."

The OECD consultation document was issued on 11 December 2017.[141] In proposing model rules, it set out a definition of a CRS Avoidance Arrangement (Chapter 1) and of an Offshore Structure (Chapter 2), with its stated purpose being:

> 1. The purpose of these model rules is to provide tax administrations with intelligence on both the design and supply of CRS Avoidance Arrangements and Offshore Structures as well as to act as a deterrent against the marketing and implementation of these type of schemes where they are being used to circumvent CRS reporting or to obscure or disguise the beneficial ownership in an offshore vehicle.

---

139  <www.oecd.org/tax/beps/oecd-seeks-input-on-new-tax-rules-requiring-disclosure-of-crs-avoidance-arrangements-and-offshore-structures.htm> accessed 20 December 2018.

140  G7 Bari Declaration on Fighting Tax Crimes and Other Illicit Financial Flows 13 May 2017 <www.g7italy.it/sites/default/files/documents/Bari%20Common%20Delaration%20On%20Fighting%20Tax%20Crimes_0.pdf> accessed 20 December 2018.

141  Draft for Public Consultation on Mandatory Disclosure Rules for Addressing CRS Avoidance Arrangements and Offshore Structures <www.oecd.org/tax/beps/Discussion-draft-mandatory-disclosure-rules-for-CRS-avoidance-arrangements-offshore-structures.pdf> accessed 20 December 2018 (Consultation Document).

It identifies the hallmarks of a CRS Avoidance Arrangement ("captures any arrangement where it is reasonable to conclude that it has been designed to circumvent or marketed as, or has the effect of, circumventing the CRS")[142] and of Offshore Structures ("specifically targets passive offshore vehicles that are held through an 'Opaque Ownership Structure'").[143] The definition of an 'Opaque Ownership Structure' "has a generic element that tests whether the ownership structure has the effect of obscuring or disguising the identity of the beneficial owner and it also specifically targets specific tax planning techniques that can be used to achieve this outcome such as the use of undisclosed nominees".[144]

The text of the draft hallmark definition of Offshore Structure is found in paragraph 33 which (so far as relevant to ownership and beneficial ownership avoidance) provides:

> 1.1 An Offshore Structure means a Passive Offshore Vehicle that is held through an Opaque Ownership Structure.
>
> 1.2 Subject to paragraph (3) below, a "Passive Offshore Vehicle" means an offshore Legal Person[145] or Legal Arrangement[146] that does not carry on

142 Ibid. para 4. The terms "design" and "marketed" are explained in para 15: "The term 'design' refers to those features of the arrangement that are included to facilitate a non-reporting outcome. A scheme should be treated as 'marketed' as a CRS Avoidance Arrangement if there is collateral evidence (e.g. written or oral statements made by a promoter) that refer to non-reporting under the CRS as one of the benefits of the arrangement. The term 'marketed' would not include providing a legal opinion given to a client on whether an existing or proposed arrangement presented by such client is subject to CRS reporting (or on the way in which an arrangement should be reported under the CRS). It would, however, include any subsequent use of that opinion to sell an investment or investment structure to a third party based on its CRS treatment".

143 Ibid. para 5.

144 Ibid. para 6. Para 41 extends the definition beyond the use of "an entity established in a jurisdiction where the lack of transparency regarding ownership makes it difficult to identify the beneficial owner" by adding "The term also includes arrangements that provide a person outside the ownership chain with indirect control over the passive offshore vehicle or its assets such as an undisclosed nominee structure". Para 46 recognises the importance of share options which "have the effect of providing the option holder with ultimate effective control over the company or those assets held by that company without being identifiable as their legal owner". The definition however takes no account of "orphan structures" (which are discussed in ch 6).

145 "Legal Person" is defined in para 33: "means any entity, including a company, body corporate, foundation, anstalt, partnership, association and other relevantly similar entity, but does not include a natural person". For the record, a partnership is not a legal person – it is a grouping of natural persons who come together in a common enterprise for profit. Nor are the entities listed in this definition in any way similar to each other. This is lazy drafting which undermines the effectiveness of the proposal.

146 "Legal Arrangement" is defined in para 33: "means an express trust or other similar legal arrangement, such as Fiducie, Treuhand and fideicomis". Not only does this evidence a fundamental misunderstanding of the nature of a trust – which is, as discussed in ch 3, readily distinguishable from its civil law counterparts, it also takes no account of Islamic Financial Structures.

a substantive economic activity that is supported by staff, equipment, assets and premises.

A Legal Person or Legal Arrangement will be treated as "offshore" for the purposes of this paragraph if it is incorporated, resident, managed, controlled or established in any jurisdiction other than the jurisdiction of residence of one or more of the Beneficial Owners and an "offshore jurisdiction" is any jurisdiction where such Legal Person or Legal Arrangement is incorporated, resident, managed and controlled or established (as applicable).

1.3 [. . .]

1.4 An Opaque Ownership Structure is an Ownership Structure for which it is reasonable to conclude that it is designed to have, marketed as having, or has the effect of allowing a natural person to be a Beneficial Owner of a Passive Offshore Vehicle while obscuring such person's Beneficial Ownership or creating the appearance that such person is not a Beneficial Owner. [. . .]

In setting out how beneficial ownership is obscured, paragraph 33 catalogues fairly standard devices – the use of nominee shareholders, "means of indirect control beyond formal ownership" (without specifying which "means"), and the location of a structure in jurisdictions with low or non-existent beneficial ownership registration or disclosure requirements.

However, paragraph 33 goes on to adopt the FATF standard, and in doing so introduces into an otherwise perceptive account of offshore structuring all the clumsiness and narrowness which the FATF definition contains:

2.2 "Beneficial Owner" shall be interpreted in a manner consistent with the Financial Action Task Force Recommendations and shall include any natural person who exercises control over a Legal Person or Legal Arrangement. In the case of a trust, such term means any settlor, trustee, protector (if any), beneficiary or class of beneficiaries and any other natural person exercising ultimate effective control over the trust, and in the case of a Legal Arrangement other than a trust, such term means persons in equivalent or similar positions.

One obvious casualty of this is the definition of "offshore", found in paragraph 39:

39. The definition of "offshore" is drafted in such a way that if any beneficial owner is resident in a jurisdiction other than the jurisdiction where the vehicle is incorporated, resident, managed, controlled or established then that vehicle will be treated as offshore with respect to all its beneficial owners. This is to prevent tax planners setting up an offshore entity with one or more local beneficial owners, simply in order to circumvent the reporting requirements of the model rules. It also means, however, that an otherwise plain vanilla domestic family trust with a single non-resident beneficiary will fall within the offshore definition.

What are "local beneficial owners"? Trust and corporate service providers ensconced offshore may be the local men of straw, but in no sense would they be beneficial owners. Furthermore, mentioning a "vanilla domestic family trust" compounds this nonsense. There is no such equitable concept as a beneficial owner of a trust.

The Public Comments were issued on 18 January 2018.[147] Of the 29 organisations submitting responses, only the following six specifically addressed issues of beneficial ownership:

- *The Alternative Investment Management Association Ltd*[148] felt the draft rules to be too broad which may result in disclosure of many structures which are inoffensive – or, indeed, which are disclosed out of caution when not required to be disclosed. Disclosures in excess of what is reasonably required would place a burden on professional advisers and intermediaries, while tax authorities would receive a significant amount of unnecessary information which they would be required to process in order to use properly. It also criticised the draft rules for making no mention of the possibility that investors may hold their interests via a fund of funds which is *itself* the investor, or by *an insurance company* as part of the assets attributable to an insurance policy funded by the investor.

- *The Business and Industry Advisory Committee to the OECD*[149] commented: A definition of the term "*beneficial ownership*" should be added, even if it is (a) an open definition or (b) a definition by reference to the FATF Guidance on Transparency and Beneficial Ownership (October 2014), as (i) that term is a common law (as opposed to civil law) term and (ii) a domestic definition of that term may not exist in some civil law jurisdictions.

- *The Financial Transparency Coalition*[150] drew attention to the artificiality of percentage thresholds in determining beneficial ownership, but offered no alternative: "Countries should require Active NFEs to be looked-through and identify/report their beneficial owners (BO), unless they were incorporated in a jurisdiction with (public) registries of beneficial ownership. The definition of BO should use lower thresholds than 25% (e.g. 5%)".

- *Tax Advisers Europe*[151] *on behalf of the Global Tax Advisers' Cooperation Forum* clung to the FATF definition of beneficial owner, resisting any attempt to improve it: "The definition of Beneficial Owner refers to the FATF recommmendations but then expands this which leads to a partial repetition. It

---

147 Public Comments on the discussion draft on Mandatory Disclosure Rules for Addressing CRS Avoidance Arrangements and Offshore Structures <www.oecd.org/tax/beps/public-comments-mandatory-disclosure-rules-for-CRS-avoidance-arrangements-offshore-structures.pdf> accessed 20 December 2018.
148 <www.aima.org> accessed 20 December 2018.
149 <www.biac.org> accessed 20 December 2018.
150 <www.FinancialTransparency.org> accessed 20 December 2018.
151 <https://taxadviserseurope.org/> accessed 20 December 2018.

would be better to adhere to the FATF glossary by repeating that definition without embellishments".

- *PWC*[152] was concerned about the treatment of trusts: "We acknowledge the reference to evidence of arrangements being set up to hide beneficial ownership for tax or other regulatory reasons, and understand the rationale for wanting to identify these. We note though that entities such as trusts are used for many purposes – to protect the interests of young or vulnerable beneficiaries, protect wealth intended for future generations – and in many cases were established a long time ago by previous generations."

- *The Society of Trust and Estate Practitioners*[153] decried duplicated effort: "We are not convinced there is any evidence at present to support the need for a separate rule relating to 'opaque offshore structures' as well as the more general hallmark relating to CRS avoidance arrangements. This is especially the case because of the widespread regulation of trust and corporate service providers in many so-called 'offshore' jurisdictions who have their own obligations to ascertain beneficial ownership of structures which they help to establish or administer".

In response to the consultation on 8 March 2018 the OECD issued Model Mandatory Disclosure Rules for CRS Avoidance Arrangements and Opaque Offshore Structures.[154] These closely reflect the OECD consultation document issued on 11 December 2017[155] but are avowedly modest in their aims, focussing on their deterrent effect:

> 3. The mandatory disclosure rules do not affect the substantive provisions of a jurisdiction's CRS Legislation or impact on any reporting outcomes under the CRS. Rather these rules are information gathering tools that seek to bolster the integrity of the CRS *by deterring advisors and other intermediaries from promoting certain schemes.* The rules seek to accomplish this by providing tax administrations and policy makers with information on schemes, their users and suppliers, for use in compliance activities, exchange with treaty partners and tax policy design.
>
> [Emphasis added]

The definitions of a CRS Avoidance Arrangement and of an Opaque Offshore Structure are set out in Rules 1.1 and 1.2. "These definitions are given a broad

---

152  <www.pwc.com> accessed 20 December 2018.
153  <www.step.org> accessed 20 December 2018.
154  <accessed>www.oecd.org/tax/exchange-of-tax-information/model-mandatory-disclo sure-rules-for-crs-avoidance-arrangements-and-opaque-offshore-structures.pdf>accessed 20 December 2018 ("Model Mandatory Rules"). In the foreword, however, the OECD, in noting that the Model Rules were approved by its Committee of Fiscal Affairs on 8 March 2018, states "This approval does not entail endorsement as a minimum standard".
155  Draft for Public Consultation on Mandatory (n 141).

scope in order to capture any type of Arrangement that has the effect of circumventing CRS Legislation or not allowing the accurate identification of the Beneficial Owners under an Opaque Offshore Structure. An Arrangement or Structure that fits within these hallmarks *will only be required to be disclosed in the reporting jurisdiction by the persons that are responsible for the design or marketing of that Arrangement or Structure, or persons who can reasonably be expected to know that the Arrangement meets the description set out in those hallmarks* [. . .]"[156] [Emphasis added].

Rule 1.1 closely follows the text in paragraph 4[157] of the Consultation Document: "A 'CRS Avoidance Arrangement' is any Arrangement for which it is reasonable to conclude that it is designed to circumvent or is marketed as, or has the effect of, circumventing CRS Legislation or exploiting an absence thereof [. . .]".

In defining "Passive Offshore Vehicle" Rule 1.2(b) departs from the text proposed in paragraph 33 of the Consultation Document and curiously drops both the word "offshore" and the definition of "offshore" and "offshore jurisdiction", resulting in something no doubt intended to be more generic but which actually opens up the possibility of any "letter box" or "brass plate" company in *any jurisdiction* being included:[158]

(b) Subject to paragraph (c) below, a "Passive Offshore Vehicle" means a Legal Person or Legal Arrangement that does not carry on a substantive economic activity supported by adequate staff, equipment, assets and premises in the jurisdiction where it is established or is tax resident.

(c) A Passive Offshore Vehicle does not include a Legal Person or Legal Arrangement (i) that is an Institutional Investor or that is wholly owned by one or more Institutional Investors or (ii) where all Beneficial Owners of that Legal Person or Legal Arrangement are only resident for tax purposes in the jurisdiction of incorporation, residence, management, control and establishment (as applicable) of the Legal Person or Legal Arrangement.

---

156 Model Mandatory Rules (n 154) para 6.
157 Draft for Public Consultation on Mandatory (n 141).
158 Para 29 of the Model Rules gives some clarification: "A vehicle is 'offshore' if it is incorporated, resident, managed, controlled or established outside the jurisdiction of residence of its Beneficial Owners. The types of entities and arrangements that will be treated as wholly-domestic (and therefore outside the intended scope of this hallmark) would generally include a locally incorporated company held only by resident shareholders and the domestic family trust with resident beneficiaries, where the trustees and others with control over the trust are all resident in the same jurisdiction as the beneficiaries". But even more curiously, in the commentary on Rule 1.2(b) contained in para 30 of the Model Rules the text of para 39 of the Consultation Document dealing with the definition of "offshore" is still included. It is wholly unclear why the word "offshore", which has disappeared from the Model Rules except in the title "Passive Offshore Vehicle", resurfaces in paras 29 and 30.

The definition of Opaque Ownership Structure in Rule 1.2 (d) follows the text in paragraph 33 of the Consultation Document but adds a reasonableness test:

> where it is reasonable to conclude that the Structure is designed to have, marketed as having, or has the effect of allowing a natural person to be a Beneficial Owner of a Passive Offshore Vehicle while not allowing the accurate determination of such person's Beneficial Ownership or creating the appearance that such person is not a Beneficial Owner.

The obvious problem with this formulation is that it is silent as to where any burden of proof lies. The words "designed to have" and "marketed as having" may have a common-sense meaning, but common sense, legal interpretation and the rules of evidence in civil and criminal proceedings are not necessarily coincident.

Rule 1.2(d)(i) and (ii) reflect the Consultation Document in referring to "the use of nominee shareholders with undisclosed nominators" and "the use of means of indirect control beyond formal ownership"; but neither indicator on closer examination is entirely satisfactory. Paragraph 33 of the Model Rules, commenting on Rule 1.2(d)(i), states:

> The FATF Guidance on Transparency and Beneficial Ownership (October 2014) identified (at paragraph 9(e)) that one of the important ways in which offshore Structures can be used to not allow the accurate determination of Beneficial Ownership is through the use of nominee shareholders where the identity of the nominator is undisclosed.

The commentary focusses on "offshore structures" whereas Rule 1.2 no longer mentions them, and the use of nominees is the least sophisticated of any ownership concealment strategy. Further, as paragraph 34 of the Model Rules makes clear: "While actively traded shares of widely held entities are often held in nominee name by brokers and custodians, such nominee arrangements would typically not be targeted by this hallmark as widely held entities are not within the scope of the Opaque Offshore Structures".

In seeking to clarify "indirect control beyond formal ownership" paragraphs 35–37 of the Model Rules either state the obvious – "These types of informal control Arrangements do not allow the accurate identification of the Beneficial Owner, either by making it difficult to identify the natural persons with direct or indirect control over the Passive Offshore Vehicle or creating the appearance that the person with such control is the Beneficial Owner when, in reality, the effective control rests with a third party or parties" – or substantially misunderstand equitable principles and the attorney-client relationship – "For example, this hallmark would capture a trustee of a trust (including a lawyer) who habitually acts under the instructions of another person even though the person is not recognised as a trustee or protector under the trust deed".

Rule 1.4(c) in defining "Beneficial Ownership" and "Beneficial Owner" follows the text in paragraph 33 of the Consultation Document but allows for a degree of evolution by referring to "the *latest* Financial Action Task Force Recommendations". As the FATF even in its most recent report "Concealment of Beneficial Ownership" issued in July 2018[159] has not updated its definition of beneficial ownership, evolution is on hold.

In summary, the Model Rules are weakened internally both by definitional shortcomings and by a blind-faith reliance on the FATF's own definitions. As to external challenges, like the FATF itself, the Model Rules make no reference to any beneficial ownership avoidance initiative.[160]

## BEPS: Tax Challenges Arising From Digitalisation

In March 2018 the OECD/G20 BEPS Project issued an Interim Report on Tax Challenges Arising from Digitalisation.[161] Though the Report does not address ownership issues expressly, it does engage with transparency. The means to achieve enhanced transparency exchanges exist, but unfortunately that existence of itself says nothing about the fitness for purpose of the information-gathering mechanisms which produce the information which is to be exchanged, and how those mechanisms may be undermined by transparency counter-initiatives. It also hints that the sheer volume of information capable of being exchanged in this way may instead of being illuminating, simply overwhelm taxation authorities:

492. Technology has also allowed for significant advances in tax transparency internationally as well as domestically, in particular through enhanced information exchange between tax administrations. The OECD's Common Reporting Standard (CRS) for the automatic exchange of financial account information (AEOI) has made available to tax authorities information on offshore transfers and accounts which was previously unknown and unknowable. Using technology available through the OECD-developed Common Transmission System, as the platform for secure bilateral exchanges of information between participating tax administrations, these exchanges now occur automatically on a periodic basis. With the large amounts of AEOI data, tax authorities must ensure it is effectively deployed, matching it with existing information sources relating to the taxpayers concerned.

493. Taking this a step further, work is now being launched by the OECD's Forum on Tax Administration to investigate innovative approaches to the analysis of the data now available under the CRS. This includes tax authorities working together to develop a more systematic analysis of behavioural patterns relating to both onshore and offshore non-compliance/evasion,

159 (n 59).
160 See the discussion on "orphan structures" in ch 5.
161 <www.oecd.org/tax/tax-challenges-arising-from-digitalisation-interim-report-9789264293083-en.htm> with the full text at <www.oecd-ilibrary.org/docserver/9789264293083-en.pdf?expires=1537700029&id=id&accname=guest&checksum=E8D2ECC0252C59C60F751C02C351E527> accessed 20 December 2018.

including with respect to different taxpayer segments such as individuals, small traders, and micro businesses. In time, such approaches will be able to not only detect existing tax evasion, but also pre-empt and deter these behaviours through the use of targeted tools.

The report also alludes to the challenges, as yet not fully scoped by the OECD, posed by the advance of blockchain technology and rise of cryptocurrencies:[162]

> 501. As with other types of technology, blockchain also presents some risks particularly as a result of the absence of a central rule-setting governance mechanism. Some of its applied uses, such as crypto-currencies, 4 may also offer a new avenue for masking the identity of those sending and receiving payments. As such, it could present new transparency risks which if unchecked may undermine progress over the last decade to tackle offshore tax evasion. More broadly, the implications of crypto-currencies for tax crime and other financial crime may be an area where further study is warranted.

Here is the paradox. What the Global Forum refers to in the OECD Global Forum 2016 Report on Tax Transparency[163] as "a flood of new information [which] will start to be provided by financial institutions all over the world" may in reality be a tsunami.

### OECD: current self-assessment

How does the OECD currently rate its own progress, and what challenges does it identify, specifically with reference to issues of beneficial ownership?

The OECD Secretary-General Report to G20 Finance Ministers and Central Bank Governors (Buenos Aires, Argentina) was issued in March 2018.[164] It is resolutely upbeat:

> There have been dramatic improvements in tax transparency over the past decade. However, challenges still remain. High profile leaks, such as the release of the "Paradise Papers", underscore the widespread use of offshore structures to hide beneficial ownership of assets and income. The rapid and widespread adoption of AEOI through the implementation of the OECD's Common Reporting Standard (CRS) is limiting taxpayers' ability to hide their income and assets offshore. However, the experience of a number of tax administrations and the information disclosed through the OECD's CRS

---

162 See ch 6 for a discussion on the interaction of beneficial ownership avoidance strategies and blockchain technology.
163 (n 107).
164 <www.oecd.org/tax/OECD-Secretary-General-tax-report-G20-Finance-Ministers-Argentina-March-2018.pdf> accessed 20 December 2018.

disclosure initiative show that a number of advisers and service providers are actively marketing schemes designed to circumvent the CRS reporting requirements. [. . .][165]

Quoting the Bari Declaration of 13 May 2017[166] which called on the OECD to start "discussing possible ways to address arrangements designed to circumvent reporting under the CRS or aimed at providing beneficial owners with the shelter of non-transparent structures", the report declares:

> The OECD has delivered. The release of a new report *Model Mandatory Disclosure Rules for CRS Avoidance Arrangements and Opaque Offshore Structures* sets out model mandatory disclosure rules that target promoters and service providers involved in arrangements designed to circumvent reporting under the Common Reporting Standard or aimed at providing beneficial owners with the shelter of non-transparent structures. [. . .]As the first exchanges under the CRS approached, close to 85 billion euros in additional tax revenue was identified as a result of voluntary compliance mechanisms and offshore investigations.[167]

Nevertheless, this report acknowledges the difficulties identified in the Global Forum report on Tax Transparency 2017[168] particularly as regards uncertainty amongst states as to how to report beneficial ownership, and the problem of under-resourcing in developing nations which necessitates further technical assistance on the part of the OECD.[169]

In its report OECD Work on Taxation 2018–2019[170] the OECD sees beneficial ownership as crucial in the stemming of illicit financial flows:

> The international movement of money, illegally or illicitly, is a global concern impacting all countries. Illicit financial flows (IFFs) have several sources and channels including bribes, tax evasion, criminal earnings, cash smuggling, shell corporations, informal value transfer systems, trade based money laundering, and fraudulent customs invoicing. [. . .] Tax transparency and exchange of information is the best universal weapon to fight IFFs, *shedding light on the legal and beneficial ownership of companies and other legal entities*

---

165 <www.oecd.org/tax/OECD-Secretary-General-tax-report-G20-Finance-Ministers-Argentina-March-2018.pdf> accessed 20 December 2018 13.
166 G7 Bari Declaration on Fighting Tax Crimes (n 140).
167 (n 165) 13.
168 OECD Global Forum Report on Tax Transparency 2017 (n 16).
169 (n 165) 32.
170 <www.oecd.org/corruption/crime/centre-for-tax-policy-and-administration-brochure.pdf> accessed 20 December 2018 23, 24.

*and arrangements located offshore*, which are most often used to carry out illegal activities that result in IFFs.

[Emphasis added]

In these two reports, the OECD clearly acknowledges the importance of and yet the *practical* difficulties inherent in its strategy of focussing on beneficial ownership. There is however no evidence in its 2018 self-assessment that the OECD is aware of the *legal and technical* shortcomings of the FATF beneficial ownership standard.

## Part four: United States of America

### *"A major money laundering haven"?*

The United States does not always see itself as others see it, though the Report of the Helsinki Commission "Incorporation Transparency" issued on 4 October 2018 highlights the difficulties facing the United States of America domestically:

> Unfortunately, the United States has no permanent policy for the collection of BOT [beneficial ownership transparency] information. Because incorporation occurs at the state level in the U.S. federal system, attempts to find a countrywide solution have been complicated.[171] Under the USA PATRIOT Act, the Department of the Treasury can issue geographic targeting orders (GTOs), which impose specific additional recordkeeping and reporting requirements to prevent money laundering, to financial institutions in certain geographic areas. [. . .]However, these orders are time-limited and are a poor substitute for a permanent BOT policy.
>
> With the one notable exception of GTOs, law enforcement in the United States has been hampered by the lack of accessible BOT information, and the country has transformed into a major money laundering haven.[172]

---

171 For an account of draft anti-money laundering and beneficial ownership disclosure legislation under review in the United States as at September 2018, see Bruce Zagaris, 'ABA Considers Options on AML Bills' 26 *STEP Journal* 7 (August/September 2018) <www. step.org/journal/step-journal-august-september-2018/aba-considers-options-aml-bills> accessed 20 December 2018 (subscription required).

172 (n 198). A detailed consideration of money laundering as it affects the United States and the wider Americas is outside the scope of this book. See for example (1) Jana Kasperkevic, 'Forget Panama: It's Easier to Hide Your Money in the US Than Almost Anywhere' *The Guardian* (6 April 2016) <accessed>www.theguardian.com/us-news/2016/apr/06/panama-papers-us-tax-havens-delaware>accessed 20 December 2018 and (2) Celina B Realuyo, *"Following the Money Trail" to Combat Terrorism, Crime, and Corruption in the Americas* (Wilson Center, Latin American Program, Mexico Institute, August 2017) <www.wilsoncenter.org/sites/default/files/follow_the_money_final_0.pdf> accessed 20 December 2018 and (3) Anders Åslund, *How the United States Can Combat Russia's Kleptocracy* (Atlantic Council, Eurasia Center July 2018) <www.atlanticcouncil.org/images/

In December 2016 the FATF issued its Mutual Evaluation Report on the United States.[173] In Recommendation 24 – Transparency and beneficial ownership of legal persons – the report concludes, rating the United States non-compliant:[174]

> In its 3rd MER [2006], the U.S. was rated non-compliant with these requirements. The technical deficiencies were the absence of any measures to ensure that there was adequate, accurate and timely information on the beneficial ownership and control of legal persons that could be obtained or accessed in a timely fashion by competent authorities. Also, there were no measures taken by those states which permit the issue of bearer shares to ensure that bearer shares were not misused for ML [money laundering]. [. . .] The major gap is the generally unsatisfactory measures for ensuring that there is adequate, accurate and updated information on BO [beneficial ownership] (as defined by the FATF) which can be obtained or accessed by competent authorities in a timely manner. Other gaps are in the areas of basic information being obtained by State registries, absence of licensing or disclosure requirements for nominee shareholders/ directors, and no requirement for companies to maintain register of shareholders within the country.

The OECD Global Forum on Transparency and Exchange of Information for Tax Purposes issued in July 2018 its Peer Review Report on the Exchange of Information on Request (Second Round) on the United States, concluding that overall the United States is largely compliant.[175] The OECD applied the FATF standard[176] when assessing the effectiveness of the United States' strategy for the identification of beneficial owners. The report is immensely thorough and provides a detailed account of federal and state beneficial ownership disclosure requirements (mainly tax driven). Nevertheless, the OECD in assessing compliance through the lens of the FATF found the United States wanting, and, in respect of the availability of ownership and identity information, only partly compliant:

> Certain beneficial ownership information (i.e. identification of the responsible party) is required to be provided by companies (including LLCs) and

---

publications/How_the_United_States_Can_Combat_Russia_s_Kleptocracy.pdf> accessed 20 December 2018.

173 Anti-money laundering and counter-terrorist financing measures United States Mutual Evaluation Report December 2016 <www.fatf-gafi.org/media/fatf/documents/reports/mer4/MER-United-States-2016.pdf> accessed 20 December 2018 (FATF US MER 2016).

174 FATF US MER 2016 222, 226.

175 <https://read.oecd-ilibrary.org/taxation/global-forum-on-transparency-and-exchange-of-information-for-tax-purposes-united-states-2018-second-round_9789264302853-en#page2> accessed 20 December 2018 (OECD US Peer Review).

176 Financial Action Task Force, 'FATF Recommendations 2012' (n 26).

partnerships upon registration with the IRS. However, not all beneficial owners are required to be identified in line with the standard. [. . .] Although the United States law requires identification of the settlor, the trustee, beneficiaries, and any person who exercises control over the trust through a combination of obligations imposed primarily under the state law, federal tax law and common law; none of these obligations explicitly requires identification of all the beneficial owners of trusts as required by the standard (i.e. including the identity of any other natural person exercising ultimate effective control over the trust through a chain of entities or arrangements).[177]

In summary, referring to the OECD Terms of Reference 2016,[178] the report observes:

> However, the 2016 Terms of Reference contain additional requirements in respect of the availability of beneficial ownership information. Certain beneficial ownership information is required to be provided to the IRS, some is available with entities or trusts themselves and some financial institutions (including banks) are required to obtain beneficial ownership information pursuant to their AML obligations. Consequently, a significant amount of beneficial ownership information is available. However, none of the beneficial ownership information required to be available fully conforms to the standard. Moreover, where beneficial ownership information is required to be maintained, appropriate procedures are not yet in place to ensure that the beneficial ownership information is adequate, accurate and up to date.[179]

This passing reference in the report to "some financial institutions (including banks)" does the United States a disservice, although this may be more as a result of the report having been compiled before the United States introduced beneficial ownership requirements for banking institutions than out of a sense of moral superiority. On 11 May 2016 the Financial Crimes Enforcement Network (FinCEN) of the US Department of the Treasury issued its Final Rule on Customer Due Diligence Requirements for Financial Institutions, under the Bank Secrecy Act (effective 11 July 2016, with all covered financial institutions required to comply by 11 May 2018).[180] This was not only a new initiative but also unprecedented in the US banking sector. Its stated purpose is unequivocal:

---

177  OECD US Peer Review Part A: Availability of Information paragraph 42. The FATF standard is muddle-headed in its assertion that the concept of beneficial ownership of a trust exists – in equity, this is a nonsense, yet the OECD Peer Review of the United States repeatedly exhorts the United States to "identify and verify the identity of all beneficial owners of a trust".

178  <www.oecd.org/tax/transparency/about-the-global-forum/publications/terms-of-reference.pdf> accessed 20 December 2018.

179  OECD US Peer Review para 7.

180  <www.gpo.gov/fdsys/pkg/FR-2016-05-11/pdf/2016-10567.pdf> accessed 20 December 2018. On 11 May 2018 the Federal Financial Institutions Examination Council

Covered financial institutions are not presently required to know the identity of the individuals who own or control their legal entity customers (also known as beneficial owners). This enables criminals, kleptocrats, and others looking to hide ill-gotten proceeds to access the financial system anonymously. The beneficial ownership requirement will address this weakness and provide information that will assist law enforcement in financial investigations, help prevent evasion of targeted financial sanctions, improve the ability of financial institutions to assess risk, facilitate tax compliance, and advance US compliance with international standards and commitments.[181]

Beneficial Owner would include each individual, if any, who, directly or indirectly, through any contract, arrangement, understanding, relationship or otherwise, owns 25% or more of the equity interests of a legal entity customer (referred to as the "ownership prong"); and a single individual with significant responsibility to control, manage, or direct a legal entity customer or senior manager, including a Chief Executive Officer, Chief Financial Officer, Chief Operating Officer, Managing Member, General Partner, President, Vice President, or Treasurer; or any other individual who regularly performs similar functions (referred to as the "control prong", to which the 25% threshold is irrelevant).[182]

The Final Rule in adopting the 25% threshold for the ownership prong and an emphasis on corporate officers for the control prong does mirror the FATF standard, but importantly it departs from the FATF civil law approach in evidencing an understanding of the equitable principles which underpin trusts:

> [U]nlike the legal entities that are subject to the final rule, a trust is a contractual arrangement between the person who provides the funds or other

---

released updated procedures for the FinCEN CDD Rule <www.ffiec.gov/press/pdf/Customer%20Due%20Diligence%20-%20Overview%20and%20Exam%20Procedures-FINAL.pdf> accessed 20 December 2018 and issued a new set of exam procedures to address the CDD Rule's beneficial ownership procedures <www.ffiec.gov/press/pdf/Beneficial%20Ownership%20Requirements%20for%20Legal%20Entity%20Customers-Overview-FINAL.pdf> accessed 20 December 2018.

181 Federal Register / Vol. 81, No. 91 / Wednesday, 11 May 2016 / Rules and Regulations 29398.

182 31 CFR 1010.230. Beneficial Ownership requirements for legal entity customers Federal Register / Vol. 81, No. 91 / Wednesday, 11 May 2016 / Rules and Regulations 29451, 29452. This ability to treat senior management as beneficial owners suffers from the same weakness as the identical approach under the FATF regime. The Tax Justice Network in its 2018 Narrative Report on the USA comments: "banks can simply rely on the beneficial ownership information provided by the representative of the client, who does not have to certify that the information is correct and merely has to supply the information to the best of their knowledge. So if the company sends an administrative assistant to fill out the paperwork and the administrative assistant doesn't know or understand the corporate structure enough to know who the beneficial owners are, he or she can simply indicate that there are no beneficial owners or guess and write down incorrect information [. . .]". <www.finan cialsecrecyindex.com/PDF/USA.pdf> accessed 20 December 2018.

assets and specifies the terms (*i.e.*, the grantor or settlor) and the person with control over the assets (*i.e.*, the trustee), for the benefit of those named in the trust deed (*i.e.*, the beneficiaries). Formation of a trust does not generally require any action by the state. [. . .] [I]dentifying a "beneficial owner" from among these parties, based on the definition in the proposed or final rule, would not be possible.[183]

Nevertheless, as long as the OECD adopts as its litmus test the standard on beneficial ownership laid down by the FATF, clear thinking like this on the part of FinCEN will be accorded insufficient weight.

In 2018 the United States was in second place behind Switzerland, and ahead of third placed Cayman Islands, in the Financial Secrecy Index issued by the Tax Justice Network.[184] The Narrative Report on the United States within the Financial Secrecy Index comments:

> The U.S. provides a wide array of secrecy and tax-free facilities for non-residents, both at a Federal level and at the level of individual states. Many of the main Federal-level facilities were originally crafted with official tolerance or approval, in some cases to help with the U.S. balance of payments difficulties during the Vietnam War; however some facilities – such as tolerance by states like Delaware or Nevada of highly secretive anonymous shell companies – are more the fruit of a race to the bottom between individual states on standards of disclosure and transparency.[185]

### *Foreign Account Tax Compliance Act 2010 (FATCA)*[186]

The focus of United States ownership and taxation disclosure regulation has been outward-looking. FATCA is an extraterritorial beneficial ownership transparency initiative of the United States of America, and as such is all the more surprising

---

183 Federal Register / Vol. 81, No. 91 / Wednesday, 11 May 2016 / Rules and Regulations 29412. Though the current interpretation of the ownership prong is that a pragmatic solution is applied, and if a trust owns directly or indirectly, through any contract, arrangement, understanding, relationship or otherwise, 25% or more of the equity interests of a legal entity customer, the beneficial owner is the *trustee* (31 CFR 1010.230(d)(2).

184 In explaining the significance of the FSI the Tax Justice Network comments: "In identifying the most important providers of international financial secrecy, the Financial Secrecy Index reveals that traditional stereotypes of tax havens are misconceived. The world's most important providers of financial secrecy harbouring looted assets are mostly not small, palm-fringed islands as many suppose, but some of the world's biggest and wealthiest countries". <www.financialsecrecyindex.com/> accessed 20 December 2018.

185 <www.financialsecrecyindex.com/PDF/USA.pdf> accessed 20 December 2018.

186 Sections 1471–1474 of the Internal Revenue Code were enacted in the Foreign Account Tax Compliance Act (Title V) of the Hiring Incentives to Restore Employment Act of 2010 (HIRE Act) (United States Public Law No. 111–147, paras 501–535).

for being out of synch with United States federal and state internal initiatives, or, rather, the lack of them.

The U.S. Department of the Treasury summarises FATCA:

> FATCA was enacted in 2010 by Congress to target non-compliance by U.S. taxpayers using foreign accounts. FATCA requires foreign financial institutions (FFIs) to report to the IRS information about financial accounts held by U.S. taxpayers, or by foreign entities in which U.S. taxpayers hold a substantial ownership interest. FFIs are encouraged to either directly register with the IRS to comply with the FATCA regulations (and FFI agreement, if applicable) or comply with the FATCA Intergovernmental Agreements (IGA) treated as in effect in their jurisdictions.[187]

FATCA represents unilateral self-protection, but when it was introduced it became, for a time, something greater than the sum of its parts: the internationally recognised global standard of cross-border information exchange (albeit the information flows only in one direction, back to the United States). It shamed the OECD into supplementing the OECD's largely ineffective exchange of information on request programme with automatic information exchange, leading to the Common Reporting Standard.[188]

FATCA uses the threat and force of steep penalties for non-disclosure to achieve its aims.[189] The sanction for non-compliance on the part of FFIs is that FATCA requires the withholding of a wide range of United States source payments to the non-compliant FFIs, regardless of whether such payments benefit US persons, non-US customers of the FFI or the FFI itself. The IGA process permits reporting by the FFIs to the tax authorities in the country in which they are located; followed by automatic information exchange between governments (thereby avoiding placing an FFI in peril of breaching, at the behest of a foreign

---

187 <www.treasury.gov/resource-center/tax-policy/treaties/Pages/FATCA.aspx> accessed 20 December 2018. This contains a list of those jurisdictions which have entered into FATCA Intergovernmental Agreements. For a useful and condensed overview see DLA Piper, *The Foreign Account Tax Compliance Act* <http://files.dlapiper.com/files/Uploads/Documents/FATCA-Alert.pdf> accessed 20 December 2018.

188 (n 111).

189 The best part of a decade elapsed before the first-ever conviction, which was on 11 September 2018, when Adrian Baron, the former Chief Business Officer and former Chief Executive Officer of Loyal Bank Ltd, an off-shore bank with offices in Budapest, Hungary and Saint Vincent and the Grenadines, pleaded guilty to conspiring to defraud the United States by failing to comply with FATCA by means of stock fraud involving multiple Belize-based brokerages, when he appeared in Court in the Eastern District of New York <www.justice.gov/usao-edny/pr/former-executive-loyal-bank-ltd-pleads-guilty-conspiring-defraud-united-states-failing> accessed 20 December 2018. For the reaction in Belize see 'Belize Brokerages Named in First FATCA Conviction' *Belize Reporter* (14 September 2018) <http://reporter.bz/2018/09/14/belize-brokerages-named-in-first-fatca-conviction/> accessed 20 December 2018.

power, contractual relationships, data protection rules, and banking and commercial secrecy laws in the country of its location).[190]

With respect to a corporation, a Substantial US Owner means any specified US person that owns, directly or indirectly, more than 10% of the stock of such corporation by vote or value. Comparable rules are provided for ownership in partnerships and trusts.[191] For Foreign Investment Vehicles, the 10% ownership rule does not apply, which means an investment by a US person below 10% is reportable. A "specified US person" includes: a US citizen and resident, a privately owned domestic corporation (but does not include a publicly traded company and its more than 50% controlled affiliates), a domestic partnership, and a domestic trust, and excludes certain other US entities.[192]

From tiny acorns mighty oaks do grow: the legislation has become Byzantine in its layered complexity. There are in excess of thirty categories of customer, requiring very granular information on each.

> FATCA's reach is truly breathtaking. Every single non-U.S. entity in the world has a FATCA classification. This is as true for a shell company with no assets or activity as it is for the biggest multinational. It is as true for the most informal two-person partnership in the most far-flung country on the planet as it is for the most massive offshore fund. And it is also true for every non-U.S. trust, even though trusts aren't really entities.[193]

---

190  It was this conflicts problem which is credited with spurring on the OECD/G20 initiative on the automatic exchange of information in the form of the Common Reporting Standard. See Itai Grinberg, 'Does FATCA Teach Broader Lessons About International Tax Multilateralism?' in Peter Dietsch and Thomas Rixen (eds), *Global Tax Governance: What Is Wrong with It and How to Fix It* (ECPR Press, 2016) ch 7.

191  The provisions are found in 26 U.S. Code Section 1473(2)(A): *(2)Substantial United States owner* (A)In general The term "substantial United States owner" means – *(i) with respect to any corporation, any specified United States person which owns, directly or indirectly, more than 10 percent of the stock of such corporation (by vote or value), (ii) with respect to any partnership, any specified United States person which owns, directly or indirectly, more than 10 percent of the profits interests or capital interests in such partnership, and (iii)*in the case of a trust – *(I) any specified United States person treated as an owner of any portion of such trust under subpart E of part I of subchapter J of chapter 1, and (II) to the extent provided by the Secretary in regulations or other guidance, any specified United States person which holds, directly or indirectly, more than 10 percent of the beneficial interests of such trust.* The definition of "trust" is expanded to include any arrangement (other than an estate) which, although not a trust, has substantially the same effect as a trust (26 U.S. Code section 2652(bv)(1)). The definition of "partnership" includes a syndicate, group, pool, joint venture, or other incorporated organisation through or by means of which any business, financial operation or venture is carried on, and which is not a corporation, trust or estate (26 U.S. Code section 761). <www.law.cornell.edu/uscode/text/26/1473> accessed 20 December 2018.

192  26 US Code section 1473(3). The United States imposes worldwide taxation on individuals based on citizenship.

193  Peter A Cotorceanu, 'FATCA and Offshore Trusts: A Second Bite of the Elephant' *Tax Analysts* (23 October 2013) <www.taxhistory.org/www/features.nsf/Articles/DA7E5C0 B6EF087B385257C0D0046A8F8?OpenDocument> accessed 20 December 2018.

The key feature from an ownership perspective, taken in isolation, is whether the mechanism in FATCA for the identification of beneficial owners suffers from defects similar to that of the flawed FATF methodology. Client due diligence as generally understood is intended to reduce the risk of money laundering and terrorist financing; FATCA's sole aim is to identify US tax evaders. There's the rub: FATCA refers to specified US persons, but provides *no methodology* as to how any specified US person is deemed connected to a structure. As with FinCEN, self-certification *as a US person* is employed, but this alone provides no guidance as to whether that person is in any sense an *owner* of a given entity. Presumably the reporting FFI is expected to apply local client due diligence procedures to identify whether or not a specified US person can be regarded as an owner or investor, and this will lead to significant inconsistencies given the multiplicity of definitions of "beneficial owner" across many regulatory systems.

> Further, FATCA offers a limited self-certification mechanism for account beneficial owners with Form W-8BEN and form W-8BEN-E. However, it is difficult to enforce the requirement that the customers accurately disclose BO information to the financial institutions. If the entity intends to hide the real beneficial owner, it can still conceal it. [. . .] For FATCA compliance, when W8 or W9 forms are required, it is overwhelming for both the customer and bank staff to handle all the information from different streams and various versions. Long turnaround time, postage costs and data management workload become a significant challenge for the bank to meet the reporting standard and timelines.[194]

FATCA is, in addition, blind to the possibility that a structure may be ownerless.

## Part five: European Union: Fifth Anti-Money Laundering Directive (Directive EU 2018/843 30 May 2018)[195]

On 30 May 2018 the EU issued EU Directive 2018/843 (amending EU Directive 2015/849[196]) (4AMLD) on the prevention of the use of the financial system for the purposes of money laundering or terrorist financing (5AMLD). 5AMLD supplements rather than replaces 4AMLD and inter alia updates the rules regarding the identification of the beneficial owners of companies and

---

194 Yunhong Liu, 'How Compliance Practices Should Adapt to Increased Beneficial Ownership Scrutiny' (n 3) 6.

195 <https://eur-lex.europa.eu/legal-content/EN/TXT/?qid=1540113903626&uri=CELEX:32018L0843> with the full text in English at <https://eur-lex.europa.eu/legal-content/EN/TXT/PDF/?uri=CELEX:32018L0843&qid=1540113903626&from=EN> accessed 20 December 2018 (5AMLD). See ch 6 for the impact of 5AMLD on cryptocurrencies.

196 <https://publications.europa.eu/en/publication-detail/-/publication/0bff31ef-0b49-11e5-8817-01aa75ed71a1/language-en> accessed 20 December 2018.

other legal persons, and of trusts. It does not however really get to grips with what it means by "beneficial owners" and does not evidence any understanding that ownership is not a normative concept and, what is more, may be absent altogether.

The genesis of 5AMLD was a spike in terrorist-related incidents in Europe which occurred after 4AMLD was introduced in 2015:

> Recent terrorist attacks have brought to light emerging new trends, in particular regarding the way terrorist groups finance and conduct their operations. [. . .] In order to keep pace with evolving trends, further measures should be taken to ensure the increased transparency of financial transactions, of corporate and other legal entities, as well as of trusts and legal arrangements having a structure or functions similar to trusts ('similar legal arrangements'), with a view to improving the existing preventive framework and to more effectively countering terrorist financing. [. . .][197]

This is compounded by difficulties inherent in the EU's enforcement mechanisms and in the non-compliant behaviour of some EU Member States:

> Though the European Union has strong laws on the books regarding BOT [beneficial ownership transparency] information collection, the European Union's compliance process can make it difficult to ensure that various member states are adequately enforcing provisions. While the European Court of Justice [. . .] has the power to hear cases in which the European Commission sues a Member State for non-implementation, non-enforcement of implemented EU legislation is a more difficult problem to remedy. Given that several states within the EU are known for their money laundering industries – especially Cyprus, Czech Republic, Latvia, and Malta – non-enforcement of anti-money laundering laws is a well-documented problem. [. . .] The United Kingdom has become so inundated with Russian money that that London is sometimes referred to by commentators as "Londongrad."[198]

---

197 5AMLD Recital 2. In its Statement issued on 19 April 2018 on the adoption of 5AMLD the European Commission made its motivation clear: "In July 2016, in the aftermath of the terrible terrorist attacks that struck the EU and the vast financial dealings uncovered by the 'Panama Papers', the Commission decided to take urgent counter-measures. The revised directive is part of that action plan". <http://europa.eu/rapid/press-release_STATE MENT-18-3429_en.htm>accessed 20 December 2018.

198 Helsinki Commission Report, *Incorporation Transparency* (n 4). The United Kingdom's response is the proposal for a publicly available register on which overseas companies owning property situated in the United Kingdom will be required to identify their beneficial owners. See David Pegg, 'Offshore Owners of British Property to Be Forced to Reveal Names' *The Guardian* (23 July 2018) <www.theguardian.com/business/2018/jul/23/offshore-owners-of-british-property-to-be-forced-to-reveal-names> accessed 20 December 2018.

In a diplomatically worded side-swipe at the implementational shortcomings of the FATF and of the OECD, 5AMLD comments:

> While there have been significant improvements in the adoption and implementation of Financial Action Task Force (FATF) standards and the endorsement of the work of the Organisation for Economic Cooperation and Development on transparency by Member States in recent years, the need to further increase the overall transparency of the economic and financial environment of the Union is clear. The prevention of money laundering and of terrorist financing cannot be effective unless the environment is hostile to criminals seeking shelter for their finances through non-transparent structures. The integrity of the Union financial system is dependent on the transparency of corporate and other legal entities, trusts and similar legal arrangements. This Directive aims not only to detect and investigate money laundering, but also to prevent it from occurring. Enhancing transparency could be a powerful deterrent.[199]

5AMLD distinguishes corporates from trusts. Member States are to ensure that registers of ultimate beneficial owners of companies and other legal persons become accessible to the general public, but not the register of ultimate beneficial owners of trusts, which will require a demonstration of legitimate interest.

4AMLD required corporates and other legal persons to obtain and retain adequate, accurate and current information on their beneficial owners, to be held on national or central registers[200] which were to be established for this purpose:

> The need for accurate and up-to-date information on the beneficial owner is a key factor in tracing criminals who might otherwise be able to hide their identity behind a corporate structure. The globally interconnected

---

199 5AMLD Recital 4.

200 The implementation at a national level of 4AMLD registration requirements is reviewed in *Status overview UBO register Europe* (NautaDutilh, 31 August 2017) <www.nautadutilh.com/sites/nautadutilh.com/files/inline-files/overview-status-implementation-ubo-register---survey-nautadutilh-31-august-2017.pdf> accessed 20 December 2018. Note the distinction between the registration of trusts on the one hand, and the ability of a trustee to register details of assets held in a trust on the other. The latter is a long-standing concept found in Article 12 of the Convention of the Law Applicable to Trusts and on their Recognition (1 July 1985) Article 12: *Where the trustee desires to register assets, movable or immovable, or documents of title to them, he shall be entitled, in so far as this is not prohibited by or inconsistent with the law of the State where registration is sought, to do so in his capacity as trustee or in such other way that the existence of the trust is disclosed.* <www.hcch.net/en/instruments/conventions/full-text/?cid=59> accessed 20 December 2018. The purpose of Article 12 is to protect trust property against the insolvency of the otherwise apparent beneficial owner (that is, the trustee in whose name the property is held). See D Hayton and others, *Underhill and Hayton Law of Trusts and Trustees* (19th Edition, LexisNexis, 2016) paragraph 100.219.

financial system makes it possible to hide and move funds around the world, and money launderers and terrorist financers as well as other criminals have increasingly made use of that possibility.[201]

5AMLD expressly acknowledges the difficulties posed by multiple legal systems in the EU with regard to trusts, many such systems being ignorant of them:

> [. . .] Due to differences in the legal systems of Member States, certain trusts and similar legal arrangements are not monitored or registered anywhere in the Union. Beneficial ownership information of trusts and similar legal arrangements should be registered where the trustees of trusts and persons holding equivalent positions in similar legal arrangements are established or where they reside. [. . .][202]

So far so good, but then the cracks begin to appear, as the EU falls into the same error as any civil law–based initiative such as the FATF and the OECD and treats corporates and trusts as if they were, structurally and in terms of ownership, substantively identical (which they are not):

> Rules that apply to trusts and similar legal arrangements with respect to access to information relating to their beneficial ownership should be comparable to the corresponding rules that apply to corporate and other legal entities. Due to the wide range of types of trusts that currently exists in the Union, as well as an even greater variety of similar legal arrangements, the decision on whether or not a trust or a similar legal arrangement is comparably similar to corporate and other legal entities should be taken by Member States.[203]

That differences do exist between corporates and trusts is acknowledged, but only in the context of *disclosure* of beneficial ownership, not in the manner in which beneficial ownership (a concept which is in any event alien to trusts) should be determined, and employing so flexible a drafting approach as to sow confusion:

> [. . .] When determining the level of transparency of the beneficial ownership information of such trusts or similar legal arrangements, Member States should have due regard to the protection of fundamental rights of individuals, in particular the right to privacy and protection of personal data. Access to beneficial ownership information of trusts and similar legal arrangements should be granted to any person that can demonstrate a legitimate interest. Access should also be granted to any person that files a written request in relation to a trust or similar legal arrangement which holds

---

201  5AMLD Recital 25.
202  Ibid. Recital 26.
203  Ibid. Recital 27.

or owns a controlling interest in any corporate or other legal entity incorporated outside the Union, through direct or indirect ownership, including
through bearer shareholdings, or through control via other means. The
criteria and conditions granting access to requests for beneficial ownership
information of trusts and similar legal arrangements should be sufficiently
precise and in line with the aims of this Directive. It should be possible
for Member States to refuse a written request where there are reasonable
grounds to suspect that the written request is not in line with the objectives
of this Directive. [. . .][204]

There is no definition of "legitimate interest" in a trust or a "controlling interest" or "control" in or of a corporation – and these are non-EU corporations (so
presumably targeted mainly at those formed in offshore financial centres). What
therefore is to be understood by the catch-all remark "It should be possible"
when there is no guidance as to how? 5AMLD tacitly admits that the EU Member States' legal systems do not (in the main) recognise or understand trusts, yet
the burden is placed on Member States to adjudicate.[205] And how shall a Member
State become competent to interpret what constitutes corporate "control" under
the laws of any number of non-EU jurisdictions?

Under 4AMLD there was however to have been limited access to such information, principally restricted to crime and regulatory enforcement bodies. 5AMLD
extends this access to any member of the public but favours a generalisation of the
information disclosed, in order not to prejudice beneficial owners:

Public access to beneficial ownership information allows greater scrutiny of
information by civil society, including by the press or civil society organisations, and contributes to preserving trust in the integrity of business transactions and of the financial system. It can contribute to combating the misuse
of corporate and other legal entities and legal arrangements for the purposes
of money laundering or terrorist financing, both by helping investigations

---

204  Ibid. Recital 28.
205  A burden not made any lighter under 5AMLD Recital 29, which states: "In order to ensure
legal certainty and a level playing field, it is essential to clearly set out which legal arrangements established across the Union should be considered similar to trusts by effect of their
functions or structure. Therefore, each Member State should be required to identify the
trusts, if recognised by national law, and similar legal arrangements that may be set up
pursuant to its national legal framework or custom and which have structure or functions
similar to trusts, such as enabling a separation or disconnection between the legal and the
beneficial ownership of assets. [. . .]". This is further compounded by 5AMLD Recitals
41 and 42 which entrust the definition of "legitimate interest" to the law of the Member
State where the trustee (or equivalent) is established or resides or (if none) by the law of
the Member State in which the beneficial ownership information is registered. There will
therefore be no overarching legitimacy principle derived from 5AMLD.

and through reputational effects, given that anyone who could enter into transactions is aware of the identity of the beneficial owners.[206]

Member States should therefore allow access to beneficial ownership information on corporate and other legal entities in a sufficiently coherent and coordinated way, through the central registers in which beneficial ownership information is set out, by establishing a clear rule of public access, so that third parties are able to ascertain, throughout the Union, who are the beneficial owners of corporate and other legal entities. It is essential to also establish a coherent legal framework that ensures better access to information relating to beneficial ownership of trusts and similar legal arrangements, once they are registered within the Union. Rules that apply to trusts and similar legal arrangements with respect to access to information relating to their beneficial ownership should be comparable to the corresponding rules that apply to corporate and other legal entities.[207]

The set of data to be made available to the public should be limited, clearly and exhaustively defined, and should be of a general nature, so as to minimise the potential prejudice to the beneficial owners.[208]

From the perspective of ownership disclosure, 5AMLD has an urgent timescale:

> Given the need to urgently implement measures adopted with a view to strengthen the Union's regime set in place for the prevention of money laundering and financing of terrorism, and seeing the commitments undertaken by Member States to quickly proceed with the transposition of Directive (EU) 2015/849, the amendments to Directive (EU) 2015/849 should be transposed by 10 January 2020. Member States should set up beneficial ownership registers for corporate and other legal entities by 10 January 2020[209] and for trusts and similar legal arrangements by 10 March 2020. Central registers should be interconnected via the European Central Platform by 10 March 2021. Member States should set up centralised automated mechanisms allowing the identification of holders of bank and payment accounts and safe-deposit boxes by 10 September 2020.[210]

Yet underlying the entire strategy is a definition of beneficial ownership which is no more sophisticated than the FATF model on which it is closely based and

---

206 5AMLD Recital 30.
207 Ibid. Recital 33; 4AMLD Article 31 (as amended).
208 5AMLD Recital 34. Disclosure exemptions will apply "where that information would expose the beneficial owner to a disproportionate risk of fraud, kidnapping, blackmail, extortion, harassment, violence or intimidation". 5AMLD Recital 36; 4AMLD Article 31(7a).
209 Under 4AMLD the original deadline for corporates had been 26 June 2017.
210 5AMLD Recital 53.

the criticisms of which can equally be applied here. It is found in Article 3(6) 4AMLD (with minor amendments made under 5AMLD):

(6) 'beneficial owner' means any natural person(s) who ultimately owns or controls the customer and/or the natural person(s) on whose behalf a transaction or activity is being conducted and includes at least:

(a)   in the case of corporate entities:

(i)   the natural person(s) who ultimately owns or controls a legal entity through direct or indirect ownership of a sufficient percentage of the shares or voting rights or ownership interest in that entity, including through bearer shareholdings, or through control via other means, other than a company listed on a regulated market that is subject to disclosure requirements consistent with Union law or subject to equivalent international standards which ensure adequate transparency of ownership information. A shareholding of 25% plus one share or an ownership interest of more than 25% in the customer held by a natural person shall be an indication of direct ownership. A shareholding of 25% plus one share or an ownership interest of more than 25% in the customer held by a corporate entity, which is under the control of a natural person(s), or by multiple corporate entities, which are under the control of the same natural person(s), shall be an indication of indirect ownership. This applies without prejudice to the right of Member States to decide that a lower percentage may be an indication of ownership or control. Control through other means may be determined, inter alia, in accordance with the criteria in Article 22(1) to (5) of Directive 2013/34/EU of the European Parliament and of the Council[211];

(ii)   if, after having exhausted all possible means and provided there are no grounds for suspicion, no person under point (i) is identified, or if there is any doubt that the person(s) identified are the beneficial owner(s), the natural person(s) who hold the position of senior managing official(s), the obliged entities shall keep records of the actions taken in order to identify the beneficial ownership under point (i) and this point;

(b)   in the case of trusts: (i) the settlor(s); (ii) the trustee(s); (iii) the protector(s), if any; (iv) the beneficiaries, or where the individuals

211 Directive 2013/34/EU of the European Parliament and of the Council of 26 June 2013 on the annual financial statements, consolidated financial statements and related reports of certain types of undertakings, amending Directive 2006/43/EC of the European Parliament and of the Council and repealing Council Directives 78/660/EEC and 83/349/ EEC (OJ L 182, 29.6.2013, p. 19).

benefiting from the legal arrangement or entity have yet to be determined, the class of persons in whose main interest the legal arrangement or entity is set up or operates; (v) any other natural person exercising ultimate control over the trust by means of direct or indirect ownership or by other means;

(c) in the case of legal entities such as foundations, and legal arrangements similar to trusts, the natural person(s) holding equivalent or similar positions to those referred to in point (b);

There is apparently no awareness of beneficial ownership avoidance techniques. The shortcomings of the FATF definition go unrecognised and hence uncorrected. In embracing standardisation, the EU adopts a flawed standard.[212]

## Part six: The Council of Europe MONEYVAL

The Council of Europe[213] consists of 47 Member States and 6 Observer States.[214] Describing itself as "the Continent's leading human rights organisation", one of its expressed values is to help Member States fight corruption and terrorism.[215]

Prime amongst its initiatives is MONEYVAL, originally established in 1997 and elevated as from 1 January 2011[216] to an independent monitoring mechanism within the Council of Europe:

The Committee of Experts on the Evaluation of Anti-Money Laundering Measures and the Financing of Terrorism – MONEYVAL is a permanent monitoring body of the Council of Europe entrusted with the task of assessing compliance with the principal international standards to counter

---

212 For a general criticism of the treatment of trusts under 5AMLD see Andres Knobel, 'The EU's Latest Agreement on Amending the Anti-money Laundering Directive: At the Vanguard of Trust Transparency, But Still Further to Go' *Tax Justice Network* (9 April 2018) <accessed>www.taxjustice.net/2018/04/09/the-eus-latest-agreement-on-amending-the-anti-money-laundering-directive-still-further-to-go/>accessed 20 December 2018 and his earlier study 'The Case for Registering Trusts – and How to Do It' *Tax Justice Network* <www.taxjustice.net/wp-content/uploads/2013/04/Registration-of-Trusts_AK.pdf> accessed 20 December 2018. See also David Pegg and Hilary Osborne, 'EU to Force Firms to Reveal True Owners in Wake of Panama Papers' *The Guardian* (15 December 2017) <www.theguardian.com/world/2017/dec/15/eu-to-force-companies-to-disclose-owners-with-directive-prompted-by-panama-papers> accessed 20 December 2018.
213 <www.coe.int/en/web/about-us/who-we-are> accessed 20 December 2018.
214 <www.coe.int/en/web/about-us/our-member-states> accessed 20 December 2018.
215 <www.coe.int/en/web/about-us/values> accessed 20 December 2018.
216 Pursuant to Resolution CM/Res(2010)12 <https://search.coe.int/cm/Pages/result_details.aspx?ObjectId=09000016805ce2da> accessed 20 December 2018 further amended in 2013 by Resolution CM/Res(2013)13 <https://search.coe.int/cm/Pages/result_details.aspx?ObjectId=09000016805c77e5> accessed 20 December 2018 and in 2017 by Resolution CM/Res(2017)19 <https://search.coe.int/cm/Pages/result_details.aspx?ObjectId=0900001680758cb9> accessed 20 December 2018.

money laundering and the financing of terrorism and the effectiveness of their implementation, as well as with the task of making recommendations to national authorities in respect of necessary improvements to their systems. Through a dynamic process of mutual evaluations, peer review and regular follow-up of its reports, MONEYVAL aims to improve the capacities of national authorities to fight money laundering and the financing of terrorism more effectively.[217]

MONEYVAL currently evaluates 28 jurisdictions which are Member States of the Council of Europe that are not members of the FATF and Member States of the Council of Europe that become members of the FATF (and request to continue to be evaluated by MONEYVAL). In addition, some non-Member States of the Council of Europe are also evaluated.[218] The evaluation has as its benchmark the FATF Core Recommendations.[219] MONEYVAL's confident assertion is that its Compliance Enhancing Procedures ensure that countries take steps to meet the international standards espoused by MONEYVAL in a timely manner.[220]

In addressing transparency and beneficial ownership, MONEYVAL clearly appreciates the nature and scope of the problem:

Legal persons and arrangements are essential for the conducting of business and are used for a broad variety of purposes. In order to enable the widest use of corporate vehicles, countries establish manifold types of legal entities and arrangements with changing structures. Nevertheless, these complex structures, as provided for by the legislation, might give criminals the possibility to hide their assets, as well as to cover them up for the purposes of entering them into the financial system. In this respect, it is essential to understand the structure of such entities, both in respect of their ownership and control over their activities. Accordingly, the concept of beneficial ownership has been developed, requiring the identification of the ultimate natural person exercising influence over the legal entity.[221]

However, the fundamental weakness in its methodology is the uncritical adoption of the FATF Recommendations, with their inherent flaws and aspirational goals:

Due to the increased interconnectivity of the global network and financial systems, international channels are at high risk of being abused for ML or

217 <www.coe.int/en/web/moneyval> accessed 20 December 2018.
218 <www.coe.int/en/web/moneyval/moneyval-brief/members> accessed 20 December 2018. Amongst the non-Member States are the UK Crown Dependencies of Guernsey, Jersey and the Isle of Man; Gibraltar and The Holy See.
219 Financial Action Task Force, 'FATF Recommendations 2012' (n 26).
220 <www.coe.int/en/web/moneyval/evaluations/compliance> accessed 20 December 2018.
221 <www.coe.int/en/web/moneyval/implementation/transparency-beneficial-ownership> accessed 20 December 2018.

TF purposes. It is therefore fundamental for all jurisdictions to cooperate in the fight against ML and TF, but also to ensure that all jurisdictions apply to maximum extent international standards in this matter on a national level in order to avoid the criminals to abuse possible lacunas. In this respect, the FATF is monitoring implementation of its standards across the globe and identifying jurisdictions with strategic weaknesses in their national AML/CFT regimes.[222]

Whereas the requirement of registration of legal persons by state authorities sets concrete obligations for countries, the remaining requirements of the FATF Recommendations merely refer to a desired outcome. Countries may therefore apply a customised approach which suits their legal system best as long as the purpose of the Recommendations is achieved.[223]

Daniel Thelesklaf, President of MONEYVAL, writing in the Introduction to the MONEYVAL Annual Report 2017[224] acknowledges that MONEYVAL is underfunded and overwhelmed:

> During this period, we have witnessed money laundering scandals that make the headlines almost on a daily basis. Countless cases of grand corruption and money laundering are brought to the attention of the general public. Major strides in technology continue to facilitate the concealment and disguise of ill-gotten funds. The alarming deterioration of the rule of law and democracy in certain quarters of our own region encourages criminals to act with impunity. One would be forgiven for believing that not only has the laundering of proceeds of organised criminality, corruption, tax fraud and other major proceeds-generating crimes not declined but it has actually intensified. [. . .] In our previous annual report, we stated that MONEYVAL was at a crossroad in light of past achievements and future expectations. This remains to be the case. We of course appreciate that the 2018–2019 Council of Europe budget foresees an additional post for the MONEYVAL's secretariat, in particular while being conscious of the overall financial situation of the organisation. At the same time, however, the FATF constantly widens the activities of the global AML/CFT network, with growing expectations on the regional bodies whose workload consequently increases. This has only worsened the situation. Given that the majority of FATF members are likewise Council of Europe member states, it is of utmost importance that MONEYVAL is sufficiently resourced to be able to meet the expectations of the global AML/CFT network.

---

222  <www.coe.int/en/web/moneyval/high-risk-and-non-cooperative-jurisdictions> accessed 20 December 2018.
223  (n 221).
224  <https://rm.coe.int/moneyval-annual-report-2017-eng/16808af3c2>    accessed    20 December 2018.

As a transparency strategy, MONEYVAL offers nothing distinctive other than to set its compliance initiatives in the context of human rights.

## Part seven: United Kingdom

The United Kingdom is not alone in the international community in having implemented beneficial ownership disclosure requirements in its domestic legislation.[225] For example, a register of beneficial owners of companies known as the People with Significant Control register was launched in 2016 under the provisions of the Small Business, Enterprise and Employment Act 2015.[226] That this legislation adopts the FATF Recommendations[227] (including a 25% threshold for deemed beneficial ownership) means that it contributes little to the substantive debate on the adequacy of "ownership" as a defining criterion in matters of regulation.

Yet the United Kingdom has introduced two unique transparency strategies – Unexplained Wealth Orders and the forcing of its Overseas Territories to reveal the names of the ultimate beneficial owners behind companies formed there.

### *Unexplained Wealth Orders*

Through the introduction of Unexplained Wealth Orders under the provisions of the Criminal Finances Act 2017[228] the United Kingdom has sidestepped the

---

225  For an overview see House of Commons briefing paper Number 8259, 24 August 2018 *Registers of beneficial ownership* <https://researchbriefings.parliament.uk/ResearchBriefing/Summary/CBP-8259>accessed 20 December 2018.

226  <www.legislation.gov.uk/ukpga/2015/26/contents> accessed 20 December 2018. This has significant teething troubles. Global Witness notes tax haven addresses being used (prohibited), inconsistencies in determining nationalities and nearly 10% of companies claiming to have no beneficial owner by taking advantage of the 25% ownership threshold: '10 Lessons from the UK's Public register of the Real Owners of Companies' *Global Witness* (23 October 2017) <www.globalwitness.org/en-gb/blog/10-lessons-uks-public-register-real-owners-companies/> accessed 20 December 2018. See also *Learning the Lessons from the UK's Public Beneficial Ownership Register* (OpenOwnership and Global Witness joint briefing, October 2017) <https://openownership.org/uploads/Learning%20the%20lessons%20briefing.pdf> accessed 20 December 2018 and the commentary on the Global Witness analysis by Will Fitzgibbon, 'Loopholes in UK Company Register Show Crime Can Still Flourish, Study Finds' *ICIJ* (2 August 2018) <www.icij.org/blog/2018/08/loopholes-in-uk-company-register-show-crime-can-still-flourish-study-finds/?utm_content=bufferc9e68&utm_medium=social&utm_source=twitter.com&utm_campaign=Buffer+-+Twitter> accessed 20 December 2018. The dangers posed by an absence of regulation in the United Kingdom of company formation agents is examined in Tom Bergin and Stephen Grey, 'Insight – How UK Company Formation Agents Fuel Fraud' *Reuters Business News* (18 March 2016) <https://uk.reuters.com/article/uk-regulations-agents-insight-idUKKCN0WK17W> accessed 20 December 2018.

227  Financial Action Task Force, 'FATF Recommendations 2012' (n 26).

228  <www.legislation.gov.uk/ukpga/2017/22/contents> accessed 20 December 2018. S 1 of the Act inserts new ss 362A to 362H into ch 2 of pt 8 of the Proceeds of Crime Act 2002.

debate on what is meant by "ownership" and has opted instead for regulation based on "control".

A person will be required to explain how specific property (with a value greater than £50,000) has been acquired, with any unsatisfactory explanation giving rise to a forfeiture order. The power of enquiry will be exercised (with the approval of the High Court) where there are "reasonable grounds to suspect" an inconsistency or disproportionality between a person's legitimate income and the extent of their assets. The United Kingdom has also reversed the burden of proof: the person must provide a statement:

(a)  setting out the nature and extent of the respondent's interest in the property in respect of which the order is made,

(b)  explaining how the respondent obtained the property (including, in particular, how any costs incurred in obtaining it were met),

(c)  where the property is held by the trustees of a settlement, setting out such details of the settlement as may be specified in the order, and

(d)  setting out such other information in connection with the property as may be so specified.[229]

Under section 362B(4) Proceeds of Crime Act the High Court must be satisfied that the person is either a politically exposed person or there are reasonable grounds for suspecting that they themselves are or have themselves been involved in serious crime (in the United Kingdom or elsewhere) or are connected with such a person.

Under section 362H Proceeds of Crime Act 2002 a person "holds" property where they have effective control over the property (meaning the exercise or ability to exercise control, or the entitlement to acquire direct or indirect control), they are the trustee of a settlement in which property is comprised or are a beneficiary (actual or potential) in relation to the settlement. Straightforward legal interest would be comprised within this wide definition of control but by no means constitute the defining characteristic. The equitable principle that a beneficiary of a trust (not being a person with a life interest – that is, someone to whom the trustees are bound to make distributions) cannot in any sense be the owner of trust assets is pragmatically disregarded.

By not relying on "ownership" tests and by reversing the burden of proof such that the person enquired of has to demonstrate that they are not "holding" the property concerned, the United Kingdom has opened up an entirely new approach. It remains to be seen how effective UWOs will be when the property under investigation is held in an "orphan structure"[230] and hence under neither the ownership nor the control of a person, but the legislation appears

---

229  Proceeds of Crime Act 2002 s 362A(3).
230  See ch 5.

sufficiently flexible to allow for amendments which will encompass even these offshore chimera.

Article 1 of the First Protocol to the European Convention on Human Rights[231] provides:

> Every natural or legal person is entitled to the peaceful enjoyment of his possessions. No one shall be deprived of his possessions except in the public interest and subject to the conditions provided for by law and by the general principles of international law.
>
> The preceding provisions shall not, however, in any way impair the right of a State to enforce such laws as it deems necessary to control the use of property in accordance with the general interest or to secure the payment of taxes or other contributions or penalties.

It remains to be seen whether in seizing the property of someone who, in the state's sole estimation, cannot adequately account for it, and given that the burden of proof rests with the person under investigation, the United Kingdom will be able to claim to be acting in the public interest or to benefit from the proviso if challenged on international human rights grounds.

### *Shades of Empire –The British Overseas Territories*[232]

The United Kingdom has historically had an uneasy relationship with its former colonial possessions, and though many of these difficulties have passed, its relationship with the British Overseas Territories and the Crown Dependencies continues to be a cause for concern on both sides.[233]

---

231 <www.echr.coe.int/Documents/Convention_ENG.pdf> accessed 20 December 2018. The Convention forms part of the domestic law of the United Kingdom under the Human Rights Act 1998 <www.legislation.gov.uk/ukpga/1998/42/contents> accessed 20 December 2018.

232 British Nationality Act 1981 Schedule 6 lists these: Anguilla; Bermuda; British Antarctic Territory; British Indian Ocean Territory; Cayman Islands; Falkland Islands; Gibraltar; Montserrat; Pitcairn, Henderson, Ducie and Oeno Islands; St Helena, Ascension and Tristan da Cunha; South Georgia and the South Sandwich Islands; The Sovereign Base Areas of Akrotiri and Dhekelia (Cyprus); Turks and Caicos Islands; Virgin Islands <www.legislation.gov.uk/ukpga/1981/61/schedule/6> accessed 20 December 2018.

233 The future of the UK Overseas Territories inquiry by the Foreign Affairs Committee of the UK Parliament was set up in late 2018. This inquiry will consider the resilience of the Overseas Territories, how effectively the Foreign and Commonwealth Office manages its responsibilities towards them and how it envisages their future. The inquiry is likely to be structured around overarching themes but may look at individual Overseas Territories, as and when appropriate. Its terms of reference and proceedings are at <www.parliament.uk/business/committees/committees-a-z/commons-select/foreign-affairs-committee/inquiries1/parliament-2017/inquiry13/> accessed 20 December 2018.

The tension has increased following the coming into force of the Sanctions and Anti-Money Laundering Act 2018, section 51[234] of which deals with public registers of beneficial ownership of companies registered in British Overseas Territories:

51 (1) For the purposes of the detection, investigation or prevention of money laundering, the Secretary of State must provide all reasonable assistance to the governments of the British Overseas Territories to enable each of those governments to establish a publicly accessible register of the beneficial ownership of companies registered in each government's jurisdiction.

(2) The Secretary of State must, no later than 31 December 2020, prepare a draft Order in Council requiring the government of any British Overseas Territory that has not introduced a publicly accessible register of the beneficial ownership of companies within its jurisdiction to do so.

(3) The draft Order in Council under subsection (2) must set out the form that the register must take.[235]

Section 62 provides for secondary legislation to address the meaning of ownership or control:

62 (4) Regulations under section 1 may make provision as to the meaning of any reference in the regulations to funds, economic resources or technology (or a particular description of funds, economic resources or technology) being – (a) owned by a person, (b) held by a person, (c) controlled by a person, or (d) made available to or for the benefit of a person.

(5) Regulations under section 1 may make provision as to the meaning of any reference in the regulations to a person "owning" or "controlling" another person.

According to Global Witness "there is overwhelming evidence that anonymous companies in the Overseas Territories help fuel a staggering amount of corruption around the world".[236]

---

234 <www.legislation.gov.uk/ukpga/2018/13/section/51> accessed 20 December 2018.
235 An attempt by Andrew Mitchell MP and Dame Margaret Hodge MP to include a reference to the Crown Dependencies was abandoned following successful lobbying from the Governments of the Isle of Man, Guernsey and Jersey. The proposed provisions were put forward in the House of Commons at the Report Stage of the Sanctions and Anti-Money Laundering Bill on 1 May 2018 and can be viewed at <https://publications.parliament.uk/pa/bills/cbill/2017-2019/0176/amend/sanctions_daily_rep_0430.1-7.html> accessed 20 December 2018. The Chief Minister of the Isle of Man issued a statement to this effect on 10 May 2018 <www.gov.im/news/2018/may/10/chief-minister-statement-on-uk-sanctions-and-anti-money-laundering-bill-and-beneficial-ownership-registers/> accessed 20 December 2018.
236 'The UK's Tax Havens: Top 10 Corruption Cases Involving Anonymous Companies' *Global Witness* (21 February 2017) <www.globalwitness.org/en/blog/uks-tax-

Reaction from the British Overseas Territories was predictably cross: "Reminiscent of the worst injustices of a bygone era of colonial despotism – we want to remove that ability for the UK to be able to randomly legislate for us" commented the Premier of the Cayman Islands, Alden McLaughlin. The Premier of Bermuda, David Burt, was equally robust: "This country does not recognise the right of the United Kingdom Parliament to legislate on matters which are internal affairs reserved to Bermuda under its constitution".[237]

Hussein Haeri of law firm Withers, instructed by the Government of the British Virgin Islands, commented: "We are confident that there are constitutional grounds for challenging the imposition of a public register of the beneficial ownership of companies and human rights issues raised by public access to the register. The BVI's consistent position is that it will not introduce public registers unless and until they become a global standard". Premier Orlando Smith of the British Virgin Islands is unequivocal in his opposition to the proposals and denies their constitutional legitimacy: "I reject the idea that our democratically elected Government should be superseded by the United Kingdom Parliament, especially in the area of financial services which has been entrusted to the BVI people. It is repugnant to the constitutional arrangements that the United Kingdom made when our new Constitution was approved in 2007 and would certainly undermine the constitutional relationship and destroy any trust between the BVI and the United Kingdom".[238]

Martin Kenney, a solicitor practising in the British Virgin Islands, expresses the scepticism which appears widespread in the British Overseas Territories:

> [C]rooks do not play by the rules – which is what makes them crooks, after all – and the money launderers and bad guys will simply elude the new systems being demanded. I have explained countless times that forcing so-called open registers across Britain's overseas territories will lead to fraudsters and other ne'er-do- ls masking their identities with nominee 'straw men' to front their companies. Their "businesses" will also migrate to jurisdictions that

---

havens-top-10-corruption-cases-involving-anonymous-companies/> accessed 20 December 2018.

237 All quotes taken from Patrick Wintour, 'British Overseas Territories in Talks to Keep Tax Haven Secrecy' *The Guardian* (13 June 2018) <www.theguardian.com/world/2018/jun/13/british-overseas-territories-in-talks-to-keep-tax-haven-secrecy> accessed 20 December 2018. The United Kingdom Parliament retains its ability to impose legislation on the British Overseas Territories but this is not true of the Crown Dependencies. The abolition of the death penalty (1991) and the decriminalisation of homosexuality (2000) in the British Overseas Territories are cases in point.

238 Government of the Virgin Islands, Statement by Premier Smith on United Kingdom Sanctions and Anti-Money Laundering Bill 30 April 2018 <http://bvi.gov.vg/media-centre/statement-premier-smith-united-kingdom-sanctions-and-anti-money-laundering-bill> accessed 20 December 2018.

care nothing about compliance and combating money laundering.[239] This will inevitably lead to the loss or destruction of extremely valuable and substantially accurate UBO identification material housed in controlled systems of transparency, such as here in the BVI.[240]

Taking the opposite stance, Alex Cobham of the Tax Justice Network points to the consequences for both the British Overseas Territories and the Crown Dependencies of the introduction by the United Kingdom of the EU 5th Anti-Money Laundering Directive.[241]

It now seems likely that the EU's 5th Anti-Money Laundering Directive, and the UK government's decision to transpose it into UK law, will make public registers irresistible in the Crown Dependencies and, we think, in the Overseas Territories alike – importantly for trusts as well as companies. [. . .] The Crown Dependencies, recognising the importance for their business

239 Such jurisdictions are not necessarily palm-fringed atolls in the grip of a financial mafia. They include major economies such as the United States and Canada: "Despite a recent commitment from the provinces to start collecting beneficial ownership data (without making it public), it is still possible in Canada today to register a corporation, open a bank account and send and receive money overseas all without disclosing your name. [. . .] Canada's corporate secrecy has inspired the international practice of 'snow washing' – hiding suspect transactions, money laundering and tax evasion behind the country's reputation for respected financial oversight institutions and a solid economy". Marco Chown Oved and Robert Cribb, describing the United Kingdom's initiative as "a stunning move", in 'Offshore Tax Havens Set to Overtake Canada in Corporate Transparency' *The Star* (7 May 2018) <www.thestar.com/amp/news/investigations/2018/05/06/offshore-tax-havens-set-to-overtake-canada-in-corporate-transparency.html?__twitter_impression=true> accessed 20 December 2018.
240 Martin Kenney, 'Crooks Are (predictably) Avoiding Open Company Registers' *The FCPA Blog* (2 October 2018) <www.fcpablog.com/blog/2018/10/2/martin-kenney-crooks-are-predictably-avoiding-open-company-r.html> accessed 20 December 2018. Martin Kenney's views are debated at length in *The Global Anticorruption Blog* beginning in May 2018 and continuing <https://globalanticorruptionblog.com/2018/05/> accessed 20 December 2018.
241 (n 195). The United Kingdom has confirmed that notwithstanding its cessation of membership of the European Union, 5AMLD will be adopted: Juliette Garside, 'UK to Adopt EU Laws on Combatting Terrorism and Money Laundering' *The Guardian* (23 July 2018) <www.theguardian.com/world/2018/jul/23/uk-eu-laws-terrorism-money-laundering-margaret-hodge> accessed 20 December 2018. See also Federico Mor, *Registers of Beneficial Ownership* (House of Commons Library, Briefing Paper Number 8259, 24 August 2018): "The UK has registers of beneficial ownership for three different types of assets: companies, properties and land, and trusts. Information on the beneficial ownership of companies is publicly available. For properties owned by overseas companies and legal entities, the Government plans to launch a public beneficial ownership register in 2021. The register for trusts is not public". <https://researchbriefings.parliament.uk/Research-Briefing/Summary/CBP-8259#fullreport> accessed 20 December 2018.

model of maintaining full access to EU markets, are likely to align with the standard.[242]

How tempting will it be for the corporate and trust service provider sectors in the Crown Dependencies, should these not align to that standard, to take on business fleeing the public transparency of the British Overseas Territories? What pressure may be brought to bear on the Governments of the Crown Dependencies by their finance sectors to resist the change?

Take Jersey as an example, where the finance sector is marshalling its arguments. Jersey Finance (which describes itself as a not-for-profit organisation formed to represent and promote Jersey as an international finance centre)[243]opposes a public register of beneficial owners, preferring to place reliance on the current private register which it says is in line with FATF standards. It holds that the call for public registers makes no distinction between the adequacy of regulatory standards which are applied in various international finance centres; that public registers are based on self-reporting and inherently open to inaccuracy and deliberate misstatement which goes unprosecuted; that public registers merely duplicate information exchange under the CRS, place information in the hands of inexpert members of the public, facilitate further criminal activity (identity theft, kidnap or extortion), create (in the absence of agreed international standards) an un-level playing field, and may breach data protection legislation.[244]

The British Overseas Territories may wish to factor in to their defence (or attack) that over £90 billion is estimated to be laundered through the United Kingdom's financial system annually, attributable in part to very lax company formation procedures:

Individuals with criminal records can still control companies here because, the Department for Business says, "Companies House does not have powers to verify the authenticity of company directors, secretaries and registered

---

242 Alex Cobham, 'UK to Introduce 5th Anti-Money Laundering Directive: Eyes Turn to Crown Dependencies and Overseas Territories' *Tax Justice Network* (23 July 2018) <www.taxjustice.net/2018/07/23/uk-to-introduce-5th-anti-money-laundering-directive-eyes-turn-to-crown-dependencies-and-overseas-territories/> accessed 20 December 2018. The *Financial Times* has described London as "the laundromat of the world, as it washes billions of pounds of dirty cash every year": Caroline Binham, 'London's Role in Danske Dirty Money Scandal Under Spotlight' *Financial Times* (25 September 2018) <www.ft.com/content/ba1a0c2a-bdb6-11e8-94b2-17176fbf93f5> accessed 20 December 2018.
243 <accessed>www.jerseyfinance.je>accessed 20 December 2018. Jersey Finance Limited was registered on 29 August 2000 as a private company under the Companies (Jersey) Law 1991. Further details are available from the JFSC Companies Registry <www.jerseyfsc.org/registry/documentSearch/NameDetail.aspx?Id=40213> accessed 20 December 2018.
244 Geoff Cook, '10 Reasons Why Public Register Arguments Are Flawed' *Jersey Finance* (20 November 2018) <www.jerseyfinance.je/ceo-blog/10-reasons-why-public-register-arguments-are-flawed?utm_medium=referral&utm_source=twitter.com&utm_campaign=CEOblog#.XCj42NL7Rph> accessed 20 December 2018.

office addresses". So this is where we are. Ministers huff and puff about combating financial crime, but in the absence of effective action by regulators with teeth, the UK cannot win the fight against money laundering.[245]

It remains to be seen whether this extraterritoriality based on the United Kingdom's ancient privilege will be open to effective challenge by the British Overseas Territories. As small economies heavily dependent on their finance sectors, their options seem constrained.[246] Should the Crown Dependencies decide (somewhat counterintuitively, from a commercial standpoint) voluntarily to adopt public disclosure, the case for the British Overseas Territories for arguing that a global standard is not in the process of being adopted will be considerably weakened.

Much will depend on how secondary legislation under section 62(5) addresses the definitions of "owner" and "controller". Should the draftsperson experience a Pavlovian conditioned response and revert to the FATF Recommendations on what constitutes ownership,[247] then the flaws in those Recommendations will taint and undermine the United Kingdom's objectives. Should, in the alternative, the definition of beneficial owner be left to be determined according to the laws of the various British Overseas Territories, inconsistency and confusion will result. And predictably perhaps, no account is taken of the global industry in beneficial ownership avoidance through the use of "orphan structures",[248] offered by the British Overseas Territories themselves, which drive a coach and four through the whole strategy.

## Part eight: Isle of Man – an offshore case study

The Isle of Man has applied international guidelines on beneficial ownership, using the FATF methodology. In doing so, it has experienced just how difficult it

245 Prem Sikka, 'Tax-haven Transparency Won't Stop Money Laundering in Britain' *The Guardian* (8 May 2018) <www.theguardian.com/commentisfree/2018/may/08/tax-haven-transparency-money-laundering-britain> accessed 20 December 2018.
246 See the discussion by Naomi Fowler, 'UK Overseas Territories Fight Back Against Financial Transparency Measures' *Tax Justice Network* (14 June 2018) <www.taxjustice.net/2018/06/14/uk-overseas-territories-fight-back-against-financial-transparency-measures/> accessed 20 December 2018. The origin and impact of the "finance curse" affecting the British Overseas Territories and the Crown Dependencies is discussed by Anthea Lawson and John Christensen, 'Yes, Britain is closing its tax havens. But let's not forget it created them in the first place' *Tax Justice Network* (4 May 2018) <www.taxjustice.net/2018/05/04/yes-britain-is-closing-its-tax-havens-but-lets-not-forget-it-created-them-in-the-first-place/> accessed 20 December 2018. And see Nicholas Shaxson, *Treasure Islands: Tax Havens and the Men Who Stole the World* (The Bodley Head, London, 2011) and Nicholas Shaxson, *The Finance Curse: How Global Finance Is Making Us All Poorer* (The Bodley Head, London, 2018).
247 Financial Action Task Force, 'FATF Recommendations 2012' (n 26).
248 Ch 5.

is in practice to turn largely aspirational policies and empty rhetoric into workable legislation or effective international cooperation.[249]

## *Beneficial Ownership Act 2017*

The Companies (Beneficial Ownership) Act 2012 (in force September 1, 2013) required every company that was not a client company of a Corporate Service Provider or covered by an exception in the Act or in the Companies (Beneficial Ownership) (Exemptions) Order 2013 (SD 235/2013) to appoint a "nominated officer", who must be an individual resident in the Isle of Man. Members of a company (whose details are to be found in the company's register of members) are required to provide the nominated officer with details of the beneficial owner(s) of the company, if beneficial ownership is not theirs.

The 2012 Act and the 2013 Order have been replaced and greatly extended by the Beneficial Ownership Act 2017.[250] The 2017 Act, which entered into force on 1 July 2017, places all Isle of Man corporate and legal entities under the same legislation regarding beneficial ownership.

The following commentary[251] was prepared by the Isle of Man Government Treasury when introducing the Beneficial Ownership Bill 2017:

> The Beneficial Ownership Bill 2017 is introduced against a background of important international developments over the last few years. Arising from a series of Action Plan Principles which were agreed at the G8 summit hosted by the UK in Lough Erne in June 2013, the Isle of Man published an Action Plan in which it agreed to review its existing provisions on beneficial ownership and consider whether the introduction of a centralised registry would improve the transparency of the ownership and control of companies in the

---

249 For an account of the constitution of the Isle of Man and its relationship with the United Kingdom, the EU and the USA, see Paul Beckett, 'Isle of Man' in T Lyons (ed), *European Cross-Border Estate Planning* (Sweet & Maxwell, London, 2019). The Isle of Man is a Member of the Inclusive Framework on BEPS <accessed>www.oecd.org/tax/beps/inclusive-framework-on-beps-composition.pdf>accessed 20 December 2018. The Isle of Man is a member of MONEYVAL, which in July 2018 published its Fifth Round of Mutual Evaluations 1st Enhanced Follow-up Report on the Isle of Man <https://rm.coe.int/moneyval-2018-9-sr-5th-round-summary-fupmer-isle-of-man/16808d3cca> accessed 20 December 2018.

250 <https://legislation.gov.im/cms/images/LEGISLATION/PRINCIPAL/2017/2017-0003/BeneficialOwnershipAct2017_3.pdf> accessed 20 December 2018.

251 <www.tynwald.org.im/business/bills/Bills/Beneficial_Ownership_Bill_2017-Notes.pdf> accessed 20 December 2018. The Isle of Man Financial Services Authority (FSA) has issued Guidance (GC 2017/0003 June 2017) ("Guidance Note") which although not law in itself is persuasive. Where a person follows the FSA Guidance, this would tend to indicate compliance with the legislative provisions: <www.gov.im/media/1357278/beneficial-ownership-act-2017-guidance-june-2017-gc-no-2017-0003.pdf> accessed 20 December 2018.

Isle of Man. [. . .] The European Union's Fourth Anti-Money Laundering Directive[252] [. . .] has subsequently raised the bar with the emergence of a new EU standard requiring the establishment of a central database of beneficial ownership accessible (at the very minimum) by law enforcement authorities. At around the same time, the G5 grouping of the five largest economies in the EU (the UK, France, Germany, Italy and Spain) announced its commitment to a pilot initiative looking at the potential for automatic exchange of beneficial ownership information; an initiative with which the Isle of Man has agreed to engage.

The 2017 Act is an advance on the 2012 Act, because it covers much more ground, but it suffers from the same word blindness as its earlier self.

In the 2017 Act, "beneficial owner" means the person who ultimately owns or controls a legal entity to which the Act applies, in whole or in part, through direct or indirect ownership or control of shares or voting rights or other ownership interest in that entity, or who exercises control via other means, and "beneficial ownership" is to be construed accordingly.

The 2017 Act defines any beneficial owner who owns or controls more than 25% of the beneficial ownership of a legal entity to which the 2017 Act applies as a "registrable beneficial owner", and the required details of any registrable beneficial owner must be submitted electronically to the Isle of Man Database of Beneficial Ownership by the nominated officer/Corporate Service Provider.[253]

There is a persuasive case that the 25% threshold is toothless.[254]

If a company has five shareholders, or a partnership five members, none is a registrable beneficial owner. The application of the 25% threshold to trusts boggles the imagination: firstly, no beneficiary under a trust is a beneficial owner of trust assets, and the trustees themselves have only legal title to them because trustees cannot benefit from the trust fund of which they are trustees. Obviously, if any trust assets are distributed to a beneficiary, then at that point beneficial ownership arises in the hands of that beneficiary but not because he or she is a beneficiary of the trust – the assets have passed out of the trust by that time.[255]

252 Directive (EU) 2015/849 of the European Parliament and of the Council of 20 May 2015 on the prevention of the use of the financial system for the purposes of money laundering or terrorist financing <http://data.europa.eu/eli/dir/2015/849/oj> accessed 20 December 2018.
253 Outline guidance is available from the Isle of Man Companies Registry <www.gov.im/categories/business-and-industries/companies-registry/beneficial-ownership/> accessed 20 December 2018.
254 The 25% threshold approach is a literal reading of the Financial Action Task Force, 'FATF Guidance on Transparency and Beneficial Ownership' (n 29) para 33a) where this percentage is used merely as an example. The Isle of Man is not alone in slavishly following what the FATF never intended to be a mandatory percentage.
255 In its Guidance Note the Isle of Man Financial Services Authority concedes this and concludes: "*Where the trust is a discretionary trust, its beneficiaries do not have an absolute right to any of the trust property, but only a right to be considered, as any benefit they receive is at the*

The intention of the 2017 Act was to identify true ownership of assets, but as the FSA tacitly concedes in its Guidance Note, this is fraught with difficulties. Neither the word "ownership" nor the word "control" is defined in the 2017 Act. The FSA grasps the nettle:

> *The term "**ownership**" is not defined in the Act, but should be construed as including beneficial ownership and/or legal ownership of the entity concerned.*
>
> *The term "**control**" is also not defined in the Act, but again should be construed broadly, as including all those individuals who, by whatever means, hold a right in respect of or are able to exercise significant influence over the decision-making process of the entity. A person may hold such a right as a result of a variety of circumstances including the provisions of the entity's constitution, the rights attached to the shares or securities which the person holds, a shareholders' agreement, some other agreement or otherwise.*[256] *Whether a person holds such a right is a matter of fact and law, which must be determined in the case of each entity.*
>
> *The term "**legal owner**" is defined in section 3 of the Act as meaning a natural or legal "person who directly owns or controls shares or voting rights or other ownership interest in that entity or who exercises direct control via other means whether or not that person is also the beneficial owner of that interest". This includes corporate shareholders and nominee shareholders holding shares on behalf of others.*[257]

- Trustees have legal ownership of a trust fund; but they are not the beneficial owners. Nevertheless, the FSA states: "*As, by operation of law, the trustees of a trust are joint legal owners of the trust assets, they will, when natural persons, be registrable beneficial owners of the company. In the case of a corporate trustee, the beneficial owners will be the shareholders of the corporate trustee.*"[258]
- Stating that control is a right which is a matter of fact and law which must be determined in the case of each entity is a recipe for disaster.

---

*discretion of the trustees. In such circumstances, the beneficiaries of the discretionary trust cannot be beneficial owners and therefore cannot be registrable beneficial owners of the company. In that case, the registrable beneficial owners will, in the case of trustees who are natural persons, be those trustees. Where the trustee is a legal person, the registrable beneficial owners may be the trust company's shareholders, if their apportioned shareholding in the company is over 25%".* <www.gov.im/media/1357278/beneficial-ownership-act-2017-guidance-june-2017-gc-no-2017-0003.pdf> accessed 20 December 2018 9.

256 The FSA concedes (Guidance Note 15): "In order to be a registrable beneficial owner of a legal entity, a natural person must own or control more than 25% of the legal entity. Whilst control by way of shareholding whether directly or indirectly held is relatively simple to quantify, [. . .] control 'via other means' is more problematic".

257 Guidance Note 3.

258 Guidance Note 8.

Does the FSA have the resources to pursue any "controller" thought to have breached the provisions of the 2017 Act when, in order to work out whether there has been a breach, that person's own unique set of circumstances must be minutely examined?[259]

- The definition of "legal owner" by including nominees undermines the whole concept of beneficial ownership. Corporate shareholders could well be beneficial owners – something which the FSA acknowledges. But what is to be made, in an Act seeking to identify beneficial ownership, of the words "*whether or not that person is also the beneficial owner of that interest*"[260]?

In truth, **trusts** simply do not fit into the approach which the 2017 Act has adopted, as the FSA concedes:

*It is important to note that a registrable beneficial owner can only be a natural person whose ownership interest or control can be quantified at more than 25% so in practice a registrable beneficial owner can only be a natural person who exercises ownership or control by direct or indirect shareholding. This will **exclude** such individuals as the **beneficiaries** of any discretionary trust which itself owns an interest in the legal entity concerned. It will also exclude **settlors** of any trust (unless the trust is a revocable trust) and may exclude **protectors**, depending on whether any powers they are given under the trust deed confers quantifiable control of over 25%. It will also exclude those who exercise control via other means unless this can be quantified as more than 25%.*[261]

The FSA applies the same logic to companies limited by guarantee, protected cell companies, limited liability companies, limited partnerships[262] and foundations

---

259 Perhaps the FSA will just make examples, like Admiral Byng of whom François-Marie Arouet de Voltaire wrote in *Candide*, "In this country it is wise to kill an admiral from time to time to encourage the others". (*Dans ce pays-ci, il est bon de tuer de temps en temps un amiral pour encourager les autres.*) (Gabriel Cramer, Geneva, 1759). On a more serious note, this is particularly important, as criminal sanctions may be imposed in the form of fines (of up to £5,000) or imprisonment (of up to two years) for non-compliance – Beneficial Ownership Act 2017 section 10; with proposals put forward by the FSA in September 2018 for the imposition of civil penalties (of up to £5,000) which will require a lower standard of proof than that required for a criminal conviction: Consultation Paper CP18–05/T17 <www.iomfsa.im/fsa-news/2018/sep/consultation-on-the-introduction-of-civil-penalties-for-some-contraventions-of-the-beneficial-ownership-act-2017/> accessed 20 December 2018.
260 Guidance Note 3.
261 Guidance Note 4.
262 "*A limited partner which owns more than 25% of the ownership interest in the partnership will be a registrable beneficial owner, despite having no control or voting rights. A general partner which controls over 25% will be a registrable beneficial owner, despite having no ownership rights*". Guidance Note 13.

(though struggles in each case to make the 2017 Act approach fit the entity in point).

Even the boundaries of **"control"** are traced in sand:[263]

> *Where the person provides advice or direction in a professional capacity; for example, as: a) a **lawyer**; b) an **accountant**; c) a **management consultant**; d) an **investment manager**; e) a **tax adviser**; or f) a **financial adviser**.*
>
> *Where the person deals with the legal entity under a third party commercial or financial agreement; for example, as: a) a **supplier**; b) a **customer**; or c) a **lender**.*
>
> *Where the person exercises a function under an enactment; for example, as: a) a **regulator**; or b) a **liquidator or receiver**.*
>
> *Where the person is an **employee** acting in the course of their employment and as nominee for their employer, including an employee, director or CEO of a third party (such as a corporate director company), which has significant influence or control over the legal entity.*
>
> *Where the person is a director of a company, including, as: a) a **managing director**; b) a **sole director**; or c) a non-executive[264] or executive director who **holds a casting vote**.*
>
> *A person who makes recommendations to shareholders on an issue, or set of issues, on a one-off occasion, which is subject to a shareholder vote.*
>
> *Rights held by all or a group of employees, for the purpose of representing the employees' interests in an employee-owned entity. Any relevant person or entity of significance in relation to any association, professional standards organisation or network of companies or firms which promulgates common rules, policies or standards to be adopted by the members of the association, organisation or network, but does not otherwise have control of members of the network.*

The FSA's exclusion wording *"where the constitution of the legal entity is particularly complicated, specific advice should be taken"*[265] speaks for itself. The 2017 Act is based on the twin concepts of beneficial ownership and control. It fails adequately to address either.

## Part nine: Conclusions

At the heart of the difficulties faced by the systems of disclosure and registration reviewed in this chapter is the use of "beneficial ownership" as the defining marker of the person who is ultimately to be held accountable. Not only is "ownership" as a concept incapable of universal definition, as explained in chapter 2, the very act of focussing attention on one defining marker makes life so much

---

263 Guidance Note 16, 17.
264 The concept of *non-executive* director is, however, unknown under Isle of Man law.
265 Guidance Note 4.

easier for structural designers. They simply find ways of eliminating owners from the equation.

In this those structural designers have been helped by regulatory bodies which have – perhaps lacking the political will (or political support) to meet the challenge head on, or simply lacking expertise and resources fully to appreciate the fundamentals of the problem – resort to mere exhortations and aspirational goals. These regulatory bodies create their own pragmatic rules of what constitutes ownership, and in doing so impose a degree of artificiality which leaves them wide open to challenge when those rules prove to be largely at odds with established law and practice.

The 2014 High-Level Principles on Beneficial Ownership Transparency are not so much "high level" as stratospheric and are vague to the point of not addressing the definition of "beneficial ownership" at all.

The FATF Recommendations make a brave stab at a universal standard definition of "beneficial owner", which begins to fall apart when applied to trusts and which in adopting a 25% ownership threshold gives a get out of jail free card to any structure with more than four "owners". The Beneficial Ownership Act 2017 of the Isle of Man – drafted to meet the FATF standard – is a case in point.

The weakness of the FATF approach then permeates the registration and disclosure initiatives of the OECD, the European Union and the Council of Europe MONEYVAL, each of which adopts that approach unquestioningly as if it were a gold standard.

The United States of America in FATCA in focussing on US Persons simply shifts the burden of determining how a US person is connected to any structure or could in any sense be considered an owner to the foreign jurisdictions in which those US Persons are resident; and if they have stayed at home, allows them to self-declare (even where the declaration is that no one is the beneficial owner – something which then goes unchecked). FATCA does not introduce any alternative to the "ownership" marker.

The United Kingdom in introducing Unexplained Wealth Orders, characterised by blunt State assertions that anyone at the receiving end of a disclosure enquiry holds illicit funds, and putting the burden of proof squarely on that person to prove otherwise, has turned pragmatism into an art form. Unexplained Wealth Orders seek to sidestep the "beneficial owner" debate. Even this pragmatism, however, yet may prove incompatible with principles of international human rights law.

If it were only a question of inherent weaknesses in the drafting of the regulations, this could with time and patience be corrected, but these "own goals" are only part of the problem. The G20, FATF, OECD, European Union and the Council of Europe MONEYVAL in their regulatory systems take no account of ownerless, so-called "orphan structures" which, as discussed in chapter 5, are being promoted by a worldwide industry in accountability avoidance. None makes any reference to Islamic financial instruments or structures, some of which, as explained in chapter 2, are ownerless.

The disclosure and registration initiatives in espousing the amorphous term "ownership" are flawed – not fatally or permanently, perhaps, as amendment is always a possibility, but flawed in our times. These initiatives present a single target, and anything "ownerless" will not be caught. They are at best to be regarded as a work in progress.

## Bibliography

### *Legislation and regulations*

Beneficial Ownership Act 2017 <https://legislation.gov.im/cms/images/LEGIS LATION/PRINCIPAL/2017/2017-0003/BeneficialOwnershipAct2017_3.pdf> accessed 20 December 2018 (Isle of Man)

Bribery Act 2010 <www.legislation.gov.uk/ukpga/2010/23/section/8> accessed 20 December 2018 (UK)

British Nationality Act 1981 sch 6 <www.legislation.gov.uk/ukpga/1981/61/schedule/6> accessed 20 December 2018 (UK)

Criminal Finances Act 2017 <www.legislation.gov.uk/ukpga/2017/22/contents> accessed 20 December 2018 (UK)

Foreign Account Tax Compliance Act 2010 (FATCA) [Sections 1471 to 1474 of the Internal Revenue Code were enacted in the Foreign Account Tax Compliance Act (Title V) of the Hiring Incentives to Restore Employment Act of 2010 (HIRE Act) (United States Public Law No. 111–147, paras 501 to 35)] (United States of America)

Human Rights Act 1998 <www.legislation.gov.uk/ukpga/1998/42/contents> accessed 20 December 2018 (UK)

Proceeds of Crime Act 2002 <www.legislation.gov.uk/ukpga/2002/29/contents> accessed 20 December 2018 (UK)

Sanctions and Anti-Money Laundering Act 2018, section 51 <www.legislation.gov.uk/ukpga/2018/13/section/51> accessed 20 December 2018 (UK)

Small Business, Enterprise and Employment Act 2015 <www.legislation.gov.uk/ukpga/2015/26/contents> accessed 20 December 2018 (UK)

### *European documents*

Fifth Anti Money Laundering Directive (Directive EU 2018/843 30 May 2018 <https://eur-lex.europa.eu/legal-content/EN/TXT/?qid=1540113903626&uri=CELEX:32018L0843>with the full text in English at <https://eur-lex.europa.eu/legal-content/EN/TXT/PDF/?uri=CELEX:32018L0843&qid=1540113903626&from=EN> accessed 20 December 2018

Fourth Anti Money Laundering Directive (Directive EU 2015/849) <https://publications.europa.eu/en/publication-detail/-/publication/0bff31ef-0b49-11e5-8817-01aa75ed71a1/language-en> accessed 20 December 2018

General Data Protection Regulation (GDPR) (May 2018) Regulation (EU) 2016/679 on the Protection of Natural Persons with Regard to the Processing of Personal Data and on the Free Movement of Such Data <https://eur-lex.europa.eu/legal-content/EN/TXT/?qid=1532348683434&uri=CELEX:02016R0679-20160504> accessed 20 December 2018

**International documents**

Convention of 1 July 1985 on the Law Applicable to Trusts and on their Recognition (Hague Convention) <www.hcch.net/en/instruments/conventions/fulltext/?cid=59> accessed 12 December 2018
Convention for the Protection of Human Rights and Fundamental Freedoms 1950 ("The European Convention on Human Rights") <www.coe.int/en/web/conventions/search-on-treaties/-/conventions/treaty/005> accessed 11 December 2018
——— First Protocol (1952) <www.coe.int/en/web/conventions/search-on-treaties/-/conventions/treaty/009> accessed 11 December 2018
Council of Europe *MONEYVAL, Compliance Enhancing Procedures* <www.coe.int/en/web/moneyval/evaluations/compliance> accessed 20 December 2018
——— Annual Report 2017 <https://rm.coe.int/moneyval-annual-report-2017-eng/16808af3c2> accessed 20 December 2018
Financial Action Task Force (FATF), The Misuse of Corporate Vehicles Including Trust and Company Service Providers' (13 October 2006) <www.fatf-gafi.org/media/fatf/documents/reports/Misuse%20of%20Corporate%20Vehicles%20including%20Trusts%20and%20Company%20Services%20Providers.pdf> accessed 20 December 2018
———FATF Risk Based Approach Guidance for Legal Professionals (October 2008) <www.fatf-gafi.org/publications/fatfrecommendations/documents/riskbasedapproachguidanceforlegalprofessionals.html> accessed 20 December 2018
——— FATF Guidance on Transparency and Beneficial Ownership' (*Financial Action Task Force*, October 2014) <www.fatf-gafi.org/media/fatf/documents/reports/Guidance-transparency-beneficial-ownership.pdf> accessed 20 December 2018
——— Anti-money laundering and counter-terrorist financing measures United States Mutual Evaluation Report December 2016 <www.fatf-gafi.org/media/fatf/documents/reports/mer4/MER-United-States-2016.pdf> accessed 20 December 2018
——— FATF Recommendations 2012 (16 February 2012) (updated to October 2018) <www.fatf-gafi.org/publications/fatfrecommendations/documents/fatf-recommendations.html> and <www.fatf-gafi.org/publications/fatfrecommendations/documents/fatf-recommendations.html#UPDATES> accessed 20 December 2018
——— (with Egmont Group) Concealment of beneficial Ownership (18 July 2018) <www.fatf-gafi.org/publications/methodsandtrends/documents/concealment-beneficial-ownership.html with the full text at www.fatf-gafi.org/media/fatf/documents/reports/FATF-Egmont-Concealment-beneficial-ownership.pdf> accessed 20 December 2018
G7 Bari Declaration on Fighting Tax Crimes and Other Illicit Financial Flows (13 May 2017) <www.g7italy.it/sites/default/files/documents/Bari%20Common%20Delaration%20On%20Fighting%20Tax%20Crimes_0.pdf> accessed 20 December 2018
G20 High-Level Principles on Beneficial Ownership Transparency' (*Australian Government, Attorney General's Department*, 2014) <www.ag.gov.au/CrimeAndCorruption/AntiCorruption/Documents/G20High-LevelPrinciplesOnBeneficialOwnershipTransparency.pdf> accessed 20 December 2018
——— High-Level Principles on Private Sector Transparency and Integrity 2015 <www.g20.org/sites/default/files/media/g20_high_level_principles_on_private_sector_transparency_and_integrity.pdf> accessed 20 December 2018

———— Communiqué, G20 Finance Ministers and Central Bank Governors Meeting held in Washington, DC, USA, 27 April 2016 <www.g20.utoronto.ca/2016/160415-finance.html> accessed 20 December 2018

———— G20 Progress Report on the Implementation of the G20/OECD High-Level Principles of Corporate Governance (July 2016) <www.g20.utoronto.ca/2016/g20-oecd-progress-report-corporate-governance.pdf> accessed 20 December 2018

———— G20 Leaders' Communiqué: Hangzhou Summit, Hangzhou, China, 5 September 2016 <www.g20.utoronto.ca/2016/160905-communique.html> accessed 20 December 2018

———— 'G20 Anti-Corruption Action Plan 2017–2018: 2016 Hangzhou Summit: Hangzhou, 5 September 2016' (University of Toronto, 2016) <www.g20.utoronto.ca/2016/160905-anticorruption.html> accessed 20 December 2018

———— G20 Hamburg Action Plan, Hamburg Summit, Hamburg, Germany 7/8 July 2017 <www.g20.utoronto.ca/2017/2017-g20-hamburg-action-plan-en.pdf> accessed 20 December 2018

———— G20 High Level Principles on the Liability of Legal Persons for Corruption, Hamburg Summit, Hamburg, Germany 7/8 July 2017 <www.g20.utoronto.ca/2017/2017-g20-acwg-liberty-legal-persons-en.pdf> accessed 20 December 2018

———— G20 Leaders' Declaration: Hamburg Summit, Hamburg, Germany 7/8 July 2017 <www.g20.utoronto.ca/2017/2017-G20-leaders-declaration.pdf> accessed 20 December 2018

———— G20 Leaders' Statement on Countering Terrorism: Hamburg Summit, Hamburg, Germany 7/8 July 2017 <www.g20.utoronto.ca/2017/2017-g20-statement-antiterror-en.pdf> accessed 20 December 2018

Helsinki Commission Report *Incorporation Transparency: The First Line of Financial Defense* 4 October 2018 <www.csce.gov/sites/helsinkicommission.house.gov/files/BOT%20Final.pdf> accessed 20 December 2018

*ILO Tripartite Declaration of Principles Concerning Multinational Enterprises and Social Policy* (5th Edition, 2017) <www.ilo.org/empent/areas/mne-declaration/lang--en/index.htm> accessed 20 December 2018

Organisation for Economic Co-operation and Development, OECD Multilateral Convention on Mutual Administrative Assistance in Tax Matters (1988, amended by Protocol 2010) <www.oecd.org/tax/exchange-of-tax-information/convention-on-mutual-administrative-assistance-in-tax-matters.htm> and <https://read.oecd-ilibrary.org/taxation/the-multilateral-convention-on-mutual-administrative-assistance-in-tax-matters_9789264115606-en#page2> accessed 20 December 2018

———— Draft for Public Consultation on Mandatory Disclosure Rules for Addressing CRS Avoidance Arrangements and Offshore Structures <www.oecd.org/tax/beps/Discussion-draft-mandatory-disclosure-rules-for-CRS-avoidance-arrangements-offshore-structures.pdf> accessed 20 December 2018

———— Explanatory Statement (BEPS) <www.oecd.org/tax/treaties/explanatory-statement-multilateral-convention-to-implement-tax-treaty-related-measures-to-prevent-BEPS.pdf> ("Explanatory Statement") accessed 20 December 2018

———— Information Brochure (BEPS) <www.oecd.org/tax/treaties/multilateral-instrument-BEPS-tax-treaty-information-brochure.pdf> accessed 20 December 2018

———— OECD Convention on Combating Bribery of Foreign Public Officials in International Business Transactions (21 November 1997) ("Anti Bribery Convention")

<www.oecd.org/corruption/oecdantibriberyconvention.htm>    accessed    20 December 2018. The full text is (in English) at <www.oecd.org/daf/anti-bribery/ ConvCombatBribery_ENG.pdf> and (in French) at <www.oecd.org/fr/daf/anti-corruption/ConvCombatBribery_FR.pdf> accessed 20 December 2018

——— *OECD* Recommendations for Further Combatting Bribery of Foreign Public Officials in International Business Transactions (2009) <www.oecd.org/daf/anti-bribery/oecdantibriberyrecommendation2009.htm> with the full text at <www. oecd.org/daf/anti-bribery/44176910.pdf> accessed 20 December 2018

——— OECD Guidelines for Multinational Enterprises (2011 Edition) <www.oecd. org/daf/inv/mne/48004323.pdf> accessed 20 December 2018

——— OECD Multilateral Competent Authority Agreement on Automatic Exchange of Financial Account Information (29 October 2014) <www.oecd. org/tax/transparency/technical-assistance/aeoi/whatisthemultilateralcompet entauthorityagreement.htm> and <www.oecd.org/tax/exchange-of-tax-infor mation/multilateral-competent-authority-agreement.htm> accessed 20 Decem ber 2018

——— 'G20/OECD Principles of Corporate Governance' (September 2015) <www. g20.utoronto.ca/2015/G20-OECD-Principles-of-Corporate-Governance.pdf> accessed 20 December 2018

——— Multilateral Convention to Implement Tax Treaty Related Measures to Pre-vent Base Erosion and Profit Shifting (2016) (BEPS) <www.oecd.org/tax/trea ties/multilateral-convention-to-implement-tax-treaty-related-measures-to-pre vent-beps.htm> with the full text at <www.oecd.org/tax/treaties/multilateral-convention-to-implement-tax-treaty-related-measures-to-prevent-BEPS.pdf> accessed 20 December 2018

——— OECD Due Diligence Guidance for Responsible Supply Chains of Miner-als from Conflict-Affected and High-Risk Areas (2016) <www.oecd.org/daf/ inv/mne/OECD-Due-Diligence-Guidance-Minerals-Edition3.pdf> accessed 20 December 2018

——— OECD Secretary-General's Report to G20 Finance Ministers, April 2016 (*OECD*, April 2016) <www.oecd.org/tax/oecd-secretary-general-tax-report-g20-finance-ministers-april-2016.pdf> accessed 20 December 2018

——— OECD Secretary-General Report to G20 Finance Ministers: Chengdu Peo-ple's Republic of China 23–24 July 2016' (*OECD*, 2016) <www.oecd.org/ctp/ oecd-secretary-general-tax-report-g20-finance-ministers-july-2016.pdf> accessed 20 December 2018

——— OECD 2016 Terms of Reference to Monitor and Review Progress Towards Transparency and Exchange of Information on Request for Tax Purposes <www. oecd.org/tax/transparency/about-the-global-forum/publications/terms-of-ref erence.pdf> accessed 20 December 2018

——— OECD Global Forum 2016 Report on Tax Transparency <www.oecd.org/ tax/transparency/GF-annual-report-2016.pdf> accessed 20 December 2018

——— Global Forum on Transparency and Exchange of Information for Tax Pur-poses: Tax Transparency 2017, Report on Progress <www.oecd.org/tax/transpar ency/global-forum-annual-report-2017.pdf> accessed 20 December 2018

——— OECD Model Tax Convention on Income and on Capital (Condensed Ver-sion, as it read on 21 November 2017) <https://read.oecd-ilibrary.org/taxation/ model-tax-convention-on-income-and-on-capital-condensed-version-2017_mtc_ cond-2017-en#page1> accessed 20 December 2018

—— OECD Standard for Automatic Exchange of Financial Account Information in Tax Matters (Second Edition, 2017) <www.oecd-ilibrary.org/docserver/9789264267992-en.pdf?expires=1537085651&id=id&accname=guest&checksum=F0474BCD55FBB8138E01DBA985F0EBBC> accessed 20 December 2018

—— Model Mandatory Disclosure Rules for CRS Avoidance Arrangements and Opaque Offshore Structures (8 March 2018) <www.oecd.org/tax/exchange-of-tax-information/model-mandatory-disclosure-rules-for-crs-avoidance-arrangements-and-opaque-offshore-structures.pdf> accessed 20 December 2018

—— OECD Secretary-General Report to the G20 Finance Ministers and Central Bank Governors (Buenos Aires, Argentina, March 2018) <www.oecd.org/tax/OECD-Secretary-General-tax-report-G20-Finance-Ministers-Argentina-March-2018.pdf> accessed 20 December 2018

—— OECD Standard for Automatic Exchange of Financial Account Information in Tax Matters Implementation Handbook (Second Edition, 2018) accessed 20 December 2018 <www.oecd.org/tax/exchange-of-tax-information/implementation-handbook-standard-for-automatic-exchange-of-financial-information-in-tax-matters.pdf> accessed 20 December 2018

—— Public Comments on the discussion draft on Mandatory Disclosure Rules for Addressing CRS Avoidance Arrangements and Offshore Structures (18 January 2018) <www.oecd.org/tax/beps/public-comments-mandatory-disclosure-rules-for-CRS-avoidance-arrangements-offshore-structures.pdf> accessed 20 December 2018

—— OECD/G20 BEPS Project Interim Report on Tax Challenges Arising from Digitalisation (March 2018) <www.oecd.org/tax/tax-challenges-arising-from-digitalisation-interim-report-9789264293083-en.htm> with the full text at <www.oecd-ilibrary.org/docserver/9789264293083-en.pdf?expires=1537700029&id=id&accname=guest&checksum=E8D2ECC0252C59C60F751C02C351E527> accessed 20 December 2018

—— OECD Due Diligence Guidance for Responsible Business Conduct (31 May 2018) <https://mneguidelines.oecd.org/due-diligence-guidance-for-responsible-business-conduct.htm> accessed 20 December 2018

—— CRS-related Frequently Asked Questions (June 2018) <www.oecd.org/tax/exchange-of-tax-information/CRS-related-FAQs.pdf> accessed 20 December 2018

—— OECD/G20 Inclusive Framework on BEPS Progress Report July 2017 – June 2018 <www.oecd.org/ctp/inclusive-framework-on-beps-progress-report-june-2017-july-2018.htm> accessed 20 December 2018

—— OECD Global Forum on Transparency and Exchange of Information for Tax Purposes: United States 2018 (Second Round) (16 July 2018) <www.oecd.org/unitedstates/global-forum-on-transparency-and-exchange-of-information-for-tax-purposes-united-states-2018-second-round-9789264302853-en.htm> accessed 20 December 2018

—— OECD Work on Taxation 2018–2019 <www.oecd.org/corruption/crime/centre-for-tax-policy-and-administration-brochure.pdf> accessed 20 December 2018

US Department of the Treasury, the Financial Crimes Enforcement Network (FinCEN) Final Rule on Customer Due Diligence Requirements for Financial Institutions, under the Bank Secrecy Act (effective 11 July 2016). Federal Register/Vol.81,

No. 91/Wednesday, 11 May 2016/Rules and Regulations 29398 <www.gpo.gov/fdsys/pkg/FR-2016-05-11/pdf/2016-10567.pdf> accessed 20 December 2018
US Federal Financial Institutions Examination Council, Updated procedures for the FinCEN CDD Rule (11 May 2018) <www.ffiec.gov/press/pdf/Customer%20Due%20Diligence%20-%20Overview%20and%20Exam%20Procedures-FINAL.pdf> accessed 20 December 2018
——— New Exam Procedures to Address the FinCEN CDD Rule's Beneficial Ownership Procedures (11 May 2018) <www.ffiec.gov/press/pdf/Beneficial%20Ownership%20Requirements%20for%20Legal%20Entity%20CustomersOverview-FINAL.pdf> accessed 20 December 2018

### United Nations documents

The United Nations Guiding Principles on Business and Human Rights 2011 (Ruggie Principles) A/HRC/17/31 <www.ohchr.org/EN/Issues/TransnationalCorporations/Pages/Reports.aspx> accessed 11 December 2018
United Nations Model Double Taxation Convention Between Developed and Developing Countries (2005, updated to 2017) <www.un.org/esa/ffd/wp-content/uploads/2018/05/MDT_2017.pdf> accessed 20 December 2018

### Secondary sources

Åslund, Anders *How the United States Can Combat Russia's Kleptocracy* (Atlantic Council, Eurasia Center July 2018) <www.atlanticcouncil.org/images/publications/How_the_United_States_Can_Combat_Russia_s_Kleptocracy.pdf> accessed 20 December 2018
Beckett, Paul 'Isle of Man' in T Lyons (ed), *European Cross-Border Estate Planning* (Sweet & Maxwell, London, 2019)
*Belize Reporter* 'Belize Brokerages Named in First FATCA Conviction' *Belize Reporter* (14 September 2018) <http://reporter.bz/2018/09/14/belize-brokerages-named-in-first-fatca-conviction/> accessed 20 December 2018
Bergin, Tom and Grey, Stephen 'Insight – How UK Company Formation Agents Fuel Fraud' *Reuters Business News* (18 March 2016) <https://uk.reuters.com/article/uk-regulations-agents-insight-idUKKCN0WK17W> accessed 20 December 2018
Binham, Caroline 'London's Role in Danske Dirty Money Scandal Under Spotlight' *Financial Times* (25 September 2018) <www.ft.com/content/ba1a0c2a-bdb6-11e8-94b2-17176fbf93f5> accessed 20 December 2018
Cobham, Alex 'UK to Introduce 5th Anti-Money Laundering Directive: Eyes Turn to Crown Dependencies and Overseas Territories' *Tax Justice Network* (23 July 2018) <www.taxjustice.net/2018/07/23/uk-to-introduce-5th-anti-money-laundering-directive-eyes-turn-to-crown-dependencies-and-overseas-territories/> accessed 20 December 2018
Cook, Geoff '10 Reasons Why Public Register Arguments Are Flawed' *Jersey Finance* (20 November 2018) <www.jerseyfinance.je/ceo-blog/10-reasons-why-public-register-arguments-are-flawed?utm_medium=referral&utm_source=twitter.com&utm_campaign=CEOblog#.XCj42NL7Rph> accessed 20 December 2018
Cotorceanu, Peter A 'FATCA and Offshore Trusts: A Second Bite of the Elephant' *Tax Analysts* (23 October 2013) <www.taxhistory.org/www/features.nsf/

Articles/DA7E5C0B6EF087B385257C0D0046A8F8?OpenDocument> accessed 20 December 2018

DLA Piper, *The Foreign Account Tax Compliance Act* <http://files.dlapiper.com/files/Uploads/Documents/FATCA-Alert.pdf> accessed 20 December 2018

Eccleston, Richard and Smith, Helen 'The G20, BEPS and the Future of International Tax Governance' in Peter Dietsch and Thomas Rixen (eds), *Global Tax Governance: What Is Wrong with it and How to Fix It* (ECPR Press, Colchester, UK, 2016)

Financial Stability Board *Thematic Review on Corporate Governance* (28 April 2017) <www.fsb.org/2017/04/thematic-review-on-corporate-governance/> accessed 20 December 2018

Fitzgibbon, Will 'Loopholes in UK Company Register Show Crime Can Still Flourish, Study Finds' *ICIJ* (2 August 2018) <www.icij.org/blog/2018/08/loopholes-in-uk-company-register-show-crime-can-still-flourish-study-finds/?utm_content=bufferc9e68&utm_medium=social&utm_source=twitter.com&utm_campaign=Buffer+-+Twitter> accessed 20 December 2018

Franklin, Joshua and O'Donnell, John 'Swiss Banks Lobby for Get-out Clause as End of Bank Secrecy Nears' *Reuters* (15 June 2017) <https://uk.reuters.com/article/uk-swiss-banks-secrecy-idUKKBN19623I> accessed 20 December 2018

Garside, Juliette 'UK to Adopt EU Laws on Combatting Terrorism and Money Laundering' *The Guardian* (23 July 2018) <www.theguardian.com/world/2018/jul/23/uk-eu-laws-terrorism-money-laundering-margaret-hodge> accessed 20 December 2018

Global Witness 'The UK's Tax Havens: Top 10 Corruption Cases Involving Anonymous Companies' *Global Witness* (21 February 2017) <www.globalwitness.org/en/blog/uks-tax-havens-top-10-corruption-cases-involving-anonymous-companies/> accessed 20 December 2018

——— '10 Lessons from the UK's Public Register of the Real Owners of Companies' *Global Witness* (23 October 2017) <www.globalwitness.org/en-gb/blog/10-lessons-uks-public-register-real-owners-companies/> accessed 20 December 2018

Government of the Virgin Islands, Statement by Premier Smith on United Kingdom Sanctions and Anti-Money Laundering Bill 30 April 2018 <http://bvi.gov.vg/media-centre/statement-premier-smith-united-kingdom-sanctions-and-anti-money-laundering-bill> accessed 20 December 2018

Grinberg, Itai 'Does FATCA Teach Broader Lessons About International Tax Multilateralism?' in Peter Dietsch and Thomas Rixen (eds), *Global Tax Governance: What Is Wrong with It and How to Fix It* (ECPR Press, Colchester, UK, 2016) ch 7

House of Commons briefing paper Number 8259, 24 August 2018 *Registers of Beneficial Ownership* <https://researchbriefings.parliament.uk/ResearchBriefing/Summary/CBP-8259> accessed 20 December 2018

Hubbard, Mark *Protectors of Trusts* (Oxford University Press, Oxford, 2013)

Huber, Andrew T 'Trust Protectors: The Role Continues to Evolve' *Probate and Property Magazine* (January/February 2017 Volume 31 No 1, Section of Real Property, Trust and Estate Law, American Bar Association) <www.americanbar.org/publications/probate_property_magazine_2012/2017/january_february_2017/2017_aba_rpte_pp_v31_1_article_huber_trust_protectors.html> accessed 20 December 2018

Isle of Man Financial Services Authority, Guidance (GC 2017/0003 June 2017) <www.gov.im/media/1357278/beneficial-ownership-act-2017-guidance-june-2017-gc-no-2017-0003.pdf> accessed 20 December 2018

Kasperkevic, Jana 'Forget Panama: It's Easier to Hide Your Money in the US Than Almost Anywhere' *The Guardian* (6 April 2016) <www.theguardian.com/us-news/2016/apr/06/panama-papers-us-tax-havens-delaware> accessed 20 December 2018

Keatinge, Tom 'We Cannot Fight Cross-border Money Laundering with Local Tools' *Financial Times* (9 September 2018) <www.ft.com/content/0397fc40-b281-11e8-87e0-d84e0d934341> accessed 20 December 2018

Kenney, Martin 'Crooks Are (predictably) Avoiding Open Company Registers' *The FCPA Blog* (2 October 2018) <www.fcpablog.com/blog/2018/10/2/martin-kenney-crooks-are-predictably-avoiding-open-company-r.html> accessed 20 December 2018

Kerzner, David S and Chodikoff, David W 'Article 26 of the OECD Model Tax Convention on Income and on Capital' in *International Tax Evasion in the Global Information Age* (Palgrave Macmillan, 2016) ch 7

―――― *Automatic Exchange of Information in International Tax Evasion in the Global Information Age* (Palgrave Macmillan, 2016) ch 8

―――― 'The OECD's War on Tax Evasion 1996–2014' in *International Tax Evasion in the Global Information Age* (Palgrave Macmillan, 2016) ch 3

Knobel, Andres 'The Case for Registering Trusts – and How to Do It' *Tax Justice Network* <www.taxjustice.net/wp-content/uploads/2013/04/Registration-of-Trusts_AK.pdf> accessed 20 December 2018

―――― 'The EU's Latest Agreement on Amending the Anti-money Laundering Directive: At the Vanguard of Trust Transparency, But Still Further to Go' *Tax Justice Network* (9 April 2018) <www.taxjustice.net/2018/04/09/the-eus-latest-agreement-on-amending-the-anti-money-laundering-directive-still-further-to-go/> accessed 20 December 2018

―――― 'It's Time for Countries to Start Publishing the Data They're Collecting Under OECD's Common Reporting Standard' *Tax Justice Network* (11 July 2018) <www.taxjustice.net/2018/07/11/its-time-for-countries-to-start-publishing-the-data-theyre-collecting-under-oecds-common-reporting-standard/> accessed 20 December 2018

Knobel, Andres, Harari, Moran and Meinzer, Markus 'The State of Play of Beneficial Ownership Registration: A Visual Overview' *Tax Justice Network* (27 June 2018) <www.taxjustice.net/wp-content/uploads/2018/06/TJN2018-BeneficialOwnershipRegistration-StateOfPlay-FSI.pdf> accessed 20 December 2018

The Law Library of Congress, Global Legal Research Center *Disclosure of Beneficial Ownership in Selected Countries* (July 2017) <www.loc.gov/law/help/beneficial-ownership/disclosure-beneficial-ownership.pdf> accessed 20 December 2018

Lawson, Anthea and Christensen, John 'Yes, Britain Is Closing Its Tax Havens. But Let's Not Forget it Created Them in the First Place' *Tax Justice Network* (4 May 2018) <www.taxjustice.net/2018/05/04/yes-britain-is-closing-its-tax-havens-but-lets-not-forget-it-created-them-in-the-first-place/> accessed 20 December 2018

Liu, Yunhong *How Compliance Practices Should Adapt to Increased Beneficial Ownership Scrutiny* (Dun & Bradstreet, 2016) <www.dnb.co.uk/content/dam/english/dnb-solutions/supply-management/beneficial-ownership-white-paper.pdf> accessed 20 December 2018

Mishcon de Reya 'Legal Challenge to Common Reporting Standard (CRS) and Beneficial Ownership (BO) Registers' (1 August 2018) <www.mishcon.com/news/

firm_news/legal-challenge-to-common-reporting-standard-crs-and-beneficial-ownership-bo-registers> accessed 20 December 2018

Mor, Federico *Registers of Beneficial Ownership* (House of Commons Library, Briefing Paper Number 8259, 24 August 2018) <https://researchbriefings.parliament.uk/ResearchBriefing/Summary/CBP-8259#fullreport> accessed 20 December 2018

NautaDutilh, *Status Overview UBO Register Europe* (NautaDutilh, 31 August 2017) <www.nautadutilh.com/sites/nautadutilh.com/files/inline-files/overview-status-implementation-ubo-register---survey-nautadutilh-31-august-2017.pdf> accessed 20 December 2018

*OpenOwnership and Global Witness, Learning the Lessons from the UK's Public Beneficial Ownership Register* (OpenOwnership and Global Witness joint briefing, October 2017) <https://openownership.org/uploads/Learning%20the%20lessons%20briefing.pdf> accessed 20 December 2018

Osborne, Hilary 'Offshore Wealth: Loopholes Found in EU Ant-tax Evasion Rules' *The Guardian* (15 October 2018) <www.theguardian.com/business/2018/oct/15/offshore-wealth-loopholes-found-eu-anti-tax-evasion-rules> accessed 20 December 2018

Oved, Marco Chown and Cribb, Robert 'Offshore Tax Havens Set to Overtake Canada in Corporate Transparency' *The Star* (7 May 2018) <www.thestar.com/amp/news/investigations/2018/05/06/offshore-tax-havens-set-to-overtake-canada-in-corporate-transparency.html?__twitter_impression=true> accessed 20 December 2018

Pegg, David 'Offshore Owners of British Property to be forced to reveal names' *The Guardian* (23 July 2018) <www.theguardian.com/business/2018/jul/23/offshore-owners-of-british-property-to-be-forced-to-reveal-names> accessed 20 December 2018

———— 'Mishcon de Reya Complains About Anti-tax Evasion Measures' *The Guardian* (2 August 2018) <www.theguardian.com/money/2018/aug/02/mishcon-de-reya-complains-about-anti-tax-evasion-measures> accessed 20 December 2018

Pegg, David and Osborne, Hilary 'EU to Force Firms to Reveal True Owners in Wake of Panama Papers' *The Guardian* (15 December 2017) <www.theguardian.com/world/2017/dec/15/eu-to-force-companies-to-disclose-owners-with-directive-prompted-by-panama-papers> accessed 20 December 2018

Realuyo, Celina B *"Following the Money Trail" to Combat Terrorism, Crime, and Corruption in the Americas* (Wilson Center, Latin American Program, Mexico Institute, August 2017) <www.wilsoncenter.org/sites/default/files/follow_the_money_final_0.pdf> accessed 20 December 2018

Shaxson, Nicholas *Treasure Islands: Tax Havens and the Men Who Stole the World* (The Bodley Head, London, 2011)

———— *The Finance Curse: How Global Finance Is Making Us All Poorer* (The Bodley Head, London, 2018)

Sikka, Prem 'Tax-haven Transparency Won't Stop Money Laundering in Britain' *The Guardian* (8 May 2018) <www.theguardian.com/commentisfree/2018/may/08/tax-haven-transparency-money-laundering-britain> accessed 20 December 2018

Society of Trust and Estate Practitioners (STEP), *CRS: Trusts Under the Common Reporting Standard – Jurisdiction X* <www.step.org/sites/default/files/Policy/Trusts_under_CRS_flowchart_Jurisdiction_X.pdf> accessed 20 December 2018

———— *Guidance Note: CRS and Trusts* (8 March 2017) <www.step.org/sites/default/files/Policy/Guidance_note_CRS_and_trusts.pdf> accessed 20 December 2018

Swiss Bankers Association 'Statement from the SBA Regarding Federal Council Decision in Favour of a Further AEOI Country List' (2 February 2017) <www.swissbanking.org/en/media/positions-and-press-releases/statement-from-the-sba-regarding-the-federal-council-decision-in-favour-of-a-further-aeoi-country-list> accessed 20 December 2018

Tax Justice Network 'TJN Responds to New OECD Report on Automatic Information Exchange' *Tax Justice Network* (13 February 2014) <www.taxjustice.net/2014/02/13/press-release-tjn-responds-new-oecd-report-automatic-information-exchange/> accessed 20 December 2018

———— Tax Justice Network Financial Secrecy Index (30 January 2018) <www.financialsecrecyindex.com/> accessed 20 December 2018

United Kingdom Parliament, Foreign Affairs Committee 'The future of the UK Overseas Territories inquiry' <www.parliament.uk/business/committees/committees-a-z/commons-select/foreign-affairs-committee/inquiries1/parliament-2017/inquiry13/> accessed 20 December 2018

United Kingdom Parliament, House of Commons, 'Report Stage of the Sanctions and Anti-Money Laundering Bill' (1 May 2018) <https://publications.parliament.uk/pa/bills/cbill/2017-2019/0176/amend/sanctions_daily_rep_0430.1-7.html> accessed 20 December 2018

United States Department of Justice, 'Former Executive of Loyal Bank Ltd Pleads Guilty to Conspiring to Defraud the United States by Failing to Comply with Foreign Account Tax Compliance Act (FATCA)' (11 September 2018) <www.justice.gov/usao-edny/pr/former-executive-loyal-bank-ltd-pleads-guilty-conspiring-defraud-united-states-failing> accessed 20 December 2018

Wintour, Patrick 'British Overseas Territories in Talks to Keep Tax Haven Secrecy' *The Guardian* (13 June 2018) <www.theguardian.com/world/2018/jun/13/british-overseas-territories-in-talks-to-keep-tax-haven-secrecy> accessed 20 December 2018

Woodward, Richard 'A Strange Revolution: Mock Compliance and the Failure of the OECD's International Tax Transparency Regime' in Peter Dietsch and Thomas Rixen (eds), *Global Tax Governance: What Is Wrong with It and How to Fix It* (ECPR Press, Colchester, UK, 2016) ch 5 108

The World Bank, van der Does de Willebois, Emile and others *Puppet Masters: How the Corrupt Use Legal Structures to Hide Stolen Assets and What to Do About It* (World Bank Publications, Washington, DC, 2011)

———— 'Corrupt Money Concealed in Shell Companies and Other Opaque Legal Entities, Finds New StAR Study' *The World Bank* (24 October 2011) <www.worldbank.org/en/news/press-release/2011/10/24/corrupt-money-concealed-in-shell-companies-and-other-opaque-legal-entities-finds-new-star-study> accessed 20 December 2018

World Customs Organization *Illicit Financial Flows via Trade Mis-invoicing Study Report 2018* <www.wcoomd.org/-/media/wco/public/global/pdf/media/newsroom/reports/2018/wco-study-report-on-iffs_tm.pdf?db=web> accessed 20 December 2018

Zagaris, Bruce 'ABA Considers Options on AML Bills' 26 *STEP Journal* 7 (August/September 2018) <www.step.org/journal/step-journal-august-september-2018/aba-considers-options-aml-bills> accessed 20 December 2018

Zucman, Gabriel *The Hidden Wealth of Nations: The Scourge of Tax Havens* (Teresa Lavender Fagan tr, The University of Chicago Press, Chicago, 2015)

# 4 Confidentiality versus concealment

## Introduction

Is there a right to maintain full anonymity of ownership? As Joseph Pulitzer cautioned, "There is not a crime, there is not a dodge, there is not a trick, there is not a swindle, there is not a vice which does not live by secrecy".[1]

In this chapter, the distinction between privacy and legitimate confidentiality on the one hand, and concealment on the other, and their legitimacy or abuse, is explained with reference to commercial and trade law and practice, principles of corporate governance and applicable business human rights.

There is a real difference between the rights of contracting parties to keep the details of their negotiations and agreements confidential between them and the claimed right of business organisations to conceal their true ownership and control. This chapter looks at the legitimate limits of commercial confidentiality.

In the second decade of the 21st century, is it any longer acceptable that a corporation or any other business structure which owes its existence to the state should have freedom to conduct itself in business in any manner it chooses? The proposed constraints of good corporate governance are reviewed, from the perspective of ownership concealment and beneficial ownership avoidance.

Finally, can the corporation strike back? Has it those same rights as a *legal* person which *natural* persons enjoy? Does having a legal personality entitle it to claim human rights, and amongst those rights, the right to privacy?

To begin with, what is understood by "privacy"?

## Privacy[2]

### *The meaning of "privacy"*

Accountability avoidance through secrecy and through the ability to exercise control over how and if information is disseminated is inherently bound up with privacy: secrecy and information control are two examples of often overlapping defining

---

1 Joseph Pulitzer, quoted in Denis Brian *Pulitzer: A Life* (John Wiley & Sons, New York, 2001) 377.
2 A comprehensive analysis of privacy is beyond the scope of this work. See Daniel J Solove, *Understanding Privacy* (Harvard University Press, Cambridge, MA, 2008) and Beate Roessler and Dorota Mokrosinska (eds), *Social Dimensions of Privacy – Interdisciplinary Perspectives* (Cambridge University Press, Cambridge, 2015).

markers of privacy. The mere concealment of ownership or full-blown beneficial ownership avoidance is rooted in a desire, legitimate or otherwise, for privacy. One approach to challenging registration and disclosure systems[3] is an assertion of the right to privacy. Yet it is commonly agreed that privacy "is a concept in disarray. Nobody can articulate what it means".[4] "Perhaps the most striking thing about the right to privacy is that nobody seems to have any clear idea what it is".[5]

It is this lack of meaning – or, perhaps, plurality of meanings – which is exploited by those seeking to avoid accountability. Countering an assertion of privacy rights is made all the more problematic when privacy "is a value so complex, so entangled in competing and contradictory dimensions, so engorged with various and distinct meanings".[6] Such assertions may on closer examination be merely "a plea for the right to misrepresent oneself to the rest of the world".[7]

The privacy rights of an individual and the privacy rights of a legal construct such as a corporation have to be distinguished. An individual does not owe their existence to the state – the state is not a primogenitor of humanity. Legal constructs such as corporations and trusts do however find their origin and enjoy their continued existence as creatures of the state. The privacy rights of a legal person may therefore be as wide or as narrow as the state which supports their existence sees fit. The state has granted corporations the benefit of limited liability – it must not be presumed that it has granted them a concomitant right to anonymity of ownership.[8] "[T]he right to privacy is a societal bequeathal, not an individual possession".[9]

> The traditional view of privacy, in which protection of individual privacy is a means of protecting individual interests, has proved a weak basis for protection of privacy in political practice: when individual privacy conflicts with broader social interests such as law enforcement, public security, or the implementation of social justice, protecting individuals' interests seems to be a luxury that society can ill afford.[10]

---

3  Discussed in ch 3.
4  Daniel J Solove, *Understanding Privacy* (n 2) 1.
5  Judith Jarvis Thomson, 'The Right to Privacy' in Ferdinand David Schoeman (ed), *Philosophical Dimensions of Privacy: An Anthology* (Cambridge University Press, Cambridge, 1984) 272, 272.
6  Robert C Post, 'Three Concepts of Privacy' 89 *Georgetown Law Journal* 2087 (2001).
7  Richard A Epstein, 'The Legal Regulation of Genetic Discrimination: Old Responses to New Technology' 74 *Boston University Law Review* 1, 12 (1994).
8  See the discussion of a "franchise from society" in ch 2 and in Privacy and corporations: an American perspective (below).
9  Richard Hixson, *Privacy in a Public Society: Human Rights in Conflict* (Oxford University Press Inc., New York, USA, 1987) xiv.
10  Dorota Mokrosinska and Beate Roessler, 'Introduction' in Beate Roessler and Dorota Mokrosinska (eds), *Social Dimensions of Privacy, Interdisciplinary Perspectives* (Cambridge University Press, Cambridge, 2015) 3.

The issue of ownership disclosure and counter-assertions of privacy is analogous to state surveillance. It is a question of what James B Rule calls "default legitimacy":

> By this I mean public acceptance of the means and ends of the project as at least minimally consistent with prevailing values. Such default legitimacy need not entail enthusiastic support or deep personal conviction on the part of the public. It may simply entail grudging public acquiescence [. . .]. In nearly every sector of life, default legitimacy has upheld the notion that collective interests in efficiency, economic growth and "innovation", state security or crime prevention may trump privacy claims.[11]

James B Rule suggests that as the results of a surveillance system come fully to light – his idea being that where there is no place to hide and where all one's actions are tracked and recorded, there can be no successful crime – public support will build. His example is the use of smartphone technology and smartcards to monitor an individual's activities.[12] His argument can be applied equally to blockchain technology (including ownership rights attaching to initial coin offerings and securitised cryptocurrencies[13]), which when applied to corporate share registration indelibly marks a security's origin and transfer.[14]

James B Rule takes a step back however from advocating that this information should be widely available, with only "government officials with authentic needs to know" permitted to access intelligence – "including members of law enforcement and counterterrorist agencies, immigration authorities, offices concerned with taxation and administration of government benefits, social welfare

---

11 James B Rule, 'Privacy: The *Longue Durée*' in Beate Roessler and Dorota Mokrosinska (eds), *Social Dimensions of Privacy, Interdisciplinary Perspectives* (Cambridge University Press, Cambridge, 2015) 18, 27.
12 Ibid. 23.
13 See ch 6 for a fuller discussion.
14 See Sujeet Indap, 'Blockchain Could Clean Up Messy Shareholder Registers' *Financial Times* (11 September 2017) <www.ft.com/content/f5cf21f6-935a-11e7-a9e6-11d2f0ebb7f0> accessed 11 December 2018 discussing the State of Delaware's initiative, which came into force on 1 August 2017, to allow companies to use blockchain technology to store their share registers. He comments, "[T]he current low-tech share bookkeeping system is indirect and esoteric. It often struggles because assigning company shares to their underlying owners is not straightforward [. . .]". See also Catherine Simard, "Delaware provides legal clarification for blockchain maintenance of corporate records – the view from Canada" (Norton Rose Fulbright, September 2017) <www.nortonrosefulbright.com/knowledge/publications/155384/delaware-provides-legal-clarification-for-blockchain-maintenance-of-corporate-records-the-view-from-canada> accessed 11 December 2018. She writes: "Blockchain technology facilitates simultaneous record-keeping and validation by providing a secure, transparent and immutable audit trail without the need for any intermediaries".

and educational services, those involved in the war on drugs and other bodies with enforcement or investigative powers".[15]

What harmful consequences would flow from the public disclosure of ownership, were this to be categorised as a privacy violation?

> Harms from data revelations range from physical violence, to retribution, to shaming. Yet a more precise taxonomy of data related harms is needed. Metrics are needed to inform decisions based on data risks, harms, and benefits. Who has the authority to make these decisions? When should privacy impact assessments be mandated (and enforced) either by government or self-regulatory mechanisms?[16]

Fundamentally, it is a question of what society considers a reasonable expectation of privacy – whether an individual or a legal person has exhibited a subjective expectation of privacy, and then assessing whether this is one that society is prepared to recognise as "reasonable".[17]

The concept of "privacy", like that of ownership accountability itself, is dynamic and evolutionary. Introducing a reasonableness test, rather than fixing the concepts of "privacy" (or, indeed, "ownership"), provides the necessary flexibility of response.

### *General Data Protection Regulation ("GDPR")*[18]

The GDPR on the protection of natural persons with regard to the processing of personal data and on the free movement of such data of 27 April 2016 became binding on all Member States of the European Union on 25 May 2018. It has been hailed by Human Rights Watch as "one of the strongest and most

---

15  James B Rule, 'Privacy: The *Longue Duré*' (n 11) 24, 25. This is a far wider category of "officials with authentic needs to know" than is currently regarded as acceptable – see the discussion in ch 3 on the dissemination and use of disclosed material and its restriction to law enforcement and fiscal authorities.

16  Mark Latonero and Zachard Gold, 'Data, Human Rights & Human Security' *Data & Society*, 5 (22 June 2015) <https://datasociety.net/pubs/dhr/Data-HumanRights-primer2015. pdf> accessed 11 December 2018.

17  The use of the reasonable expectation of privacy is one found predominantly in United States jurisprudence on the Fourth Amendment to the United States Constitution: "The right of the people to be secure in their persons, houses, papers, and effects, against unreasonable searches and seizures, shall not be violated, and no warrants shall issue, but upon probable cause, supported by oath or affirmation, and particularly describing the place to be searched, and the persons or things to be seized". See the discussion of the reasonable expectation of privacy in *Katz v United States*, 389 US 347, 361 (1967).

18  <https://eur-lex.europa.eu/legal-content/EN/TXT/HTML/?uri= CELEX:02016R0679-20160504&from=EN> accessed 11 December 2018. Guidance provided by the European Commission is available at <https://ec.europa.eu/commission/ priorities/justice-and-fundamental-rights/data-protection/2018-reform-eu-data-protec tion-rules_en> accessed 11 December 2018.

comprehensive attempts globally to regulate the collection and use of personal data by both governments and the private sector. If robustly implemented and enforced, it can bolster the right to privacy in Europe and serve as a useful model for countries such as the United States that have comparatively weak protections for personal data".[19]

A full review of the GDPR is outside the scope of this work, but, focussing on ownership, to what extent does the GDPR impede any transparency strategies? The answer is, barely at all.

The permitted restrictions found in Article 23 permit a Member State to restrict the protections offered in the GDPR:

> [. . .] when such a restriction respects the essence of the fundamental rights and freedoms and is a necessary and proportionate measure in a democratic society to safeguard:
>
> (a)  national security;
> (b)  defence;
> (c)  public security;
> (d)  the prevention, investigation, detection or prosecution of criminal offences or the execution of criminal penalties, including the safe-guarding against and the prevention of threats to public security;
> (e)  other important objectives of general public interest of the Union or of a Member State, in particular an important economic or finan-cial interest of the Union or of a Member State, including monetary, budgetary and taxation matters, public health and social security;
> (f)  to (j) [. . .]

The terms "national security" and "public security" are not defined in the GDPR and taken together with "the prevention, investigation, detection or prosecution of criminal offences" and "monetary, budgetary and taxation matters" pose no obstacle to a government wishing to override any claimed rights of privacy or anonymity on the part of owners. Nor in such a case is a government prevented from transferring personal data to a third country or an international organisation provided the European Commission has decided that these afford an "adequate level of protection"[20] (Art 45). "International organisation" is not defined, which

---

19  'EU: Data Protection Rules Advance Privacy' *Human Rights Watch* (6 June 2018) <www.hrw.org/news/2018/06/06/eu-data-protection-rules-advance-privacy> accessed 11 December 2018.

20  Art 45 para 2 provides: "When assessing the adequacy of the level of protection, the Com-mission shall, in particular, take account of the following elements:

(a) the rule of law, respect for human rights and fundamental freedoms, relevant legislation, both general and sectoral, including concerning public security, defence, national security and criminal law and the access of public authorities to personal data, as well as the implementation of such legislation, data protection rules, professional rules and security measures, including

broadens the scope for transfers even further. Such a transfer requires no specific authorisation.

## Principles of commercial confidentiality[21]

The placing on public record of the identity of the owners of an enterprise is a question quite distinct from requiring an enterprise to bring into the public domain its business details.

The disclosure of information about the privacy of an individual – relevant to questions of ownership, the identity of a shareholder or ultimate beneficial owner – is on a different legal foundation from that where a person's confidential information in the sense of that person's commercial and trading *activities* is disclosed.

The contractual underpinnings of trading activities of an enterprise are neither public property nor matters of public knowledge, and so are confidential. But this is not necessarily true when it comes to questions of ownership disclosure. In the context of accountability avoidance the public interest protecting confidence may be outweighed by some other countervailing public interest which favours disclosure.

### *English Common Law approach*

What are the defining characteristics of "confidential information"? The common law is pragmatic.

On the first test in *Coco v AN Clark (Engineers) Ltd* [1969] RPC 41 a case for an actionable breach of confidence will need to establish that the information has

---

rules for the onward transfer of personal data to another third country or international organisation which are complied with in that country or international organisation, case-law, as well as effective and enforceable data subject rights and effective administrative and judicial redress for the data subjects whose personal data are being transferred; (b) the existence and effective functioning of one or more independent supervisory authorities in the third country or to which an international organisation is subject, with responsibility for ensuring and enforcing compliance with the data protection rules, including adequate enforcement powers, for assisting and advising the data subjects in exercising their rights and for cooperation with the supervisory authorities of the Member States; and (c) the international commitments the third country or international organisation concerned has entered into, or other obligations arising from legally binding conventions or instruments as well as from its participation in multilateral or regional systems, in particular in relation to the protection of personal data".

21  For a general discussion of confidentiality see Tanya Aplin, Lionel Bentley, Phillip Johnson and Simon Malynicz, *Gurry on Breach of Confidence: The Protection of Confidential Information* (Oxford University Press, 2012) and for a practical guide see Mark Anderson and Victor Warner, *Drafting Confidentiality Agreements* (3rd Edition, The Law Society, 2014). Both books predate the introduction of Directive (EU) 2016/943 on the protection of undisclosed know-how and business information (trade secrets) against their unlawful acquisition, use and disclosure. (See n 28.)

the "necessary quality of confidence about it" and "must not be something which is public property and public knowledge".[22]

The issue of the right to *protect* confidential information was considered by the House of Lords in *OBG Ltd and another v Allan and others 2007.*[23]

> [255] As the law has developed breach of confidence, or misuse of confidential information, now covers two distinct causes of action, protecting two different interests: privacy, and secret ('confidential') information. It is important to keep these two distinct. In some instances information may qualify for protection both on grounds of privacy and confidentiality. In other instances information may be in the public domain, and not qualify for protection as confidential, and yet qualify for protection on the grounds of privacy. Privacy can be invaded by further publication of information or photographs already disclosed to the public. Conversely, and obviously, a trade secret may be protected as confidential information even though no question of personal privacy is involved. This distinction was recognised by the Law Commission in its report on Breach of Confidence (Law Com no 110) (Cmnd 8388) (1981), pp 5–6. (per Lord Nicholls of Birkenhead)[24]
>
> [272] I now turn to breach of confidence. This House has quite recently reaffirmed that English law knows no common law tort of invasion of privacy (see Wainwright v Home Office [2003] UKHL 53, [2003] 4 All ER 969, [2004] 2 AC 406). But the law of confidentiality has been, and is being developed in such a way as to protect private information. [. . .] The most important single step in the course of the law's recent development has been the speech of Lord Goff of Chieveley in A-G v Guardian Newspapers Ltd (No 2) [1988] 3 All ER 545, [1990] 1 AC 109 [. . .] Lord Goff stated a broad general principle of confidence subject to three limiting principles: (1) 'the principle of confidentiality only applies to information to the extent that it is confidential;' (2) '[it] applies neither to useless information, nor to trivia;' and (3) the public interest protecting confidence 'may be outweighed by some other countervailing public interest which favours disclosure' (per Lord Walker of Gestingthorpe).[25]

It is a "balancing operation":

> [A]lthough the basis of the law's protection of confidence is that there is a public interest that confidences should be preserved and protected by the law, nevertheless that public interest may be outweighed by some other

---

22  [1969] RPC 41 at 47 per Megarry J.
23  *OBG Ltd and another v Allan and others; Douglas and another v Hello! Ltd and others (No 3); Mainstream Properties Ltd v Young and others* [2007] UKHL 21; [2007] 4 All ER 545.
24  [2007] 4 All ER 545 at 607.
25  Ibid. at 610.

countervailing public interest which favours disclosure. This limitation may apply, as the judge pointed out, to all types of confidential information. It is this limiting principle which may require a court to carry out a balancing operation, weighing the public interest in maintaining confidence against a countervailing public interest favouring disclosure.

(per Lord Goff of Chieveley)[26]

Where anonymity (or outright absence) of ownership with the aim of avoiding accountability is in issue, and where it is reasonable to assume that the anonymity strategy is motivated by the desire to avoid or evade taxation, to facilitate money laundering, to fund terrorism, or any similar avowedly antisocial activity, then the public interest may better be served by favouring disclosure.[27]

### *Directive (EU) 2016/943 – trade secrets*[28]

On 8 June 2016, in line with a proposal from the European Commission, the European Parliament and the EU Council adopted Directive (EU) 2016/943 on the protection of undisclosed know-how and business information (trade secrets) against their unlawful acquisition, use and disclosure. Its aim and scope are summarised by the European Commission:[29]

The Directive harmonises the definition of trade secrets in accordance with existing internationally binding standards. It also defines the relevant forms of misappropriation and clarifies that reverse engineering and parallel innovation must be guaranteed, given that trade secrets are not a form of exclusive intellectual property right.

Without establishing criminal sanctions, the proposal harmonises the civil means through which victims of trade secret misappropriation can seek protection, such as:

- stopping the unlawful use and further disclosure of misappropriated trade secrets

---

26  *Attorney General v Guardian Newspapers and others (No 2)* [1988] 3 All ER 545 at 659.
27  In a case dealing with the right of the police to circulate a suspect's photograph, Laws J stated "The police have acted well within the scope of such obligation as the law imposes upon them in relation to the plaintiff's photograph. What they did was obviously and unarguably in the public interest: it was reasonably directed to the prevention of crime". *Hellewell v Chief Constable of Derbyshire* [1995] 4 All ER 473 at 480.
28  Directive (EU) 2016/943 on the protection of undisclosed know-how and business information (trade secrets) against their unlawful acquisition, use and disclosure <https://eur-lex.europa.eu/legal-content/EN/TXT/HTML/?uri=CELEX:32016L0943&from=EN> accessed 11 December 2018.
29  <http://ec.europa.eu/growth/industry/intellectual-property/trade-secrets_en> accessed 11 December 2018.

- the removal from the market of goods that have been manufactured on the basis of a trade secret that has been illegally acquired
- the right to compensation for the damages caused by the unlawful use or disclosure of the misappropriated trade secret.[30]

"Trade secrets" is the compendium term for all aspects of confidential information – the Directive in recital (6) acknowledges that "there are important differences in the Member States' legislation as regards the protection of trade secrets against their unlawful acquisition, use or disclosure by other persons" and cites definitional remedial inconsistencies.

The deadline for EU Member States to implement the Directive was 9 June 2018, and on that date in the United Kingdom the Directive took effect, supplementing the English common law approach to confidentiality with the coming into force of the Trade Secrets (Enforcement, etc.) Regulations 2018,[31] thereby affording statutory protection to "trade secrets" for the first time. "Trade secret" is defined in Regulation 2:

> "trade secret" means information which – (a) is secret in the sense that it is not, as a body or in the precise configuration and assembly of its components, generally known among, or readily accessible to, persons within the circles that normally deal with the kind of information in question, (b) has commercial value because it is secret, and (c) has been subject to reasonable steps under the circumstances, by the person lawfully in control of the information, to keep it secret. [32]

Expressly, the Directive preserves in Article 1 2(b) and Article 5(b) the public interest exception to confidentiality:

> 2. This Directive shall not affect: [. . .] (b) the application of Union or national rules requiring trade secret holders to disclose, for reasons of public interest, information, including trade secrets, to the public or to administrative or judicial authorities for the performance of the duties of those authorities; [. . .]
>
> 5. Member States shall ensure that an application for the measures, procedures and remedies provided for in this Directive is dismissed where the alleged acquisition, use or disclosure of the trade secret was carried out in any of the following cases: [. . .] (b) for revealing misconduct, wrongdoing or illegal activity, provided that the respondent acted for the purpose of protecting the general public interest.

---

30 However, the Directive in Recital (37) stresses that it "does not aim to establish harmonised rules for judicial cooperation, jurisdiction, the recognition and enforcement of judgments in civil and commercial matters, or deal with applicable law".

31 <www.legislation.gov.uk/uksi/2018/597/contents/made> accessed 11 December 2018.

32 The definition reproduces that in the Directive, Article 2(1).

*Anonymity – a commercial right?*

Neither the English common law nor the Directive or the Regulations makes any reference to ownership of the entity as being amongst trade secrets to be protected. On the contrary, both systems recognise the need to protect the general public interest. Neither therefore affords any support to an assertion that details of the ownership of an entity constitute a form of commercial confidential information worthy of or entitled to protection.

## Principles of corporate governance

To what extent have international, and national, standards of corporate governance focussed on the question of ownership, or even acknowledged its relevance? Bad people can make good money from legitimate enterprises, to put towards evil purposes. It is naïve to assume that they would put all their commercial eggs in one corporate basket. The question is therefore to what extent commercial enterprises which strive for legitimacy and which seek to observe corporate governance codes are required under such codes to look back over their shoulder to see who – if anyone – owns them, and whether in their quest for legitimacy they are merely fuelling the illegitimate.

The problem is at its most acute in the context of publicly listed companies and international financial markets:

> Investor confidence in financial markets depends in large part on the existence of an accurate disclosure regime that provides transparency in the beneficial ownership and control structures of publicly listed companies. This is particularly true for corporate governance systems that are characterised by concentrated ownership. On the one hand, large investors with significant voting and cash-flow rights may encourage long-term growth and firm performance. On the other hand, however, controlling beneficial owners with large voting blocks may have incentives to divert corporate assets and opportunities for personal gain at the expense of minority investors. [. . .] Stakeholder rights (e.g. employees and creditors) cannot be properly exercised if ultimate decision-makers in a company's affairs cannot be identified. The accountability of the board may also be seriously endangered if stakeholders and the general public are unaware of decision-making and ultimate control structures. Finally, regulators and supervisory agencies have a strong interest in knowing beneficial owners – in order to determine the origin of investment flows, to prevent money laundering and tax evasion and to settle issues of corporate accountability. A good corporate governance infrastructure should combine transparency, accountability and integrity and this requires knowledge of beneficial ownership.[33]

---

33 Erik P M Vermeulen, 'Beneficial Ownership and Control: A Comparative Study – Disclosure, Information and Enforcement' *OECD Corporate Governance Working Papers*, No. 7 (OECD Publishing, 2013) Executive Summary 5 <http://dx.doi.org/10.1787/5k4dkhwckbzv-en> accessed 11 December 2018.

There is no world shortage of corporate governance codes, principles and guidelines. Whether on an international and national level, state issued or private sector initiatives, secular or faith-based, concerned with the merely internal administrative or the external moral outcomes of trade, a range of standards have been put forward.[34]

Sampling these, by way of example:

- The United Nations Global Compact (2000)[35] and the United Nations Convention Against Corruption (2004).[36]
- The United Nations Guiding Principles on Business and Human Rights 2011 (more commonly known as the "Ruggie Principles") which seek to define the international human rights responsibilities of corporations.
- The IGCN Global Governance Principles (2017, 5th edition) and Global Stewardship Principles (2016) issued by the International Corporate Governance Network (an example of private sector corporate governance initiatives).
- The Guiding Principles on Corporate Governance for Institutions Offering Only Islamic Financial Services (IFSB-3) (December 2006), Guiding Principles on Governance for Islamic Collective Investment Schemes (IFSB-6) (December 2008) and Guiding Principles on Disclosure Requirements for Islamic Capital Market Products (*ṣukūk* and Islamic Collective Investment Schemes) (IFSB-19) (April 2017) issued by the Islamic Financial Services Board.
- The UK Corporate Governance Code issued by the Financial Reporting Council in July 2018.

From the perspective of a corporation, if it chooses to abide by these standards (which are soft law guidelines and not mandatory[37]) in pursuing its business

---

34  The *OECD Corporate Governance Factbook 2017* provides a comparative analysis of a wide range of countries' institutional, legal and regulatory frameworks. This includes the corporate governance landscape, covering ownership patterns, the role of stock exchanges and regulators and the cross-border application of listing requirements. The perspective of the Factbook is however that of key ownership functions, in the sense of the rights and duties of shareholders in the governance of the corporation (paragraph 3.1): "The informed use of shareholder rights and the effective exercise of the ownership function are key elements of corporate governance". The impact on a corporation of dispersed or concentrated ownership is considered, and it is acknowledged that (paragraph 1.1) "Considering the existence of multi-layer ownership structures and interconnections among shareholders through the use of control-enhancing mechanisms, a simple dichotomy between 'concentrated' and 'dispersed' ownership might be too simplified to allow a deeper understanding of the diversity of ownership structures" but "ownership" in the sense of *beneficial* ownership is not addressed. <www.oecd.org/daf/ca/Corporate-Governance-Factbook.pdf> accessed 11 December 2018.

35  <www.unglobalcompact.org/what-is-gc/mission> accessed 11 December 2018.

36  <accessed>www.unodc.org/documents/treaties/UNCAC/Publications/Convention/08-50026_E.pdf>accessed 11 December 2018.

37  An exception to the soft law approach is found in the Companies Act 2006 of the UK which in s 172(1) provides: *"(1) A director of a company must act in the way he considers, in good*

activities, then from an operational standpoint it will be compliant; but what these codes exhibit is that the significance of *beneficial* ownership is underplayed, ill-defined or entirely ignored.

### The United Nations Global Compact (2000) and the United Nations Convention Against Corruption (2004)

The United Nations Global Compact was launched in 2000, and its current mission statement is "to support companies to (1) do business responsibly by aligning their strategies and operations with Ten Principles on human rights, labour, environment and anti-corruption, and (2) take strategic action to advance broader societal goals, such as the UN Sustainable Development Goals, with an emphasis on collaboration and innovation". The Global Compact is not a trade association or a regulator charged with enforcing rules on others: participation is voluntary.

As of December 2018, 9,500 businesses and over 3,000 non-business enterprises (civil society organisations, business associations, labour organisations, academic institutions and cities) are participants in the Global Compact.[38] The take-up of membership over an eighteen-year period is not impressive: for example, in its first decade of existence overall implementation rates for the human rights principles stood at 27%.[39] The Global Compact Office has itself been aware from the outset that enthusiasm could diminish, and the Global Compact be rendered impotent as participant energy fades (and thousands of companies have been de-listed for failure to fulfil their commitment to submit progress reports).[40] The United Nations nevertheless regards the Global Compact Office as having a vital role in strengthening the capacity of the United Nations to partner strategically with the private sector, particularly in the potential to develop global

---

faith, would be most likely to promote the success of the company for the benefit of its members as a whole, and in doing so have regard (amongst other matters) to – (a) the likely consequences of any decision in the long term, (b) the interests of the company's employees, (c) the need to foster the company's business relationships with suppliers, customers and others, (d) the impact of the company's operations on the community and the environment, (e) the desirability of the company maintaining a reputation for high standards of business conduct, and (f) the need to act fairly as between members of the company". (Emphasis added) Though s 172(3) reminds the directors that the interests of creditors must also be considered, s 172(1) in imposing corporate governance standards on the directors does so for the benefit of the members and is silent as to the impact on the broader community which is a concomitant of ownership itself. <www.legislation.gov.uk/ukpga/2006/46/section/172> accessed 11 December 2018.
38 <www.unglobalcompact.org/what-is-gc/participants> accessed 11 December 2018.
39 2011 Global Compact Implementation Survey (June 2012) <www.unglobalcompact.org/docs/news_events/8.1/2011_Global_Compact_Implementation_Survey.pdf> accessed 11 December 2018.
40 Steve Waddell, *The Global Compact: An organizational innovation to realize UN Principles* (Global Compact Governance Papers Series, November 2011, United Nations Global Compact, New York, USA) 15.

partnerships between the United Nations and the private sector in addressing the challenges of development.[41]

The Global Compact's Ten Principles are derived from the Universal Declaration of Human Rights,[42] the International Labour Organisation's Declaration on Fundamental Principles and Rights at Work,[43] the Rio Declaration on Environment and Development[44] and the United Nations Convention Against Corruption.[45]

Principle 10, which was adopted in 2004, deals with anti-corruption: "*Businesses should work against corruption in all its forms, including extortion and bribery*".[46] It commits Global Compact participants not only to avoid bribery, extortion and other forms of corruption, but also to develop proactively policies and concrete programmes to address corruption internally and within their supply chains. The underlying legal instrument for Principle 10 is the United Nations Convention Against Corruption (2005) (UNCAC).

However, from an ownership perspective, and the concealment or outright avoidance of beneficial ownership, the Global Compact and the UNCAC are not wholly engaged. Stakeholders are mentioned, but not in terms of *who* they are, but instead of *what damage they may suffer*:

> There are many reasons why the elimination of corruption has become a priority within the business community. Confidence and trust in business among investors, customers, employees and the public have been eroded by recent waves of business ethics scandals around the globe. Companies are learning the hard way that they can be held responsible for not paying enough attention to the actions of their employees, associated companies, business partners and agents.
>
> The rapid development of rules of corporate governance around the world is also prompting companies to focus on anti-corruption measures as part of their mechanisms to express corporate sustainability and to protect their reputations and the interests of their stakeholders. Their anti-corruption systems are increasingly being extended to a range of ethics and integrity issues, and a growing number of investment managers are looking to these systems

41 Resolution of the UN General Assembly 66/223 (28 March 2012) *Towards Global Partnerships* <www.unglobalcompact.org/docs/about_the_gc/government_support/FINAL_A_RES_66_223.pdf> accessed 11 December 2018.

42 <www.un.org/en/universal-declaration-human-rights/index.html> accessed 11 December 2018.

43 <www.ilo.org/declaration/lang--en/index.htm> accessed 11 December 2018.

44 <https://sustainabledevelopment.un.org/rio20/futurewewant> accessed 11 December 2018.

45 <www.unodc.org/unodc/en/treaties/CAC/index.html> accessed 11 December 2018.

46 <www.unglobalcompact.org/what-is-gc/mission/principles/principle-10> accessed 11 December 2018.

as evidence that the companies undertake good and well-managed business practice.[47]

To combat associated legal, reputational and financial risks, and the erosion of internal trust and confidence which flows from unethical behaviour, companies are urged to introduce anti-corruption policies and to join forces with industry peers and other stakeholders "to scale up anti-corruption efforts, level the playing field and create fair competition for all".[48]

This includes signing the Anti-Corruption Call to Action[49] which was launched in 2014 to urge governments to underscore anti-corruption and good governance as fundamental pillars of a sustainable and inclusive global economy (particularly in regard to the 2030 Agenda for Sustainable Development[50]). The Anti-Corruption Call to Action focusses on procurement and contract processes and the need for greater transparency in relation to revenues received by governments from private sector companies. The impact has however not been great – by December 2018 over 250 companies and investors worldwide had signed, but self-evidently this leaves a vast number which have not.

At no point does the Anti-Corruption Call to Action address the question of the significance of ownership of those companies and how the manipulation of ownership structures (or ownership avoidance) can in itself be corrupt. The concentration is on how businesses conduct themselves and not on for whom they operate.

The UNCAC does address issues of beneficial ownership but exclusively as regards banks and non-bank financial institutions in the context of money laundering:

*Article 14. Measures to prevent money-laundering*

1. Each State Party shall:

    (a) Institute a comprehensive domestic regulatory and supervisory regime for banks and non-bank financial institutions, including natural or legal persons that provide formal or informal services for the transmission of money or value and, where appropriate, other bodies particularly susceptible to money laundering, within its competence, in order to deter and detect all forms of money-laundering, which regime shall emphasize requirements for customer and, where appropriate, beneficial owner identification, record-keeping and the reporting of suspicious transactions;

---

47  Taken from <www.unglobalcompact.org/what-is-gc/mission/principles/principle-10> accessed 11 December 2018.
48  Ibid.
49  <www.unglobalcompact.org/take-action/action/anti-corruption-call-to-action>  accessed 11 December 2018.
50  <https://sustainabledevelopment.un.org/post2015/transformingourworld/publication> accessed 11 December 2018.

*Article 52. Prevention and detection of transfers of proceeds of crime*

1. Without prejudice to article 14 of this Convention, each State Party shall take such measures as may be necessary, in accordance with its domestic law, to require financial institutions within its jurisdiction to verify the identity of customers, to take reasonable steps to determine the identity of beneficial owners of funds deposited into high-value accounts and to conduct enhanced scrutiny of accounts sought or maintained by or on behalf of individuals who are, or have been, entrusted with prominent public functions and their family members and close associates. Such enhanced scrutiny shall be reasonably designed to detect suspicious transactions for the purpose of reporting to competent authorities and should not be so construed as to discourage or prohibit financial institutions from doing business with any legitimate customer.

No method of beneficial ownership identification (or definition of either "beneficial" or "ownership") is suggested in the UNCAC, this being left to the competence of the States Parties.[51]

The approach of the UN is therefore to concentrate on an enterprise's activities, without paying much heed to the question of by whom (or for whose benefit) those enterprises are in existence. Ten years after the Global Compact, this absence of requiring an enterprise to look back over its shoulder to see who ultimately stands behind it was again the case, this time not in the field of corruption and criminality, but with the United Nations Guiding Principles on Business and Human Rights.

## *The United Nations Guiding Principles on Business and Human Rights 2011*[52]

In response to the growing concern over corporate responsibility and accountability for the violation of human rights, in 2005 the United Nations appointed Professor John Ruggie as the Secretary General's Special Representative on business and human rights. On 18 June 2008, the UN Human Rights Council

---

51 The United Nations Office on Drugs and Crime in November 2017 released a second edition of its study *"State of Implementation of the United Nations Convention Against Corruption: Criminalisation, Law Enforcement and International Cooperation"* based on the findings and results emanating from the first cycle reviews of the implementation of the UNCAC by 156 States parties (2010–2015) It does not as such address beneficial ownership of entities, though it does review States measures to identify mismatches between a person's known sources of income and their ownership or possession of moveable or immoveable property and assesses the effectiveness of national laws with regard to "the concealment of the true nature, source, location, disposition, movement or ownership of or rights with respect to property" <www.unodc.org/unodc/en/corruption/tools_and_publications/state_of_uncac_implementation.html> at 55, 70 accessed 11 December 2018.
52 Guiding Principles on Business and Human Rights 2011 A/HRC/17/31 <www.ohchr.org/EN/Issues/TransnationalCorporations/Pages/Reports.aspx> accessed 11 December 2018.

unanimously welcomed the framework proposed by John Ruggie. The United Nations Guiding Principles on Business and Human Rights, more commonly known as the Ruggie Principles, were unanimously endorsed by the UN Human Rights Council on 16 June 2011. It was in many ways a false dawn.

The policy framework comprises *three core pillars.*

> *Pillar 1* – the *State duty to protect* against human rights abuses by third parties, including business, through appropriate policies, regulation, and adjudication;
> *Pillar 2* – the *corporate responsibility to respect* human rights, which means to avoid infringing on the human rights of others and addressing adverse human rights impacts with which they are involved; and
> *Pillar 3* – the need for *greater access by victims to effective remedy*, judicial and non-judicial.

The Ruggie Principles are designed so that all three of these pillars interconnect:

> Each pillar is an essential component in an inter-related and dynamic system of preventative and remedial measures: the State duty to protect because it lies at the very core of the international human rights regime; the corporate responsibility to respect because it is the basic expectation society has of business in relation to human rights; and access to remedy because even the most concerted efforts cannot prevent all abuse.[53] [. . .] These Guiding Principles apply to all States and to all business enterprises, both transnational and others, regardless of their size, sector, location, ownership and structure.[54]

Pillar 1 is sufficiently vague to be open to the interpretation that the State's responsibility to regulate includes the regulation of ownership structures, but Foundational Principle 1 makes it clear that the involvement of the State is to be at the operational level of the corporation, not the structural:

> 1. States must protect against human rights abuse within their territory and/ or jurisdiction by third parties, including business enterprises. This requires taking appropriate steps to prevent, investigate, punish and redress such abuse through effective policies, legislation, regulations and adjudication.

The access by victims to effective remedy urged by Pillar 3 is similarly constrained if that remedy is against the corporation itself and not against those who (if there at all) stand behind it.

---

53 Introduction paragraph 6.
54 Foundational Principles, paragraph 14: "*The responsibility of business enterprises to respect human rights applies to all enterprises regardless of their size, sector, operational context, ownership and structure. Nevertheless, the scale and complexity of the means through which enterprises meet that responsibility may vary according to these factors and with the severity of the enterprise's adverse human rights impacts*".

Nearly a decade on from the UN endorsement of the Ruggie Principles, they have not yet had the impact which enthusiasts at the time of their introduction anticipated.[55] Up to 1 January 2019 only eighteen countries, thirteen of which are from Europe, have adopted National Action Plans implementing the Ruggie Principles: the United Kingdom (2013, revised 2016), the Netherlands (2013), Denmark (2014), Finland (2014), Lithuania (2015), Sweden (2015), Norway (2015), Colombia (2015), Switzerland (2016), Germany (2016), Italy (2016), the United States of America (2016), Indonesia (2017), Spain (2017), Chile (2017), the Czech Republic (2017), Ireland (2017) and Georgia (2018). Several other governments including Argentina, Australia, Belgium, Japan, Kenya, Mexico, Peru and Poland are drafting or have drafted National Action Plans.[56] Africa and Asia remain almost wholly unengaged.

John Ruggie gamely continues to promote the Principles which bear his name and to argue that human rights in a business development context ought not to be sidelined, and that "[. . .] far from being at the 'immature' end of a transformative trajectory of business models, respect for human rights, respect for the dignity of every person, is at the very core of the people part of sustainable development".[57]

From an ownership and accountability perspective, the Ruggie Principles are of very limited assistance. They are focussed on what a corporation does, and whether in doing what it does it infringes international human rights norms. Accountability is seen to lie with the corporation itself as a legal person. Yet in most cases a corporation enjoys limited liability.

55 See the dissemination and implementation strategy put forward by the United Nations on 12 August 2012 *Human rights and transnational corporations and other business enterprises* A/67/285 accessible via the General Assembly 67th session <www.ohchr.org/EN/HRBodies/SP/Pages/GA67session.aspx> accessed 11 December 2018. In his 14 November 2016 address to the UN Forum on Business and Human Rights John Ruggie drew attention to the disconnect between the United Nations 2030 Social Development Goals and the Guiding Principles, noting that the Social Development Goals make only "[. . .] a passing reference to relevant standards and agreements that address corporate accountability for human rights harm, including the Guiding Principles". <www.shiftproject.org/resources/viewpoints/globalization-sustainable-development-goals-business-respect-human-rights/> accessed 11 December 2018.
56 *Implementation of the UN Guiding Principles on Business and Human Rights* (European Parliament, Directorate-General for External Policies, February 2017) 8: "Certainly, less declaration and more real political will is needed on the side of governments, as so far their commitments to develop National Action Plans (NAPs) implementing the Guiding Principles have been far too slow to materialise". <www.europarl.europa.eu/RegData/etudes/STUD/2017/578031/EXPO_STU(2017)578031_EN.pdf> accessed 11 December 2018. The Business & Human Rights Resources Centre publishes up-to-date news on the adoption of National Action Plans, including those which adopt the Ruggie Principles <www.business-humanrights.org/en/un-guiding-principles/implementation-tools-examples/implementation-by-governments/by-type-of-initiative/national-action-plans/latest-news-on-national-action-plans/?dateorder=datedesc&page=2&componenttype=all> accessed 1 January 2019.
57 <www.shiftproject.org/resources/viewpoints/globalization-sustainable-development-goals-business-respect-human-rights/> accessed 11 December 2018.

"Ownership and structure" are referred to in Foundational Principle 14, but this serves only to indicate that such considerations may be set aside.[58] The possibility that those who own the corporation may be wholly unaccountable (or that the corporation may have no owner at all) is not in contemplation.

Suggestions that the voluntary dissemination by corporations of their data would be in the spirit of the Ruggie Principles and constitute an act of corporate philanthropy[59] are unlikely to obtain any traction when it comes to ownership disclosure.

### IGCN Global Governance Principles[60] and IGCN Global Stewardship Principles[61]

The ICGN[62] Global Governance Principles 2017 (5th edition) in referring to the beneficial ownership of shares do so in conventional, and arguably perfunctory, terms:

#### 8.12 Shareholder identification

The board should ensure that the company maintains a record of the registered owners of its shares or those holding voting rights over its shares.

58 The commentary on Foundational Principle 14 concentrates on the size of an enterprise rather than its ownership, though it strikes a glancing blow at group structures without pursuing the idea any further: *"The means through which a business enterprise meets its responsibility to respect human rights will be proportional to, among other factors, its size. Small and medium-sized enterprises may have less capacity as well as more informal processes and management structures than larger companies, so their respective policies and processes will take on different forms. But some small and medium-sized enterprises can have severe human rights impacts, which will require corresponding measures regardless of their size. Severity of impacts will be judged by their scale, scope and irremediable character. The means through which a business enterprise meets its responsibility to respect human rights may also vary depending on whether, and the extent to which, it conducts business through a corporate group or individually. However, the responsibility to respect human rights applies fully and equally to all business enterprises"*. Guiding Principles on Business (n 52).
59 Matt Stempeck, 'Sharing Data Is a Form of Corporate Philanthropy' *Harvard Business Review* (24 July 2014) <https://hbr.org/2014/07/sharing-data-is-a-form-of-corporate-philanthropy> accessed 11 December 2018 referred to in Mark Latonero and Zachard Gold, 'Data, Human Rights & Human Security' (n 16).
60 <http://icgn.flpbks.com/icgn-global-governance-principles-2017/> accessed 11 December 2018.
61 <http://icgn.flpbks.com/icgn-global-stewardship-principles/#p=1> accessed 11 December 2018.
62 <www.icgn.org/> accessed 11 December 2018. Established in 1995, ICGN describes itself as "an investor-led organisation" whose "mission is to promote effective standards of corporate governance and investor stewardship to advance efficient markets and sustainable economies world-wide". Its register of members, who are said to be "drawn from more than 43 markets" is available at <www.icgn.org/members/our-members> accessed 11 December 2018.

Registered shareholders, or their agents, should provide the company (*where anonymity rules do not preclude this*) with the identity of beneficial owners or holders of voting rights when requested in a timely manner. Shareholders should be able to review this record of registered owners of shares or those holding voting rights over shares. *It is ultimately the shareholders' responsibility to identify themselves by ensuring they appear on the shareholder register directly in their own name and in any call for vote confirmation.* (emphasis added)

*8.17 Vote confirmation*

Companies should confirm to shareholders (*where the beneficial owner appears on the share register*) whether or not their votes have been validly recorded and formally counted. *This normally can only be provided where the institutional investors hold shares in their own names rather than through pooled or omnibus accounts which commingle the securities of multiple investors.* (emphasis added)

Although this is evidence of an acknowledgement that the ultimate ownership of a corporation is relevant for purposes of corporate governance, placing the responsibility on the shareholders to reveal whether they are beneficially entitled to the shares, and acknowledging that institutional investors may hold shares for undisclosed multiple investors, robs these principles of much of their effectiveness. Providing an exemption "where anonymity rules do not preclude this" further weakens the position. In any event, a corporation may be under no obligation to look behind the names on its share register to ascertain any trustee or nominee relationship.

The principles come closer to the mark when dealing with related party transactions ("RPTs") but offer no guidance as to what "beneficial" or "controlling" means:

*8.5 Shareholder approval of RPTs*

Shareholders should have the right to approve significant RPTs above an appropriate materiality threshold, and this should be based on the approval of a majority of disinterested shareholders.

The board should submit the transaction for shareholder approval in the notice of the meeting and disclose (both before concluding the transaction and in the company's annual report):

a)  the identity of the ultimate beneficiaries including any controlling owner and any party affiliated with the controlling owner with any direct/indirect ownership interest in the company;

b)  other businesses in which the controlling shareholder has a significant interest; and

c) shareholder agreements (e.g. commitments to related party payments such as licence fees, service agreements and loans).

Principle 8.5c) is however a timely reminder that even in the case of a registered shareholder who is (in English legal terminology) both legal and equitable owner, they may have relinquished the benefit of such ownership through encumbering the shareholding, thereby making an undisclosed third party the de facto beneficial owner.[63]

The IGCN Global Stewardship Principles (2016) are wholly silent on beneficial ownership.

## Guiding Principles issued by the Islamic Financial Services Board[64]

The Islamic Financial Services Board (IFSB)[65] describes itself as "an international standard-setting organisation that promotes and enhances the soundness and stability of the Islamic financial services industry by issuing global prudential standards and guiding principles for the industry, broadly defined to include banking, capital markets and insurance sectors".

The following guidance encompasses the main themes addressed by the IFSB:

- Guiding principles on corporate governance for institutions offering only Islamic financial services (excluding Islamic insurance (Takaful) institutions and Islamic mutual funds) (IFSB-3, December 2006)
- Guiding principles for Islamic collective investment schemes (IFSB-6, January 2009)
- Guiding principles on conduct of business for institutions offering Islamic financial services (IFSB-9, December 2009)
- Guiding principles on Shari'ah governance systems for institutions offering Islamic financial services (IFSB-10, December 2009)
- Revised guidance on key elements in the supervisory review process of institutions offering Islamic financial services (excluding Islamic insurance (Takaful) institutions and Islamic collective investment schemes) (IFSB-16, March 2014)
- Guiding principles on disclosure requirements for Islamic capital market products (*ṣukūk* and Islamic collective investment schemes) (IFSB-19, April 2017)

IFSB-3 (paragraph 65(ii))[66] recommends that institutions offering only Islamic financial services ("IIFS") make individual account holders aware, inter alia, of

---

63 See the discussion on nominee shareholders and de facto ownership in ch 2.
64 All publications of the IFSB are available online in Arabic and in English at <www.ifsb.org/published.php> accessed 11 December 2018.
65 <www.ifsb.org/> accessed 11 December 2018.
66 Similar wording is found in IFSB-6 paragraph 35(iii).

the "basic ownership structure – for example, major share ownership and voting rights, beneficial owners, major shareholder participation on the board or in senior management positions, shareholder meetings". It contains no guidance on how to ascertain what constitutes a *beneficial* owner however. Nevertheless, there is a strong emphasis on corporate governance (paragraph 71):

> While the notion of "corporate governance" could be considered as a modern creation, the norms and values that are attached to this notion are already synonymous with Islam. Within its comprehensively prescribed way of life, Islam has always promoted good ethics, strong morals, unshakeable integrity and honesty of the highest order. The concern of the proponents of good governance that the separation of ownership and management of a firm may lead to an agency problem has long been addressed in the Qur'ān, which enshrines the importance of ethics not only in contracts and residual contracts but, ultimately, in accountability to God.

IFSB-9 does not expressly address legal or beneficial ownership, but in Principle 4 (paragraphs 33 to 36) states:

### *Principle 4: Information about Clients*

An IIFS shall take steps to ensure that it understands the nature and circumstances of its clients, so that it offers those products most suitable for their needs, as well as offering financing only for Shari'ah-compliant projects.

33. The principle of "know your customer" (KYC) is well known in banking circles and has particular relevance in the context of avoiding money laundering and transactions intended to finance criminal or terrorist organisations. In these Guiding Principles, the principle regarding information about clients obviously includes KYC but has a broader import, as it also includes having the capability of understanding a client's needs in order to avoid mis-selling (see Principles 1 and 2).11 In addition, an IIFS needs to know that its customers' businesses and the purpose of any financing provided are consistent with the Shari'ah.

IFSB-10 also addresses corporate governance, from a uniquely Islamic perspective. It focusses exclusively on the competence, independence, confidentiality and conduct of members of the Shari'ah Board, which is a corporate governance body within a corporation, separate from its board of directors:[67]

---

67 IFSB-10 para 22 states: "As the legal framework in most jurisdictions holds the BOD as the body ultimately responsible with regard to the governance of an IIFS, the *Shari'ah* board has to be clear on the limits of its own power. Respect for each other's role and function is crucial, as good governance requires all organs of governance to work *with*, and not against, one another. The BOD, the *Shari'ah* board, the management and the supervisory authority,

*(Paragraph 10)*

10. The IFSB has consistently required in its standards and guiding principles that every IIFS shall have adequate and effective access to a Shari'ah board, who will have a clear mandate and responsibility for ensuring that the IIFS adheres to Shari'ah rules and principles with respect to all Islamic financial products and services that it offers.[. . .]

*(Paragraph 14)*

14. In line with internationally recognised corporate governance standards such as those issued by the OECD, IIFS should exercise proper discretion in choosing Shari'ah governance structures so that they appropriately safeguard the fulfilment of fiduciary duties including good faith, care, skill and diligence towards all their stakeholders. [. . .]

Though IFSB-16, augmenting IFSB-3, deals extensively with risk assessment and risk management, including related party transactions, risk is perceived largely in investment terms as financial and reputational. Risks associated with the ownership of the IIFS are addressed in terms of "know your customer" reputational risk but without reference to issues of *beneficial ownership*:

*(Paragraph 247)*

247. Supervisory authorities should expect an IIFS to identify potential sources of reputational risk to which it is exposed and appropriate policies to manage such risk. These potential sources include the IIFS's business lines, liabilities, affiliated operations and failure to apply rigorous customer acceptance procedures (i.e. any deficiency in Know-Your-Customer (KYC) procedures and acceptance of customers with higher risk profiles or inadequate documentation), off-balance sheet vehicles [. . .] and the markets in which it operates.

IFSB-19 when setting disclosure requirements for Islamic capital market products, specifically the *ṣukūk*,[68] stresses in Principle 3 (section 2.4.4) that "the structure of the *ṣukūk* should be described with sufficient clarity to allow an investor

---

as well as other stakeholders such as the customers, suppliers and the public, should always seek to improve communications among themselves in order to avoid misunderstandings and confusion, in line with the *Quranic* injunction in *Surah Al-Maidah* verse 2: '*Help ye one another in righteousness and piety, but help ye not one another in sin and rancour; Fear Allah, for Allah is strict in punishment*'".

68 IFSB-19 p 31 defines a *ṣukūk* as: "Certificates that represent a proportional undivided ownership right in tangible assets, or a pool of tangible assets and other types of assets. These assets

to understand it and assess any risks associated with it, including any legal risks associated with the interactions of multiple parties within the *ṣukūk* structure under various agreements". In doing so, the IFSB seeks to break free from what it appears to regard as terminology unfit for purpose:

*(Paragraph 104)*

104. The precise legal interests of the issuer and ṣukūk holders in the asset should be disclosed, without solely relying on terms such as "legal owner-ship", "beneficial ownership" or "usufruct right", whose meanings may vary across jurisdictions. In addition, any particular rationale for choosing a more limited legal interest where a more extensive one exists should be explained.

The IFSB goes further, and in relation to a *ṣukūk* proposes:

*(Paragraph 106)*

106. Where a trustee or delegate trustee or agent is appointed to act for ṣukūk holders, disclosure should describe:

(a) the rights, obligations and powers of the trustee, delegate trustee or agent;
(b) the circumstances and prerequisites for the trustee, delegate trustee or agent acting on behalf of ṣukūk holders (e.g. requirements for valid instructions and indemnity requirements);
(c) the role of the trustee, delegate trustee or agent in default, accelera-tion, enforcement or restructuring of the ṣukūk;
(d) provisions for change or termination of the trustee, delegate trustee or agent; and
(e) which party will be responsible for the fees and expenses of the trus-tee, delegate trustee or agent.

The work of the IFSB stands out amongst corporate governance initiatives in placing so high an emphasis on ethics. Preferring not to rely on flexibly defined terms such as "legal ownership", "beneficial ownership" or "usufruct right" it looks to "precise legal interests", and in this context addressed the role of trustees and agents. This is clearly an evolutionary approach and one which appears not to exclude the possibility of a future code aimed specifically at those who own, control or manipulate structures.

---

could be in a specific project or specific investment activity that is Sharī'ah-compliant". See ch 2 for a fuller description of a *ṣukūk*.

### The UK Corporate Governance Code (July 2018)[69]

The UK Corporate Governance Code (July 2018) is issued by the Financial Reporting Council ("FRC")[70] The stated application of the Code is "to all companies with a premium listing, whether incorporated in the UK or elsewhere" and applies to accounting periods beginning on or after 1 January 2019.

The Code focusses exclusively on the proper functioning of a corporation's board of directors, which must be "effective and entrepreneurial"; on how responsibilities within a board are divided; on the adoption of "a formal, rigorous and transparent procedure and an effective succession plan" for board membership; on audit, risk and internal controls; and on remuneration. In the Introduction to the Code, it is made clear that the "shareholders' role in governance is to appoint the directors and the auditors and to satisfy themselves that an appropriate governance structure is in place". To this end, the board must report to the shareholders on its adherence to corporate governance requirements under the Code, and ensure that it has a clear understanding of the views of shareholders, with specific reference to section 172 Companies Act 2006.[71]

The Code has no statutory force, and in referring to section 172 Companies Act 2006 acknowledges that it adds nothing to existing statutory provisions.

No questions relating to share ownership, beneficial or otherwise, are addressed. This unconsciously (or perhaps disingenuously) betrays the fatal flaw in perpetuating the shareholder-centric myth: in the case of "premium listed" companies any shareholding may be transitory, based on short-term returns, and a shareholder may have only a minimal understanding of the company's trading activities during such a relatively brief period of ownership. Correspondingly, the corporation will have no incentive to monitor the beneficial ownership of its shares.[72]

### Corporate governance and beneficial ownership

With the sole exception of the IFSB, beneficial ownership transparency is not a priority under these sampled codes of corporate governance. When mentioned

---

69  <www.frc.org.uk/getattachment/88bd8c45-50ea-4841-95b0-d2f4f48069a2/2018-UK-Corporate-Governance-Code-FINAL.pdf> accessed 11 December 2018.
70  The FRC (<www.frc.org.uk> accessed 11 December 2018) states in the introduction to the Code: "The FRC's mission is to promote transparency and integrity in business. The FRC sets the UK Corporate Governance and Stewardship Codes and UK standards for accounting an actuarial work; monitors and takes action to promote the quality of corporate reporting; and operates independent arrangements for accountants and actuaries. As the Competent Authority for audit in the UK the FRC sets auditing and ethical standards and monitors and enforces audit quality".
71  See n 37.
72  See Prem Sikka, 'Why the New Code Governing Corporations Isn't Worth the Paper It's Written on' *Left Foot Forward* (18 July 2018) <https://leftfootforward.org/2018/07/why-the-new-code-governing-corporations-isnt-worth-the-paper-its-written-on-frc-caril lion-bhs/> accessed 11 December 2018.

at all, it is either regarded as the shareholders' responsibility to identify themselves, or where beneficial ownership is recognised as an issue, no accountability mechanism is proposed. Neither is of the slightest practical use as a transparency strategy. As with the seemingly comprehensive work of the G20,[73] there is on closer examination mere lip service and good intentions, with very little legal or commercial substance and no compelling evidence of a genuine desire on the part of those framing the codes to compel an enterprise to understand fully whom it is ultimately benefitting.

## Privacy and business human rights[74]

The well-spring of privacy as a human right is Article 12 of the Universal Declaration of Human Rights (1948)[75] which states:

> No one shall be subjected to arbitrary interference with his privacy, family, home or correspondence, nor to attacks upon his honour and reputation. Everyone has the right to the protection of the law against such interference or attacks.

This was formalised in international law in the International Covenant on Civil and Political Rights 1966[76] ("ICCPR"). Article 17 of the ICCPR states:

1   No one shall be subjected to arbitrary or unlawful interference with his privacy, family, home or correspondence, nor to unlawful attacks on his honour and reputation.
2   Everyone has the right to the protection of the law against such interference or attacks.[77]

---

73  See ch 3.
74  A full review of business and human rights is outside the scope of this book. See Nadia Bernaz, *Business and Human Rights: History, Law and Policy – Bridging the Accountability Gap* (Routledge, London and New York, 2017).
75  <www.un.org/en/universal-declaration-human-rights/> accessed 11 December 2018.
76  <www.ohchr.org/en/professionalinterest/pages/CCPR.aspx> accessed 11 December 2018. The current signatories to the ICCPR are shown at <https://treaties.un.org/Pages/ViewDetails.aspx?chapter=4&clang=_en&mtdsg_no=IV-4&src=IND> accessed 11 December 2018.
77  Near identical wording is found in the American Convention on Human Rights (1969) *Article 11. Right to Privacy 1. Everyone has the right to have his honor respected and his dignity recognised. 2. No one may be the object of arbitrary or abusive interference with his private life, his family, his home, or his correspondence, or of unlawful attacks on his honor or reputation. 3. Everyone has the right to the protection of the law against such interference or attacks.* <www.cidh.oas.org/basicos/english/basic3.american%20convention.htm> accessed 11 December 2018. The Charter of Fundamental Rights of the European Union (2000) is briefer: *Everyone has the right to respect for his or her private and family life, home and communications* (Art 7) and *the right to protection of personal data* (Art 8), and is forward-thinking in crossing the line into commerce by recognising *the freedom to conduct business in accordance with*

Three decades ago Article 17 was the subject of CCPR General Comment No. 16, issued by the then UN Human Rights Committee.[78] It is a far-sighted commentary on the threats posed by excessive surveillance and the arbitrary collection and storage of personal data, and the need to curb "interference" as far as possible. It takes pains to define "unlawful" and "arbitrary interference", but concedes the relativism of "privacy":

> 7. As all persons live in society, the protection of privacy is necessarily relative. However, the competent public authorities should only be able to call for such information relating to an individual's private life the knowledge of which is essential in the interests of society as understood under the Covenant. [. . .]

However, as far as concerns the ICCPR, what is meant by "privacy" remains largely undefined over half a century after Article 17 was formulated. In the words of Sarah Joseph and Melissa Castan:[79]

> Privacy is a notoriously difficult term to define. [. . .] A compromise definition could be that a right to privacy comprises 'freedom from unwarranted and unreasonable intrusions into activities that society recognizes as belonging to the realm of individual autonomy'.[80] The 'sphere of autonomy' has been described as 'the field of action [that] does not touch upon the liberty of others' [. . .][81]

The basic difficulty therefore in assessing the human right to privacy in the context of business activities is that the concept of privacy in human rights jurisprudence remains more of an art than a science.

In 2009 the UN Human Rights Council examined the promotion and protection of human rights and fundamental freedoms while countering terrorism, and Special Rapporteur Martin Scheinin reviewed the interrelationship between privacy and human rights in broader terms:

*Community law and national laws and practices* (Art16) <www.europarl.europa.eu/charter/pdf/text_en.pdf> accessed 11 December 2018. The concept is absent from the African Charter on Human and Peoples' Rights (the Banjul Charter) (1981) however <www.achpr.org/instruments/achpr/> accessed 11 December 2018.

78 <https://tbinternet.ohchr.org/_layouts/treatybodyexternal/Download.aspx?symbolno=INT%2fCCPR%2fGEC%2f6624&Lang=en> accessed 11 December 2018.

79 *The International Covenant on Civil and Political Rights* (3rd Edition, Oxford University Press, Oxford, 2013) paragraph 16.01.

80 Quoting S E Wilborn, 'Revisiting the Public/Private Distinction: Employee Monitoring in the Workplace' 32 *Georgia Law Review* 825 (1998) 83.

81 Quoting M Novak, *UN Covenant on Civil and Political Rights: CPPR Commentary* (2nd Edition, N.P. Engel Verlag, Kehl am rhein, Germany, 2005) 378.

11. *Privacy is a fundamental human right that has been defined as the presumption that individuals should have an area of autonomous development, interaction and liberty, a "private sphere" with or without interaction with others and free from State intervention and free from excessive unsolicited intervention by other uninvited individuals.*[82] The right to privacy has evolved along two different paths. Universal human rights instruments have focused on the negative dimension of the right to privacy, prohibiting any arbitrary interference with a person's privacy, family, home or correspondence, while some regional and domestic instruments have also included a positive dimension: everyone has the right to respect for his/her private and family life, his/her home and correspondence, or the right to have his/her dignity, personal integrity or good reputation recognized and respected. While privacy is not always directly mentioned as a separate right in constitutions, nearly all States recognize its value as a matter of constitutional significance. In some countries, the right to privacy emerges by extension of the common law of breach of confidence, the right to liberty, freedom of expression or due process. In other countries, the right to privacy emerges as a religious value. *The right to privacy is therefore not only a fundamental human right, but also a human right that supports other human rights and forms the basis of any democratic society*[83]

(emphasis added)

The Special Rapporteur acknowledges (in paragraph 13) that "the right to privacy is not an absolute right" and that there are "situations where States have a legitimate power to limit the right of privacy under international human rights law". Nevertheless, "[e]very instance of interference needs to be subject to critical assessment".

In the international human rights context of the ownership debate, the assertion that privacy is a mere expression of autonomy is open to question, if for no other reason than the exploitation of confidentiality and anonymity has as its goal the avoidance of accountability which ownership embodies and hence a constriction of the liberty of others.

---

82 Quoted from Lord Lester and D Pannick (eds), *Human Rights Law and Practice* (Butterworth, London, 2004) para 4.82.

83 A/HRC/13/37 *Report of the Special Rapporteur on the promotion and protection of human rights and fundamental freedoms while countering terrorism, Martin Scheinin* 28 December 2009 paras 11 and 13 <http://www2.ohchr.org/english/bodies/hrcouncil/docs/13session/a-hrc-13-37.pdf> accessed 11 December 2018. This approach is followed in the context of the use of mass surveillance as a counter-terrorism initiative in A/69/397 *Promotion and protection of human rights and fundamental freedoms while countering terrorism* 23 September 2014 para 28 <www.un.org/ga/search/view_doc.asp?symbol=A/69/397> accessed 11 December 2018.

*Convention for the Protection of Human Rights and Fundamental Freedoms 1950 ("the European Convention on Human Rights")*[84]

What privacy and property human rights may be called upon are established by international and regional declaration and convention. A comprehensive, comparative review of the vast body of human rights instruments is outside the scope of this book. The European Convention on Human Rights serves as an example.

It must be borne in mind that the European Convention on Human Rights was drafted and adopted at a time when following the disruption caused by the Second World War there was a genuine threat to European liberalism. The ideals of the liberal state espoused by the larger part of Western Europe had been threatened by totalitarianism and barbarism and were confronting a rapidly expanding communist Eastern Europe. The European Convention on Human Rights is as much a battle cry for economic liberalism and democracy as it is a shield and sword for individual human rights.

> *It would be meaningless to disconnect the Convention's democratic model from the core values of a capitalist system since it embraces the value system of the liberal state, in which the company as protagonist of private enterprise has a natural place.*[85]

Article 8 of the European Convention on Human Rights states:

## Right to respect for private and family life

1    Everyone has the right to respect for his private and family life, his home and his correspondence.
2    There shall be no interference by a public authority with the exercise of this right except such as in accordance with the law and is necessary in a democratic society in the interests of national security, public safety or *the economic well-being of the country*, for the prevention of disorder *or crime*, for the protection of health or morals, *or for the protection of the rights and freedoms of others*. (emphasis added)[86]

---

84  <www.coe.int/en/web/conventions/search-on-treaties/-/conventions/treaty/005> accessed 11 December 2018.
85  Marius Emberland, *The Human Rights of Companies* (Oxford University Press, Oxford, 2005) 42.
86  For a discussion on the jurisprudence of the European Court of Human Rights in relation to Article 8 and the meaning of privacy see Kirsty Hughes, 'The Social Value of Privacy' in Beate Roessler and Dorota Mokrosinska (eds), *Social Dimensions of Privacy, Interdisciplinary Perspectives* (Cambridge University Press, Cambridge, 2015) ch 12.

The First Protocol to the European Convention on Human Rights (1952)[87] states in Article 1:

> Every natural or legal person is entitled to the peaceful enjoyment of his possessions. No one shall be deprived of his possessions except in the public interest and subject to the conditions provided for by law and by the general principles of international law.
>
> The preceding provisions shall not, however, in any way impair the right of a State to enforce such laws as it deems necessary to control the use of property in accordance with the general interest *or to secure the payment of taxes or other contributions or penalties.* (emphasis added)

Even if "peaceful enjoyment" were deemed to include the right of ownership anonymity, and that right of anonymity were characterised as a possession, this would in no way impair the right of the State to require disclosure if thought to be for the economic well-being of the country, the prevention of crime or to secure the payment of taxes.[88]

## *The human rights of companies*

That business structures such as corporations have human rights in their own right, and not merely through the rights of those who own them, may seem counter-intuitive. Certainly, the current vogue is to concentrate on corporate governance and the role which corporations play in the breaches of the human rights of others. But in the battle to preserve anonymity of ownership and concomitant accountability avoidance, corporations may pray in aid their human rights. Just as their adherence to international standards of corporate governance may provide them with a shield, the pursuit of human rights furnishes corporations and other "legal persons" with a sword.

The phrase "the human rights of companies" seems on first hearing to be absurd. A company, unlike a human person, has no soul to be dammed and no body to be kicked. The man in the street would say that human rights are for human beings not for non-human persons. However, the European Convention on Human Rights is not merely a treaty for the protection of "human rights" but

---

87  <www.coe.int/en/web/conventions/search-on-treaties/-/conventions/treaty/009> accessed 11 December 2018.

88  See the discussion in Reuven S Avi-Yonah and Gianluca Mazzoni, *Taxation and Human Rights: A Delicate Balance* (University of Michigan Public Law Research Paper No. 520, 5 September 2016) <https://papers.ssrn.com/sol3/papers.cfm?abstract_id=2834883> accessed 11 December 2018. The authors comment: "The right to privacy does not share the same scope of protection between tax and non-tax context. The notion of privacy in tax law is not as broad as in tort law or in constitutional law. Taxpayers cannot claim the right to be let alone or be free from unwarranted governmental intrusion. The reason is that, at stake, there is also the country's economic wellbeing to be protected".

additionally of "fundamental freedoms". It is not disputed that individuals need protection from governmental excesses and that human rights apply to natural persons and in particular the weak and vulnerable. But this is not the whole story.

Article 34 of the European Convention on Human Rights states

> The Court may receive applications from any person, non-governmental organization or group of individuals claiming to be the victim of a violation [. . .]

A common law interpretation of "person" would include legal persons such as companies. The authentic[89] French text however refers to "personne physique", and so companies are brought within the scope of European Convention protection by being "non-governmental organizations".

This is reinforced by the wording of Article 1 of the European Convention which states that the signatories shall secure to *everyone* (*toute personne*) within their jurisdiction the rights and freedoms of the European Convention:

> The High Contracting Parties shall secure to everyone within their jurisdiction the rights and freedoms defined in Section I of this Convention.
>
> Les Hautes Parties contractantes reconnaissent à toute personne relevant de leur juridiction les droits et libertés définis au titre I de la présente Convention.

Common law statutes are interpreted literally – that is to say the words on the page are given their ordinary and reasonable meaning, and no account is taken of any debate which led up to the drafting of the statute or of any policy which prompted its being enacted. This is not the case in Civil Law jurisdictions. The European Court of Human Rights in Strasburg[90] adopts the European teleological approach which means that regardless of the wording set down in the European Convention the Court must examine the purpose which the European Convention was intended to achieve and can reflect in determining those purposes how the original aims of the European Convention drafters have been augmented by evolved social and political changes since the 1950s.

The "travaux preparatoires" of the European Convention (records of the many meetings and sittings out of which the text of the European Convention emerged) make it plain that corporate bodies were intended to be included.[91]

---

89 *La Cour peut être saisie d'une requête par toute personne physique, toute organisation non gouvernementale ou tout groupe de particuliers qui se prétend victime d'une violation [. . .]* <www.echr.coe.int/Documents/Convention_FRA.pdf> accessed 11 December 2018. Only the English and French versions of the European Convention and the Protocols are authentic, as confirmed at <www.echr.coe.int/pages/home.aspx?p=basictexts> accessed 11 December 2018.
90 <www.echr.coe.int/Documents/Court_in_brief_ENG.pdf> accessed 11 December 2018.
91 The full text may be accessed at <www.echr.coe.int/Documents/Library_TravPrep_Table_ENG.pdf> accessed 11 December 2018. The discussion concerning draft Art 25(1) which was

*"Piercing the corporate veil"*[2]

The European Court of Human Rights does not generally speaking pierce the corporate veil. Shareholders cannot achieve "victim" status under Article 34 of the European Convention for matters which concern the *corporate person* and not directly their own rights. In the case of *Agrotexim Hellas SA and Others v Greece 1995*[93] the Court stated:

> The piercing of the corporate veil or the disregarding of a company's legal personality will be justified only in exceptional circumstances, in particular where it is clearly established that it is impossible for the company to apply to the Convention Institutions through the organs set up under its Articles of Incorporation or – in the event of liquidation – through its liquidators.

The concomitant of this is that a human rights assessment of a corporation will not depend on the human rights profile of its shareholders (let alone its beneficial owners). It follows that the European Convention on Human Rights does not compel ownership disclosure as a pre-condition of protection.

## Privacy and corporations: an American perspective

Over a century ago the US Courts ruled unambiguously on privacy and corporations as legal entities: privacy does not apply to them, because they are creatures of the State, and their very existence, let alone their rights, is wholly dependent on the will of the State.

> Conceding that the witness was an officer of the corporation under investigation, and that he was entitled to assert the rights of the corporation with respect to the production of its books and papers, we are of the opinion that *there is a clear distinction in this particular between an individual and a corporation, and that the latter has no right to refuse to submit its books and papers for an examination at the suit of the State.* The individual may stand upon his constitutional rights as a citizen [. . .] Upon the other hand, the corporation is a creature of the State. It is presumed to be incorporated for the benefit of the public. It receives certain special privileges and franchises, and holds them subject to the laws of the State and the limitations of its charter [. . .] It would be a strange anomaly to hold that a State, having chartered a corporation to make use of certain franchises, could not in the exercise of its sovereignty inquire how these franchises had been employed, and whether

---

to become Art 34 is available (only in French) at <www.echr.coe.int/LibraryDocs/Travaux/ECHRTravaux-ART25-1-DH(64)1-FR3806984.pdf> accessed 11 December 2018.

92 See ch 2 for a discussion of this concept.

93 [1995] ECHR 42.

they had been abused, and demand the production of the corporate books and papers for that purpose.

> (*Hale v. Henkel* 201 U.S. 43, 74–75 (1906)) [Emphasis added]

While they may and should have protection from unlawful demands made in the name of public investigation, *corporations can claim no equality with individuals in the enjoyment of a right to privacy.* They are endowed with public attributes. They have a collective impact upon society, from which they derive the privilege of acting as artificial entities. The Federal Government allows them the privilege of engaging in interstate commerce. Favors from government often carry with them an enhanced measure of regulation. Even if one were to regard the request for information in this case as caused by nothing more than official curiosity, nevertheless law-enforcing agencies have a legitimate right to satisfy themselves that corporate behaviour is consistent with the law and the public interest.

> (*California Bankers Ass'n v. Shultz 94 S.Ct. 1494, 1519–20,*
> *416 U.S. 21, 65–66 (U.S.Cal. 1974)* [Emphasis added]

The conscious rejection, in the context of privacy, of a distinction between physical (or natural) persons and legal persons found in Article 34 of the European Convention on Human Rights[94] is alien to American jurisprudence.

## Conclusions

Is there a right to maintain full anonymity of beneficial ownership under commercial trade law and practice, principles of corporate governance and applicable business human rights? It does appear those who, from whatever motive and whatever it is they wish to conceal, assert rights of privacy have merely to choose the forum most favourable to themselves, and sit tight.

In terms of *commercial trade law*, the ownership of a corporation and the activities which that corporation undertakes are compartmentalised. The contractual underpinnings of trading activities of an enterprise are neither public property nor matters of public knowledge, and so are confidential (although the broad-brush approach in American jurisprudence would suggest otherwise). In the context of accountability avoidance the public interest protecting confidence may be outweighed by some other countervailing public interest which favours disclosure. That this is a balancing act is not necessarily true when it comes to questions of ownership disclosure. There is no common or international law ground for an assertion that details of the ownership of an entity constitute a form of commercial confidential information worthy of or entitled to protection.

---

94  See n 91.

With the singular exception of Islamic finance, beneficial ownership is underplayed, ill-defined or entirely ignored in *codes of corporate governance*. Where it is occasionally referred to, this is in the context of funds flow for anti-money laundering purposes, rather than addressing asset ownership or stops short at self-disclosure by shareholders. None provides a working definition of "beneficial ownership" or proposes any accountability mechanism. None requires a corporation to look over its shoulder to those who own, control or benefit from them.

In terms of *international human rights*, the United Nations recognises privacy as a fundamental human right and attempts a definition. Corporations have human rights in their own right and not merely through the rights of those who own them. Just as their adherence to international standards of corporate governance may provide them with a shield, the pursuit of human rights furnishes corporations and other "legal persons" with a sword. Ownership disclosure is not a pre-condition of a right to protection.

The fundamental weakness is the overuse of the word "privacy". There is no clear definition of "privacy", whether the approach is philosophical, commercial or based in human rights, for the very reason that the concept of "privacy", in the same way as the concept of "ownership", is not amenable to a monolithic multi-jurisdictional, multi-disciplinary definition.

## Bibliography

### Cases

*Agrotexim Hellas SA and Others v Greece 1995* [1995] ECHR 42
*Attorney General v Guardian Newspapers and Others (No 2)* [1988] 3 All ER 545
*California Bankers Ass'n v. Shultz 94 S.Ct. 1494, 1519–20, 416 U.S. 21, 65–66 (U.S.Cal. 1974)*
*Coco v AN Clark (Engineers) Ltd* [1969] RPC 41
*Hale v. Henkel 201 U.S. 43, 74–75 (1906)*
*Hellewell v Chief Constable of Derbyshire* [1995] 4 All ER 473
*Katz v United States*, 389 U.S. 347 (1967)
*OBG Ltd and another v Allan and others; Douglas and another v Hello! Ltd and others (No 3); Mainstream Properties Ltd v Young and others* [2007] UKHL 21

### Legislation and regulations

Companies Act 2006 <www.legislation.gov.uk/ukpga/2006/46/> accessed 11 December 2018 (UK)
Trade Secrets (Enforcement, etc.) Regulations 2018 <www.legislation.gov.uk/uksi/2018/597/contents/made> accessed 11 December 2018 (UK)

### European documents

Directive (EU) 2016/943 on the Protection of Undisclosed Know-how and Business Information (trade secrets) Against Their Unlawful Acquisition, Use and

Disclosure. <https://eur-lex.europa.eu/legal-content/EN/TXT/HTML/?uri=C ELEX:32016L0943&from=EN> accessed 11 December 2018

European Commission *2018 Reform of EU Data Protection Rules* <https:// ec.europa.eu/commission/priorities/justice-and-fundamental-rights/ data-protection/2018-reform-eu-data-protection-rules_en> accessed 11 December 2018

———— Trade Secrets <http://ec.europa.eu/growth/industry/intellectual-prop erty/trade-secrets_en> accessed 11 December 2018

General Data Protection Regulation (GDPR) 27 April 2016 <https://eur-lex. europa.eu/legal-content/EN/TXT/HTML/?uri=CELEX:02016R0679-20160504&from=EN> accessed 11 December 2018

*Implementation of the UN Guiding Principles on Business and Human Rights* (Euro-pean Parliament, Directorate-General for External Policies, February 2017) <www.europarl.europa.eu/RegData/etudes/STUD/2017/578031/EXPO_ STU(2017)578031_EN.pdf> accessed 11 December 2018

## International documents

African Charter on Human and Peoples' Rights (the Banjul Charter) (1981) <www. achpr.org/instruments/achpr/> accessed 11 December 2018

American Convention on Human Rights (1969) <www.cidh.oas.org/basicos/eng-lish/basic3.american%20convention.htm> accessed 11 December 2018

Convention for the Protection of Human Rights and Fundamental Freedoms 1950 ("The European Convention on Human Rights") <www.coe.int/en/web/conven tions/search-on-treaties/-/conventions/treaty/005> accessed 11 December 2018

———— First Protocol (1952) <www.coe.int/en/web/conventions/search-on-trea ties/-/conventions/treaty/009> accessed 11 December 2018

International Labour Organisation's Declaration on Fundamental Principles and Rights at Work 1998 <www.ilo.org/declaration/lang--en/index.htm> accessed 11 December 2018

## United Nations documents

A/69/397 *Promotion and Protection of Human Rights and Fundamental Freedoms While Countering Terrorism* (23 September 2014) <www.un.org/ga/search/view_ doc.asp?symbol=A/69/397> accessed 11 December 2018

A/HRC/13/37 *Report of the Special Rapporteur on the Promotion and Protection of Human Rights and Fundamental Freedoms While Countering Terrorism*, Mar-tin Scheinin (28 December 2009) <www2.ohchr.org/english/bodies/hrcouncil/ docs/13session/a-hrc-13-37.pdf> accessed 11 December 2018

CCPR General Comment No. 16 (Right to Privacy) <https://tbinternet.ohchr. org/_layouts/treatybodyexternal/Download.aspx?symbolno=INT%2fCCPR%2fG EC%2f6624&Lang=en> accessed 11 December 2018

*Human Rights and Transnational Corporations and Other Business Enterprises* A/67/285 accessible via the General Assembly 67th session <www.ohchr.org/ EN/HRBodies/SP/Pages/GA67session.aspx> accessed 11 December 2018

International Covenant on Civil and Political Rights 1966 <www.ohchr.org/en/ professionalinterest/pages/CCPR.aspx> accessed 11 December 2018

Resolution of the UN General Assembly 66/223 (28 March 2012) *Towards Global Partnerships* <www.unglobalcompact.org/docs/about_the_gc/government_support/FINAL_A_RES_66_223.pdf> accessed 11 December 2018

Rio Declaration on Environment and Development A/RES/66/288 (2012) <https://sustainabledevelopment.un.org/rio20/futurewewant> accessed 11 December 2018

United Nations Convention Against Corruption (2004) < www.unodc.org/documents/treaties/UNCAC/Publications/Convention/08-50026_E.pdf> accessed 11 December 2018

The United Nations Global Compact (2000) <www.unglobalcompact.org/what-is-gc/mission> accessed 11 December 2018

The United Nations Guiding Principles on Business and Human Rights 2011 (Ruggie Principles) A/HRC/17/31 <www.ohchr.org/EN/Issues/TransnationalCorporations/Pages/Reports.aspx> accessed 11 December 2018

United Nations Office on Drugs and Crime "*State of Implementation of the United Nations Convention Against Corruption: Criminalisation, Law Enforcement and International Cooperation*" (2nd Edition, November 2017) <www.unodc.org/unodc/en/corruption/tools_and_publications/state_of_uncac_implementation.html> accessed 11 December 2018

Universal Declaration of Human Rights 1948 <www.un.org/en/universal-declaration-human-rights/> accessed 11 December 2018

### Secondary sources

Anderson, Mark and Warner, Victor *Drafting Confidentiality Agreements* (3rd Edition, The Law Society, London, 2014)

Aplin, Tanya, Bentley, Lionel, Johnson, Phillip and Malynicz, Simon *Gurry on Breach of Confidence: The Protection of Confidential Information* (Oxford University Press, Oxford, 2012)

Avi-Yonah, Reuven S and Mazzoni, Gianluca *Taxation and Human Rights: A Delicate Balance* (University of Michigan Public Law Research Paper No. 520, 5 September 2016) <https://papers.ssrn.com/sol3/papers.cfm?abstract_id=2834883> accessed 11 December 2018

Bernaz, Nadia *Business and Human Rights: History, Law and Policy – Bridging the Accountability Gap* (Routledge, London and New York, 2017)

Brian, Denis *Pulitzer: A Life* (John Wiley & Sons, New York, USA, 2001)

Emberland, Marius *The Human Rights of Companies* (Oxford University Press, Oxford, 2005)

Epstein, Richard A 'The Legal Regulation of Genetic Discrimination: Old Responses to New Technology' 74 *Boston University Law Review* 1, 12 (1994)

Financial Reporting Council, UK Corporate Governance Code (July 2016) <www.frc.org.uk/getattachment/88bd8c45-50ea-4841-95b0-d2f4f48069a2/2018-UK-Corporate-Governance-Code-FINAL.pdf> accessed 11 December 2018

Hixson, Richard *Privacy in a Public Society: Human Rights in Conflict* (Oxford University Press Inc., New York, USA, 1987)

Hughes, Kirsty 'The Social Value of Privacy' in Beate Roessler and Dorota Mokrosinska (eds), *Social Dimensions of Privacy, Interdisciplinary Perspectives* (Cambridge University Press, Cambridge, 2015)

Human Rights Watch, 'EU: Data Protection Rules Advance Privacy' *Human Rights Watch* (6 June 2018) <www.hrw.org/news/2018/06/06/eu-data-protection-rules-advance-privacy> accessed 11 December 2018

Indap, Sujeet 'Blockchain Could Clean Up Messy Shareholder Registers' *Financial Times* (11 September 2017) <www.ft.com/content/f5cf21f6-935a-11e7-a9e6-11d2f0ebb7f0> accessed 11 December 2018

International Corporate Governance Network (IGCN) Global Governance Principles 2017 (5th Edition) <http://icgn.flpbks.com/icgn-global-governance-principles-2017/> accessed 11 December 2018

——— Global Stewardship Principles 2016 <http://icgn.flpbks.com/icgn-global-stewardship-principles/#p=1> accessed 11 December 2018

Islamic Financial Services Board, Guiding Principles on Corporate Governance for Institutions Offering Only Islamic Financial Services (excluding Islamic insurance (Takaful) institutions and Islamic mutual funds (IFSB-3, December 2006) <www.ifsb.org/published.php> accessed 11 December 2018

——— Guiding Principles for Islamic Collective Investment Schemes (IFSB-6, January 2009) <www.ifsb.org/published.php> accessed 11 December 2018

——— Guiding Principles on Conduct of Business for Institutions Offering Islamic Financial Services (IFSB-9, December 2009) <www.ifsb.org/published.php> accessed 11 December 2018

——— Guiding Principles on Shari'ah Governance Systems for Institutions Offering Islamic Financial Services (IFSB-10, December 2009) <www.ifsb.org/published.php> accessed 11 December 2018

———Revised Guidance on Key Elements in the Supervisory Review Process of Institutions Offering Islamic Financial Services (excluding Islamic insurance (Takaful) institutions and Islamic collective investment schemes) (IFSB-16, March 2014) <www.ifsb.org/published.php> accessed 11 December 2018

——— Guiding Principles on Disclosure Requirements for Islamic Capital Market Products (*ṣukūk* and Islamic collective investment schemes) (IFSB-19, April 2017) <www.ifsb.org/published.php> accessed 11 December 2018

Joseph, Sarah and Castan, Melissa *The International Covenant on Civil and Political Rights* (3rd Edition, Oxford University Press, Oxford, 2013)

Latonero, Mark and Gold, Zachard 'Data, Human Rights & Human Security' (Data & Society, 22 June 2015) 5 <https://datasociety.net/pubs/dhr/Data-HumanRights-primer2015.pdf> accessed 11 December 2018

Lord Lester and Pannick, D (eds), *Human Rights Law and Practice* (Butterworth, London, 2004)

Novak, M *UN Covenant on Civil and Political Rights: CPPR Commentary* (2nd Edition, N. P. Engel Verlag, Kehl am rhein, Germany, 2005)

*OECD Corporate Governance Factbook 2017* <www.oecd.org/daf/ca/Corporate-Governance-Factbook.pdf> accessed 11 December 2018

Post, Robert C 'Three Concepts of Privacy' 89 *Georgetown Law Journal*, 2087 (2001)

Roessler, Beate and Mokrosinska, Dorota (eds), *Social Dimensions of Privacy – Interdisciplinary Perspectives* (Cambridge University Press, Cambridge, 2015)

Ruggie, John *Address to the UN Forum on Business and Human Rights* (14 November 2016) <www.shiftproject.org/resources/viewpoints/globalization-sustainable-development-goals-business-respect-human-rights/> accessed 11 December 2018

Rule, James B 'Privacy: The *Longue Dure'* in Beate Roessler and Dorota Mokrosinska (eds), *Social Dimensions of Privacy, Interdisciplinary Perspectives* (Cambridge University Press, Cambridge, 2015) 18

Sikka, Prem 'Why the New Code Governing Corporations Isn't Worth the Paper It's Written on' *Left Foot Forward* (18 July 2018) <https://leftfootforward. org/2018/07/why-the-new-code-governing-corporations-isnt-worth-the-paper-its-written-on-frc-carillion-bhs/> accessed 11 December 2018

Simard, Catherine "Delaware Provides Legal Clarification for Blockchain Maintenance of Corporate Records – the View from Canada" (Norton Rose Fulbright, September 2017) <www.nortonrosefulbright.com/knowledge/publications/155384/delaware-provides-legal-clarification-for-blockchain-maintenance-of-corporate-records-the-view-from-canada> accessed 11 December 2018

Solove, Daniel J *Understanding Privacy* (Harvard University Press, Cambridge, MA, 2008)

Stempeck, Matt 'Sharing Data Is a Form of Corporate Philanthropy' *Harvard Business Review* (24 July 2014) <https://hbr.org/2014/07/sharing-data-is-a-form-of-corporate-philanthropy> accessed 11 December 2018

Thomson, Judith Jarvis 'The Right to Privacy' in Ferdinand David Schoeman (ed), *Philosophical Dimensions of Privacy: An Anthology* (Cambridge University Press, Cambridge, 1984)

Vermeulen, Erik P M 'Beneficial Ownership and Control: A Comparative Study – Disclosure, Information and Enforcement' *OECD Corporate Governance Working Papers*, No. 7 (OECD Publishing, 2013) Executive Summary 5 <http://dx.doi.org/10.1787/5k4dkhwckbzv-en> accessed 11 December 2018

Waddell, Steve *The Global Compact: An Organizational Innovation to Realize UN Principles* (Global Compact Governance Papers Series, United Nations Global Compact, New York, USA, November 2011)

Wilborn, S E 'Revisiting the Public/Private Distinction: Employee Monitoring in the Workplace' 32 *Georgia Law Review* 825 (1998)

# 5 "Orphan Structures"

## Introduction

This chapter reviews the burgeoning global fiduciary services promotion of own-erless entities, sold expressly to those wanting to be held wholly unaccountable. So-called "orphan structures" render any beneficial ownership registration or dis-closure system toothless.

What are "orphan structures", where are they located and how do they wholly avoid there being a beneficial owner?

The chapter sets "orphan structures" in their jurisdictional context and exam-ines how they are further privileged in terms of immunity from lawsuit, absence of public registration, impunity concerning fraudulent transfers of property and protection against "whistle-blowers".

## Tools of abuse

The immunities and privileges offered to "orphan structures" are as significant in the context of debating whether "ownership" is an effective regulatory marker as are the very characteristics of the "orphan structures" themselves. An "orphan structure" both by definition and by design has no owner, at least as far as the law of the jurisdiction in which it exists is concerned. Other jurisdictions may beg to differ, and so to make absolutely sure that the "orphan structures" are not blasted out of offshore waters by the gunships of foreign courts and international regula-tors, very special treatment is afforded to them.

The following tools of abuse are wholly or in part common to many of the "orphan structures" and in most cases have been consciously applied in domestic legislation:

- The structures are subject to artificially low levels of domestic taxation or are wholly exempt from income and capital taxes or customs duties.
- Reciprocal enforcement of foreign judgments in domestic courts is limited or dis-applied altogether (and domestic court proceedings may be held in secret).

- Limitation periods (the time within which a claim may be brought, at the expiration of which that right is extinguished) may be so short as to preclude in practice the preparation and filing of a claim.
- Foreign rules on forced heirship (a system common in civil law jurisdictions whereby heirs have a fixed entitlement to the property of the deceased, regardless of the deceased's preferences to the contrary) are dis-applied.
- Domestic remedies relating to fraudulent transfers (the transfer of property into a structure which either intentionally defeats or is deemed in law to defeat the interests of legitimate creditors and other claimants) are dis-applied.
- The structure may be aggressively asset protective, and assets held within it may not be capable of being alienated or passed by bankruptcy, insolvency or liquidation or liable to be seized, sold, attached, or otherwise taken in execution by process of law.
- The requirement to place details of the structure, its existence, its finances and its activities in the public domain (in the form of a publicly accessible register) may be minimal or entirely absent.
- Structures which under generally accepted legal principles have a limited life span (such as private trusts) may be given perpetual existence.
- Fiduciary responsibilities of those administering or managing structures – be they directors, trustees or any other responsible officer – may be dis-applied, or, if applied, those otherwise responsible may, through a combination of manipulated limitation periods and indulgences, be deemed not culpable or culpable but absolved.
- The structure may take a form unknown under generally accepted legal principles or may have the power to shape-shift.

## The "Orphan Structures"

- Seychelles IBC
- Bahamas Executive Entities
- Cayman STAR Trusts
- BVI VISTA Trusts
- Non-charitable purpose trusts
- Foundations: Liechtenstein and Panama
- Nevis Multiform Foundation

### Seychelles IBC: absence of information on public record

Many tax havens have very loose public filing requirements for companies (an extreme example being the Principality of Liechtenstein, which has no companies' registry at all[1]), and the Seychelles International Business Company

---

1 Liechtenstein Chamber of Commerce and Industry, 'Commercial Registry' (*Liechtenstein Chamber of Commerce and Industry*, 15 September 2015) <www.lihk.li/CFDOCS/cms/cmsout/index.cfm?u=1&GroupID=20&meID=75> accessed 12 December 2018.

('Seychelles IBC') serves as an example. Seychelles IBCs originated in 1994[2] and are now governed by the International Business Companies Act 2016.[3] It is not "chimeric" strictly speaking but is an example of the limits to which an otherwise legitimate form can be taken to achieve accountability avoidance.

The Seychelles IBC has very wide trading powers, which it need not specify, though it is not permitted to trade within the Seychelles itself. Neither meetings of members nor board meetings of directors are required. The use of nominee shareholders is common. Its accounts are not publicly filed, and there is no audit requirement. Details of directors and shareholders are maintained by the company itself, but these are neither available for public access nor filed publicly. There is no "annual return" (an annual report commonly found in mainstream jurisdictions, filed at the relevant company's registry, which provides details of officers and members). There is no requirement to file publicly details of any mortgages or charges against the company. The Seychelles IBC is wholly exempt from taxation in the Seychelles.

The Seychelles IBC is therefore typical of the opacity afforded to many corporate forms in the tax havens, concealing purpose, governance, ownership, financial and accounting status, and, above all, accountability.

### Bahamas Executive Entities

Bahamas Executive Entities ('BEE') are a bizarre, artificial creation, unique to The Bahamas, the design of which was commissioned by the Bahamian government from leading London lawyers in 2010 to fill what the government believed to be a gap in the offshore products market.[4]

---

2  International Business Companies Act 1994 (repealed).

3  <www.seylii.org/sc/legislation/act/2016/15> accessed 12 December 2018. Since 1994 it is estimated that the Seychelles has registered around 180,000 IBCs, with over 18,000 in 2015 alone. The Seychelles IBC is ranked fourth in the global tax-exempt company market (the first three rankings being the US State of Delaware, the British Virgin Islands and the Republic of Panama. See Peter Burian, 'Seychelles: Beating the Odds' *Offshore Investment* (2016).

4  Danielle Levy, 'Lawrence Graham Seeks to Revolutionise Offshore Trust Structures' (*City-wire*, 23 April 2010) <http://citywire.co.uk/wealth-manager/news/lawrence-graham-seeks-to-revolutionise-offshore-trust-structures/a395505/print?section=wealth-manager> accessed 12 December 2018. "As baby boomers come of age, they are looking to protect their assets for the next generation. [. . .] In the Bahamas, finding the most suitable tool to protect wealth is easy, thanks to the availability of highly qualified professionals and legislative support. Following the introduction of [the BEE] ultra-high-net-worth individuals can now be even more confident when it comes to securing their assets". *The Bahamas Investor Magazine* 13 July 2011. The article quotes Heather Thompson, at Higgs & Johnson [<https://higgsjohnson.com/person/heather-l-thompson/> accessed 12 December 2018] as saying "No other jurisdiction, to my knowledge, is using executive entities. We came up with it first. [. . .] We are giving clients everything on a plate". <www.thebahamasinvestor.com/2011/securing-succession/> accessed 12 December 2018.

BEEs were introduced under the Executive Entities Act 2011,[5] with the intention of facilitating the establishment, operation, management and termination of a new private wealth structure. A BEE is defined as 'a legal person established by a Charter to perform only executive functions and registered in accordance with the Act' and is 'able to sue and be sued in its own name'.

The BEE is therefore simply a vehicle to carry out executive functions, primarily in wealth and asset holding structures. Executive Functions are defined in s 2 as:

(a) any powers and duties of an executive, administrative, supervisory, fiduciary and office holding nature including, but not limited to, the powers and duties of –

   (i) an enforcer, protector, trustee, investment advisor and the holder of any other office (and a committee of any of the aforementioned) of any trust, and
   (ii) the holder of any office (and a committee of the aforementioned) of any legal person; and

(b) the ownership, management and holding of (i) executive entity assets; and (ii) trust assets.

The BEE is created by a founder and may have officers and a supervisory council. It has unlimited capacity and is of perpetual existence.

No estate, inheritance, succession or gift tax, rate, duty, levy or other charge is payable by a founder or any other person with respect to any interest given to or received from a BEE. The BEE is statutorily immune to foreign forced heirship rights, challenges to fraudulent dispositions or the application reciprocally of foreign judgments.

In practice this means that if assets have been transferred into the ownership of a BEE, the validity of that transfer cannot be challenged. This opens the possibility that anyone seeking to avoid accountability – including breaches of corporate governance standards on the Ruggie Principles[6] – has a clear home run: the transfer may clearly have been made with the express intent to defraud a known or ascertainable creditor (the victims of the breach) by denuding the abuser of substantial assets, but no foreign judgment upholding a claim brought on this

---

5 <http://laws.bahamas.gov.bs/cms/images/LEGISLATION/PRINCI PAL/2011/2011-0052/ExecutiveEntitiesAct2011_1.pdf> accessed 12 December 2018, together with the Executive Entities Regulations 2012, SI 13 of 2012 <http://laws.bahamas. gov.bs/cms/images/LEGISLATION/SUBORDINATE/2012/2012-0013/ExecutiveEn titiesRegulations2012_1.pdf> accessed 12 December 2018.
6 Guiding Principles on Business and Human Rights 2011 A/HRC/17/31 <www.ohchr.org/ EN/Issues/TransnationalCorporations/Pages/Reports.aspx> accessed 12 December 2018.

ground will have any effect on the BEE in the Bahamas, and no claim based on a fraudulent transfer can be brought against the BEE in the Bahamas courts.[7]

Fundamentally, from an accountability perspective, a BEE is an 'orphan' structure: there are no shareholders or members of any kind and no beneficiaries. It is the corporate equivalent of the non-charitable purpose trust.

### Cayman STAR trusts

Cayman STAR Trusts derive their name from the Special Trusts (Alternative Regime) Law 1997, now replaced by Part VIII Trusts Law (2011 Revision)[8] as amended by the Trusts (Amendment) Law 2016 with effect from 24 October 2016,[9] which introduced the concept of private purpose trusts into a jurisdiction which up to that point recognised trusts only for beneficiaries or for charitable purposes, drawing its strength from English common law.[10]

It is another example of an artificial construction – no doubt justified locally as an evolutionary step – to serve the demands of the burgeoning Cayman finance and fiduciaries industries and to provide what is perceived to be a competitive edge.

Cayman sees itself somewhat differently. Jude Scott, CEO of Cayman Finance, issued a statement on 23 October 2017:

> Cayman is a premier global financial hub, efficiently connecting law abiding users and providers of investment capital and financing around the world. Cayman is an excellent extender of value for the US, UK and other major

---

7  This sits uneasily with the role of the Bahamas as a founding member in June 2015 of the Association of Integrity Commissions and Anti-Corruption Bodies in the Commonwealth Caribbean (the other members being Antigua and Barbuda, Barbados, Belize, Dominica, Grenada, Guyana, Jamaica, Saint Lucia, St Kitts and Nevis, St Vincent and the Grenadines and Trinidad and Tobago). The Commonwealth 'Caribbean Integrity Commissions Form New Commonwealth Body to Fight Corruption' (*The Commonwealth*, 25 June 2015) <https://shar.es/1QVznK> accessed 12 December 2018; and see Bruce Zagaris, 'Changes in International Regulatory Regimes on Caribbean Corporate, Financial Regulatory and Transparency Law' 263 *Offshore Investment* (2016).

8  <www.gov.ky/portal/pls/portal/docs/1/11524845.PDF> accessed 12 December 2018.

9  Access to Cayman Islands legislation and to the decisions of its courts is obtainable on subscription from Cayman Islands Judicial Administration <www.judicial.ky> accessed 12 December 2018.

10 When STAR Trusts were first introduced, based on drafts prepared for the Cayman Islands government by Anthony Duckworth, a lively debate on the efficacy and legitimacy of STAR Trusts ensued between him and Paul Matthews. To explore that debate in detail is outside the scope of this work, but the debate nevertheless repays the reader: (1) Paul Matthews, 'Shooting STAR: The New Special Trusts Regime from the Cayman Islands' 11 *Trust Law International* 3, 67 (1997); (2) Anthony Duckworth, 'STAR WARS: The Colony Strikes Back' 12 *Trust Law International* 1, 16 (1998); (3) Paul Matthews, 'STAR: Big Bang or Red Dwarf?' 12 *Trust Law International* 2, 98 (1998); (4) Anthony Duckworth, 'STAR WARS: Smiting the Bull' 13 *Trust Law International* 3, 158 (1999).

economies, helping to pool global investment capital and financing for major initiatives like infrastructure development.

Cayman is a transparent jurisdiction due to our combination of a verified beneficial ownership regime, the adoption of more than twenty global financial standards and adherence to both US FATCA and the EU's Common Reporting Standards. Cayman also is participating in the OECD's BEPS initiative and will be introducing Country-by-Country Reporting by December 2017. We meet none of the descriptions used by entities such as the OECD or Transparency International to define a tax haven. In fact, our system purposefully lacks any laws or regulations like double taxation treaties or foreign incentives that support the shifting of tax base by foreign entities to avoid corporate taxes in their home jurisdictions.[11]

The Cayman STAR Trust shares many of the characteristics of a non-charitable purpose trust, save that beneficiaries are possible. There is no limitation on the number of beneficiaries or of purposes (whether charitable or not). One such purpose can be wholly self-referring: the preservation of the trust assets. The trust is enforced by an Enforcer – again a similarity with the non-charitable purpose trust – to the exclusion, however, of any rights in equity of the beneficiaries themselves to seek to enforce its terms, to have information concerning the trust disclosed to them, or to challenge the trust in any way. The Cayman STAR Trust is, if desired, perpetual and because it is open to constant re-interpretation by the trustees (with or without court assistance) it can never fail or be held void ab initio for perceived uncertainty.

The beneficiaries will have a right to be considered by the trustees for a distribution but have no means to enforce this – men and women of straw in any enforcement action in which they seek to attach trust assets. The Enforcer has no proprietary rights, in law or in equity, in the trust assets and exists merely to monitor decisions of the trustees the parameters of which they themselves have set.

*In other words, the legislation takes away from persons who can enjoy the property almost all the main incidents of that enjoyment, including the opportunity to protect it by court action, and gives all those powers of protection and complaint to persons who have no chance of enjoying the property. [. . .] This legislation at first sight seems to pare down the property rights of beneficiaries to such a level that all they are left with is the bare enjoyment, if they actually do receive it and (which is the more surprising) no-one thereafter takes it away from them by force. [. . .] It is utterly precarious.[12]*

11 <www.cayman.finance/2017/10/cayman-finance-response-us-pirg-report-caymans-commitment-global-transparency-standards-makes-strong-international-partner/> accessed 12 December 2018.
12 Paul Matthews, 'Shooting STAR: the new special trusts regime from the Cayman Islands' (n 10), at 68.

In terms of accountability therefore, the settlor of a Cayman STAR Trust can warehouse assets within the trust for any purpose and section off assets for beneficiaries who have no means of influencing the administration of the trust, generation following generation.[13] In addition, those assets which are held for a *purpose* will have no beneficial owner in any sense of the words and in addition will, from a corporate perspective, be 'off balance sheet'. In consequence, they will be completely un-attachable. As there is no requirement for Cayman STAR Trusts to be registered publicly, even their very existence is concealed.

The Cayman STAR Trust may hold shares in a private trust company (that is, a company established solely to act as trustee of a particular trust), and it is not beyond the bounds of imagination that this itself may be the trustee of a non-charitable purpose trust. Thus is the ownerless itself made ownerless, ad infinitum.

### BVI VISTA trusts

The VISTA[14] trust is created and subject to the Virgin Islands Special Trusts Act 2003, as amended most recently in 2013.[15] It is a creation of statute, unique to the BVI, and hence not naturally occurring in any accepted body of trust law. Specifically designed for, and confined to, the holding of company shares, it has therefore the chimeric qualities of many of these genetically engineered tax haven structures. Though not a true "orphan" – there are beneficiaries – the VISTA trust is marketed as a "blind" trust: a trust in name only.

It is a long-established principle of trust law that a trustee is under a duty of care and must act prudently when making decisions concerning the assets in a trust fund.[16] In the case of trustees holding shares in a company, their duty to act as prudent businesspersons is paramount: speculative, bordering on reckless, behaviour by trustee shareholders is a breach of their fiduciary duty. Similarly, speculative or reckless conduct on the part of the directors of the company, who

---

13 A lack of influence which thereby provides aid and comfort to a beneficiary needing to demonstrate this to a revenue authority, creditors, a trustee in bankruptcy, a foreign court, financial regulators and law enforcement authorities. It also therefore places the beneficiaries under no obligation to trace assets which may, for example, have been embezzled by the trustee and passed to third parties – even if those third parties are in some way connected to the beneficiaries. It is a black-hole strategy.

14 VISTA is simply the acronym for the Act.

15 Virgin Islands Special Trusts Act 2003 <www.bvifsc.vg/sites/default/files/virgin_islands_special_trusts_act_2003.pdf> accessed 12 December 2018 and Virgin Islands Special Trusts (Amendment) Act 2013 <www.bvifsc.vg/sites/default/files/virgin_islands_special_trusts_amendment_act_2013.pdf> accessed 12 December 2018.

16 In some jurisdictions this equitable principle has been enshrined as a statutory duty of care: Trustee Act 2000 (United Kingdom) <www.legislation.gov.uk/ukpga/2000/29/contents> accessed 12 December 2018, pt 1; Trustee Act 2001 (Isle of Man) <https://legislation.gov.im/cms/images/LEGISLATION/PRINCIPAL/2001/2001-0018/TrusteeAct2001_1.pdf> accessed 12 December 2018, pt 1.

have its management and control, can be monitored by the trustee shareholders and reined in when felt not to be in the best commercial interests of the company or of its stakeholders. Those stakeholders include not only the shareholders themselves, but also the likes of creditors, suppliers and the company's customer base (not forgetting overriding principles of good corporate governance).

In the case of a VISTA trust, this principle is dis-applied. It is a form of trust for holding shares in companies where it is intended that the shares will be held indefinitely, and the trustee is not intended, other than in special and defined circumstances, to intervene in the conduct of the affairs of the underlying company or companies. The trustees as shareholders, regardless of any countervailing provisions of BVI company law (as VISTA applies only to BVI companies), have no management responsibility, leaving the directors with unconstrained authority. The trustees have a statutory duty to retain the shares. Even the appointment of directors is limited by 'office of director' rules contained in the trust deed which specify how the trustee shareholders must exercise their votes in respect of the appointment, removal and remuneration of directors. All authority is therefore vested in the directors.

The shareholder trustees have no fiduciary duty in relation to the assets or affairs of the company.[17] Though the VISTA trust is permitted only to hold shares in a BVI company and no other assets, there is no restriction on the assets which the BVI company itself may hold, which may of course include shares in non-BVI companies.

For a period of up to 20 years, the trustees are denied the right under the long-established common-law rule in *Saunders v Vautier* 1841[18] to vary or terminate the trust.[19]

No trust deed under BVI law is subject to public registration.

One of the marketing advantages claimed for the VISTA trust is the creation of blind trusts for politicians, who can thereby distance themselves from the companies in which they have a financial interest and easily refute accusations that they abuse their position of influence.

In terms of accountability, this claimed advantage is pernicious. Any entity or individual which or who but for the VISTA trust would hold shares directly in an abusive corporation remains with clean hands throughout and will be wholly

---

17 In one jurisdiction, the Isle of Man, the rule is diametrically opposed to this. The position of creditors in relation to assets owned by a company that is itself wholly owned by a trust is subject to the *corporate-trust fusion principle* established on 19 September 2002 in *Re Poyiadjis* 2001–03 MLR 316. Under the corporate-trust fusion principle where trustees hold 100% of the issued share capital in a company, and may even themselves be the directors of that company, their fiduciary responsibility in relation to the shares extends to the company's own assets, requiring that those assets be dealt with as if directly held in the trust itself.
18 [1841] EWHC J82, [1841] 4 Beav 115.
19 Exceptionally, if an 'interested person' (e.g. a beneficiary) calls upon the VISTA trustee to intervene in the company's affairs then the trustee must do so if the interested person has a 'permitted ground of complaint' which must be specified in the trust instrument.

absolved from responsibility in the company's affairs as only the directors are empowered.

### Non-charitable purpose trusts[20]

A trust is a simple triangle. A settlor, wishing to benefit a beneficiary, transfers property to a trustee, who takes that property into their name but who holds it for the benefit of the beneficiary.

The beneficiary has no rights of ownership in law over the property, and the trustee has no right to benefit from the property either in law or in equity. The beneficiary has an expectation that in equity they will receive the property (or the income it generates, or both).[21]

The 'three certainties' which are required for the creation and constitution of a trust are thereby present – certainty of having an intention to create a trust, certainty as to what property is to be placed in the trust and certainty of the identity of who will benefit. It is possible for the beneficiary, instead of being a person, to be a charitable cause – something which can objectively be identified even though at any one time no individual is in mind.

This analysis falls asunder in the case of a non-charitable purpose trust, under which for the duration of such trusts there is a complete absence of beneficial ownership of any asset held (for example, shares in a company) because such a trust cannot be for the benefit of any individual or identifiable group of legal or moral persons, but exists simply for its own stated purpose. That purpose may simply be the holding of the very shares in a company which form the trust fund – Ouroborus conceptualised as an equitable Möbius curve.[22] That the *form*

---

20  For a general discussion see J Glister and J Lee, *Hanbury & Martin: Modern Equity* (20th Edition, Sweet & Maxwell, 2015) ch 16 'Non-Charitable Purpose Trusts'. On the origins of non-charitable purpose trusts in English law and their early offshore proliferation, see Paul Mathews, 'The New Trust: Obligations Without Rights?' in A J Oakley (ed), *Trends in Contemporary Trust Law* (Oxford University Press, Oxford, 1996) 1.

21  This simple equitable truth has not proved apparent, for example, to the European Union. In their Directive (EU) 2015/849 of the European Parliament and of the Council of 20 May 2015 on the prevention of the use of the financial system for the purposes of money laundering or terrorist financing, amending Regulation (EU) No 648/2012 of the European Parliament and of the Council [known as the EU 4th Anti-Money Laundering Directive], and repealing Directive 2005/60/EC of the European Parliament and of the Council and Commission Directive 2006/70/EC (Text with EEA relevance) [2015] OJ L141, 5.6.2015, 'beneficial owner' in relation to trusts is identified as the settlor, trustees, beneficiaries and protector (art 3(6)(b) and art 31(1)). Not only is this wholly at odds with the equitable principles which give rise to trusts, it takes no account of beneficial ownership avoidance strategies using non-charitable purpose trusts, seemingly unaware that such trusts having no beneficiaries are widely available. Indeed, the concept of beneficial ownership avoidance is entirely absent from the Directive. See ch 3, pt 5 for a general discussion on the EU 4th and 5th Anti-Money Laundering Directives.

22  For example the use of a non-charitable purpose trust to hold special purpose vehicles – that is, companies set up to perform a specific task or to hold a specific asset – used in off-balance

of the assets ought not in theory to equate to the *purpose* of the trust – that the *purpose* should be what the assets *are applied to* – has not troubled the legislators. It is a question of attracting offshore business:

> *We must see trusts – and the purpose trust in particular – in this light. It is a product, serving a commercial need. To some extent, like all law and legal institutions, it is a conjuring trick. It is a way of making another legal institution – ownership – disappear, or half disappear. First it is refracted into legal ownership and beneficial enjoyment, and then beneficial enjoyment seems to dissolve into thin air.*[23]

Traditionally, a trust in which the beneficiaries could not be clearly identified, or for purposes which were not charitable (and so capable of benefitting persons identified not by name but by classification), would be void. The NCPT takes the triangle and cuts off the third corner.

The crucial issue is that any asset held under a purpose trust is not beneficially owned. Not until after the purpose trust has terminated will ownership of those assets once again be possible, in the form of the distribution of a surplus. Those future recipients of surplus, even if identified in the purpose trust deed itself (by name or by the use of a formula from which identity can be deduced) are in no sense beneficiaries. Their status is activated only after the event.[24]

The practical effect is substantial. It is common to find that the entire issued share capital in a company, 'ABC Limited', is held in an NCPT. *ABC Limited therefore has no beneficial owner whilst the NCPT is in existence.*[25] The recipient of surplus may be the very company ('Parent Limited') of which ABC Limited

---

sheet transactions where the beneficial interest in a special purpose vehicle may be said to be "ownerless" – see the discussion by Carey Olsen of Jersey non-charitable purpose trusts in this context: 'A Guide to Non-Charitable Purpose Trusts in Jersey' (*Carey Olsen*, 23 March 2017) <www.careyolsen.com/downloads/Non_charitable_purpose_trusts_in_Jersey.pdf> accessed 12 December 2018.

23 Paul Mathews, 'The New Trust: Obligations without Rights?' (n 10) 31.

24 They are therefore invisible, and wholly outside the scope of, e.g., (1) the OECD's Common Reporting Standard [OECD 'Standard for Automatic Exchange of Financial Account Information in Tax Matters' (*OECD*, 14 July 211AD) <www.oecd.org/ctp/exchange-of-tax-information/standard-for-automatic-exchange-of-financial-account-information-for-tax-matters-9789264216525-en.htm> accessed 12 December 2018] and (2) the United Kingdom's PSC (people with significant control) regime [United Kingdom Government, Companies House, 'PSC Requirements for Companies and Limited Liability Partnerships' (*gov.uk*, 27 January 2016) <www.gov.uk/government/publications/guidance-to-the-people-with-significant-control-requirements-for-companies-and-limited-liability-partnerships> accessed 12 December 2018].

25 The initiative taken by the United Kingdom Government under the Small Business Enterprise and Employment Act 2015 [<www.legislation.gov.uk/ukpga/2015/26/contents> accessed 12 December 2018] to establish a register of people with significant control would be wholly thwarted by this. United Kingdom Government, Companies House, 'Keeping Your People with Significant Control (PSC) Register' (*gov.uk*, 6 April 2016) <www.

would have been a subsidiary, but which Parent Limited prefers to keep off balance sheet. Investigating the books of Parent Limited during the life of the purpose trust will give no indication whatsoever of the existence of ABC Limited. Yet ABC Limited is destined to become the property of Parent Limited. Until that time, Parent Limited has no legal responsibility for the good governance of, or any economic connection with, ABC Limited.

A common use of ABC Limited would be to place under its ownership hazardous assets, such as bulk cargo tankers or brownfield, toxic development sites or politically sensitive projects such as mining or rain forest development: ABC Limited has by its very nature limited liability, and apart from the assets which it holds has no means to satisfy any claims which could be brought against it. Parent Limited, which will ultimately benefit from any profits and capital gains made by ABC Limited, remains wholly invisible and inviolate throughout.[26]

NCPTs are now available worldwide in both offshore and onshore jurisdictions under legislation which bears a universal similarity.

The NCPT is an offshore development which was not foreseen by the Hague Convention on the Law Applicable to Trusts and their Recognition (1 July 1985).[27]Whether a jurisdiction which has ratified the Hague Convention must under Article 2 concede that NCPTs are indeed trusts is moot.[28] The suggestion that non-charitable purpose trusts ought *not* to be regarded as true trusts

---

gov.uk/government/news/keeping-your-people-with-significant-control-psc-register> accessed 12 December 2018.

26  Take as an example a situation which the author has not infrequently encountered in practice – the development of urban brownfield sites. The site is potentially hazardous. The property developer prefers that it remain off balance sheet. Title to the site is therefore vested in a company incorporated for the purpose (a "special purpose vehicle" or "SPV"), which in turn is held under an NCPT. For the duration of the NCPT there is no equitable (and hence no beneficial) owner. On the termination of the NCPT – the triggering event may be the granting of planning permission, which is an acknowledgement that the brownfield site has morphed into a non-hazardous development site – the surplus assets held by the NCPT need to be distributed. The NCPT has ended. The trustees, under provisions in the relevant NCPT statute, transfer the surplus to a designated recipient of surplus. That recipient can under the relevant NCPT statute at no time during the life of the NCPT have been a beneficiary. The surplus comprises or includes the shares in the SPV. From the point of distribution, the SPV will have both a legal and equitable (hence beneficial) owner, and the public register of the SPV (if one is maintained in the relevant jurisdiction) will reveal this fact. The recipient of surplus is, predictably, the property developer.

27  See ch 2 for a fuller discussion of the Hague Convention <www.hcch.net/en/instruments/conventions/full-text/?cid=59> accessed 12 December 2018.

28  Donovan Waters, 'The Hague Trusts Convention Twenty Years On' in Michele Graziadei, Ugo Mattei and Lionel Smith (eds), *Commercial Trusts in European Private Law* (Cambridge University Press, Cambridge, 2005) 56, at 95 takes a positive view: "That is the style of the Convention. The interpretation of the Convention is always facilitative, offering a way forward to recognition for those who will take it". It must nevertheless be borne in mind that very few countries have ratified the Hague Convention (see ch 3 Appendix Two), and those which have not will apply their own laws on the classification and recognition of trusts when confronted with NCPTs.

in jurisdictions which recognise trusts in their classic form but which do not have comparative legislation does not find favour with all commentators: "Provided that the trust has an appointed enforcer, there is someone who can compel the trustee to fulfil his duties; and though an English court might dislike the tying up of capital for non-charitable purposes, it is by no means impossible to give effect to the trust".[29]

> *Underlying and underpinning the trust obligation is the fundamental principle that just as a car needs an engine, so a trust needs an enforcer (whether the enforcer be a beneficiary or the Attorney-General or the Charity Commissioners or some person expressly appointed by the settlor to be enforcer with locus standi positively to enforce the trust). Is it seriously to be suggested that the English court would invoke the orthodox beneficiary principle to refuse to give effect to a foreign non-charitable purpose trust of English assets where under the foreign governing law as a result of legislation (like that of Jersey or Bermuda or the Isle of Man or the Cayman Islands or the British Virgin Islands) such a trust is valid where the trust instrument expressly provides for an enforcer? Would the English court really hold the assets to be subject to a resulting trust for the settlor? It is submitted that, because the beneficiary principle should be regarded as the "enforcer principle", the English court would regard the foreign trust concept neither as repugnant to the English trust concept nor contrary to English public policy, the trust being one that the English court can "both enforce and control".[30]*

A long-standing argument that an NCPT would be void as lasting beyond applicable perpetuity periods[31] – a privilege reserved in equity, as a matter of public policy founded in their public beneficial nature, to charitable purpose trusts – is falling by the wayside. Many of the NCPT statutes contain a statutory perpetuity period. The perpetuity period itself is increasingly thought of as an anachronism.[32]

Dis-applying the concept of beneficial ownership means there is no possibility of transparency. The Principles – and in particular Principle 5 on trust structures[33] – can be wholly sidelined and disclosure of beneficial ownership

29  D Hayton and others, *Underhill and Hayton Law of Trusts and Trustees* (19th Edition, LexisNexis, 2016) para 100.205.

30  David J Hayton, 'Developing the Obligation Characteristic of the Trust' 117 *LQR*, 96 (January 2001), at 100.

31  J Glister and J Lee, *Hanbury & Martin* (n 20) para 16–022.

32  For example, the Isle of Man Purpose Trusts Act 1996 imposes a perpetuity period of 80 years. For trusts other than NCPTs in the Isle of Man the perpetuity period has been abolished: Perpetuities and Accumulations Act 1968 s 1A (introduced by the Trusts (Amendment) Act 2015 s 5) <https://legislation.gov.im/cms/images/LEGISLATION/PRINCIPAL/1968/1968-0008/PerpetuitiesandAccumulationsAct1968_2.pdf> accessed 12 December 2018.

33  '5. Countries should ensure that trustees of express trusts maintain adequate, accurate and current beneficial ownership information, including information of settlors, the protector

defeated. The non-charitable purpose trust (NCPT) takes concealment to a new and dangerous level, not by simply hiding the identity of a beneficial owner, but by abolishing the concept of beneficial ownership altogether: "purpose trust legislation simply encourages hidden ownership by putting assets into no-man's land [. . .] there is a feeling that pure purpose trusts may be hijacked for shady dealings involving hiding beneficial ownership".[34] In the absence of beneficiaries, and with an enforcer who may be a person of straw – "a creature of your own making (and paying) [. . .] In practice, no one is going to complain. But if *that* is the point, it is, to say the least, rather tacky".[35]

As concerns transparency strategies, it is immediately apparent that no principles of beneficial ownership tracing and declaration are of the slightest utility if there are in fact no beneficial owners.

### Case study: Isle of Man Purpose Trusts Act 1996

In the Isle of Man,[36] NCPTs are amongst the longest established. The Purpose Trusts Act 1996[37] provides for the creation of NCPTs. The operational mechanics of an Isle of Man purpose trust do not differ in any material respect from the mechanics of similar structures in other jurisdictions.

Purpose trusts are not trusts in the classical sense and are designed to be used as adjuncts to taxation planning structures and risk avoidance in various ways, including:

(a)  holding shares in a company which can then be voted in accordance with the terms of the trust (of particular importance in circumstances where an individual may not wish beneficially to own such assets);

(b)  protection of subsidiaries where a parent company borrows – the shares of the subsidiary are placed in trust until the loan is repaid, thereby protecting the subsidiary from creditors of its parent;

---

(if any) trustees and beneficiaries. These measures should also apply to other legal arrangements with a structure or function similar to express trusts'.

34  D Hayton (ed), *Modern International Developments in Trust Law* (Kluwer Law International, Alphen aan den Rijn, Netherlands, 1999) at 12 and 305, quoted in J Glister and J Lee, *Hanbury & Martin* (n 20) para 16–022.

35  Paul Mathews, 'The New Trust: Obligations without Rights?' (n 20) 29. It is the practical reality of the offshore trusts industry which is the problem, not the theory: "The basis of the trust is the unilateral transfer of assets by a settlor to a person voluntarily undertaking the office of trustee with the benefits and burdens attaching to such office. It should make no difference whether the burdens are enforceable by the beneficiaries or by the Attorney-General or the Charity Commissioners or by the designated enforcer". David J Hayton, 'Developing the Obligation Characteristic of the Trust' (n 30) 96, at 102.

36  The Isle of Man is merely one of an increasing number of jurisdictions which within the past twenty years have introduced legislation supporting the creation of non-charitable purpose trusts. This is a global phenomenon. See the Appendix.

37  <www.legislation.gov.im/cms/images/LEGISLATION/PRINCIPAL/1996/1996-0009/PurposeTrustsAct1996_1.pdf> accessed 12 December 2018.

(c)  protection of the lender where a parent company borrows – the shares of the subsidiary can be placed in a purpose trust until the loan is repaid, thereby preventing the ownership of the subsidiary from changing;

(d)  capital financing and securitisation projects in which the trust assets are off the balance sheet of one or more parties to the transaction; or

(e)  holding toxic or high-risk assets (e.g. untreated brownfield development sites, bulk carriers) in a special purpose vehicle the shares in which are held in a purpose trust.

At common law, a non-charitable purpose trust would be void for want of identifiable beneficiaries to enforce it and for breach of the rule against perpetuities.[38] The Act provides for the creation of purpose trusts. The purpose must be certain, reasonable and possible and must not be unlawful, contrary to public policy or immoral (s1(1)(a)).

The following are not capable of being regarded as purpose trusts (s 9(1)), those made:

(a)  for the benefit of a particular person (whether or not immediately ascertainable);

(b)  for the benefit of some aggregate of persons identified by reference to some personal relationship; or

(c)  for charitable purposes.[39]

The purpose must be certain, reasonable and possible; and must not be unlawful, contrary to public policy or immoral.[40]

The following are *not* capable of being regarded as NCPTs; those made:

(a)  for the benefit of a particular person (whether or not immediately ascertainable);

---

38  Note that the rule against perpetuities, under which property in trust (other than one for exclusively charitable purposes) had to vest in the beneficiaries within a fixed period of time, has been abolished in certain jurisdictions including the Isle of Man: Perpetuities and Accumulations Act 1968 (as amended) <https://legislation.gov.im/cms/images/LEGISLATION/PRINCIPAL/1968/1968-0008/PerpetuitiesandAccumulationsAct1968_2.pdf> accessed 12 December 2018, s 1A.

39  The NCPT owes its origin and continued popularity in part to the perceived weakness of charitable trusts as offshore planning vehicles. Possibly (though by no means always) genuine and correctly constituted, such charitable trusts would exist only for a relatively short period. Assets would be transferred to the trustees for a commercial purpose, which when achieved would render the charitable trust redundant in offshore planning terms. This left them open to the accusation of being mere shams. They are also subject to external supervision, in most cases from state-appointed charity commissioners: "*Not* an attractive prospect for international businessmen trying to carry through commercial purposes that were not only complex and confidential, but also, how shall we say, economical with the taxes. It *might* be lawful, but the magician never wants to reveal to the audience how the trick is done". Paul Mathews, 'The New Trust: Obligations without Rights?' (n 20) 28.

40  s 1(1)(a).

(b)  for the benefit of some aggregate of persons identified by reference to some personal relationship; or
(c)  for charitable purposes.

The purpose of the trust itself is not the issue: anything lawful, compatible with public policy and moral will suffice. The purpose may be – and most often is – simply to hold the shares in a company. The issue is that *there are no beneficiaries.* This is something more than simply saying that an individual cannot "own" the trust fund, but that he or she could at some point in time (at the discretion of the trustees) be eligible to receive a distribution. There is *no one* who owns the trust fund. For the duration of the NCPT,[41] although the legal title to the assets in the trust is held in the names of the trustees, there is no beneficial owner.

The trust must be created by deed or by a will which is capable of being, and which is, admitted to probate in the Isle of Man (or in the alternative in respect of which letters of administration are capable of being and are granted) (s1(1)(b)).

There must be two or more trustees, of whom at least one must be a person falling to one of the categories designated under the Act: an Advocate, a foreign registered legal practitioner, a qualified auditor, a member of the Chartered Institute of Management Accountants, a member of the Institute of Chartered Secretaries and Administrators, a fellow or associate member of the Institute of Bankers or a trust corporation (ss 1(1)(c) and 9(1)).

To enforce the trust there must be an 'enforcer'. The trust instrument must provide for the enforcer to have an absolute right of access to any information or document which relates to the trust, the assets of the trust or the administration of the trust (ss 1(1)(d)(i) and 1(1)(e)).[42]

The trust instrument must specify the event upon the happening of which the trust terminates and must provide for the disposition of surplus assets of the trust upon its termination (s 1(1)(f)).

The designated person must keep a copy of the trust (including supplemental instruments), a register (specifying the creator of the trust, its purpose and the details of the enforcer), and trust accounts. These accounts are to be open to inspection by the Attorney General (or anyone authorised by the Attorney General). Public inspection is, however, not required (s2).

---

41  A maximum of 80 years – s 1(1).
42  In his study made contemporaneously with the introduction of the earliest NCPT legislation offshore, Paul Matthews was sceptical: "Of course, we are talking of a theoretical position. In commercial practice an enforcer will be a stooge, provided by an offshore trust and corporate services organisation, just like the trustee, the protector (if there is one), and any company directors and nominee shareholders that may be needed. [. . .] [T]he great bulk of such trusts will never come under the microscope at all, much less be subject to attacks. If one in 100 questionable 'trusts' is ever set aside, that is probably a high proportion. Indeed, the invention of these statutory purpose trusts is in part an attempt to improve the statistics, to make it less likely that any such trust will be attacked, by removing one source [i.e. beneficiaries] of superintendence and complaint". Paul Mathews, 'The New Trust: Obligations without Rights?' (n 20) 27.

Should the enforcer die or become incapable, the Attorney General must be informed, and he may apply to the High Court of Justice of the Isle of Man to appoint a successor (s 3).

No land or any interest in land in the Isle of Man may be held, directly or indirectly, in a purpose trust (s 5).

At the end of the trust period, the trust fund, which is now regarded no longer as a trust fund (because the trust has terminated) but as surplus assets, passes to an individual or institution ('the recipient of surplus') who is either named in the purpose trust deed or who can be identified using a descriptive formula contained in the trust deed, such as 'the spouse and issue of the Grantor'.

This opens up various planning possibilities, including:

(a) holding shares in a company which can then be voted in accordance with the terms of the trust (of particular importance in circumstances where an individual may not wish beneficially to own such assets);
(b) Protection of subsidiaries where a parent company borrows – the shares of the subsidiary are placed in trust until the loan is repaid, thereby protecting the subsidiary from creditors of its parent;
(c) Protection of the lender where a parent company borrows – the shares of the subsidiary can be placed in trust until the loan is repaid, thereby preventing the ownership of the subsidiary from changing;
(d) Capital financing and securitisation projects in which the trust assets are off the balance sheet of one or more parties to the transaction.

## *Foundations*

### *Liechtenstein private-benefit foundation*[43]

The Liechtenstein Foundation, the archetype upon which all later foundation laws have been based and by the degree of their divergence from which archetype the radicalisation of this offshore structure can be assessed, are created under Personen und Gesellschaftsrecht 1926 as most recently amended (the new foundations law) by the Stiftungs Gesetz 2009.[44]

A private-benefit foundation may be purely to benefit a family or may be in a mixed form which serves both the family and other charitable and non-charitable purposes. The foundation itself cannot in general terms trade but may hold the shares in a trading company – and as such is then designated a holding

---

43 See also ch 2.
44 LGBl. 2008 no 220 <www.gesetze.li> accessed 12 December 2018 (Further amended, but not germane to this topic, by the Gesetz vom 1. Dezember 2016 über die Abänderung des Personen – und Gesellschaftsrechts). See Paolo Panico, *Private Foundations, Law and Practice* (Oxford University Press, Oxford, 2014).

foundation. The minimum foundation capital is 30,000 euros, Swiss francs or US dollars.

In the case of private-benefit foundations, registration is not required – the foundation has legal personality upon being established. All that is required of the foundation is that it give notice of its formation – its name and purpose, details of its Liechtenstein-based registered agent and the identity of the members of the foundation council (the body which administers and represents the foundation). No beneficiary details need be notified. Nothing held at the Liechtenstein Land and Public Register Office is made available to the public: all that it is permitted to reveal to third parties is that the unregistered foundation exists.

It is common for a fiduciary to act as founder, its name appearing in the documentation establishing the foundation, which means that the actual founder has the option of remaining anonymous. The actual founder may sit on the foundation council and may be a beneficiary (possibly the sole beneficiary).

The foundation is of perpetual duration, but this irrevocability on the part of the actual founder can be countered by provisions in the foundation's articles that the founder retains the right both to revoke and to amend – not only its administrative provisions, but also the identity of the beneficiaries. Dissolution (in most cases at the instance of the foundation council) is also an option. On a revocation or dissolution, the assets within the foundation pass to the actual founder as ultimate beneficiary (unless other provisions have been included to the contrary). Alternatively, the re-domiciliation of the foundation is permitted, subject to the laws of the foreign jurisdiction allowing the foundation to re-domicile as a continuing entity not deemed to have been liquidated and re-established.

There is no audit requirement, unless the private-benefit foundation were voluntarily to submit to the supervision of the Foundation Supervisory Authority.[45] However, a control body may at the founder's option be appointed to verify annually that the foundation assets are being managed and distributed in accordance with the purpose(s) of the foundation: the control body can be the founder him- or herself, an auditor appointed by the court or a specialist adviser.

The new Liechtenstein foundation law places particular emphasis on good corporate governance, which in the case of private-benefit foundations focuses on internal management controls and the information rights of beneficiaries and in the case of those which have submitted voluntarily to supervision by the Foundation Supervisory Authority to provide the Authority upon request with information and with access to the foundation's books.

Forced heirship avoidance is absent. Every contribution to the assets of a foundation is open to challenge by the donor's heirs, where those heirs have forced heirship rights (either under the law of Liechtenstein itself or under foreign law, in which case the provisions of the Liechtenstein Private International Law Act

---

45 Amt für justiz, Fürstentum Liechtenstein, 'Stiftungsaufsichtsbehörde' (*Amt für justiz, Fürstentum Liechtenstein*) <www.stifa.li/en/> accessed 12 December 2018.

will be applied). A claim against the foundation for payment of the relevant compulsory portion has to be made to the Princely Court of Justice.[46]

Liechtenstein has extremely limited provisions for the recognition and enforceability of foreign judgments (Switzerland and Austria), and this lack of reciprocity is seen as an advantage for foundations, against which an action must, with the exception of Swiss and Austrian judgments, be brought in the Liechtenstein courts. Significantly, and positively, there is no provision which would automatically prevent the re-litigation before the Liechtenstein courts of a foreign, non-reciprocal judgment.

Asset protection is contemplated in the new law but in a conscious effort to weight the rights of legitimate creditors against the rights of the founder and of the foundation. There is no duty to preserve the foundation assets, but no distribution is permitted if as a result the foundation were left with funds inadequate to meet its debts. Claims against the foundation, if successful, will attach to foundation assets, but successful claims against the founder or against beneficiaries in their personal capacities will not.

## Panama Private Foundation

Panama Private Foundations ('PPF') are a creation of La Ley por la cual Se Regulan las Fundaciones de Interés Privado 1995 ('Law by which Private Interest Foundations Are Regulated').[47] There are no restrictions on the purposes for which they may be formed, but they cannot engage in commercial or for-profit activities as a day-to-day activity.

A PPF may take effect on its incorporation or may instead become active on a later event, such as the death of the founder. The asset minimum upon incorporation is a lowly US$10,000.[48] Any inheritance laws in the jurisdiction where the founder or any of the beneficiaries are domiciled are dis-applied. Equally, in the event of any judgment or other seizure of assets of the founder, the assets of the PPF are inviolate.[49] Unlike the Bahamian BEE, for example, the transfer of assets into a PPF is open to challenge by creditors on the basis that it was done fraudulently to defeat the rights of those creditors, but subject to a limitation period of three years from the date on which the transfer of those assets was made (bearing in mind that such a transfer can occur throughout the life of the

---

46 Fürstliche Gerichte Fürstentum Liechenstein, 'News' (*Fürstliche Gerichte Fürstentum Liechenstein*) <www.gerichte.li/> accessed 12 December 2018.

47 <http://docs.panama.justia.com/federales/leyes/25-de-1995-jun-14-1995.pdf> accessed 12 December 2018.

48 La Ley por la cual Se Regulan las Fundaciones de Interés Privado 1995 (n 56) art 5(2).

49 "En ningún caso responderán [los bienes de la fundación] por obligaciones personales del fundador o de los beneficiarios" [In no case shall [the foundation assets] attract liability for the personal obligations of the founder or of the beneficiaries] La Ley por la cual Se Regulan las Fundaciones de Interés Privado 1995 (n 56) art 11.

PPF) – beyond that date, no claims will be heard before the Panamanian courts. In respect of non-Panamanian assets, the PPF is tax exempt in Panama.

The administrative workings of the PPF are found in its Charter, in which the names of the founder, the foundation council and (if appointed) protector are contained. Only the names of the founder and council members need be made public – the option exists that the protector may be appointed privately. The beneficiary provisions are contained in its Regulations, which are wholly private.

Founders have the right themselves (or to appoint third parties to exercise the right) to dismiss members of the foundation council and to appoint new or additional ones.[50] Further control is afforded to a founder who may wish to become a member of a protector, committee or other supervisory body (*protector, comité o cualquier otro órgano de fiscalización*) whose consent is required for the exercise of one or more powers of the foundation council[51] (which is strikingly similar to the role of the protector in many offshore trust systems).

A PPF is subject[52] to a state duty of confidentiality, without limit as to time, which binds not only the members of the foundation council and any protector, but also any person in a civil service or private capacity who has knowledge of the activities of the PPF. Violation of this duty incurs a six-month jail sentence plus a fine of US$50,000 in addition to any civil penalties.[53] Woe betide the whistle-blower.

The separation of ownership and control in a PPF is absolute, and neither the founder (as former owner of the foundation assets) nor the beneficiaries are in any sense of the term "owners" of foundation assets. However, a more nuanced analysis reveals that through the power of the founder to control the composition of the foundation council and to exercise powers of veto and authorisation as a protector, and to restrict information flows, the control which the founder exercised over their property survives its transfer to the PPF undiminished. Using ownership as a regulatory marker in such a case is therefore wholly ineffective.

---

50 La Ley por la cual Se Regulan las Fundaciones de Interés Privado 1995 (n 56) art 21.
51 Ibid. art 19. Furthermore, under art 19 the members of the foundation council are held wholly blameless if they act in accordance with the authorisation given by the *protector, comité o cualquier otro órgano de fiscalización:* "Los miembros del Consejo de Fundación no serán responsables por pérdida o deterioro de los bienes de la fundación, ni por los daños o perjuicios causados, cuando la mencionada autorización haya sido debidamente obtenida".
52 Ibid. art 35. "Los miembros del Consejo de Fundación y de los órganos de fiscalización, si los hubiere, así como los servidores públicos o privados que tuviesen conocimiento de las actividades, transacciones u operaciones de las fundaciones, deberán mantener reserva y confidencialidad al respecto, en todo momento. Las infracciones a este deber serán sancionadas con prisión de 6 meses y multa de cincuenta mil balboas (B/.50,000.00), sin perjuicio de la responsabilidad civil correspondiente".
53 Though beneficiaries have the right under La Ley por la cual Se Regulan las Fundaciones de Interés Privado 1995 (n 56) art 18 para 3 to be informed about the economic situation of the foundation [la situación patrimonial] this is subject to any contrary provisions in the Charter [según lo establezca el acta fundacional o sus reglamentos], which therefore offers the founder ample opportunity to restrict information flow in any manner he chooses in the drafting of that Charter.

## Nevis Multiform Foundation

The Nevis Multiform Foundation (NMF) is a creation of the Nevis Multiform Foundations Ordinance 2004.[54] It is the ultimate chameleon, and it has the ability to designate itself as a trust, a company, a limited liability company, or a general or limited partnership.[55] If none of these forms is specified, then the foundation is governed by the terms of the Ordinance as a foundation plain and simple, but if so designated, then the relevant laws of Nevis apply to each designated form.[56]

The NMF throughout its life is a shape-shifter. Only one multiform may be adopted at a time, but following establishment or, as the case may be, continuation or transformation or conversion or consolidation or merger, a stated multiform may be changed by amendment to the constitution, together with, if appropriate, a change in name.

There may be any purpose, or more than one purpose, whatsoever, be it charitable or non-charitable, commercial or non-commercial, so long as not contrary to public policy in Nevis. There is no requirement to have a beneficiary.[57]

Nevis is robust in its defence of the NMF. No NMF governed by the law of Nevis, and no subscription of property to an NMF which is valid under the law of Nevis, is void, voidable, or liable to be set aside or defective in any manner by reference to the law of a foreign jurisdiction.[58] Expressly, the fact that the laws of any foreign jurisdiction prohibit or do not recognise the concept of a foundation, a multiform foundation or any stated multiform will be disregarded.

54 <www.liburddash.com/legislation/MFO,%202004.pdf> accessed 12 December 2018.
55 Nevis Multiform Foundations Ordinance 2004 s 10.
56 "Nevis, a solitary volcano in the Caribbean with a population of just 11,000, which has been implicated in some of the most sordid financial scams of modern times. [. . .] The story of Nevis reveals the difficulties the world faces in trying to put an end to tax evasion, fraud and kleptocracy. [. . .] In the world of offshore, Nevis is a bottom-feeder. It specialises in letting its clients create corporations with greater anonymity than almost anywhere else on earth". Oliver Bullough, 'Nevis: How the World's Most Secretive Offshore Haven Refuses to Clean Up' *The Guardian* (12 July 2018) <www.theguardian.com/news/2018/jul/12/nevis-how-the-worlds-most-secretive-offshore-haven-refuses-to-clean-up> accessed 12 December 2018.
57 Nevis Multiform Foundations Ordinance 2004 s 11. *"11. (1) A foundation established under this Ordinance as a multiform foundation shall have any purpose or object whatsoever and may have more than one purpose or object, and which purpose or object shall be set out in its memorandum of establishment, provided that such purpose or object is permissible and not contrary to public policy under the law of Nevis. (2) A subscriber or beneficiary may or may not benefit from any purpose or object of the multiform foundation as set out in its memorandum of establishment and such purpose or object may be for a charitable or non-charitable purpose or object, or may be for a commercial or non-commercial purpose or object or a combination of any or all of the foregoing or as may be otherwise prescribed in its memorandum of establishment, subject to the provisions of subsection (1) above. (3) There shall be no requirement for a multiform foundation to have a beneficiary".*
58 Ibid. s 46.

In many jurisdictions, heirs have fixed rights to the deceased's estate – a civil law concept known as 'forced heirship'. In the case of the NMF these rights are expunged.

There is a state duty of confidentiality,[59] without limit as to time, which binds any person in possession of or having control over any information relating to the NMF. Violation of this duty incurs a six-month jail sentence or a fine of US$50,000, or both, in addition to any civil penalties. Further, the Confidential Relationships Act, No. 2 of 1985 of St Christopher and Nevis[60] applies to every NMF established under the Ordinance. All judicial proceedings, other than criminal proceedings, relating to NMFs are to be heard in camera (that is, without members of the public present), and no details of the proceedings are to be published by any person without leave of the court. This takes the persecution of whistle-blowers to a level of ferocity way beyond that in Panama.

Hard wired into the ordinance is a wide range of asset protective features:[61]

- The NMF itself and the beneficiaries are tax exempt in Nevis.
- There is a right to silence: a person may refuse to answer any question put to them pursuant to any provision of the Ordinance if that person's answer would or might tend to expose that person, or the spouse of that person, to proceedings under the law of Nevis or elsewhere for an offence or for the recovery of any penalty.
- Acting honestly, in the opinion of the Court, is a full defence to an action against any member of the foundation's management for negligence, default, or breach of duty.
- Notwithstanding that it is proved beyond reasonable doubt by a creditor that an NMF was subscribed to by or on behalf of a subscriber with principal intent to defraud the creditor of the subscriber and did at the time such subscription take place render the subscriber insolvent or without property by which that creditor's claim (if successful) could have been satisfied, such subscription will not be regarded by the court as void or voidable, and the NMF shall instead itself be liable to satisfy the creditor's claim. Such liability is, however, limited to the extent of the interest that the subscriber had in the property representing or comprising the subscription prior to subscription.
- If a creditor has a cause of action (wherever this arises, and not merely in Nevis) against a subscriber to the NMF, and the subscription into the NMF was made more than one year after that cause arose, the matter is time barred. If the subscription is made within that year, the creditor must commence the action no later than six months from the date of the subscription or be time barred.

---

59  Ibid. s 113.
60  <www.nexus.ua/images/legislation/Nevis_Confidential_1985.pdf> accessed 12 December 2018.
61  Nevis Multiform Foundations Ordinance 2004 pt XV.

- No assets or property of the NMF available for distribution to a beneficiary are to be alienated or pass by bankruptcy, insolvency or liquidation or be liable to be seized, sold, attached or taken in execution by process of law.[62]
- The constitution of an NMF may provide that any beneficiary, creditor of the beneficiary, trustee-in-bankruptcy or liquidator of the beneficiary shall forfeit his beneficial entitlement in the event that they or any creditor of the beneficiary, trustee-in-bankruptcy or liquidator of the beneficiary challenges the creation of the multiform foundation, any subscriptions to the multiform foundation, the constitution or any provision thereof or any decision of the management board or the supervisory board.
- No foreign judgment against the NMF, its management or the beneficiaries will be enforced in Nevis.
- The Statute of Elizabeth[63] (enactment entitled 13 Elizabeth 1 Ch 5 (1571)) which renders void any fraudulent transfer of property, and which would otherwise apply under the laws of Nevis, has no application to any multiform foundation which takes the form of a trust, nor to any subscription to such a multiform foundation.

This begs the question, as a shapeshifter, in what form may an NMF be litigated against successfully? Should the claim be brought against the NMF in the form it took at the time of the action giving rise to the complaint, or alternatively in the form it takes at the time the claim is brought? For example, in a claim based on an allegation of ultra vires dealings on the part of the NMF, may an NMF in its defence claim that though it may have been liable by virtue of dealing ultra vires in its earlier form, its current form affords it far wider powers and these are, vis-à-vis the claimant, curative of any earlier defect? Would the claim still be actionable? The law of Nevis is silent on the point.

The Financial Services Regulatory Commission of Nevis comments on its website[64]:

> *The Nevis Multiform Foundation Ordinance is a very unique and cutting-edge legislation which was designed to remedy some of the problems seen in other foundation products.*
>
> *The Nevis Multiform Foundations Ordinance provides that each Nevis Foundation will have a stated 'multiform'. This means that the constitution of the foundation will state how it is to be treated whether as a trust, a company, a partnership or an ordinary foundation. Through the 'multiform' concept the stated identity of the Foundation can be changed during its lifetime, thus*

62 Ibid. s 47(1).
63 Wikipedia, 'Fraudulent Conveyances Act 1571' <https://en.wikipedia.org/wiki/Fraudulent_Conveyances_Act_1571> accessed 12 December 2018.
64 <www.nevisfsrc.com/products/foundations/legal-framework> accessed 12 December 2018.

*allowing for there to be greater flexibility in its use and application. Generally, the Nevis Multiform Foundation product can be used for estate planning, charity, financing and special investment holding arrangements.*

To apply ownership as a regulatory marker to such a chimeric structure, which owes its very existence to the marketing drive of a small offshore jurisdiction, to become "very unique and cutting-edge" is inappropriate. As analysed in Chapter 3, ascertaining "ownership" and "beneficial ownership" in the context of corporations, trusts, and foundations is not a one-size-fits-all process and in addition to which the complexities of charitable and non-charitable purposes have to be factored in. Such an analysis would be sufficiently taxing when applying it to a structure which is immutable in form. It becomes well-nigh impossible when applying it to one which may take any one or more forms at any point in time and which as a result has to be assessed not as it is at the point of enquiry but how it was positioned in a spectrum of opportunities as to form at the time of the action under investigation.

Even if found culpable (which on the basis of the limitations of liability, procedural dead ends and exemptions provided under Nevis Multiform Foundations Ordinance 2004 pt XV appears improbable) would the NMF *in the form it took at the date of the activity which is the basis of that finding* be susceptible to penalty or to any act for recovery *in the form it takes when enforcement is attempted*? It reduces the level of international regulation to that of shadow boxing.

## Conclusions

Orphan structures go to the heart of the matter: unaccountable, mysterious and unapproachable. They have been engineered not merely to disguise or postpone ownership, but to eliminate ownership altogether. They are a targeted response on the part of the offshore jurisdictions to transparency strategies.[65]

They are generated by no social need in the jurisdictions in which they are promoted; they are the love children of the finance sectors by which these jurisdictions have been captured and to which, economically and politically, they are in thrall.

Yet no transparency strategy – global, regional or national – makes any provision for structures which are designed to be ownerless. None of the structures reviewed in this chapter, other than vanilla foundations, is referred to in the multiplicity of codes, regulations, guidance and general exhortations. All of the transparency strategies use ownership as the defining regulatory criterion, and even where "control" supplements pure ownership, this is ineffective when faced with the ultimate counter-initiative, the counter-intuitive orphans.

---

65 See the discussion of transparency strategies in ch 3.

# Appendix

## Non-charitable purpose trust jurisdictions (sampled)

| Jurisdiction | Statute |
| --- | --- |
| Belize | Trusts Act 1992 |
| British Virgin Islands | Trustee Act (Cap. 303) as amended by Trustee (Amendment) Act 2013 |
| Barbados | International Trusts Act 1995 |
| Cayman Islands | Introduced into the Cayman Islands via the Special Trusts (Alternative Regime) Law, 1997, now embedded in Part VIII of the Trusts Law (2011 Revision) ("STAR Trusts") |
| Cook Islands[66] | International Trusts Amendment Act 1995–96, s 8 |
| Guernsey | Trusts (Guernsey) Law 2007, s 12 |
| Isle of Man | Purpose Trusts Act 1996 |
| Jersey | Trusts (Jersey) Law 1984 (as amended by Trusts (Amendment No. 3) (Jersey) Law 1996 with effect from 24 May 1996) |
| Labuan | Labuan Trusts Act 1996 (as amended, 2010) s 11A |
| Mauritius | Trusts Act 2001, s 19 |
| Niue | Trustee Companies Act 1994, s31 |
| Samoa | Trusts Act 2014, s 66 |
| Turks and Caicos Islands | Trusts Ordinance 2016 |
| USA, Delaware | Del. Code tit. 12, s 3556 |
| USA, New Hampshire | N.H. Rev. Stat. s 564-B |
| USA, South Dakota | South Dakota Codified laws s 55–1–20 |
| USA, Wyoming | Wyo. Stat. s 4–10–410 |

66 Pacific Islands Legal Information Institute <www.paclii.org> accessed 12 December 2018.

# Bibliography

## Cases

*Re Poyiadjis* 2001–03 MLR 316
*Saunders v Vautier* [1841] EWHC J82, [1841] 4 Beav 115


## Legislation and regulations

Confidential Relationships Act, No. 2 of 1985 of St Christopher and Nevis <www.nexus.ua/images/legislation/Nevis_Confidential_1985.pdf> accessed 12 December 2018

The Executive Entities Act 2011 <http://laws.bahamas.gov.bs/cms/images/LEG ISLATION/PRINCIPAL/2011/2011-0052/ExecutiveEntitiesAct2011_1.pdf> accessed 12 December 2018 (Bahamas)

Executive Entities Regulations 2012, SI 13 of 2012 <http://laws.bahamas.gov. bs/cms/images/LEGISLATION/SUBORDINATE/2012/2012-0013/Execu tiveEntitiesRegulations2012_1.pdf> accessed 12 December 2018 (Bahamas)

International Business Companies Act 2016 <www.seylii.org/sc/legislation/ act/2016/15> accessed 12 December 2018 (Seychelles)

La Ley por la cual Se Regulan las Fundaciones de Interés Privado 1995 ('Law by which Private Interest Foundations Are Regulated' <http://docs.panama.justia.com/fed erales/leyes/25-de-1995-jun-14-1995.pdf> accessed 12 December 2018 (Panama)

Nevis Multiform Foundations Ordinance 2004 <www.liburddash.com/legislation/ MFO,%202004.pdf> accessed 12 December 2018 (Nevis)

Part VIII Trusts Law (2011 Revision) <www.gov.ky/portal/pls/portal/ docs/1/11524845.PDF> accessed 12 December 2018 (Cayman Islands)

Perpetuities and Accumulations Act 1968 <https://legislation.gov.im/cms/images/ LEGISLATION/PRINCIPAL/1968/1968-0008/PerpetuitiesandAccumula tionsAct1968_2.pdf> accessed 12 December 2018 (Isle of Man)

Personen und Gesellschaftsrecht 1926 and Stiftungs Gesetz 2009 LGBl. 2008 no 220 <www.gesetze.li> accessed 12 December 2018 (Principality of Liechtenstein)

Purpose Trusts Act 1996 <https://legislation.gov.im/cms/images/LEGISLA TION/PRINCIPAL/1996/1996-0009/PurposeTrustsAct1996_1.pdf> accessed 12 December 2018 (Isle of Man)

Small Business Enterprise and Employment Act 2015 <www.legislation.gov.uk/ ukpga/2015/26/contents> accessed 12 December 2018 (UK)

The Statute of Elizabeth 13 Elizabeth 1 Ch 5 (1571) Wikipedia 'Fraudulent Conveyances Act 1571' <https://en.wikipedia.org/wiki/Fraudulent_Conveyances_ Act_1571> accessed 12 December 2018

Trustee Act 2000 <www.legislation.gov.uk/ukpga/2000/29/contents> accessed 12 December 2018 (UK)

Trustee Act 2001 <https://legislation.gov.im/cms/images/LEGISLATION/ PRINCIPAL/2001/2001-0018/TrusteeAct2001_1.pdf> accessed 12 December 2018 (Isle of Man)

United Kingdom Government, Companies House, 'PSC Requirements for Companies and Limited Liability Partnerships' (*gov.uk*, 27 January 2016) <www.gov.uk/govern ment/publications/guidance-to-the-people-with-significant-control-requirements-for-companies-and-limited-liability-partnerships> accessed 12 December 2018

—— 'Keeping Your People with Significant Control (PSC) Register' (*gov.uk*, 6 April 2016) <www.gov.uk/government/news/keeping-your-people-with-signifi cant-control-psc-register> accessed 12 December 2018

Virgin Islands Special Trusts Act 2003 <www.bvifsc.vg/sites/default/files/ virgin_islands_special_trusts_act_2003.pdf> accessed 12 December 2018 and Virgin Islands Special Trusts (Amendment) Act 2013 <www.bvifsc.vg/sites/ default/files/virgin_islands_special_trusts_amendment_act_2013.pdf> accessed 12 December 2018 (British Virgin Islands)

## European documents

Fifth Anti Money Laundering Directive (Directive EU 2018/843 30 May 2018 <https://eur-lex.europa.eu/legal-content/EN/TXT/?qid=1540113903626&ur i=CELEX:32018L0843>with the full text in English at <https://eur-lex.europa. eu/legal-content/EN/TXT/PDF/?uri=CELEX:32018L0843&qid=154011390 3626&from=EN> accessed 20 December 2018

Fourth Anti Money Laundering Directive (Directive EU 2015/849) <https://pub-lications.europa.eu/en/publication-detail/-/publication/0bff31ef-0b49-11e5-8817-01aa75ed71a1/language-en> accessed 20 December 2018

## International documents

Convention of 1 July 1985 on the Law Applicable to Trusts and on their Recog-nition (Hague Convention) <www.hcch.net/en/instruments/conventions/full-text/?cid=59> accessed 12 December 2018

OECD 'Standard for Automatic Exchange of Financial Account Information in Tax Matters' (OECD, 21 July 2014) <www.oecd.org/ctp/exchange-of-tax-infor mation/standard-for-automatic-exchange-of-financial-account-information-for-tax-matters-9789264216525-en.htm> accessed 12 December 2018

## United Nations documents

The United Nations Guiding Principles on Business and Human Rights 2011 (Ruggie Principles) A/HRC/17/31 <www.ohchr.org/EN/Issues/Transnational Corporations/Pages/Reports.aspx> accessed 11 December 2018

## Secondary sources

Boal, Catherine 'Securing Succession' *The Bahamas Investor* (13 July 2011) <www. thebahamasinvestor.com/2011/securing-succession/> accessed 12 December 2018

Bullough, Oliver 'Nevis: How the World's Most Secretive Offshore Haven Refuses to Clean Up' *The Guardian* (12 July 2018) <www.theguardian.com/news/2018/ jul/12/nevis-how-the-worlds-most-secretive-offshore-haven-refuses-to-clean-up> accessed 12 December 2018

Burian, Peter 'Seychelles: Beating the Odds' *Offshore Investment* 265 (April 2016) <http://www.offshoreinvestment.com/seychelles-beating-the-odds-archive/> (subscription service only) accessed 12 March 2019

The Commonwealth 'Caribbean Integrity Commissions Form New Commonwealth Body to Fight Corruption' (*The Commonwealth*, 25 June 2015) <https://shar. es/1QVznK> accessed 12 December 2018

Duckworth, Anthony 'STAR WARS: The Colony Strikes Back' 12 *Trust Law International* 1, 16 (1998)

——— 'STAR WARS: Smiting the Bull' 13 *Trust Law International* 3, 158 (1999)

Glister, J and Lee, J *Hanbury & Martin: Modern Equity* (20th Edition, Sweet & Maxwell, London, 2015) ch 16 'Non-Charitable Purpose Trusts'

Hayton, D (ed), *Modern International Developments in Trust Law* (Kluwer Law International, Alphen aan den Rijn, Netherlands, 1999)

Hayton, D and others, *Underhill and Hayton Law of Trusts and Trustees* (19th Edition, LexisNexis, London, 2016)

Hayton, David J 'Developing the obligation characteristic of the trust' 117 *LQR*, 96 (January 2001)

Levy, Danielle 'Lawrence Graham Seeks to Revolutionise Offshore Trust Structures' (*Citywire*, 23 April 2010) <http://citywire.co.uk/wealth-manager/news/ lawrence-graham-seeks-to-revolutionise-offshore-trust-structures/a395505/ print?section=wealth-manager> accessed 12 December 2018

Matthews, Paul 'The New Trust: Obligations Without Rights?' in A J Oakley (ed), *Trends in Contemporary Trust Law* (Oxford University Press, Oxford, 1996)

——— 'Shooting STAR: The New Special Trusts Regime from the Cayman Islands' 11 *Trust Law International* 3, 67 (1997)

——— 'STAR: Big Bang or Red Dwarf?' 12 *Trust Law International* 2, 98 (1998)

Olsen, Carey 'A Guide to Non-Charitable Purpose Trusts in Jersey' (*Carey Olsen*, 23 March 2017) <www.careyolsen.com/downloads/Non_charitable_purpose_trusts_ in_Jersey.pdf> accessed 12 December 2018

Panico, Paolo *Private Foundations, Law and Practice* (Oxford University Press, Oxford, 2014)

Scott, Jude 'Cayman Finance Response to US PIRG Report: Cayman's Commitment to Global Transparency Standards Makes It a Strong International Partner' *Cayman Finance* <www.cayman.finance/2017/10/cayman-finance-response- us-pirg-report-caymans-commitment-global-transparency-standards-makes- strong-international-partner/> accessed 12 December 2018

Waters, Donovan 'The Hague Trusts Convention Twenty Years On' in Michele Graziadei, Ugo Mattei and Lionel Smith (eds), *Commercial Trusts in European Private Law* (Cambridge University Press, Cambridge, 2005)

Zagaris, Bruce 'Changes in International Regulatory Regimes on Caribbean Corporate, Financial Regulatory and Transparency Law' 263 *Offshore Investment* (2016)

# 6 Cryptocurrency and the blockchain – transient ownership

## Introduction

Earlier chapters in this book have looked at what it means in law and in equity to be an "owner", how a fundamental misunderstanding (or excessive pragmatism) on the part of regulatory authorities of the concept of "ownership" has undermined transparency strategies and how a global industry in ownerless structures is burgeoning.

There remains one more counter-initiative. If ownership is merely fleeting, passing from one person to another in minutes, if an owner can place a girdle round the earth in far, far less than forty,[1] then accountability is correspondingly brief. This is the phenomenon of *transient ownership* made possible through the use of cryptocurrency and the blockchain.[2]

This chapter looks at the challenges faced in identifying ownership and attributing accountability where transactions are funded through cryptocurrency or evidenced only on the blockchain.[3]

---

1 William Shakespeare, *Midsummer Night's Dream* Act II, Scene 1, 547.
2 Blockchains cannot yet handle millisecond performance on transactions. As of April 2018, various forms of distributed ledger technologies carry between a two- and ten-minute processing time. (Source: *Blockchain Beyond the Hype. A Practical Framework for Business Leaders* (World Economic Forum, April 2018) <http://www3.weforum.org/docs/48423_Whether_Blockchain_WP.pdf> 7 accessed 29 December 2018). By anyone's standards, however, a maximum of ten minutes as owner is transient.
3 Publications on cryptocurrency and the blockchain now run into the thousands, and so this chapter assumes a basic understanding of each concept. For a comprehensive overview of the subject see *Deciphering cryptocurrencies* (Norton Rose Fulbright, 2015–2016) <https://knowledgeproducts.nortonrosefulbright.com/nrf/deciphering-cryptocurrencies> accessed 29 December 2018 and *Unlocking the Blockchain* (Norton Rose Fulbright, 2018) <https://knowledgeproducts.nortonrosefulbright.com/nrf/unlocking-the-blockchain> accessed 29 December 2018. Numbers of bibliographies are available, amongst which are: *Blockchain & Society* <https://blockchain-society.science/blockchain-bibliography/> accessed 29 December 2018; *Cite This for Me* <www.citethisforme.com/topic-ideas/technology/Cryptocurrency-47844035> accessed 29 December 2018; *Crypto Law Review* <https://medium.com/cryptolawreview/blockchain-governance-bibliography-360efc52d3f9> accessed 29 December 2018; Giovanni Perani, *Blockchain: Bibliography* (Queen Mary University of London,

The questions to be answered concern both the nature of cryptocurrency and blockchain transactions and how existing regulations and legal analysis are capable of adapting to the new technology. What transparency strategies are being pioneered regionally and nationally? Is virtual currency merely a medium of exchange, redeemable against a purchase? Or does virtual currency go further than this, and in the form of a token have property rights attached which give it the characteristics of securities? If so, are 'virtual' securities susceptible to banking and investment regulation? How is this evidenced in the case of initial coin offerings – are these so closely analogous to initial public offerings that they should be subject to existing securities regulation? What threats are posed by the anonymity (or pseudoanonymity) of blockchain transactions? Are blockchain transactions "outlaws" in the sense that they are subject to the laws of no single jurisdiction, or no jurisdiction at all, and hence unaccountable?

Fundamentally, is the very evolution of cryptocurrency technology and the blockchain a counter-initiative to ownership transparency strategies and therefore a means of avoiding accountability?

## Cryptocurrency

The public response to the emergence of cryptocurrencies has been ambiguous, "Letting 'I dare not' wait upon 'I would', Like the poor cat I' the adage".[4] Virtual currencies have been described as "tomorrow's tax havens".[5]

> Cryptocurrencies, in large part, got their start when some investors wanted to create money no central bank could control – and no government agency could tax. Blockchain has, for the most part, enabled crypto investors to fly under the regulatory radar. With virtual coins counted in the blockchain all over the world and no overarching authority to control their value or monitor transactions, cryptocurrencies have looked like a potential tax haven.[6]

---

School of Law) <www.diritto.net/blockchain-bibliography/> accessed 29 December 2018; Pedro Franco, *Understanding Bitcoin: Cryptography, Engineering and Economics* (John Wiley & Sons Ltd., 2015), the bibliography for which is available at <https://onlinelibrary.wiley.com/doi/pdf/10.1002/9781119019138.biblio accessed 29 December 2018>; Stephan K Johansen, *A Comprehensive Literature Review on the Blockchain as a Technological Enabler for Innovation* (Mannheim University, Department of Information Systems, November 2016) <www.researchgate.net/publication/312592741_A_Comprehensive_Literature_Review_on_the_Blockchain_Technology_as_an_Technological_Enabler_for_Innovation> accessed 29 December 2018.

4  William Shakespeare, *Macbeth* Act I, Scene 7, 35.
5  Tara Mandjee, 'Bitcoin, Its Classification and Its Regulatory Framework' 15 *Journal of Business & Securities Law* 2, 158 (2015), at 186,187.
6  Paul Banker, 'Blockchain Can't Hide Cryptocurrency Revenues from the IRS' (CPA Practice Advisor, 14 December 2018) <www.cpapracticeadvisor.com/article/12437776/blockchain-cant-hide-cryptocurrency-revenues-from-the-irs> accessed 29 December 2018.

They have not yet found universal acceptance, particularly in the international finance sector:

> Last year Jamie Dimon, the chief executive of JP Morgan, said Bitcoin was a fraud and only fit for use by drug dealers, murderers and people living in places such as North Korea. He said: "The currency isn't going to work. You can't have a business where people can invent a currency out of thin air and think that people who are buying it are really smart."[7]

On 12 February 2018 the European Securities and Markets Authority, the European Banking Authority and the European Insurance and Occupational Pensions Authority issued a joint warning on the risks of virtual currencies, citing extreme volatility and bubble risk, absence of regulatory protection, lack of exit options or of price transparency, misleading information and unsuitability of virtual currencies for most purposes including investment or retirement planning.[8] This was closely followed on 15 March 2018 by the publication by the European Banking Authority of a FinTech Roadmap setting out the establishment of a Fin-Tech Knowledge Hub "to enhance knowledge sharing and foster technological neutrality in regulatory and supervisory approaches". This includes addressing consumer issues arising from FinTech and includes "the appropriateness of the current regulatory framework for virtual currencies".[9] Yet this may not be all that it at first sight appears. Speaking in March 2018 shortly before the publication of the FinTech Roadmap, Andrea Enria, chief executive of the European

---

7 Quoted by Angela Monaghan, 'Time to Regulate Bitcoin, Says Treasury Committee Report' *The Guardian* (19 September 2018) <www.theguardian.com/technology/2018/sep/19/time-to-regulate-bitcoin-says-treasury-committee-report> accessed 29 December 2018.

8 The full text of the warning is available via a hyperlink contained in a press release dated 12 February 2018 issued by the European Securities and Markets Authority <www.esma.europa.eu/press-news/esma-news/esas-warn-consumers-risks-in-buying-virtual-currencies> accessed 29 December 2018. An earlier study by the European Banking Authority issued on 4 July 2014 *EBA Opinion on 'virtual currencies'* EBA/Op/2014/08 identified multiple risks: "The risks, by contrast, are manifold. More than 70 risks were identified across several categories, including risks to users; risks to non-user market participants; risks to financial integrity, such as money laundering and other financial crime; risks to existing payment systems in conventional FCs, and risks to regulatory authorities". (Executive Summary, 5) <https://eba.europa.eu/documents/10180/657547/EBA-Op-2014-08+Opinion+on+Virtual+Currencies.pdf> accessed 29 December 2018. A contrasting view is taken by the Financial Stability Board, which whilst giving full weight to national and regional warnings issued to retail consumers concerning the volatility and risk associated with investment in cryptocurrencies, is nevertheless of the view "that crypto-assets do not pose a material risk to global financial stability at this time" *Crypto-asset Markets: Potential Channels for Future Financial Stability Implications* (10 October 2018) 14 <www.fsb.org/wp-content/uploads/P101018.pdf> accessed 29 December 2018.

9 EBA published its Roadmap on FinTech 15 March 2018 <https://eba.europa.eu/-/eba-publishes-its-roadmap-on-fintech> accessed 29 December 2018. The full text is at <https://eba.europa.eu/documents/10180/1919160/EBA+FinTech+Roadmap.pdf> accessed 29 December 2018.

Banking Authority, suggested it would be more effective to prevent banks and other regulated financial institutions from holding or selling cryptocurrencies rather than regulating the virtual currencies themselves:

> Recently, several central banks have argued that cryptocurrencies lack the institutional back-up of a central bank and cannot fulfil the traditional functions of money. [. . .] I am yet to be convinced that this is a sufficiently strong argument to attract cryptocurrencies under the full scope of regulation. [. . .] An excessive extension of the regulatory perimeter [. . .] is likely to be a sub-optimal solution. It would risk excessively constraining financial innovation, as the compliance burden placed on banks is not sustainable for small innovative start-ups.[10]

One foot firmly fixed on the moral high ground, yet one eye sharply focussed on the prize, the attitude of the United Kingdom Parliament is not untypical of many jurisdictions. In its report *Crypto-assets* published on 12 September 2018[11] the House of Commons Treasury Committee could not conceal its scepticism, even refusing to classify virtual currency as a form of currency at all:

> 5. However, despite the widespread use of the term, the Committee heard that there are no "cryptocurrencies" that perform the functions that are generally understood to define the term "currency". Martin Etheridge, Head of Note Operations at the Bank of England, told the Committee that:
>
> They [so-called cryptocurrencies] are not acting as a medium of exchange; they are not particularly good as a store of value, given the volatility; and they are certainly not being used as a unit of account. Although about 500 independent shops might say they accept bitcoin, you do not see many people pricing or receiving their wages in Bitcoin.
>
> Mr. Etheridge said that the term "crypto-assets" was therefore more accurate. Izabella Kaminska, editor at *The Financial Times* Alphaville, agreed with Mr. Etheridge, adding that:
>
> In the current environment, it looks like [cryptocurrencies] are mostly being used for speculation and as vehicles for potentially relatively quick gains or losses. They are definitely [on] the asset side.
>
> 6. For the purposes of this report, the term 'crypto-assets' will be used in place of 'crypto-currencies'.
>
> [. . .]

10  Quoted in Caroline Binham, 'EU body strikes back at cryptocurrency regulation' *Financial Times* (9 March 2018) <www.ft.com/content/bc48eafc-2301-11e8-ae48-60d3531b7d11> accessed 29 December 2018.
11  <https://publications.parliament.uk/pa/cm201719/cmselect/cmtreasy/910/910.pdf> accessed 29 December 2018.

13. Functioning currencies are generally understood to serve as a store of value, a medium of exchange and a unit of account. As yet, there are no so-called "cryptocurrencies" that serve all these functions. Well-functioning cryptocurrencies currently exist only as a theoretical concept, and the term "crypto-assets" is more helpful and meaningful in describing Bitcoin, and the many hundreds of other 'altcoins' that have emerged over the past decade.

The Committee clearly felt that the virtual currency sector has its fair share of cowboys:

129. Crypto-assets have been embedded in certain pockets of society and industry, and it is highly likely that they are here to stay. The UK Government and financial services regulators appear to be deciding whether they will allow the current "wild west" situation to continue, or whether they are going to introduce regulation. The current ambiguity surrounding the Government's and the regulators' positions is clearly not sustainable.

Somewhat disingenuously, and perhaps not entirely immune to the seductive qualities of this emerging technology, the report concludes:

134. If the UK develops an appropriate and proportionate regulatory environment for crypto-assets and if future innovations in crypto-assets proved themselves as beneficial to society and industry, the UK could be well placed to become a global centre for this activity, providing that the crypto-asset market adhered to high standards and was not associated with criminality.

The speed with which the cryptocurrency industry has developed[12] is matched only by the speed of the transactions which it facilitates. Garrick Hileman and Michel Rauchs in their ground-breaking Global Cryptocurrency Benchmarking Study (2017) comment

The findings are both striking and thought-provoking. First, the user adoption of various cryptocurrencies has really taken off, with billions in market cap and millions of wallets estimated to have been 'active' in 2016. Second, the cryptocurrency industry is both globalised and localised, with borderless exchange operations, as well as geographically clustered mining activities.

12 A review of the 10 cryptocurrencies with highest market capitalisation as at July 2018 is contained in section 3.2 of Robby Houben and Alexander Snyers, *Cryptocurrencies and Blockchain: Legal Context and Implications for Financial Crime, Money Laundering and Tax Evasion* (European Parliament, Policy Department for Economic, Scientific and Quality of Life Policies, July 2018) <www.europarl.europa.eu/cmsdata/150761/TAX3%20Study%20 on%20cryptocurrencies%20and%20blockchain.pdf> accessed 29 December 2018.

Third, the industry is becoming more fluid, as the lines between exchanges and wallets are increasingly 'blurred' and a multitude of cryptocurrencies, not just bitcoin, are now supported by a growing ecosystem, fulfilling an array of functions. Fourth, issues of security and regulatory compliance are likely to remain prevalent for years to come.[13]

### Technical definition

*Cryptocurrency* (also known as digital or virtual currency)[14] is an electronically issued currency the transferability of which into fiat currency[15] is not guaranteed by the state. Jan Lansky of the University of Finance and Administration in Prague defines cryptocurrency as a system which meets the following six conditions:

1   The system does not require a central authority, distributed achieve consensus on its state.
2   The system keeps an overview of cryptocurrency units and their ownership.
3   The system defines whether new cryptocurrency units can be created. If new cryptocurrency units can be created, the system defines the circumstances of their origin and how to determine the ownership of these new units.
4   Ownership of cryptocurrency units can be proved exclusively cryptographically.
5   The system allows transactions to be performed in which ownership of the cryptographic units is changed. A transaction statement can only be issued by an entity proving the current ownership of these units.
6   If two different instructions for changing the ownership of the same cryptographic units are simultaneously entered, the system performs at most one of them.[16]

---

13  Ibid. 4.
14  "While the various forms of what are broadly known as 'cryptocurrencies' are similar in that they are primarily based on the same type of decentralized technology known as blockchain with inherent encryption, the terminology used to describe them varies greatly from one jurisdiction to another. Some of the terms used by countries to reference cryptocurrency include: digital currency (Argentina, Thailand and Australia), virtual commodity (Canada, China and Taiwan), crypto-token (Germany), payment token (Switzerland), cyber currency (Italy and Lebanon), electronic currency (Colombia and Lebanon), and virtual asset (Honduras and Mexico)". *Regulation of Cryptocurrency Around the World* (The Law Library of Congress, Global Legal Research Centre, June 2018) 1 <www.loc.gov/law/help/crypto currency/cryptocurrency-world-survey.pdf> accessed 29 December 2018.
15  "Paper money or coins of little or no intrinsic value in themselves and not convertible into gold or silver, but made legal tender by fiat (order) of the government. Fiat money is an intrinsically worthless object, such as paper money, that is deemed to be money by law". *Ft. com/lexicon* <http://lexicon.ft.com/Term?term=fiat-money> accessed 29 December 2018.
16  Jan Lansky, 'Possible State Approaches to Cryptocurrencies' *Journal of Systems Integration* 1 (2018) 19 <www.researchgate.net/publication/322869220_Possible_State_Approaches_to_Cryptocurrencies> accessed 29 December 2018.

The four key cryptocurrency industry sectors[17] are:

- Exchanges – the purchase, sale and trading of cryptocurrency.
- Wallets – storage of cryptocurrency.
- Payments – facilitating payments using cryptocurrency.
- Mining – securing the global ledger (blockchain) generally by computing large amounts of hashes[18] to find a valid block that is added to the blockchain.

## *Cryptocurrency from an ownership perspective*

The state authorisation and use of bearer securities has declined in recent years for the self-evident reason that a bearer security, regarded as being owned by the person who has possession of it, is anonymous, travels freely and neatly avoids detection. Cryptocurrencies represent a renaissance in the bearer security industry, unrestrained by geography or jurisdiction,[19] and a facilitator of transient ownership and fraud:

> Cryptocurrencies are digital bearer assets that once transferred cannot easily be recovered (i.e., the payment cannot be reversed unless the recipient decides to do so). The surge in market prices of cryptocurrencies in recent years has made exchanges a popular target for criminals as they handle and store large amounts of cryptocurrencies. Numerous events have led to the

---

17 Garrick Hileman and Michel Rauchs, *Global Cryptocurrency Benchmarking Study* (Cambridge Centre for Alternative Finance, University of Cambridge Judge Business School, 2017) Table 2, 21 <www.jbs.cam.ac.uk/fileadmin/user_upload/research/centres/alternative-finance/downloads/2017-global-cryptocurrency-benchmarking-study.pdf> accessed 29 December 2018.

18 "Hash" is a function that converts an input of letters and numbers into an encrypted output of a fixed length – created using an algorithm. "The blockchain only contains validated transactions, which prevents fraudulent transactions and double spending of the currency. The validation process relies on data being encrypted using algorithmic hashing. The resulting encrypted value is a series of numbers and letters that does not resemble the original data, and is called a hash". *Investopedia* <www.investopedia.com/terms/h/hash.asp> accessed 29 December 2018.

19 An overview of the problems of determining which laws of which jurisdiction, if any, govern a cryptocurrency transaction is found in Leigh Sagar, *Fighting Over Nothing: Cryptocurrency Litigation Issues* <www.chba.org.uk/for-members/library/overseas-seminars/cryptocurrency-litigation-issues> accessed 29 December 2018. Indeed, cryptocurrency may stand outside the national/international dichotomy altogether: "For the regulatory authorities, the concern is to reconcile the limited jurisdictional reach of their powers with international (*anational*) and distributed nature of the cryptocurrency sector. The transnational nature of cryptocurrencies complicates the task by requiring almost universal consensus among the states holding radically different positions on cryptocurrencies". Michael McKee, DLA Piper, *Regulation of Virtual Currencies* (15 May 2018) <www.ucl.ac.uk/laws/sites/laws/files/02_mckee_ucl-blockchain.pdf< accessed 29 December 2018.

loss of exchange customer funds, and a wide variety of schemes have been employed ranging from outside server breaches to insider theft.[20]

The main property of a reasonably decentralised cryptocurrency is that the native token constitutes a censorship-resistant, digital bearer asset [. . .]. It is a *bearer asset* in the sense that the person who controls the respective private key[21] controls the particular amount of cryptocurrency associated with the corresponding public key, and *censorship-resistant* in the sense that, in theory, nobody can freeze or confiscate cryptocurrency funds nor censor transactions performed on the integrated payment network. As cryptocurrency systems are not bound to a particular location or jurisdiction, the integrated payment network has a global reach and can be used to transfer funds within a short time (ranging from seconds to several minutes depending on a variety of factors) all over the world.[22]

Ascertaining where ownership information may be located amongst the industry sectors of exchanges, wallets, payments and mining has become far more complex with the development of *universal* cryptocurrency platforms:

> It can be observed that wallets are progressively integrating exchange services within the wallet interface as a means to load the wallet, while exchanges often also provide a means to securely store newly acquired cryptocurrency within their platform. Similarly, payment companies increasingly offer fully fledged money transfer platforms that enable the storage and transfer of

---

20 Garrick Hileman and Michel Rauchs, *Global Cryptocurrency Benchmarking Study* (Cambridge Centre for Alternative Finance, University of Cambridge Judge Business School, 2017) 38 <www.jbs.cam.ac.uk/fileadmin/user_upload/research/centres/alternative-finance/downloads/2017-global-cryptocurrency-benchmarking-study.pdf> accessed 29 December 2018.

21 "Cryptocurrencies can be owned through cryptocurrency accounts. A cryptocurrency account consists of a combination of a private key and a cryptocurrency account address. The cryptocurrency account address functions similarly to a bank account number for fiat currencies. The private key is similar to a secret Personal Identification Number (PIN), which can be used to check that the account owner is using the account. [. . .] Private key is a random number within the range of 1 to $2^{256}$. There are more possible private keys than atoms in the universe". Jan Lansky 'Possible State Approaches to Cryptocurrencies' (n 21) 21.

22 Garrick Hileman and Michel Rauchs, *Global Cryptocurrency Benchmarking Study* (Cambridge Centre for Alternative Finance, University of Cambridge Judge Business School, 2017) 106 <www.jbs.cam.ac.uk/fileadmin/user_upload/research/centres/alternative-finance/downloads/2017-global-cryptocurrency-benchmarking-study.pdf> accessed 29 December 2018. But note that some jurisdictions are seeking to develop their own system of cryptocurrencies: China; the Eastern Caribbean Central Bank (ECCB) member states (Anguilla; Antigua and Barbuda; Dominica; Grenada; Montserrat; Saint Kitts and Nevis; Saint Lucia; Saint Vincent and the Grenadines); Ireland; Lithuania; the Marshall Islands and Venezuela. *Regulation of Cryptocurrency Around the World* (The Law Library of Congress, Global Legal Research Center, June 2018) Comparative Summary <www.loc.gov/law/help/cryptocurrency/cryptocurrency-world-survey.pdf> accessed 29 December 2018.

cryptocurrencies, and often include an integrated currency exchange service. As a result, putting cryptocurrency companies into fixed categories can represent a challenging task in some cases.[23]

A further shift into even greater secrecy is the use of "off-chain" transactions:

[A] rising number of cryptocurrency transactions are not performed '*on-chain*' (i.e., directly on the blockchain network), but '*off-chain*' via internal accounting systems operated by centralised exchanges, wallets and payment companies. These off-chain transactions do not appear on a public ledger.[24]

Storage, sending and receiving of cryptocurrencies is by means of a wallet. When referring to "owners" of cryptocurrency, it is the "owner" of a wallet which is meant. It is reasonable to assume that the provider of the wallet holds appropriate ownership information on each wallet and even that there may be a global procedural standard for determining ownership. None exists, however, and the industry resembles a free for all:

Each cryptocurrency has a reference implementation that includes basic wallet functionality (e.g., Bitcoin Core for Bitcoin, Mist browser for Ethereum). However, for a variety of reasons the reference implementation wallet is simply not practical for many users. As a result, a multitude of wallet providers have emerged in recent years to facilitate the storage of cryptocurrencies and make wallets easier to use. These wallets range from open-source projects run by volunteer developers to ones created by venture capital backed registered corporations.[25]

The problem of identifying cryptocurrency users and holders is made yet more complex by the use of multiple wallets and exchange accounts:

Estimating both the number of cryptocurrency holders and users is a difficult endeavour as individuals can use multiple wallets from several providers at the same time. Moreover, one single user can have multiple wallets and exchange accounts for different cryptocurrencies and thus be counted multiple times. In addition, many individuals are using centralised wallet,

23 Garrick Hileman and Michel Rauchs, *Global Cryptocurrency Benchmarking Study* (Cambridge Centre for Alternative Finance, University of Cambridge Judge Business School, 2017) 24 <www.jbs.cam.ac.uk/fileadmin/user_upload/research/centres/alternative-finance/downloads/2017-global-cryptocurrency-benchmarking-study.pdf> accessed 29 December 2018.
24 Ibid. 26.
25 Ibid. 50.

exchange or payment platforms that pool funds together into a limited number of large wallets or addresses, which further complicates the picture.[26]

The result is that no one wallet provider has the whole picture. Moreover, the majority of wallets are not controlled by the wallet provider but by the user, who is given control of the private key.[27] The use of hardware wallets, which store private keys in a secure hardware device, further augments both portability and anonymity. If the wallet offers a multi-signature facility (a mechanism to split control over an address amongst multiple private keys, with a minimum number of keys needed to unlock funds – a procedure which is intended to function as a security protection) the true owner may be any one amongst many straw names. Cryptocurrency experts' concern with the vulnerability of private key information stems from the risk of a hacking attack, as a consumer protective issue:

> Unlike in traditional banking, owner security is weakened because the cryptocurrency account address can be calculated from the private key, and thus the very knowledge of the private key is sufficient to acquire control of cryptocurrency units stored; this is not true of the banking PIN, where the knowledge of the bank account number is also required. [. . .] Cryptocurrency technology does not distinguish between the legitimate owner and a successful attacker who has acquired the private key from the owner as a result of the owner's fault. Both the owner and the successful attacker can use the cryptocurrency units stored in the attacked cryptocurrency account for their benefit.[28]

This however assumes that the private key information has been obtained against the user's will. There is nothing to prevent the user from sharing the private key information with anyone or holding that information on anyone's behalf. It is the simplest way of ensuring that ownership is transient. Somewhere on the carousel of successive key holders sits the beneficial owner. The wallet provider recognises

---

26 Ibid. 27. Jan Lasky comments: "One individual can even own millions of cryptocurrency accounts for a single cryptocurrency, created by a few seconds. The quantity of cryptocurrency units held by one individual is limited only by the total amount of cryptocurrency units (*e.g.* Bitcoin has 21 million units). A newly created account does not include any cryptocurrency units. The creation of a new account initially guarantees the owner's full anonymity. The term anonymity means that nobody (except the owner) can identify the account owner from the account data. It is recommended to use an account for one transaction only, which implies that an individual will have tens to hundreds of thousands of accounts over the course of his or her life". Jan Lansky, 'Possible State Approaches to Cryptocurrencies' (n 16) 21.
27 Only 15% of wallets take full custody of user funds – Garrick Hileman and Michel Rauchs, *Global Cryptocurrency Benchmarking Study* (Cambridge Centre for Alternative Finance, University of Cambridge Judge Business School, 2017) 55 <www.jbs.cam.ac.uk/fileadmin/user_upload/research/centres/alternative-finance/downloads/2017-global-cryptocurrency-benchmarking-study.pdf> accessed 29 December 2018.
28 Jan Lansky, 'Possible State Approaches to Cryptocurrencies' (n 16) 21.

the key holders but is unable to look through them to equate this with ownership in any sense of the word.[29]

A further layer of complexity – and impenetrability – is added by the introduction of so-called anonymous coins. An example is DASH (formerly known as Darkcoin), a cryptocurrency with built-in privacy functions.[30] DASH runs on a permissionless blockchain and is freely convertible into fiat currency. Transparent by default, it offers a user feature known as PrivateSend which obscures the origins of a user's funds through a process known as "mixing":

> PrivateSend gives you true financial privacy by obscuring the origins of your funds. All the Dash in your wallet is comprised of different "inputs", which you can think of as separate, discrete coins. PrivateSend uses an innovative process to mix your inputs with the inputs of two other people, without having your coins ever leave your wallet. You retain control of your money at all times.
> [. . .] The PrivateSend process works like this:
>
> 1    PrivateSend begins by breaking your transaction inputs down into standard denominations. These denominations are 0.01 DASH, 0.1 DASH, 1 DASH and 10 DASH – much like the paper money you use every day.
> 2    Your wallet then sends requests to specially configured software nodes on the network, called "masternodes". These masternodes are informed then that you are interested in mixing a certain denomination. No identifiable information is sent to the masternodes, so they never know "who" you are.
> 3    When two other people send similar messages, indicating that they wish to mix the same denomination, a mixing session begins. The masternode mixes up the inputs and instructs all three users' wallets to pay the now-transformed input back to themselves. Your wallet pays that denomination directly to itself, but in a different address (called a change address).

---

29  Anonymity is however not necessarily absolute. Jan Lansky prefers the term "pseudo-anonymity": "A user who follows the relevant rules [. . .] when executing cryptocurrency transactions cannot be easily identified. However, users may reveal their identity either negligently or knowingly, or outside actors may use external data to identify users, and then the cryptocurrency conversely ensures that their transactions are transparent". Ibid. 20. There is nothing "pseudo" however about the availability of anonymous coins. A brief but illuminating account of the interplay of anonymity and human error in the United States Federal Bureau of Investigation's breaking of the Silk Road (a Bitcoin market facilitating the sale of UDS1 billion in illegal drugs) see John Bohannon, 'Why Criminals Can't Hide Behind Bitcoin' *Science* (9 March 2016) <www.sciencemag.org/news/2016/03/why-criminals-cant-hide-behind-bitcoin> accessed 29 December 2018.
30  Explained by Evan Duffield and Daniel Diaz, *Dash: A Payment-Focused Cryptocurrency* <https://github.com/dashpay/dash/wiki/Whitepaper> accessed 29 December 2018.

4   In order to fully obscure your funds, your wallet must repeat this process a number of times with each denomination. Each time the process is completed, it's called a "round". Each round of PrivateSend makes it exponentially more difficult to determine where your funds originated. The user may choose between 1–16 rounds of mixing.

5   This mixing process happens in the background without any intervention on your part. When you wish to make a transaction, your funds will already be anonymized. No additional waiting is required.[31]

### *Cryptocurrency: due diligence and regulation*

Where cryptocurrency engages with the non-virtual world, as for example in fiat currency to cryptocurrency exchanges and vice versa, compliance programmes may be in place – imposed by the regulatory authorities in that non-virtual world. Where however the activity is cryptocurrency-focused, entirely along the blockchain, transactions – in so far as they can be ascertained at all – appear wholly unregulated and possibly (by virtue of their anonymity) not susceptible to state regulation. Self-regulation is possible, but is this "regulation"? Jan Lansky comments:

> Because of its lack of central authority, a cryptocurrency cannot be abolished or regulated by force; a cryptocurrency can only cease to exist by itself, when users of the cryptocurrency lose confidence in it (*e.g.* technical attacks, hacks). Nevertheless, individual users of a cryptocurrency can voluntarily decide for a form of regulation of the transactions executed by them.[32]

Self-regulation appears to be honoured more in the breach than in the observance:

> All wallets that provide centralised national-to-cryptocurrency exchange services (i.e., directly executing currency exchange) have a compliance program. In the case of wallets that integrate a third-party exchange, the third-party exchange may be responsible for user verification and compliance

---

31  <https://docs.dash.org/en/latest/introduction/features.html#privatesend> accessed 29 December 2018.

32  Jan Lansky, 'Possible State Approaches to Cryptocurrencies' (n 16) 20. An example of self-regulation is CryptoUK. In February 2018 a number of coin exchanges in the United Kingdom established this self-regulatory body representing the interests of exchanges, trading platforms/brokers, comparison sites (websites which provide data to compare the different rates of cryptocurrencies), intermediaries and asset managers. CryptoUK does not currently represent initial coin offerors. It has issued a high-level Code of Conduct, which includes inter alia the requirement to undertake checks "to ensure that investors are fit and proper to undertake transactions" and "in line with anti-money laundering regulations, members commit to undertaking due diligence checks on platform users to protect against illegal activity, including the financing of terrorism". <www.cryptocurrenciesuk.info/code-of-conducts/> accessed 29 December 2018.

requirements, while there is no clear legal framework that applies to wallets with built-in P2P exchange services as trades are happening directly between users. As a result, these wallets generally have less compliance programs than wallets providing centralised exchange services.[33]

State regulation of cryptocurrency advances apace. In June 2018 the Law Library of Congress, Global Legal Research Center published *Regulation of Cryptocurrency Around the World*, a survey of 130 countries as well as some regional organisations that have issued laws or policies on the subject. The focus of the report is on government-issued notices about the pitfalls of investing in cryptocurrency markets. However, in the opening Comparative Summary of the report, the relevance of ownership is not overlooked:

> Many of the warnings issued by various countries also note the opportunities that cryptocurrencies create for illegal activities, such as money laundering and terrorism. Some of the countries surveyed go beyond simply warning the public and have expanded their laws on money laundering, counterterrorism, and organized crimes to include cryptocurrency markets, and require banks and other financial institutions that facilitate such markets to conduct all the due diligence requirements imposed under such laws. For instance, Australia, Canada, and the Isle of Man recently enacted laws to bring cryptocurrency transactions and institutions that facilitate them under the ambit of money laundering and counter-terrorist financing laws.[34]

The intention is honourable, but the execution of it is flawed. No cryptocurrency regulation initiative reinvents the FATF "golden standard" of what constitutes ownership. This is to be expected, as those jurisdictions applying their anti-money laundering and counter-terrorist financing laws to cryptocurrencies see no need to adapt those laws to fit the unique characteristics of cryptocurrencies. However, the combination of transient ownership and an FATF ownership standard which is not fit for purpose[35] still affords the promoters and users of cryptocurrencies considerable scope for beneficial ownership avoidance.

---

33 Garrick Hileman and Michel Rauchs, *Global Cryptocurrency Benchmarking Study* (Cambridge Centre for Alternative Finance, University of Cambridge Judge Business School, 2017) 63 <www.jbs.cam.ac.uk/fileadmin/user_upload/research/centres/alternative-finance/downloads/2017-global-cryptocurrency-benchmarking-study.pdf> accessed 29 December 2018.

34 <www.loc.gov/law/help/cryptocurrency/world-survey.php> with the full text of the Report at <www.loc.gov/law/help/cryptocurrency/cryptocurrency-world-survey.pdf> accessed 29 December 2018. For a briefer overview see Arjun Kharpal 'Cryptocurrencies: Regulating the New Economy' *CNBC* (9 August 2018) <www.cnbc.com/2018/08/09/cryptocurrencies--regulating-the-new--economy.html> accessed 29 December 2018. See also Jeffrey H Matsuura, *Digital Currency: An International Legal and Regulatory Compliance Guide* (Bentham Science Publishers Ltd., Sharjah, UAE, 2016).

35 See ch 3.

*European Union: Fifth Anti-Money Laundering Directive (Directive EU 2018/843 30 May 2018)*[36]

On 30 May 2018 the EU issued EU Directive 2018/843 (amending EU Directive 2015/849)[37] (4AMLD) on the prevention of the use of the financial system for the purposes of money laundering or terrorist financing (5AMLD). 5AMLD supplements rather than replaces 4AMLD, and inter alia updates the rules regarding the identification of the beneficial owners of companies and other legal persons and of trusts.[38]

5AMLD addresses the issue of virtual currencies and their potential to further anti-money-laundering and terrorist-financing purposes. It adds to Article 3 of the Fourth Anti-Money Laundering Directive EU Directive 2015/849[39] (4AMLD) the following definitions:

> (18) "virtual currencies" means a digital representation of value that is not issued or guaranteed by a central bank or a public authority, is not necessarily attached to a legally established currency and does not possess a legal status of currency or money, but is accepted by natural or legal persons as a means of exchange and which can be transferred, stored and traded electronically.
>
> (19) "custodian wallet provider" means an entity that provides services to safeguard private cryptographic keys on behalf of its customers, to hold, store and transfer virtual currencies.

The motivation for the changes, reflecting an advance in the EU's approach to the potential of digital systems to disrupt the economy and advance fraud, is set out in the following recitals to 5AMLD:

> (8) Providers engaged in exchange services between virtual currencies and fiat currencies (that is to say coins and banknotes that are designated as legal tender and electronic money, of a country, accepted as a medium of exchange in the issuing country) as well as custodian wallet providers are under no Union obligation to identify suspicious activity. Therefore, terrorist groups may be able to transfer money into the Union financial system or within virtual currency networks by concealing transfers or by benefiting from a certain degree of anonymity on those platforms. It is therefore essential to extend the scope

---

36  <https://eur-lex.europa.eu/legal-content/EN/TXT/?qid=1540113903626&uri=CEL EX:32018L0843> with the full text in English at <https://eur-lex.europa.eu/legal-con tent/EN/TXT/PDF/?uri=CELEX:32018L0843&qid=1540113903626&from=EN> ('© European Union, https://eur-lex.europa.eu, 1998–2019') accessed 29 December 2018 (5AMLD). See chapter 6 for the impact of 5AMLD on cryptocurrencies.

37  <https://publications.europa.eu/en/publication-detail/-/publication/0bff31ef-0b49-11e5-8817-01aa75ed71a1/language-en> accessed 29 December 2018.

38  See ch 3, Part Five for a fuller discussion.

39  <https://publications.europa.eu/en/publication-detail/-/publication/0bff31ef-0b49-11e5-8817-01aa75ed71a1/language-en> accessed 29 December 2018.

of Directive (EU) 2015/849 [4AMLD] so as to include providers engaged in exchange services between virtual currencies and fiat currencies as well as custodian wallet providers. For the purposes of anti-money laundering and countering the financing of terrorism (AML/CFT), competent authorities should be able, through obliged entities, to monitor the use of virtual currencies. Such monitoring would provide a balanced and proportional approach, safeguarding technical advances and the high degree of transparency attained in the field of alternative finance and social entrepreneurship.

(9) The anonymity of virtual currencies allows their potential misuse for criminal purposes. The inclusion of providers engaged in exchange services between virtual currencies and fiat currencies and custodian wallet providers will not entirely address the issue of anonymity attached to virtual currency transactions, as a large part of the virtual currency environment will remain anonymous because users can also transact without such providers. To combat the risks related to the anonymity, national Financial Intelligence Units (FIUs) should be able to obtain information allowing them to associate virtual currency addresses to the identity of the owner of virtual currency. In addition, the possibility to allow users to self-declare to designated authorities on a voluntary basis should be further assessed.

10) [. . .] Although virtual currencies can frequently be used as a means of payment, they could also be used for other purposes and find broader applications such as means of exchange, investment, store-of-value products or use in online casinos. The objective of this Directive is to cover all the potential uses of virtual currencies.

This is to be achieved as set out in Article 47, paragraph 1 4AMLD, which is replaced:

> 1. Member States shall ensure *that providers of exchange services between virtual currencies and fiat currencies, and custodian wallet providers, are registered*, that currency exchange and cheque cashing offices, and trust or company service providers are licensed or registered, and that providers of gambling services are regulated.
>
> [Emphasis added]

The effect of the changes is that virtual currency exchange platforms and custodian wallet providers become designated persons under the EU's anti-money laundering and countering the financing of terrorism rules must therefore meet client due diligence requirements when on-boarding new customers and report suspicious transactions.

On closer examination, however, these provisions are to a degree aspirational.

- How does the EU propose that competent authorities monitor the use of virtual currencies, as referred to in recital (8) when such use is by its very nature designed to favour anonymity?

- The closing words of recital (9) also lack any implementation mechanism, which the substantive provisions of 4AMLD and 5AMLD do not themselves provide: "To combat the risks related to the anonymity, national Financial Intelligence Units (FIUs) should be able to obtain information allowing them to associate virtual currency addresses to the identity of the owner of virtual currency. In addition, the possibility to allow users to self-declare to designated authorities on a voluntary basis should be further assessed". This sits uneasily with the transient nature of ownership of virtual currencies and provides no guidance as to how to associate virtual currency addresses and ownership. Nor does it explain why persons bent on subverting the regulation of anti-money laundering or terrorist financing by using virtual currencies should suddenly find within themselves a well of public spirit and voluntarily spill the digital beans.
- The new provisions relate to exchange services between virtual currencies and fiat currencies, and take no account of P2P (peer to peer) transactions – bartering between one cryptocurrency type and another, which does not interface at all with fiat currencies or involve the investment or banking sectors at any stage.

The wider issue, as discussed in chapter 3, part five, is the reliance of 4AMLD and 5AMLD on the flawed ownership standards set by FATF, which fundamentally weakens their effectiveness. If the very concept of what constitutes an owner is obscure, then exhorting competent authorities to monitor the owners of virtual currencies amounts to little more than asking them to take a shot in the dark web.

In July 2018 a study requested by the TAX3 Committee of the European Parliament on cryptocurrencies and the blockchain was published.[40] The authors acknowledge the key issue as being anonymity:

> The key issue that needs to be addressed is the anonymity surrounding cryptocurrencies. This anonymity, varying from complete anonymity to pseudo-anonymity, prevents cryptocurrency transactions from being adequately monitored, allowing shady transactions to occur outside of the regulatory perimeter and criminal organisations to use cryptocurrencies to obtain easy access to "clean cash". Anonymity is also the major issue when it comes to tax evasion. When a tax authority does not know who enters into the taxable transaction, because of the anonymity involved, it cannot detect nor sanction this tax evasion.

They are uncritical of 5AMLD's definition of virtual currencies, which "is sufficient to combat money laundering, terrorist financing and tax evasion via cryptocurrencies", whilst recognising that the definition must remain fluid and "a sufficient one going forward". Blind spots do not go unnoticed:

---

40  Robby Houben and Alexander Snyers, *Cryptocurrencies and Blockchain* (n 12).

When we look at the key players in cryptocurrency markets, we can see that a number of those are not included in AMLD5, leaving blind spots in the fight against money laundering, terrorist financing and tax evasion. The examples are numerous and include miners, pure cryptocurrency exchanges that are not also custodian wallet providers, hardware and software wallet providers, trading platforms and coin offerors. Persons with malicious intent could look up these blind spots. If that would happen and it would appear to have a (material) adverse effect on the fight against money laundering, terrorist financing and tax evasion, expanding the scope of AMLD5 should be considered.[41]

It is fairly safe to assume that "persons with malicious intent" are on the prowl, and that the defects in 4AMLD and 5AMLD need urgently to be addressed. As the authors of the study themselves point out: "There are simply no rules unveiling the anonymity associated with crypto-currencies, making the question whether they are taken at the right level or to whom they apply a superfluous one".[42]

## *Financial Action Task Force*[43]

Following its plenary meeting 21–23 February 2018 the FATF issued a brief statement that it had "considered a report on the AML/CFT risks associated with virtual currencies and the regulatory measures being taken in different countries. The improved understanding of the misuse and risk of virtual currencies will lead to FATF undertaking additional work streams".[44] At its plenary meeting 17–19 October 2018 matters had become more focussed, but remained at a high level:

> The FATF Plenary discussed and adopted amendments to the FATF Standards to respond to the increasing use of virtual assets for money laundering and terrorist financing and at the request of the G20 Ministers. This includes an amendment to the FATF Recommendations and glossary to clarify to which businesses and activities the FATF requirements apply in the case of virtual assets. Exchanges and wallet providers will be required to implement AML/CFT controls, and to be licensed or registered and supervised or monitored by national authorities. Strengthening the standards is part of a

---

41 All the quotations are from the Executive Summary to Robby Houben and Alexander Snyers, Ibid.

42 Ibid. para 4.1.4, 'Cryptocurrencies are falling between the cracks'.

43 (*Financial Action Task Force*) <www.fatf-gafi.org/about> accessed 29 December 2018. For a fuller discussion on the methodology adopted by FATF in relation to the designation and identification of owners, see ch 3, Part Two.

44 <www.fatf-gafi.org/publications/fatfgeneral/documents/outcomes-plenary-february-2018.html> accessed 29 December 2018.

comprehensive approach that the FATF has developed to prevent the misuse of virtual asset activities for money laundering and terrorist financing.

As a next step, the FATF will update its Guidance to assist countries with the full and effective implementation of these requirements of the FATF Standards. All countries are encouraged to swiftly take the necessary steps to prevent the misuse of virtual assets. Given the speed of innovation, and to ensure that the FATF Standards remain relevant, the FATF will review its standards as they apply to the virtual asset sector in 12 months.[45]

On 19 October 2018 the FATF issued a statement on the regulation of virtual assets, in response to calls for greater clarity about which FATF standards apply in this context. Other than adding definitions to its recommendations, the FATF has produced little of substance and nothing which addresses the shortcomings in the methodology it employs in the identification of "owner". The burden of designing implementation strategies is placed on the FATF member states, with no attempt at inter-state co-ordination and no clear guidance on how virtual assets or virtual asset service providers are to be classified for the purposes of regulation:

> Given the urgent need for an effective global, risk-based response to the AML/CFT risks associated with virtual asset financial activities, the FATF has adopted changes to the FATF Recommendations and Glossary[46] that clarify how the Recommendations apply in the case of financial activities involving virtual assets. These changes add to the Glossary new definitions of "virtual assets" and "virtual asset service providers" – such as exchanges, certain types of wallet providers, and providers of financial services for Initial Coin Offerings (ICOs). These changes make clear that jurisdictions should ensure that virtual asset service providers are subject to AML/CFT regulations, for example conducting customer due diligence including ongoing monitoring, record-keeping, and reporting of suspicious transactions. They should be licensed or registered and subject to monitoring to ensure compliance. *The FATF will further elaborate on how these requirements should be applied in relation to virtual assets.*
>
> *All jurisdictions should urgently take legal and practical steps to prevent the misuse of virtual assets.* This includes assessing and understanding the risks associated with virtual assets in their jurisdictions, applying risk-based AML/CFT regulations to virtual asset service providers and identifying effective systems to conduct risk-based monitoring or supervision of virtual asset service providers. [. . .] *The FATF emphasises that jurisdictions have flexibility to decide under which AML/CFT category of regulated activities virtual asset*

45 Ibid.
46 <www.fatf-gafi.org/publications/fatfrecommendations/documents/fatf-recommendations.html> accessed 29 December 2018.

*service providers should be regulated, e.g. as financial institutions, DNFBPs, or as another, distinctive category.*[47]

[Emphasis added]

On the FATF's to-do list for 2019, as set out in its statement, is that it:

> will provide clarification to jurisdictions in managing the ML and TF risks of virtual assets, while creating a sound AML/CFT regulatory environment in which companies are free to innovate. As part of a staged approach, the FATF will prepare updated guidance on a risk-based approach to regulating virtual asset service providers, including their supervision and monitoring; and guidance for operational and law enforcement authorities on identifying and investigating illicit activity involving virtual assets.

Pending such clarification, the newly added second paragraph to FATF Recommendation 15 is all that there is:

> To manage and mitigate the risks emerging from virtual assets, countries should ensure that virtual asset service providers are regulated for AML/CFT purposes, and licensed or registered and subject to effective systems for monitoring and ensuring compliance with the relevant measures called for in the FATF Recommendations.

## Isle of Man: a case study in the regulation of cryptocurrency

Sometimes the road to regulation is indirect. Ownership transparency strategies in relation to cryptocurrency are faced with the many obstacles which are discussed in this chapter. The problem of how to identify the owners of cryptocurrency, from moment to moment, or even at all, seems insurmountable. Pull back the camera for a wider perspective, away from the owners so that the service providers come into view, and a solution presents itself. The burden of identifying the owners is placed on the service providers, and if they do not discharge that responsibility, their oxygen is cut off. They are refused the right to trade.

### CONSTITUTIONAL BACKGROUND

The Isle of Man, together with the United Kingdom, the Channel Islands and the Republic of Ireland form the geographical area known as the British Isles. Although the Isle of Man acknowledges the sovereign of the United Kingdom to be its head of state, the island is politically and constitutionally not part of the United Kingdom. It is a Crown Dependency. As such, it is independent in

---

47 <www.fatf-gafi.org/publications/fatfrecommendations/documents/regulation-virtual-assets.html> accessed 29 December 2018.

all matters except foreign affairs and defence, which are the responsibility of the United Kingdom government. In particular, no legislation on taxation or other revenue matters of the United Kingdom Parliament applies in the Isle of Man.[48]

The Isle of Man has had a special relationship with the EU, of which it has never been a member. The Treaty of Rome 1957[49] provides for its application to all European territories for whom a member state is responsible. In the case of the United Kingdom, however, a Third Protocol was added to the United Kingdom Treaty of Accession of Denmark, Ireland and the United Kingdom 1972.[50] This provides that the Treaty of Rome does not apply to the Isle of Man save that the Isle of Man is included within the customs territory of the EU and is subject to the rules on the free movement of goods. This relationship between the Isle of Man and the EU ceases upon the withdrawal of the United Kingdom from membership of the European Union.

The Isle of Man has a Customs and Excise Agreement with the UK dating from November 1979 (amended in August 1994 and October 2007),[51] and the two countries therefore constitute a common customs area. In anticipation of the withdrawal of the United Kingdom from membership of the European Union the 1979 Agreement has been further amended by the Crown Dependencies Customs Union (Isle of Man) (EU Exit) Order 2018[52] (agreed on 26 November 2018) which will come into effect upon an exchange of letters between the two governments. It provides for a continuing customs union between the Isle of Man and the United Kingdom.

The Isle of Man is a member of the Organisation for Economic Co-operation and Development (OECD), the United Kingdom Government at the request of the Isle of Man Government having declared in 1990 that the OECD Convention applies to the Isle of Man.[53] Since 2012, the Isle of Man, as a non-member State of the Council of Europe, has been evaluated by MONEYVAL.[54]

---

48 For a fuller analysis of the characteristics of the Isle of Man, see Paul Beckett, *Tax Havens and International Human Rights* (Routledge, London and New York, October 2017) and Paul Beckett, 'Isle of Man' in Timothy Lyons (ed), *European Cross Border Estate Planning* (Sweet & Maxwell, London, Release 87, October 2018).

49 <https://ec.europa.eu/romania/sites/romania/files/tratatul_de_la_roma.pdf> accessed 29 December 2018.

50 <https://eur-lex.europa.eu/legal-content/EN/TXT/PDF/?uri=OJ:L:1972:073:FULL&from=EN> ('© European Union, https://eur-lex.europa.eu, 1998–2019') accessed 29 December 2018.

51 <www.gov.im/media/80147/customs_agreement1979.pdf> accessed 29 December 2018.

52 <www.legislation.gov.uk/ukdsi/2018/9780111175156> accessed 29 December 2018.

53 See OECD *Global Forum on Transparency and Exchange of Information for Tax Purposes: Isle of Man 2017 (Second Round)* <www.oecd.org/countries/isleofman/global-forum-on-transparency-and-exchange-of-information-for-tax-purposes-isle-of-man-2017-second-round-9789264283770-en.htm> accessed 29 December 2018.

54 <www.coe.int/en/web/moneyval/moneyval-brief/members> accessed 29 December 2018 and see the most recent follow-up report on the Isle of Man (7 September 2018) at <www.coe.int/en/web/human-rights-rule-of-law/-/moneyval-publishes-a-follow-up-report-on-the-isle-of-man> accessed 29 December 2018.

REGULATION OF CRYPTOCURRENCY

The Isle of Man was amongst the first jurisdictions to introduce legislation to regulate cryptocurrencies. As such, it was in largely uncharted territory. It has done so by not seeking to reinvent the wheel. In summary, regulation has been effected by bringing the virtual currency sector within the ambit of the Proceeds of Crime Act 2008,[55] which in turn makes it subject to the provisions of the Designated Businesses (Registration and Oversight) Act 2015,[56] from the combination of which it must comply with the Anti-Money Laundering and Countering the Financing of Terrorism Code 2015 (as amended 2018).[57]

Responsibility for ensuring adherence to regulatory, supervisory and registration regimes in the Isle of Man is that of the Isle of Man Financial Services Authority.[58]

The Isle of Man distinguishes between four different types of online currencies:

- Digital currency refers to any electronic representation of a fiat currency, and this can include representations of virtual currency.
- Virtual currency is a narrower asset and is a digital representation of value which can be traded digitally. The nature of a virtual currency means that it does not need to be centrally controlled or administered. Virtual currency can be either convertible or non-convertible.
- Convertible virtual currency, which includes cryptocurrency, can be converted into a fiat currency, either directly or through an exchange. For a currency to be convertible, there does not need to be a set rate or an established benchmark, merely that a market exists and the ownership rights can be transferred from one person to another, whether for consideration or not.
- Non-convertible virtual currency, once purchased, cannot be transferred to another person and cannot be redeemed for fiat currency, either directly or through an exchange.

---

55  <https://legislation.gov.im/cms/images/LEGISLATION/PRINCIPAL/2008/2008-0013/ProceedsofCrimeAct2008_18.pdf> accessed 29 December 2018.

56  <https://legislation.gov.im/cms/images/LEGISLATION/PRINCIPAL/2015/2015-0009/DesignatedBusinessesRegistrationandOversightAct2015_7.pdf> accessed 29 December 2018 and see the guidance issued by the Isle of Man Financial Services Authority at <www.iomfsa.im/designated-business/overview/> accessed 29 December 2018. Sch 1, Part 1 of the Act lists businesses which are designated. Para 1(1)(l) provides: "the business of issuing, transmitting, transferring, providing safe custody or storage of, administering, managing, lending, buying, selling, exchanging or otherwise trading or intermediating convertible virtual currencies, including cryptocurrencies or similar concepts where the concept is accepted by persons as a means of payment for goods or services, a unit of account, a store of value or a commodity".

57  <www.iomfsa.im/media/1590/antimoneylaunderingandterrorist.pdf> accessed 29 December 2018.

58  <www.iomfsa.im/about/about-us/> accessed 29 December 2018.

The Proceeds of Crime Act 2008 was amended in 2015 to include virtual currency businesses within its regulated sector as a "designated business",[59] specifically those that are in the business of issuing, transmitting, transferring, providing safe custody or storage of, administering, managing, lending, buying, selling, exchanging or otherwise trading or intermediating convertible virtual currencies, including cryptocurrencies or similar concepts where the concept is accepted by persons as a means of payment for goods.[60] By virtue of being included in Schedule 4 to the Proceeds of Crime Act 2008, virtual currency business is subject to the requirements of the Anti-Money Laundering and Countering the Financing of Terrorism Code 2015 (as amended 2018).

This amendment brought businesses that engaged in these activities, including those that wish to offer initial coin offerings (ICOs),[61] within the ambit of the Designated Businesses (Registration and Oversight) Act 2015, requiring the use of know-your-customer practices, such as collecting identifying information, knowing the beneficial owner of any currency and record keeping and reporting requirements for certain transactions.[62] Businesses registered under this Act are required to submit annual returns that show compliance with anti-money laundering laws.

The classification of virtual currency business as designated business means that any person undertaking this business must be registered with the Isle of Man Financial Services Authority prior to commencing business. The impact of the requirement to register as a designated business, as a tool for weeding out undesirables wishing to enter the virtual currency sector in the Isle of Man, cannot be underestimated. No person who is not deemed "fit and proper" by the Isle of Man Financial Services Authority will be registered – and in the case of a company seeking registration, the test will be applied to the directors and other officers, shareholders and (if different) beneficial owners of that company:

> The fit and proper test is both an initial test at the time of registration and a continuing test in relation to the compliance with AML/CFT legislation of designated business.
>
> It should be noted that the fit and proper test for designated businesses is much narrower than the test for the Authority's licence holders. Section 9 of the Act states that when assessing the fitness and propriety of an applicant the Authority would take into consideration whether the applicant:

---

59  Isle of Man Financial Services Authority, *Questions & Answers in Respect of Persons Seeking to Launch an Initial Coin Offering in or from The Island* (Updated 5 October 2018) at 1, <www.iomfsa.im/media/2365/icoguidanceforapplicants.pdf> accessed 29 December 2018.

60  Proceeds of Crime Act 2008 Schedule 4, paragraph 1(1)(mm).

61  Isle of Man Financial Services Authority, *Questions & Answers* (n 59).

62  Isle of Man Financial Services Authority, *Virtual Currency Business: Sector Specific AML/CFT Guidance Notes* (October 2016) <www.iomfsa.im/media/1606/virtualcurrencyguidance.pdf> accessed 29 December 2018.

- has been convicted of an offence –
- under AML/CFT legislation[63];
- under the law of a country or territory outside the Island if the conduct giving rise to the offence would constitute an offence under [AML/CFT legislation] if it had occurred in the Island;
- involving dishonesty (whether under the law of the Island or elsewhere);
- under a relevant Act;[64] or
- of perjury or conspiracy to pervert the course of justice (whether under the law of the Island or elsewhere);
- is or has been the subject of any action with respect to any breach of a relevant Act (as defined) or AML/CFT legislation;
- has knowingly or recklessly provided misleading or false information in the application for registration; or
- is otherwise considered by the Authority not to be fit and proper for reasons related to the risk of money laundering or the financing of terrorism.[65]

There must also be a real presence and substance to a business if it is to be registered:

In order for the IOMFSA to be able to successfully undertake its statutory duty of overseeing the compliance of designated businesses with the AML/ CFT legislation, designated businesses must have sufficient real presence to facilitate oversight. Given the nature of CVC[66] business, and in order to ensure oversight can effectively take place, with effect from 5 October 2018

---

63 (a) the Anti-Terrorism and Crime Act 2003; (b) Part 3 (money laundering) of the Proceeds of Crime Act 2008; (c) the Terrorist Asset-Freezing etc. Act 2010 (of Parliament) as applied to the Island; (d) the Terrorism and Other Crime (Financial Restrictions) Act 2014; (e) any instrument of a legislative character made under one of the Acts mentioned in paragraphs (a) to (d). [Designated Businesses (Registration and Oversight) Act 2015 section 3(2)].

64 (a) the Advocates Acts 1976; (b) the Advocates Act 1995; (c) the Collective Investment Schemes Act 2008; (d) the Estate Agents Acts 1975; (e) the Financial Services Act 2008; (f) the Insurance Act 2008; (g) the Legal Practitioners Registration Act 1986; (h) the Money-lenders Act 1991; (i) the Online Gambling Regulation Act 2001; (j) the Retirement Benefits Schemes Act 2000; (k) any other Act that is relevant to the regulation of a designated business; (l) any legislation in any other country or territory that is equivalent to any of the above Acts [Designated Businesses (Registration and Oversight) Act 2015 section 3(3)].

65 <www.iomfsa.im/designated-business/registration-policy/> accessed 29 December 2018. The Isle of Man Financial Services Authority Designated Business Registration Policy (Version 4, 5 October 2018) is at <www.iomfsa.im/media/1424/dnfbpregistrationpolicy.pdf> accessed 29 December 2018.

66 CVC is defined in the Glossary to the Isle of Man Financial Services Authority Designated Business Registration Policy as convertible virtual currency including cryptocurrencies or similar concepts where the concept is accepted by persons as a means of payment for goods or services, a unit of account, a store of value or a commodity.

the IOMFSA will not register a CVC business unless the following two conditions of registration are met:

a)  the CVC business must have (and continue to have) at least 2 IoM resident directors; and
b)  management and control of the CVC business must be in the Island. Because of the limitation of the IOMFSA's ability to oversee CVC businesses which lack substance or real presence on the Island, such a characteristic is considered to pose an unacceptably high risk of money laundering and terrorist financing.[67]

ICOs are subject to strict registration conditions:

It is the IOMFSA's policy to refuse to register an applicant which engages in the CVC business of issuing a CVC (of whatever type) where the CVC issued provides no benefit to the purchaser other than the CVC itself.
Examples of this include, but are not restricted to:

- ICOs which convey –

    a)  limited or no rights to the income generated from a project;
    b)  limited or no rights to use the assets developed, purchased or acquired from the funds raised by the ICO;

- ICOs where there is no reasonable basis for any expected capital growth of the value of the CVC.

Such characteristics are generally considered by the IOMFSA to pose an unacceptably high risk that the money raised from the CVC issuance could be used for unanticipated and illegal purposes, as well as posing a risk to consumers. It is because of these risks that it is the policy of the IOMFSA to refuse to register this type of business.[68]

OWNERSHIP PERSPECTIVE

By requiring virtual currency businesses to comply with its AML/CFT legislation, the Isle of Man has extended the identification of beneficial ownership to the holders of cryptocurrency. The burden is placed on the service provider to identify those beneficial owners. The penalty for non-compliance is a refusal to permit that service provider to trade in or from the Isle of Man.

---

67 <www.iomfsa.im/media/1424/dnfbpregistrationpolicy.pdf> accessed 29 December 2018 para 4.1.1.
68 Ibid. para 4.1.2.

So far, so good, but as the Isle of Man applies the methodology of FATF, as adopted by both the OECD and by the Council of Europe MONEYVAL, then (in common with all jurisdictions which do so) it has imported the fundamental weaknesses of that FATF methodology.[69] This is reflected in the guidance on what constitutes beneficial ownership and control set out in paragraph 3 of the Anti-Money Laundering and Countering the Financing of Terrorism Code 2015 (as amended 2018)[70]

> "beneficial owner" means the natural person who ultimately owns or controls the customer or on whose behalf a transaction or activity is being conducted and includes but is not restricted to – (a) in the case of a legal person other than a company whose securities are listed on a recognised stock exchange, a natural person who ultimately owns or controls (whether through direct or indirect ownership or control, including through bearer share holdings) 25% or more of the shares or voting rights in the legal person; (b) in the case of any legal person, a natural person who otherwise exercises ultimate effective control over the management of the legal person; (c) in the case of a legal arrangement, the trustee or other person who exercises ultimate effective control over the legal arrangement; and (d) in the case of a foundation, a natural person who otherwise exercises ultimate effective control over the foundation;

Add to this the inherent difficulties in identifying ownership of cryptocurrency which are discussed in this chapter, and the weight of the burden placed on the service providers is clear.

Nevertheless, as a transparency strategy in relation to cryptocurrency, focussing on the service provider and imposing on that service provider AML/CFT and beneficial ownership disclosure requirements which themselves apply across the board in the Isle of Man is innovative. It strikes at the root of the problem.

## Blockchain

### *Technical definition*

*Blockchain* is a record of all validated transactions grouped into blocks, each cryptographically linked to predecessor transactions down to the genesis block, thereby creating a 'chain of blocks'.[71]

---

69 See the discussion in ch 3, Part Two.
70 <www.iomfsa.im/media/1590/antimoneylaunderingandterrorist.pdf> accessed 29 December 2018.
71 Garrick Hileman and Michel Rauchs, *Global Cryptocurrency Benchmarking Study* (Cambridge Centre for Alternative Finance, University of Cambridge Judge Business School, 2017) 13 <www.jbs.cam.ac.uk/fileadmin/user_upload/research/centres/

Blockchain is described by the World Economic Forum as follows:

> Currently, most people use a trusted middleman such as a bank to make a transaction. But blockchain allows consumers and suppliers to connect directly, removing the need for a third party. Using cryptography to keep exchanges secure, blockchain provides a decentralized database, or "digital ledger", of transactions that everyone on the network can see. This network is essentially a chain of computers that must all approve an exchange before it can be verified and recorded. In the case of Bitcoin, blockchain stores the details of every transaction of the digital currency, and the technology stops the same Bitcoin being (duplicated and) spent more than once. The technology can work for almost every type of transaction involving value, including money, goods and property. Its potential uses are almost limitless: from collecting taxes to enabling migrants to send money back to family in countries where banking is difficult. Blockchain could also help to reduce fraud because every transaction would be recorded and distributed on a public ledger for anyone to see.[72]

### *The Fourth Industrial Revolution*

The importance of blockchain cannot be overstated. In the opinion of the World Economic Forum Centre for the Fourth Industrial Revolution,[73] "Blockchain has the potential to upend entire systems". This is seen as a positive:

> Blockchain, a relatively nascent technology that enables the decentralized and secure storage and transfer of information, has already proven itself to be a powerful tracking and transaction tool, which can minimize friction, reduce corruption, increase trust and empower users. Cryptocurrencies built on this distributed ledger platform, despite still being in their infancy, have emerged as potential gateways to new wealth creation and disrupters across financial markets.[74]

On 8 June 2018 the Directorate for Financial and Enterprise Affairs Competition Committee of the OECD[75] published an Issues Paper *Blockchain Technology*

---

alternative-finance/downloads/2017-global-cryptocurrency-benchmarking-study.pdf> accessed 29 December 2018.

72 Rosamond Hutt, *All You Need to Know About Blockchain, Explained Simply* (World Economic Forum, 17 June 2016) <www.weforum.org/agenda/2016/06/blockchain-explained-simply/> accessed 29 December 2018. And see OECD *Blockchain Primer* <www.oecd.org/finance/OECD-Blockchain-Primer.pdf> accessed 29 December 2018.

73 <www.weforum.org/centre-for-the-fourth-industrial-revolution/> accessed 29 December 2018.

74 *Blockchain and Distributed Ledger Technology* (World Economic Forum Centre for the Fourth Industrial Revolution) <www.weforum.org/communities/blockchain-and-distributed-ledger-technology> accessed 29 December 2018.

75 Links to all materials published by the OECD on blockchain and competition policy are available at <www.oecd.org/daf/competition/blockchain-and-competition-policy.htm> accessed 29 December 2018.

*and Competition Policy.*[76] The tone is as resolutely upbeat as that of the World Economic Forum, seeing significant advantages from a competition perspective in the apparent transparency of the blockchain and seeking to distance blockchain technology from specific cryptocurrency use:

1   Blockchain is a general-purpose technology that threatens to disrupt markets and institutions across the world. Where the internet enabled the publishing and digital transfer of information, blockchain authenticates the ownership of assets, makes them unique, traceable, and facilitates the digital transfer and hence trading of assets by providing trust in the transaction and reducing uncertainty (through its use of trustworthy self-executing code).
2   The most prominent example of a blockchain thus far is Bitcoin, a crypto-currency that uses blockchain technology to act as an alternative payment system. Bitcoin is a non-permissioned or public blockchain, meaning that there is no restriction on who can spend Bitcoin or take part in verifying the authenticity of blocks of transactions in the blockchain [. . .]. [T]he block-chain is transparent in the sense that everyone can view the chain (though identities are anonymised). Largely as result of this anonymity, Bitcoin has proved controversial and been banned in some countries. However, it is worth noting that many concerns around Bitcoin's anonymity and energy usage are characteristics of Bitcoin and not necessarily the wider blockchain technology.[77]

The Issues Paper addresses the question of ownership indirectly, in terms of how the technology could be used at government level. In essence, however, this is about the ownership of information rather than of assets:

4. [. . .] helping enforcers to clamp down on avoidance of tax and other laws and regulations; to support monetary and fiscal policy via sovereign-backed cryptocurrency; to create digital land titling and other registries, to help citizens prove their identity and vote, and to increase the efficiency and transparency of public services. Pension and social security payments might be made more cheaply and transparently via blockchain, while health records might be shared securely between a patient and all relevant doctors.

Is this optimism realistic? The devil is in the detail.

There has been an overwhelming amount of hype surrounding blockchain over the past year. It has been proposed as a solution to such a dizzying array of problems and industries that it is increasingly difficult to keep up, let alone develop a reasoned and sensible approach to the technology. One of the

76 <https://one.oecd.org/document/DAF/COMP/WD(2018)47/en/pdf> accessed 29 December 2018.
77 Ibid. 2.

most unique aspects of blockchain is its high number of evangelists – people who believe blockchain can solve everything from global financial inequality to access to financing for start-ups, the provision of ID for refugees, to solving supply chain problems and enabling people to sell their houses without needing an estate agent. It has started to seem that the most intractable of the world's problems have merely been waiting for blockchain to arrive. This is not only misleading and untrue but also becomes a barrier to decision-makers in taking a balanced perspective on the technology.[78]

Blockchain technology goes far beyond cryptocurrencies, tokens and finance generally, and will be applied across a broad spectrum of commercial activity.[79]

> The areas where major blockchain progress is taking place are as diverse as the applications they are creating. The global nature of blockchain's development can help distribute opportunities for wealth creation and economic development more widely than before. It is important for governments to develop the right policies to harness the potential benefits of this technology while mitigating its risks and potential for misuse. To do so, it is essential for countries to cooperate in order to share best practices and ensure interoperability. Regulatory fragmentation will hinder the progress towards useful applications of blockchain technology.[80]

In the identification of ownership and the attribution of accountability, regulatory fragmentation, and in consequence the potential of blockchain transactions to anonymize the parties with impunity is of great concern.

### Anonymity: an absence of ownership transparency

Everyone can view the chain, though identities are anonymised. The anonymisation of identity is from the outside looking in. Between participants themselves in the blockchain, identities are not necessarily unknown. The use of "smart contracts" typifies this:

---

78 Blockchain Beyond the Hype (n 2) 3.
79 See for example the discussions at the OECD Blockchain Policy Forum held on 4–5 September 2018 <www.oecd.org/finance/oecd-blockchain-policy-forum-2018.htm> accessed 29 December 2018.
80 OECD *Blockchain Primer* <www.oecd.org/finance/OECD-Blockchain-Primer.pdf> accessed 29 December 2018. The current extent of use of blockchain technology by governments worldwide is surveyed by the Illinois Blockchain Initiative <https://sites.google.com/view/blockchain-govt-tracker> accessed 29 December 2018 and available in tabular form at <https://airtable.com/shreIXQjzluCxam37/tbl7qVDFKKiEcFFrc> accessed 29 December 2018. The list is not yet particularly extensive: Brazil, Canada, Ghana, Honduras, Hong Kong, India, Japan, Netherlands, Republic of Georgia, Russia, Sweden, Ukraine, United Kingdom and the United States (Cook County Recorder of Deeds). The majority use is in relation to their respective Land Title Registries.

Smart contracts are self-executing contracts with the terms of the agreement between buyer and seller being directly written into lines of code. The code and the agreements contained therein exist across a distributed, decentralized blockchain network. Smart contracts permit trusted transactions and agreements to be carried out among disparate, anonymous parties without the need for a central authority, legal system, or external enforcement mechanism. They render transactions traceable, transparent, and irreversible.[81]

The "disparate, anonymous parties" clearly need to know – and do know – who each other are, because they are in a peer-to-peer contractual relationship. Yet the transaction is unregulated and literally outside the law. To the external observer, the contracting parties are unknowable. An IP address may be traceable from computer to computer, but this is not the same thing as tracing from person to person.[82]

From an ownership perspective this is the key: transactions on permissioned, private, shared systems are "traceable, transparent and irreversible" *between the parties to the transaction* but not otherwise.[83]

81 <www.investopedia.com/terms/s/smart-contracts.asp> accessed 29 December 2018. Smart contracts are still in their infancy, and as such teething troubles remain to be overcome: because they are immediately effective, there is no room for renegotiation of terms (transmission of the smart contract and completion of that contract are simultaneous); those persons coding the smart contracts are unlikely to be lawyers and misinterpretation of contractual provisions when reducing these to code form will have legal consequences unforeseen by the parties; smart contracts can be hacked. For a discussion of the issues surrounding smart contracts see Artificial Lawyer, *Smart Contracts* <www.artificiallawyer.com/category/smart-contracts/> accessed 29 December 2018. Smart contract service providers (Clause, Legaler, LegalThings, Monax and OpenLaw) are reviewed by Artificial Lawyer at <www.artificiallaw yer.com/al-100-directory/smart-contracts/> accessed 29 December 2018.
82 Technology is already freely available which will obscure access to IP addresses. For example: "Kovri is a free, decentralized, anonymity technology developed by Monero. Currently based on I2P's open specifications, Kovri uses both garlic encryption and garlic routing to create a private, protected overlay-network across the internet. This overlay-network provides users with the ability to effectively hide their geographical location and internet IP address. Essentially, Kovri covers an application's internet traffic to make it anonymous within the network". <https://getkovri.org/> accessed 29 December 2018.
83 A detailed analysis of types of distributed ledger technology and their accessibility is outside the scope of this book. The following definitions are taken from Blockchain Beyond the Hype (n 2) 5 (1) *Permissionless, public, shared systems* are those that allow anyone to join the network, to write to the network and to read the transactions from those networks. These systems have no single owner – everyone on the network has an identical copy of the "ledger" (e.g. Bitcoin); (2) *Permissioned, public, shared systems* are a form of hybrid system that provide for situations where whitelisted access is required but all the transactions should be publicly viewable. Examples of this are government applications where only certain people should be able to write to the network but all transactions can be publicly verified; (3) *Permissioned, private, shared systems* are those that have whitelisted access, meaning that only those people with permission can read or write to such systems. They may have one or many owners – often consortia are formed to manage the ownership.

Patterns in blockchain transactions may be discerned, and precautionary measures can be introduced by blockchain service providers to block any transactions which arouse suspicion, but user identity (and hence ownership) remains anonymous.

> Arnold Spencer, former U.S. federal prosecutor and currently general counsel for Coinsource, cautions that avoiding taxes or concealing the nature, source, location, ownership or control of finances (elements of money laundering under U.S. law) is still entirely possible with blockchain technology. Both the government and the general public can use the blockchain to support their agendas, but neither can use blockchain to conquer the other. We need to remember that a government's power to investigate is only as strong as its power to compel or collect information. Although a government can obtain a copy of a decentralized blockchain, it cannot obtain the identity of a blockchain participant in a foreign country that refuses to cooperate (e.g., a tax haven).[84]

Advisors to the European Parliament writing in July 2018 seem oblivious to the potential for abuse of the blockchain stemming from its absence of a central authority, of an applicable legal system and of an external enforcement mechanism. Their focus of concern is cryptocurrency alone:

> As regards blockchain, it would be too blunt to associate blockchain with money laundering, terrorist financing or tax evasion. It is just technology, on which a large number of cryptocurrencies run, but which is not designed to launder money, facilitate terrorist financing or evade taxes. Blockchain has numerous applications throughout the whole lawful economy. It would not be wise to discourage future innovations in this respect by submitting blockchain and fintech's exploring its use cases to burdensome requirements, simply because of one of the applications using blockchain technology, cryptocurrencies, is used illicitly by some. Therefore, blockchain should be left untouched from a money laundering, terrorist financing and tax evasion perspective. The fight against money laundering, terrorist financing and tax evasion should focus on the illicit use cases of cryptocurrencies.[85]

Blockchain is however not "just technology, on which a large number of cryptocurrencies run". It is an unregulated, anonymised medium of international trade and commerce, immune to the laws which govern those practices in the non-virtual world, extending far beyond cryptocurrencies. To advocate that

---

84 Michael Chang, 'Blockchain Could Be a Powerful Tool for Shrinking Pervasive Global Money Laundering' *Entrepreneur* (19 July 2018) <www.entrepreneur.com/article/316691> accessed 29 December 2018.
85 Executive Summary to Robby Houben and Alexander Snyers, *Cryptocurrencies and Blockchain* (n 12).

blockchain transactions "should be left untouched from a money laundering, terrorist financing and tax evasion perspective" betrays a very limited understanding, bordering on the shamefully naïve.

### United States of America: Delaware – blockchain maintenance of corporate records

The State of Delaware is proud of its Division of Corporations:

> The State of Delaware is a leading domicile for U.S. and international corporations. More than 1,000,000 business entities have made Delaware their legal home. More than 66% of the Fortune 500 have chosen Delaware as their legal home. [. . .] The Delaware General Corporation Law is the most flexible business formation statute in the nation.[86]

An aspect of that flexibility is that the former Governor of Delaware, Jack Markell, on 2 May 2016 announced the Delaware Blockchain Initiative – "a comprehensive program to provide an enabling regulatory and legal environment for the development of blockchain technology and to welcome blockchain companies to locate in the state". This would include "clarifications of the Delaware corporate law to address and enable the authorization of 'distributed leger shares' by Delaware corporations. This move is especially significant given the state's role as the legal home of 66% of Fortune 500 companies, 85% of U.S. initial public offerings, and many startup and venture capital backed businesses around the world".[87]

Blockchain technology applied with an eye to wider regulatory issues has the potential to be a huge improvement on what Sujeet Indap calls "the current low-tech share bookkeeping system [which] is indirect and esoteric. It often struggles because assigning company shares to their underlying owners is not straightforward [. . .]":

> When stock trading exploded in the 1970s, moving around paper stock certificates became impractical. Banks and brokerages set up depositories and stocked them with jumbo certificates that represented bulk shares. Today, just one depository remains, DTC, and almost all US stock certificates are issued in the name of DTC's nominee, Cede & Co. Shares are fungible across institutions which have customer accounts. But that means that individuals are not quite official share owners. [. . .] In a blockchain ledger, the DTC layer is eliminated. Ownership rosters are updated transparently and in real time.[88]

---

86  <https://corp.delaware.gov/aboutagency/> accessed 29 December 2018.
87  <www.prnewswire.com/news-releases/governor-markell-launches-delaware-blockchain-initiative-300260672.html> accessed 29 December 2018.
88  Sujeet Indap, 'Blockchain Could Clean Up Messy Shareholder Registers' *Financial Times* (11 September 2017) <www.ft.com/content/f5cf21f6-935a-11e7-a9e6-11d2f0ebb7f0> accessed 29 December 2018.

Title 8 of the Delaware Code, Corporations, Chapter 1 General Corporation Law was duly amended on 1 August 2017 and now provides in section 224:[89]

> *224 Form of records.*
>
> Any *records administered by or on behalf of the corporation* in the regular course of its business, including its stock ledger, books of account, and minute books, may be kept on, or by means of, or be in the form of, any information storage device, method, or 1 or more electronic networks or databases (*including 1 or more distributed electronic networks or databases*), provided that the records so kept can be converted into clearly legible paper form within a reasonable time, and, with respect to the stock ledger, that the records so kept (i) can be used to prepare the list of stockholders specified in §§ 219 and 220 of this title, (ii) record the information specified in §§ 156, 159, 217(a) and 218 of this title, and (iii) record transfers of stock as governed by Article 8 of subtitle I of Title 6. Any corporation shall convert any records so kept into clearly legible paper form upon the request of any person entitled to inspect such records pursuant to any provision of this chapter. When records are kept in such manner, a clearly legible paper form prepared from or by means of the information storage device, method, or 1 or more electronic networks or databases (including 1 or more distributed electronic networks or databases) shall be valid and admissible in evidence, and accepted for all other purposes, to the same extent as an original paper record of the same information would have been, provided the paper form accurately portrays the record. [Emphasis added]

Absent from the text is now any reference to officers of a corporation having to be in charge of the securities register or of records having to be maintained by the corporation itself. The reference to records "administered by or on behalf of a corporation" ensures that blockchain technology can be used for these purposes instead of relying on a corporate officer. In short, private corporations incorporated in Delaware are now empowered to track share issues and transfers using blockchain.

There is however no guidance as to whether public "permissionless" blockchains or alternatively private "permissioned" blockchains are indicated. If the former, then all interested parties could view changes to a corporation's share ownership in real time, and registered ownership will be transparent. However, if the latter, then the ownership of Delaware corporations availing themselves of this new facility will become opaque and accessible only to those within the corporation itself or to authorised employees of the blockchain service provider which it engages.

---

89 <http://delcode.delaware.gov/title8/c001/sc07/> accessed 29 December 2018.

The implications for ownership transparency are obvious but merit repeating: there is every possibility that ownership of stocks and shares in such a corporation will be transient. There will be no involvement of the corporation's officers – and so no opportunity for a proposed transfer to be rejected as not being in the corporation's best commercial interests. Shareholders will have unrestricted liberty to trade their shares for all practical purposes unobserved. If challenged whether they own shares, a person can confidently reply that they did so ten minutes ago, and may do so again ten minutes from now, but, for the moment, they do not. This is neither a natural nor a necessary concomitant of blockchain share registers. Delaware has by sleight of hand allowed officers to slip the leash of corporate accountability. Perhaps unwittingly Delaware has handed to ultimate beneficial owners who wish to distance themselves from registered ownership an ever-changing, readily available cast of nominees able at a moment's notice – and without restraint – to pass the baton one to another.

## Initial Coin Offerings

### *The nature of an ICO and its associated risks*

The challenges posed by cryptocurrency in the identification of owners have become massively more fragmented and numerous with the rise of Initial Coin Offerings (also known as Initial Token Offerings) ("ICOs"). ICOs borrow the language of Initial Public Offerings[90] but are largely unregulated and are highly unstable as investments. The debate currently rages as to whether these ICOs should be regulated as securities offerings or whether in the alternative they are merely the sale of redeemable tokens akin to any store credit. Either way, the aim of the issuer of digital tokens (the branding of which is specific to the issuer) is to raise as much value as possible in the virtual world, to be converted into Bitcoin or ether or into fiat currency for use by the issuer to fund its commercial project.

> Most ICOs work by having investors send funds (usually bitcoin or ether) to a smart contract that stores the funds and distributes an equivalent value in the new token at a later point in time.[91] There are few, if any, restrictions on who can participate in an ICO, assuming that the token is not, in fact, a security. And since you're taking money from a global pool of investors, the sums raised in ICOs can be astronomical. A fundamental issue with ICOs is the fact that most of them raise money pre-product. This makes the

---

90 An Initial Public Offering is the process of offering shares in a corporation to the public for the first time – the issuer works closely with banks and underwriting firms to determine the number of shares, the form of the security to be offered and the offering price. IPOs are regulated as securities offerings. See John Jagerson, 'Initial Public Offering' – IPO *Investopedia* (7 December 2018) <www.investopedia.com/terms/i/ipo.asp> accessed 29 December 2018.
91 The smart contract takes the form of a branded digital token.

investment extremely speculative and risky. The counter argument is that this fundraising style is particularly useful (even necessary) in order to incentivize protocol development.[92]

*Ownership perspective*

From an ownership perspective the problem is immediately evident. If ICOs are to be regulated as securities offerings, then it is reasonable to expect that procedures for the identification of ownership in the relevant jurisdictions will be applicable, and anti-money laundering and the countering of the financing of terrorism, tax evasion, fraud, bribery and criminality generally will be addressed. However, if ICOs are not to be regulated as securities offerings, it will be a free for all.

> Legally, ICOs have existed in an extremely gray area because arguments can be made both for and against the fact that they're just new, unregulated financial assets. [ . . . ] In some cases, the token is simply a utility token, meaning it gives the owner access to a specific protocol or network; thus it may not be classified as a financial security. On the other hand, if the token is an equity token, meaning that its only purpose is to appreciate in value, then it looks a lot more like a security.[93]

The digital tokens, as smart contracts, can have attached to them any number of legal rights. They need not simply be tokens which can be exchanged for services offered by the issuer – something akin to a non-transferable purchase token[94] – but are capable of replicating the most sophisticated share and securities

---

92 *What Is an ICO?* (Bitcoin Magazine) <https://bitcoinmagazine.com/guides/what-ico/> accessed 29 December 2018.
93 Ibid. A detailed consideration of the case for and against the classification of ICO digital tokens as securities and associated investor risks is outside the scope of this book. See Dirk Zetzsche, Ross Buckley, Douglas Arner and Linus Föhr, 'The ICO Gold Rush: It's a Scam, It's a Bubble, It's a Super Challenge for Regulators' (24 July 2018). University of Luxembourg Law Working Paper No. 11/2017; UNSW Law Research Paper No. 17–83; University of Hong Kong Faculty of Law Research Paper No. 2017/035; European Banking Institute Working Paper Series 18/2018; 63 *Harvard International Law Journal* 2 (2019). SSRN:<https://ssrn.com/abstract=3072298> or <http://dx.doi.org/10.2139/ssrn.3072298> accessed 29 December 2018; Jonathan Rohr and Aaron Wright, 'Blockchain-Based Token Sales, Initial Coin Offerings, and the Democratization of Public Capital Markets' Cardozo Legal Studies Research Paper No. 527; University of Tennessee Legal Studies Research Paper No. 338 (4 October 2017). SSRN:<https://ssrn.com/abstract=3048104> or <http://dx.doi.org/10.2139/ssrn.3048104> accessed 29 December 2018; Philipp Hacker and Chris Thomale, 'Crypto-Securities Regulation: ICOs, Token Sales and Cryptocurrencies Under EU Financial Law' (22 November 2017). European Company and Financial Law Review Forthcoming. SSRN:<https://ssrn.com/abstract=3075820> or <http://dx.doi.org/10.2139/ssrn.30758200> accessed 29 December 2018.
94 A characteristic of which would have to be technical limitations to the transfer of token ownership which prevent the effective assignment of tokens to third parties.

offerings. The principal provider of such smart contracts is Etherium, which was launched in July 2015. Etherium offers a "design and issue your own cryptocurrency" service which makes clear that the holder of such cryptocurrency may have unlimited real-world property rights (whilst at the same time blurring the distinction between cryptocurrency and digital tokens): "Create a tradeable digital token that can be used as a currency, a representation of an asset, virtual shares, a proof of membership or anything at all. These tokens use a standard coin API so your contract will be automatically compatible with any wallet, other contract or exchange also using this standard".[95]

Here is the heart of the matter. Digital tokens, like cryptocurrency, are *bearer* instruments. The smart contract is freely transferable, and from the point of view of the issuer, whoever holds the private key to a given digital token is the owner.[96] Etherium digital tokens are tradable on so-called coin exchanges.[97] Ownership can swiftly pass from person to person, limited only by the speed of the blockchain itself. In order for the issuer to keep track of owners, the issuer will have to make an effort to trace back all transfers.[98] In the absence of regulation requiring

---

95 Etherium Blockchain App Platform <www.ethereum.org/> accessed 29 December 2018. Digital tokens therefore differ fundamentally from cryptocurrency. The sole purpose of a coin is to exchange value, and it has limited functionality beyond that. A digital token created in Etherium is a smart contract, which has a functionality beyond an exchange of value – it has the capacity to represent any asset.

96 "Owner" in this context does not mean that the holder of the digital token owns the issuer (which, were that person a shareholder, would be the case). There is no legal ownership stake in the issuer, but undoubtedly the holder of the digital token is in a position analogous to that of a shareholder from an economic perspective. "Even though some of the tokens issued as part of these ICOs bear some of the attributes of equity securities (bestowing voting rights or even rights to the issuer's 'profits'), they do not provide access to the capital of a commercial company. This said, tokens may be legally classed as equity securities if they bestow the same economic and governance rights as those traditionally attached to shares or preference shares". French Autorité des Marchés Financiers (AMF), 'Discussion Paper on Initial Coin Offerings (ICOs)' (26 October 2017) <www.amf-france.org/en_US/Publications/Consultationspubliques/Archives?docId=workspace%3A%2F%2FSpacesStore%2Fa2b 267b3-2d94-4c24-acad-7fe3351dfc8a> accessed 29 December 2018 7.

97 Coin exchanges (also known as crypto exchanges) take one of two forms. A centralised exchange is one where funds can be stored and exchanged – for example, Bitcoin for other coins and tokens. A decentralised exchange has no middleman, being automated and peer to peer, with an emphasis on privacy in a "trustless environment" driven by smart contracts. 'Crypto Trading, Explained' *Cointelegraph* (15 June 2018) <https://cointelegraph.com/explained/crypto-trading-explained> accessed 29 December 2018.

98 "As tokens come under many different forms, and as the law applicable to their transfer will vary from case to case, it is difficult to say in general whether good faith acquisition of tokens is possible.[. . .] However, the blockchain itself provides for a perfect substitute. It contains and cryptographically secures the exact chain of ownership for each and every issued token. Each transfer of ownership is transparently recorded on the blockchain. It is the very essence of tokenization that ownership of claims is inherently linked to tokens that are directly registered on the blockchain. Therefore, the criterion of sufficient protection against invalid transfer of ownership is clearly fulfilled in blockchain-based tokens". Philipp Hacker and Chris Thomale, 'Crypto-Securities Regulation: ICOs, Token Sales and Cryptocurrencies under EU Financial Law' (n 93) 22.

this, perhaps an issuer will simply take a commercially pragmatic approach and demur.

Describing the issuing of digital tokens as "a project with a trustless crowdsale" ("trustless" refers to automated, peer-to-peer transactions with no intermediary) Etherium comments:

> [W]ho would lend money to someone they don't trust? Using Etherium, you can create a contract that will hold a contributor's money until any given date or goal is reached. Depending on the outcome, the funds will either be released to the project or safely returned back to the contributors. All of this is possible without requiring a centralized arbitrator, clearinghouse or having to trust anyone.[99]

The contributor may be long gone, the digital token having been traded many times over. If the funds are returned, the likelihood of them being returned to the original contributor is questionable. Unless a coin exchange is required by law to update the issuer in real time as to who owns the traded digital token, the issuer will have no means of knowing to whom its obligations are owed. It is a system of ownership vulnerable to the most basic laundering and terrorist financing initiatives: A buys a digital token, transfers it to B (via however many other intermediate holders), and B receives from the issuer the original amount contributed. This is not to suggest that Etherium intends to promote or to facilitate criminal activity. Etherium is simply the medium.[100] Criminals are perfectly capable of identifying opportunities by themselves.

### *Ownership as an ICO regulatory criterion*

In 2018, substantial progress was made in addressing the "grey areas" of ICO regulation, and specifically the potential for ICOs to be used both as an ownership and as an accountability avoidance mechanism. For those jurisdictions not yet fully engaged in a regulatory process, the conceptual guidelines are becoming clearer.[101] Switzerland and the United States have tackled the issue of whether

---

99 Etherium Blockchain App Platform <ttps://www.ethereum.org/> accessed 29 December 2018.
100 Etherium's development is promoted and supported by the Etherium Foundation, a Swiss non-profit organisation: "The Ethereum Foundation's mission is to promote and support Ethereum platform and base layer research, development and education to bring decentralized protocols and tools to the world that empower developers to produce next generation decentralized applications (dapps), and together build a more globally accessible, more free and more trustworthy Internet". <www.ethereum.org/foundation> accessed 29 December 2018.
101 It is outside the scope of this book to deal in depth with the many and varied jurisdictional approaches to ICOs, which are at the present time tentative. The International Organization of Securities Commissions (IOSCO) in its Annual Report 2017 has published statements on ICOs which have been issued by Regulators in (inter alia) Abu Dhabi, Andorra,

ICOs ought to be regulated as security offerings (with the concomitant need to identify beneficial ownership seamlessly applied). Bermuda has introduced ICO-specific legislation requiring, inter alia, ICO ownership transparency.[102] Shariah law scholars have reimagined ICOs in terms of existing ownership and investment structures.

## Switzerland

On 16 February 2018 the Swiss Financial Market Supervisory Authority (FINMA) issued guidelines on how it intends to apply financial market legislation to ICOs, noting an increase in ICOs in Switzerland and the absence of ICO-specific regulation.

FINMA focusses on anti-money laundering and securities regulations:

> Money laundering risks are especially high in a decentralised blockchain-based system, in which assets can be transferred anonymously and without any regulated intermediaries.
>
> Securities regulation is intended to ensure that market participants can base their decisions about investments on a reliable minimum set of information.

FINMA follows what has become the standard triple classification of tokens:

- *Payment tokens* are synonymous with cryptocurrencies [. . .]. For ICOs where the token is intended to function as a means of payment and can already be transferred, FINMA will require compliance with anti-money laundering regulations. FINMA will not, however, treat such tokens as securities.
- *Utility tokens* are tokens which are intended to provide digital access to an application or service. These tokens do not qualify as securities only if their sole purpose is to confer digital access rights to an application or service and if the utility token can already be used in this way at the point of issue. If a utility token functions solely or partially as an investment in economic terms, FINMA will treat such tokens as securities (i.e. in the same way as asset tokens).

---

Argentina, Australia, Austria, Belgium, Brazil, Canada, China, Denmark, Dubai, European Union, France, Germany, Gibraltar, Hong Kong, Ireland, Isle of Man, Israel, Japan, Jersey, Kenya, Kuwait, Liechtenstein, Macau, Malaysia, Malta, Mexico, Netherlands, New Zealand, Poland, Portugal, Saudi Arabia, Singapore, Slovenia, Spain, Switzerland, Thailand, United Arab Emirates, United Kingdom and the United States <www.iosco.org/publications/?subsection=ico-statements> accessed 29 December 2018. In most cases these take the form of warnings, their primary focus being investor protection, or indicate that the jurisdiction concerned is contemplating the introduction of ICO-specific legislation.

102  See also the approach of the Isle of Man, adopting the designation and registration of virtual currency businesses (including ICOs), discussed in this chapter.

- *Asset tokens* represent assets such as participations in real physical underlyings [sic], companies, or earnings streams, or an entitlement to dividends or interest payments. In terms of their economic function, the tokens are analogous to equities, bonds or derivatives. FINMA regards asset tokens as securities, which means that there are securities law requirements for trading in such tokens, as well as civil law requirements under the Swiss Code of Obligations (e.g. prospectus requirements).[103]

The FINMA Guidelines in paragraph 3.7 expressly address the question of beneficial ownership transparency:

> Anti-money laundering regulation gives rise to a range of due diligence requirements including the requirement to establish the identity of the beneficial owner and the obligation either to affiliate to a self-regulatory organisation (SRO) or to be subject directly to FINMA supervision. These requirements can be fulfilled by having the funds accepted via a financial intermediary who is already subject to the AMLA[104] in Switzerland.[105]

International response to the Swiss initiative has not been unfavourable. The *Financial Times* at the date of the launch of the FINMA Guidelines suggested that the very nature of ICOs, cryptocurrency and underlying blockchain ledger technology, was "to facilitate tax avoidance, money laundering and fraud" and that in such a context the FINMA Guidelines "make broad sense".[106]

From 2019 a new Swiss FinTech licence[107] has been introduced under which small financial institutions (having gross revenues under CHF1.5 million) which accept public deposits of up to CHF100 million but which do not invest funds or pay interest will be subject to relaxed anti-money laundering requirements. Though the position is not entirely clear, ICOs are unlikely to

---

103 All the quotations from FINMA are taken from FINMA Press Release *FINMA publishes ICO guidelines* 16 February 2018 <www.finma.ch/en/news/2018/02/20180216-mm-ico-wegleitung/> accessed 29 December 2018.

104 Federal Act on Combating Money Laundering and Terrorist Financing (Anti-Money Laundering Act, AMLA) of 10 October 1997, in force 1 April 1998. A non-authoritative English translation together with an English/German/French/Italian language comparison is available at <www.admin.ch/opc/en/classified-compilation/19970427/index.htm> accessed 29 December 2018. See generally *Regulatory Aspects of Initial Coin Offerings (ICOs) in Switzerland* (Baker McKenzie, 2018) <www.bakermckenzie.com/en/-/media/files/insight/publications/2018/03/regulatory-aspects-ico-switzerland/br_switzerland_regulatoryaspectsico_mar2018.pdf> accessed 29 December 2018.

105 The full text of the Guidelines is hyperlinked from the FINMA Press Release (n 103).

106 'Bringing Swiss Order to Initial Coin Offerings' *Financial Times* (19 February 2018) <www.ft.com/content/36ef310c-1566-11e8-9e9c-25c814761640> accessed 29 December 2018.

107 FINMA Press Release *FinTech licence: FINMA publishes guidelines* <www.finma.ch/en/news/2018/12/20181203-aktuell-fintech-bewilligung/> accessed 29 December 2018. The full text of the FinTech Guidelines is hyperlinked from this press release.

be affected by the changes and will continue to be regulated under the FINMA Guidelines.[108]

## United States of America[109]

On 21 August 2018 the U.S. Securities and Exchange Commission ("SEC") issued generalised consumer guidance on ICOs.[110] Principally, "ICOs, based on specific facts, may be securities offerings, and fall under the SEC's jurisdiction of enforcing federal securities laws". On 11 December 2017 SEC Chairman Jay Clayton had issued a personal statement on cryptocurrencies and ICOs.[111]

> I believe that initial coin offerings – whether they represent offerings of securities or not – can be effective ways for entrepreneurs and others to raise funding, including for innovative projects. However, any such activity that involves an offering of securities must be accompanied by the important disclosures, processes and other investor protections that our securities laws require. A change in the structure of a securities offering does not change the fundamental point that when a security is being offered, our securities laws must be followed. Said another way, replacing a traditional corporate interest recorded in a central ledger with an enterprise interest recorded through a blockchain entry on a distributed ledger may change the form of the transaction, but it does not change the substance.
>
> [. . .] [C]ertain market professionals have attempted to highlight utility characteristics of their proposed initial coin offerings in an effort to claim that their proposed tokens or coins are not securities. Many of these assertions appear to elevate form over substance. Merely calling a token a "utility" token or structuring it to provide some utility does not prevent the token from being a security. Tokens and offerings that incorporate features and marketing efforts that emphasize the potential for profits based on the entrepreneurial or managerial efforts of others continue to contain the hallmarks of a security under U.S. law.

---

108 Brenna Hughes Neghaiwi, 'Swiss Watchdog to Propose Looser Anti-money Laundering Rules for Fintechs' *Reuters* (28 August 2018) <www.reuters.com/article/us-swiss-fintech/swiss-watchdog-to-propose-looser-anti-money-laundering-rules-for-fintechs-idUSKCN-1LD14W> accessed 29 December 2018.
109 A detailed account of the regulation of cryptocurrency and blockchain technologies at a state and federal level in the United States of America is outside the scope of this book. See Rosario Girasa, *Regulation of Cryptocurrencies and Blockchain Technologies: National and International Perspectives* (Palgrave Macmillan, New York, 2018).
110 <www.sec.gov/ICO> accessed 29 December 2018.
111 <www.sec.gov/news/public-statement/statement-clayton-2017-12-11> accessed 29 December 2018.

On 16 November 2018 the SEC issued a press release, announcing settled charges against two companies – CarrierEQ Inc (trading as Airfox)[112] and Paragon Coin Inc.[113] Both companies had sold digital tokens in ICOs. These are the SEC's first cases imposing civil penalties solely for ICO securities offering registration violations. The SEC's position is unambiguous:

> According to the SEC's orders, both CarrierEQ Inc. (Airfox) and Paragon Coin Inc. conducted ICOs in 2017 after the Commission warned that ICOs can be securities offerings in its DAO Report of Investigation.[114] Airfox, a Boston-based startup, raised approximately $15 million worth of digital assets to finance its development of a token-denominated "ecosystem" starting with a mobile application that would allow users in emerging markets to earn tokens and exchange them for data by interacting with advertisements. Paragon, an online entity, raised approximately $12 million worth of digital assets to develop and implement its business plan to add blockchain technology to the cannabis industry and work toward legalization of cannabis. Neither Airfox nor Paragon registered their ICOs pursuant to the federal securities laws, nor did they qualify for an exemption to the registration requirements. "We have made it clear that companies that issue securities through ICOs are required to comply with existing statutes and rules governing the registration of securities," said Stephanie Avakian, Co-Director of the SEC's Enforcement Division.[115]

Through the application of existing securities regulation, by analogy with the regulation of initial public offerings, the SEC seamlessly applies ownership and accountability criteria to ICOs.

## Bermuda

On 9 July 2018 the Companies and Limited Liability Company (Initial Coin Offering) Amendment Act 2018[116] came into force.[117] The accompanying

---

112 SEC Release No. 10575/ 16 November 2018 <www.sec.gov/litigation/admin/2018/33-10575.pdf> accessed 29 December 2018.

113 SEC Release No. 10574/ 16 November 2018 <www.sec.gov/litigation/admin/2018/33-10574.pdf> accessed 29 December 2018.

114 SEC Release No. 81207/ 25 July 2017 <www.sec.gov/litigation/investreport/34-81207.pdf> accessed 29 December 2018. This seminal analysis concluded that the tokens issued by DAO were securities, fulfilling the three criteria of an investment contract under s 2(a)(1) Securities Act of 1933 and s 3(a)(10) of the Securities Exchange Act of 1934, namely an investment of money in a common enterprise with a reasonable expectation of profits to be derived from the entrepreneurial or managerial efforts of others. (DAO refers to a Decentralised Autonomous Organisation, which is a term used to describe a "virtual" organisation embodied in computer code and executed on a distributed ledger or blockchain).

115 <www.sec.gov/news/press-release/2018-264> accessed 29 December 2018.

116 <www.bermudalaws.bm/laws/Annual%20Laws/2018/Acts/Companies%20and%20Limited%20Liability%20Company%20(Initial%20Coin%20Offering)%20Amendment%20Act%202018.pdf> accessed 29 December 2018.

117 Companies and Limited Liability Company (Initial Coin Offering) Amendment Act 2018 Commencement Day Notice 2018 <www.bermudalaws.bm/laws/Annual%20

Companies (Initial Coin Offering) Regulations 2018 ("ICO Regulations")[118] were published the following day. With this, Bermuda took an innovative lead in the regulation of ICOs, its methodology being to do so by close analogy with the regulation of initial public offerings. When examined in detail, the new regulatory regime – at least from an ownership transparency perspective – does have a distinctly "offshore lite" feel to it.

Only companies and limited liability companies formed under the Companies Act 1981[119] (new section 34B) or the Limited Liability Company Act 2016[120] (new section 85B) are permitted to issue an Initial Coin Offering in or from within Bermuda.

Initial Coin Offering is defined identically in the case both of companies (new section 34A Companies Act 1981) and limited liability companies (new section 85A Limited Liability Company Act 2016) as an offer to the public to purchase or otherwise acquire digital assets.

Digital assets are defined in those same sections as:

> "digital asset" means anything that exists in binary format and comes with the right to use it and includes a digital representation of value that –
>
> (a) is used as a medium of exchange, unit of account, or store of value and is not legal tender, whether or not denominated in legal tender;
> (b) is intended to represent assets such as debt or equity in the promoter;
> (c) is otherwise intended to represent any assets or rights associated with such assets; or
> (d) is intended to provide access to an application or service or product by means of blockchain;
>
> but does not include –
>
> (e) a transaction in which a person grants value as part of an affinity or rewards program, which value cannot be taken from or exchanged with the person for legal tender, bank credit or any digital asset; or
> (f) a digital representation of value issued by or on behalf of the publisher and used within an online game, game platform, or family of games sold by the same publisher or offered on the same game platform.

---

Laws/2018/Statutory%20Instruments/Companies%20and%20Limited%20Liability%20Company%20(Initial%20Coin%20Offering)%20Amendment%20Act%202018%20Commencement%20Day%20Notice%202018.pdf> accessed 29 December 2018.

118 <www.bermudalaws.bm/laws/Annual%20Laws/2018/Statutory%20Instruments/Companies%20(Initial%20Coin%20Offering)%20Regulations%202018.pdf> accessed 29 December 2018. There are as yet no separate Regulations for Limited Liability Companies.
119 <www.bermudalaws.bm/laws/consolidated%20laws/companies%20act%201981.pdf> accessed 29 December 2018.
120 <www.bermudalaws.bm/laws/Annual%20Laws/2016/Acts/Limited%20Liability%20Company%20Act%202016.pdf> accessed 29 December 2018.

From an ownership perspective, the new legislation is unambiguous. Both in relation to companies (new section 34H(1) Companies Act 1981) and limited liability companies (new section 85H(1) Limited Liability Company Act 2016):

1.   A company shall, in relation to an Initial Coin Offering, ensure that it applies appropriate measures relating to identification and verification of the identity of persons participating in the Initial Coin Offering.

Those "appropriate measures" are set out in Part 3, Compliance measures, of the ICO Regulations. A person's identity must be verified on the basis of documents, data or information obtained from a reliable and independent source, and in the case of a legal person those natural persons behind it must also be identified. The same applies to any person acting as a duly authorised representative (ICO regulation 9).

The ICO offeror must verify the identity of participants before the digital asset is issued: though this is a weak point in the legislation. The regulations suffer from internal inconsistencies and in addition leave a great deal to the discretion of the offeror at the point of issuance. ICO Regulation 10(3) provides:

3.   Such verification may be completed after the issue of a digital asset if –

   (a)   the rights and functionalities are such that the digital asset can only be used for services and products provided by the ICO issuer;
   (b)   this is necessary not to interrupt the normal conduct of business;
   (c)   there is little risk of money laundering or terrorist financing occurring, provided that the verification is completed as soon as practicable after the digital asset is issued;
   (d)   any money laundering or terrorist financing risks that may arise are effectively managed; and
   (e)   it appears that a participant, or any person purporting to act on behalf of the participant, is not or does not appear to be anonymous or fictitious.

In ICO Regulation 11 there is more than a hint of shutting the stable door after the horse has bolted. This requires an issuer who finds itself unable to apply appropriate measures not to transact with or issue digital assets to that person and to terminate any existing business relationship with that person. This begs the question, however, if the appropriate measures are taken after issuance under ICO Regulation 10(3) and only at that point a problem in verification becomes apparent, surely it is too late?

Under ICO Regulation 12 enhanced due diligence is required if a person or transaction is from a country identified by the FATF as having a higher risk or is a country which "represents a higher risk of money laundering, corruption, terrorist financing or [is] subject to international sanctions". The regulation adds "in any other situation which by its nature may present a higher risk of money laundering or terrorist financing" or where the issuer suspects this. The ICO

Regulations however provide no guidance as to whether the test is the subjective opinion of the issuer or whether it is objective in the sense that any issuer in possession of such information would consider enhanced due diligence necessary.

Announcing the coming of the new legislation, the Bermuda Minister of National Security announced:

> By being one of the few countries in the world to specifically regulate ICOs, we believe that the proposed regulatory framework will provide legal certainty to companies looking to conduct ICOs in Bermuda. [. . .] Embracing this new world with responsible regulation could lead to the attraction of new companies and capital investment to Bermuda; additional Government revenues; new career, employment and training opportunities for Bermudians; and the laying of a foundation for a prosperous future for our next generation of Bermudians. [. . .]This promises to be an exciting evolution for Bermuda, and we're pleased it's being carried forward with careful legislation, contemporary regulatory oversight, and most of all, the type of collaboration our market is renowned for.[121]

In short, driven by market forces, the ICO Regulations are not lacking in wiggle room.

### Shariah law analysis

> If the tokens entitle one to a *service*, use of something or utility on a protocol, then the utility tokens would be classified as al-Huquq al-'Urfiy yah (customary rights). According to the classical Maliki, Shafi'i and Hanbali jurists, such tokens would be classified as Māl (property). [. . .] *Equity tokens* represent a share in a company that has completed a token sale. This will be similar to trading in shares and investing in IPOs. [. . .] From a Shariah perspective, the same rulings which apply to shares will apply to equity tokens. A business activity screening and a financial screening will be required before investing in such an ICO or network. [. . .] If there are no assets whatsoever and the ICO is purely a crowd-funding exercise where the underlying assets in the ICO will be cash only, the pooling of resources together can possibly create a shirkat al-milk (co-ownership) of the pooled resources evidenced by the equity tokens. *Asset tokens* are digital tokens that represent a physical asset or product. The tokenisation of assets allows greater liquidity. Tokenisation is

---

121 Government of Bermuda, Department of Communications, Media Release, *Government Tables Landmark Legislation* 13 April 2018. Bermuda is far from being alone in seizing the commercial possibilities afforded by the new technology. See for example Nathaniel Popper, 'Have a Cryptocurrency? Bermuda, Malta or Gibraltar Wants You' *New York Times* (29 July 2018) <www.nytimes.com/2018/07/29/technology/cryptocurrency-bermuda-malta-gibraltar.html> accessed 29 December 2018. "Now the race is on to become the go-to destination for cryptocurrency companies that are looking for shelter from regulatory uncertainty in the United States and Asia".

effectively securitisation. The transfer of ownership and risk can be realised through the transfer of the tokens. The owner of the tokens will have constructive possession (Takhliya) as discussed in AAOIFI standard No.18 on possession (Qabd).[122] When trading such a token, the Shariah principles of buying and selling must be considered before trading such tokens.[123]

This analysis does not attempt to define what is meant by "owner" or to address the consequences of transient ownership, but by applying an existing legal analysis to ICOs, far more subtle than the simple securities/tokens dichotomy, Shariah law principles on ownership are imported.[124]

## Conclusions

Underlying any analysis of the role played by cryptocurrencies and by blockchain transactions in the avoidance of accountability is the problem of defining what ownership means and of beneficial ownership avoidance strategies.[125] Whether intentional or not, and whether or not it is the primary purpose, the very evolution of cryptocurrency technology and the blockchain compounds that problem. The new digital technology has the capacity to function as a counter-initiative to ownership transparency strategies and therefore as a means of avoiding accountability.

Cryptocurrencies represent a renaissance in the bearer security industry, unrestrained by geography or jurisdiction, and a facilitator of transient ownership and fraud. The identification of cryptocurrency users and holders is in itself complex, and a key holder is not necessarily an owner in any sense of the word. The availability of so-called anonymous coins presents an almost impenetrable barrier to ownership identification.

State regulation of cryptocurrencies consists in the main of consumer protective measures, from the perspective of platform security and investment volatility. No initiative reinvents the flawed FATF "golden standard" of what constitutes ownership. This is apparent in 5AMLD issued by the European Union, which in the opinion of the TAX3 Committee of the European Parliament leaves blind spots in the fight against money laundering, terrorist financing and tax evasion. FATF has barely addressed the problem, merely calling on its members to ensure that virtual asset service providers are regulated for the purposes of anti-money laundering and the countering of terrorist financing but acknowledging the FATF members' "flexibility" in how they go about this. One of the early innovators of

122 Accounting and Auditing Organization for Islamic Financial Institutions (AAOIFI), Shariah Standards (as at Safar 1439 A.H. – November 2018) <http://aaoifi.com/shariaa-standards/?lang=en> accessed 29 December 2018.
123 *Decoding Compliance of an Iconic Offering (ICO)* (Shariyah Review Bureau, April 2018) <https://islamicmarkets.com/publications/initial-coin-offerings-icos-shariah-compliance> accessed 29 December 2018.
124 For the Shariah law perspective on ownership see ch 2.
125 See chs 2 and 5.

state regulation, the Isle of Man, has brought the virtual currency sector within the ambit of its proceeds of crime legislation and imposed registration requirements on virtual currency service providers, but whether this approach finds favour globally remains to be seen.

Blockchain technology is seen as having incepted the Fourth Industrial Revolution. It goes far beyond cryptocurrencies, tokens and finance generally and will be applied across a broad spectrum of commercial activity. In particular, self-executing "smart contracts" are available and claimed to be traceable, transparent and irreversible. However, this is true only between the parties to the transaction but not to an observer – user identity (and hence ownership) remains anonymous. In the United States, Delaware has seized on this to create what amount to peer-to-peer share transfers which slip the leash of corporate accountability.

The challenges posed by cryptocurrency in the identification of owners have become massively more fragmented and numerous with the rise of Initial Coin Offerings. If these are to be regulated as securities offerings, as is the case in Switzerland and the United States, regulations analogous to those governing initial public offerings will apply. Anti-money laundering, the countering of the financing of terrorism, tax evasion, fraud, bribery and criminality generally will be addressed. If they are not to be regulated as securities, ICOs will be a free for all. ICO-specific legislation such as that introduced by Bermuda appears driven by market forces and has such a degree of in-built room to manoeuvre that the effective curtailment of abuse is far from certain. The more subtle and nuanced approach under Shariah law, closely identifying ICOs with existing legal structures, thereby importing Shariah law principles on ownership, may prove to be a more universal template.

## Bibliography

### *Legislation and regulations*

Anti-Money Laundering and Countering the Financing of Terrorism Code 2015 (as amended 2018) <www.iomfsa.im/media/1590/antimoneylaunderingandterrorist.pdf> accessed 29 December 2018 (Isle of Man)

Companies Act 1981 <www.bermudalaws.bm/laws/consolidated%20laws/compa nies%20act%201981.pdf> accessed 29 December 2018 (Bermuda)

Companies and Limited Liability Company (Initial Coin Offering) Amendment Act 2018 <www.bermudalaws.bm/laws/Annual%20Laws/2018/Acts/Compa nies%20and%20Limited%20Liability%20Company%20(Initial%20Coin%20Offer ing)%20Amendment%20Act%202018.pdf> accessed 29 December 2018 (Bermuda)

Companies (Initial Coin Offering) Regulations 2018 <www.bermudalaws.bm/laws/Annual%20Laws/2018/Statutory%20Instruments/Companies%20(Initial%20Coin%20Offering)%20Regulations%202018.pdf> accessed 29 December 2018 (Bermuda)

The Crown Dependencies Customs Union (Isle of Man) (EU Exit) Order 2018 <www.legislation.gov.uk/ukdsi/2018/9780111175156> accessed 29 December 2018 (UK/Isle of Man)

Designated Businesses (Registration and Oversight) Act 2015 <https://legislation. gov.im/cms/images/LEGISLATION/PRINCIPAL/2015/2015-0009/DesignatedBusinessesRegistrationandOversightAct2015_7.pdf> accessed 29 December 2018 (Isle of Man)

Federal Act on Combating Money Laundering and Terrorist Financing (Anti-Money Laundering Act, AMLA) of 10 October 1997. A non-authoritative English translation together with an English/German/French/Italian language comparison is available at <www.admin.ch/opc/en/classified-compilation/19970427/index. htm> accessed 29 December 2018 (Switzerland)

Limited Liability Company Act 2016 <www.bermudalaws.bm/laws/Annual%20 Laws/2016/Acts/Limited%20Liability%20Company%20Act%202016.pdf> accessed 29 December 2018 (Bermuda)

Proceeds of Crime Act 2008 <https://legislation.gov.im/cms/images/LEGISLATION/PRINCIPAL/2008/2008-0013/ProceedsofCrimeAct2008_18.pdf> accessed 29 December 2018 (Isle of Man)

Title 8 of the Delaware Code, Corporations, Chapter 1 General Corporation Law <http://delcode.delaware.gov/title8/c001/sc07/> accessed 29 December 2018 (Delaware, USA)

### European documents

European Banking Authority (4 July 2014) *EBA Opinion on 'Virtual Currencies'* EBA/Op/2014/08 <https://eba.europa.eu/documents/10180/657547/EBA-Op-2014-08+Opinion+on+Virtual+Currencies.pdf> accessed 29 December 2018
——— Roadmap on FinTech 15 March 2018 <https://eba.europa.eu/-/eba-publishes-its-roadmap-on-fintech> accessed 29 December 2018. The full text is at <https://eba.europa.eu/documents/10180/1919160/EBA+FinTech+Roadmap.pdf> accessed 29 December 2018

European Securities and Markets Authority, the European Banking Authority and the European Insurance and Occupational Pensions Authority Joint Warning (12 February 2018). The full text of the warning is available via a hyperlink contained in a press release dated 12 February 2018 issued by the European Securities and Markets Authority<www.esma.europa.eu/press-news/esma-news/esas-warn-consumers-risks-in-buying-virtual-currencies> accessed 29 December 2018

Fifth Anti Money Laundering Directive (Directive EU 2018/843 30 May 2018 <https://eur-lex.europa.eu/legal-content/EN/TXT/?qid=1540113903626&uri=CELEX:32018L0843>with the full text in English at <https://eur-lex.europa. eu/legal-content/EN/TXT/PDF/?uri=CELEX:32018L0843&qid=154011390 3626&from=EN> accessed 20 December 2018

Fourth Anti Money Laundering Directive (Directive EU 2015/849) <https://publications.europa.eu/en/publication-detail/-/publication/0bff31ef-0b49-11e5-8817-01aa75ed71a1/language-en> accessed 20 December 2018

Treaty of Accession of Denmark, Ireland and the United Kingdom 1972 <https:// eur-lex.europa.eu/legal-content/EN/TXT/PDF/?uri=OJ:L:1972:073:FULL&from=EN> (© European Union, https://eur-lex.europa.eu, 1998–2019) accessed 29 December 2018

*Treaty of Rome 1957* <https://ec.europa.eu/romania/sites/romania/files/tratatul_de_la_roma.pdf> accessed 29 December 2018

## International documents

Accounting and Auditing Organization for Islamic Financial Institutions (AAOIFI), Shariah Standards (as at Safar 1439 A.H. – November 2018) <http://aaoifi.com/shariaa-standards/?lang=en> accessed 29 December 2018

Financial Action Task Force, Recommendations 2012 <www.fatf-gafi.org/publica tions/fatfrecommendations/documents/fatf-recommendations.html> accessed 29 December 2018

——— Regulation of Virtual Assets (19 October 2018) <www.fatf-gafi.org/publica tions/fatfrecommendations/documents/regulation-virtual-assets.html> accessed 29 December 2018

*OECD Global Forum on Transparency and Exchange of Information for Tax Purposes: Isle of Man 2017 (Second Round)* <www.oecd.org/countries/isleofman/global-forum-on-transparency-and-exchange-of-information-for-tax-purposes-isle-of-man-2017-second-round-9789264283770-en.htm> accessed 29 December 2018

——— *Blockchain Primer* <www.oecd.org/finance/OECD-Blockchain-Primer.pdf> accessed 29 December 2018

——— Issues Paper *Blockchain Technology and Competition Policy* (8 June 2018) <https://one.oecd.org/document/DAF/COMP/WD(2018)47/en/pdf> accessed 29 December 2018

## Secondary sources

Artificial Lawyer *Smart Contracts* <www.artificiallawyer.com/category/smart-contracts/> accessed 29 December 2018

Autorité des Marchés Financiers (AMF) 'Discussion Paper on Initial Coin Offerings (ICOs)' (26 October 2017) <www.amf-france.org/en_US/Publications/Consultationspubliques/Archives?docId=workspace%3A%2F%2FSpacesStore%2Fa 2b267b3-2d94-4c24-acad-7fe3351dfc8a> accessed 29 December 2018

Baker McKenzie, *Regulatory Aspects of Initial Coin Offerings (ICOs) in Switzerland* (Baker McKenzie, 2018) <www.bakermckenzie.com/en/-/media/files/insight/publications/2018/03/regulatory-aspects-ico-switzerland/br_switzerland_regulatoryaspectsico_mar2018.pdf> accessed 29 December 2018

Banker, Paul 'Blockchain Can't Hide Cryptocurrency Revenues from the IRS' (CPA Practice Advisor, 14 December 2018) <www.cpapracticeadvisor.com/arti cle/12437776/blockchain-cant-hide-cryptocurrency-revenues-from-the-irs> accessed 29 December 2018

Binham, Caroline 'EU Body Strikes Back at Cryptocurrency Regulation' *Financial Times* (9 March 2018) <www.ft.com/content/bc48eafc-2301-11e8-ae48-60d3531b7d11> accessed 29 December 2018

Bohannon, John 'Why Criminals Can't Hide Behind Bitcoin' *Science* (9 March 2016) <www.sciencemag.org/news/2016/03/why-criminals-cant-hide-behind-bitcoin> accessed 29 December 2018

Chang, Michael 'Blockchain Could Be a Powerful Tool for Shrinking Pervasive Global Money Laundering' *Entrepreneur* (19 July 2018) <www.entrepreneur.com/article/316691> accessed 29 December 2018

Cointelegraph 'Crypto Trading, Explained' *Cointelegraph* (15 June 2018) <https://cointelegraph.com/explained/crypto-trading-explained> accessed 29 December 2018

*Decoding Compliance of an Iconic Offering (ICO)* (Shariyah Review Bureau, April 2018) <https://islamicmarkets.com/publications/initial-coin-offerings-icos-shariah-compliance> accessed 29 December 2018

Delaware Blockchain Initiative, Statement of Former Governor of Delaware, Jack Markell, on 2 May 2016 <www.prnewswire.com/news-releases/governor-markell-launches-delaware-blockchain-initiative-300260672.html> accessed 29 December 2018

Duffield, Evan and Diaz, Daniel *Dash: A Payment-Focussed Cryptocurrency* <https://github.com/dashpay/dash/wiki/Whitepaper> accessed 29 December 2018

Financial Stability Board, *Crypto-asset Markets: Potential Channels for Future Financial Stability Implications* (10 October 2018) 14 <www.fsb.org/wp-content/uploads/P101018.pdf> accessed 29 December 2018

*Financial Times*, 'Bringing Swiss Order to Initial Coin Offerings' *Financial Times* (19 February 2018) <www.ft.com/content/36ef310c-1566-11e8-9e9c-25c814761640> accessed 29 December 2018

FINMA Guidelines on Initial Coin Offerings (16 February 2018) (Swiss Financial Market Supervisory Authority) <www.finma.ch/en/news/2018/02/20180216-mm-ico-wegleitung/> accessed 29 December 2018

——— FinTech licence, guidelines (2019) FINMA Press Release *FinTech licence: FINMA publishes guidelines* <www.finma.ch/en/news/2018/12/20181203-aktuell-fintech-bewilligung/> accessed 29 December 2018

Girasa, Rosario *Regulation of Cryptocurrencies and Blockchain Technologies: National and International Perspectives* (Palgrave Macmillan, 2018)

Hacker, Philipp and Thomale, Chris 'Crypto-Securities Regulation: ICOs, Token Sales and Cryptocurrencies Under EU Financial Law' (22 November 2017). European Company and Financial Law Review Forthcoming. SSRN:<https://ssrn.com/abstract=3075820> or <http://dx.doi.org/10.2139/ssrn.30758200> accessed 29 December 2018

Hileman, Garrick and Rauchs, Michel *Global Cryptocurrency Benchmarking Study* (Cambridge Centre for Alternative Finance, University of Cambridge Judge Business School, Cambridge, 2017)

Houben, Robby and Snyers, Alexander *Cryptocurrencies and Blockchain: Legal Context and Implications for Financial Crime, Money Laundering and Tax Evasion* (European Parliament, Policy Department for Economic, Scientific and Quality of Life Policies, Brussels, July 2018)

House of Commons Treasury Committee (United Kingdom Parliament), *Crypto-assets* <https://publications.parliament.uk/pa/cm201719/cmselect/cmtreasy/910/910.pdf> accessed 29 December 2018

Hutt, Rosamond *All You Need to Know About Blockchain, Explained Simply* (World Economic Forum, 17 June 2016) <www.weforum.org/agenda/2016/06/blockchain-explained-simply/> accessed 29 December 2018

Illinois Blockchain Initiative <https://sites.google.com/view/blockchain-govt-tracker> accessed 29 December 2018 and available in tabular form at <https://airtable.com/shreIXQjzluCxam37/tbl7qVDFKKiEcFFrc> accessed 29 December 2018

Indap, Sujeet 'Blockchain Could Clean Up Messy Shareholder Registers' *Financial Times* (11 September 2017) <www.ft.com/content/f5cf21f6-935a-11e7-a9e6-11d2f0ebb7f0> accessed 29 December 2018

International Organization of Securities Commissions (IOSCO) Annual Report 2017 <www.iosco.org/publications/?subsection=ico-statements> accessed 29 December 2018

Isle of Man Financial Services Authority, *Virtual Currency Business: Sector Specific AML/CFT Guidance Notes* (October 2016) <www.iomfsa.im/media/1606/virtualcurrencyguidance.pdf> accessed 29 December 2018

———— Designated Business Registration Policy (Version 4, 5 October 2018) <www.iomfsa.im/media/1424/dnfbpregistrationpolicy.pdf> accessed 29 December 2018

———— *Questions & Answers in Respect of Persons Seeking to Launch an Initial Coin Offering in or from The Island* (Updated 5 October 2018) <www.iomfsa.im/media/2365/icoguidanceforapplicants.pdf> accessed 29 December 2018

Kharpal, Arjun 'Cryptocurrencies: Regulating the New Economy' *CNBC* (9 August 2018) <www.cnbc.com/2018/08/09/cryptocurrencies--regulating-the-new--economy.html> accessed 29 December 2018

Lansky, Jan 'Possible State Approaches to Cryptocurrencies' *Journal of Systems Integration* 1, 19 (2018) <www.researchgate.net/publication/322869220_Possible_State_Approaches_to_Cryptocurrencies> accessed 29 December 2018

The Law Library of Congress, *Regulation of Cryptocurrency Around the World* (The Law Library of Congress, Global Legal Research Centre, June 2018) 1 <www.loc.gov/law/help/cryptocurrency/cryptocurrency-world-survey.pdf> accessed 29 December 2018

Mandjee, Tara 'Bitcoin, Its Classification and Its Regulatory Framework' 15 *Journal of Business & Securities Law* 2, 158 (2015)

Matsuura, Jeffrey H *Digital Currency: An International Legal and Regulatory Compliance Guide* (Bentham Science Publishers Ltd, Sharjah, UAE, 2016)

McKee, Michael DLA Piper *Regulation of Virtual Currencies* (15 May 2018) <www.ucl.ac.uk/laws/sites/laws/files/02_mckee_ucl-blockchain.pdf> accessed 29 December 2018

Monaghan, Angela 'Time to Regulate Bitcoin, Says Treasury Committee Report' *The Guardian* (19 September 2018) <www.theguardian.com/technology/2018/sep/19/time-to-regulate-bitcoin-says-treasury-committee-report> accessed 29 December 2018

Neghaiwi, Brenna Hughes 'Swiss Watchdog to Propose Looser Anti-money Laundering Rules for Fintechs' *Reuters* (28 August 2018) <www.reuters.com/article/us-swiss-fintech/swiss-watchdog-to-propose-looser-anti-money-laundering-rules-for-fintechs-idUSKCN1LD14W> accessed 29 December 2018

Norton Rose Fulbright, *Deciphering Cryptocurrencies* (Norton Rose Fulbright, 2015–2016) <https://knowledgeproducts.nortonrosefulbright.com/nrf/deciphering-cryptocurrencies> accessed 29 December 2018

———— *Unlocking the Blockchain* (Norton Rose Fulbright, 2018) <https://knowledgeproducts.nortonrosefulbright.com/nrf/unlocking-the-blockchain> accessed 29 December 2018

Popper, Nathaniel 'Have a Cryptocurrency? Bermuda, Malta or Gibraltar Wants You' *New York Times* (29 July 2018) <www.nytimes.com/2018/07/29/technology/cryptocurrency-bermuda-malta-gibraltar.html> accessed 29 December 2018

Rohr, Jonathan and Wright, Aaron 'Blockchain-based Token Sales, Initial Coin Offerings, and the Democratization of Public Capital Markets' Cardozo Legal Studies Research Paper No. 527; University of Tennessee Legal Studies Research

Paper No. 338 (4 October 2017). SSRN: <https://ssrn.com/abstract=3048104> or<http://dx.doi.org/10.2139/ssrn.3048104> accessed 29 December 2018

Sagar, Leigh *Fighting Over Nothing: Cryptocurrency Litigation Issues* <www.chba.org.uk/for-members/library/overseas-seminars/cryptocurrency-litigation-issues> accessed 29 December 2018

U.S. Securities and Exchange Commission, Consumer Guidance on Initial Coin Offerings (21 August 2018) <www.sec.gov/ICO> accessed 29 December 2018

——— DAO Report of Investigation SEC Release No. 81207/ 25 July 2017 <www.sec.gov/litigation/investreport/34-81207.pdf> accessed 29 December 2018

——— Press Release on CarrierEQ Inc (trading as Airfox) SEC Release No. 10575/ 16 November 2018 <www.sec.gov/litigation/admin/2018/33-10575.pdf> accessed 29 December 2018

——— Press Release on Paragon Coin Inc. SEC Release No. 10574/ 16 November 2018 <www.sec.gov/litigation/admin/2018/33-10574.pdf> accessed 29 December 2018

*What Is an ICO?* (Bitcoin Magazine) <https://bitcoinmagazine.com/guides/what-ico/> accessed 29 December 2018

World Economic Forum, *Blockchain Beyond the Hype: A Practical Framework for Business Leaders* (World Economic Forum, April 2018) <http://www3.weforum.org/docs/48423_Whether_Blockchain_WP.pdf 7> accessed 29 December 2018

——— *Blockchain and Distributed Ledger Technology* (World Economic Forum Centre for the Fourth Industrial Revolution) <www.weforum.org/communities/blockchain-and-distributed-ledger-technology> accessed 29 December 2018

Zetzsche, Dirk Buckley, Ross Arner, Douglas and Föhr, Linus 'The ICO Gold Rush: It's a Scam, It's a Bubble, It's a Super Challenge for Regulators' (24 July 2018). University of Luxembourg Law Working Paper No. 11/2017; UNSW Law Research Paper No. 17–83; University of Hong Kong Faculty of Law Research Paper No. 2017/035; European Banking Institute Working Paper Series 18/2018; 63 *Harvard International Law Journal* 2 (2019). SSRN: <https://ssrn.com/abstract=3072298> or <http://dx.doi.org/10.2139/ssrn.3072298> accessed 29 December 2018

### Further bibliographies

*Blockchain & Society* <https://blockchain-society.science/blockchain-bibliography/> accessed 29 December 2018

*Cite This for Me* <www.citethisforme.com/topic-ideas/technology/Cryptocurrency-47844035> accessed 29 December 2018

*CryptoLawReview*<https://medium.com/cryptolawreview/blockchain-governance-bibliography-360efc52d3f9> accessed 29 December 2018

Franco, Pedro *Understanding Bitcoin: Cryptography, Engineering and Economics* (John Wiley & Sons Ltd., 2015) the bibliography for which is <https://onlinelibrary.wiley.com/doi/pdf/10.1002/9781119019138.biblio accessed 29 December 2018>

Johansen, Stephan K *A Comprehensive Literature Review on the Blockchain as a Technological Enabler for Innovation* (Mannheim University, Department of Information Systems, November 2016) <www.researchgate.net/publication/312592741_A_Comprehensive_Literature_Review_on_the_Block

chain_Technology_as_an_Technological_Enabler_for_Innovation> accessed 29 December 2018

Perani, Giovanni *Blockchain: Bibliography* (Queen Mary University of London, School of Law) <www.diritto.net/blockchain-bibliography/> accessed 29 December 2018

# 7 Concluding Recommendations

In the previous six chapters various issues have been highlighted which both lend themselves to further academic research and demonstrate a pressing need for action to be taken. In this chapter the author presents his overarching conclusions, and outlines his research recommendations for future scholars and his policy recommendations to states, international organisations and other stakeholders.

Whether viewed from the perspective of the common law, civil law or Shariah law, ownership is a complex, multi-layered and shape-shifting concept, which only grudgingly lends itself to deconstruction. Beneficial ownership on closer examination proves incapable of exact legal definition.

These challenges are compounded by attempts on the part of non-Islamic regulators to construct a working definition of ownership, employing convenient fictions and flying in the face of legal and equitable principles. Islamic regulators seek to apply existing Shariah concepts of ownership to structures and situations which could not have been in contemplation when those Shariah concepts were developed.

Added to this is the burgeoning global industry in beneficial ownership avoidance structures, which are designed with the express purpose of removing altogether anyone approaching the status of an "owner" from the equation. In so doing, the promotors of these chimera empower their clients neatly to sidestep ownership-based regulatory systems.[1]

Surely there should come a point when if a hypothesis proves unworkable, another should be substituted. Nevertheless, "ownership" has been chosen by national and international regulators as the touchstone, the litmus test in the fight back against tax evasion, money laundering, organised crime, terrorism, bribery, corruption and gross human rights abuses. The prevailing assumptions are that an owner by definition must possess something for which they are accountable and that everything is owned.

---

1 An international (more accurately, meta-jurisdictional) counter strategy to beneficial ownership avoidance, employing human rights principles, is discussed in Paul Beckett, *Tax Havens and International Human Rights* (Routledge, London and New York, 2017).

The conclusion is self-evident. The fundamental weakness of this approach is that it stakes everything on the turn of a single card: ownership. Constructing a regulatory system on ownership is to build on sand.

## Recommendation 1

Members of the G20 must revisit the 2014 G20 High-Level Principles on Beneficial Ownership Transparency, which are not fit for purpose. The principles are not so much "high level" as stratospheric and are vague to the point of not addressing the definition of "beneficial ownership" at all. Confining these principles to reviews of nominee shareholdings and shadow directors – tools of the seventies and eighties – and to the registration of beneficial owners shows a lack of awareness on the part of the draftspersons of the range and complexity of avoidance options available in the tax havens. The High-Level Principles themselves are vague and overlapping: aspirational but lacking any implementation strategy. By existing in this inadequate form, the High-Level Principles fill a political space which should be better occupied. The members of the G20 refer to them as if they are the last word on the subject, when clearly the problem of beneficial ownership avoidance has yet to be addressed.

## Recommendation 2

The FATF Recommendations make a brave stab at a universal standard definition of "beneficial owner", which begins to fall apart when applied to trusts and which in adopting a 25% ownership threshold gives a get-out-of-jail free card to any structure with more than four "owners". The ineptitude of the FATF approach then permeates and fatally undermines registration and disclosure initiatives – not the least of which are those of the OECD, the European Union, the Council of Europe MONEYVAL and the Islamic Financial Services Board. Each of them adopts the FATF Recommendations unquestioningly as if they were a "gold standard". The FATF should undertake an impact assessment of its methodology. Weak links in chains do not come much weaker than this.

## Recommendation 3

The United States of America in FATCA by focussing on US persons simply shifts to the foreign jurisdictions in which those US persons are resident the burden of determining how a US person is connected to any structure or could in any sense be considered an owner. If they have stayed at home, FATCA allows them to self-certify, even where their declaration is that *no one* is the beneficial owner – assertions which go unchecked. Self-certification *as a US person* provides no guidance as to whether that person is in any sense an *owner* of a given entity. FATCA provides *no methodology* as to how any specified US person is deemed connected to a structure. Having to apply local client due diligence procedures to identify whether or not a specified US person can be regarded as an owner or investor will lead to significant inconsistencies given the multiplicity (and, often, inadequacy) of definitions of "beneficial owner" across many regulatory systems. FATCA is, in addition, blind to the possibility that a structure may be *ownerless*. FATCA should be augmented by the introduction of ownership identification criteria – but should not compound the difficulties of their present absence by slavishly following the flawed FATF "golden standard".

## Recommendation 4

The European Union Fifth Anti-Money Laundering Directive (Directive EU 2018/843 30 May 2018) (5AMLD) updates the rules regarding the identification of the beneficial owners of companies and other legal persons and of trusts. 5AMLD does not however really get to grips with what it means by "beneficial owners" and does not evidence any understanding that ownership is not a normative concept and, what is more, may be absent altogether. 5AMLD in Recital 4 takes a diplomatically worded side-swipe at the implementational shortcomings of the methodologies employed by the FATF and the OECD. In recital 26 5AMLD expressly acknowledges the difficulties posed by multiple legal systems in the EU with regard to trusts, many such systems being ignorant of them. The EU is therefore aware of the challenges yet to be addressed. The EU ought not to lose momentum but should urgently implement consultation across its member states to augment and remedy 5AMLD.

## Recommendation 5

The growing use of so-called "orphaned structures" (such as non-charitable purpose trusts and the Bahamas Enterprise Entity), specifically designed to facilitate accountability avoidance and aggressively marketed to promote this, should be curbed. None of these structures is born of domestic need in the jurisdictions which have adopted them, perhaps other than a desire to boost the incomes of their financial and fiduciary sectors (to which many if not all tax havens find themselves in thrall). Compounding the problem, there is a general unawareness of these structures other than within the charmed circle of the tax havens themselves and on the part of those who operate through the tax havens. In September 2016 and again in September 2018 the author gave presentations on beneficial ownership avoidance counter-strategies to groups of distinguished corporate and commercial law and tax specialist academics at the Annual Conference of the Society of Legal Scholars. None of those present had heard of non-charitable purpose trusts or of the concept of beneficial ownership avoidance. Just how many elephants have to be in the room before someone notices?

## Recommendation 6

Underlying any analysis of the role played by cryptocurrencies and by blockchain transactions in the avoidance of accountability is the problem of defining what ownership means and of beneficial ownership avoidance strategies. Whether or not evasive by intention, and whether or not it is the primary purpose, the very evolution of cryptocurrency technology and the blockchain compounds that problem. The new digital technology has the capacity to function as a counter-initiative to ownership transparency strategies and therefore as a means of avoiding accountability. The challenges posed by cryptocurrency in the identification of owners have become massively more fragmented and numerous with the rise of Initial Coin Offerings (ICOs). In the case of initial public offerings (IPOs) of shares and other securities, sophisticated consumer protection measures are applied. In this way, anti-money laundering, the countering of the financing of terrorism, tax evasion, fraud, bribery and criminality generally will be addressed. ICOs should follow the IPO model (which is already the case in Switzerland and the United States). If they are not to be regulated as securities, ICOs will be a free for all.

## Recommendation 7

The apparently "outlaw" characteristics of blockchain transactions – specifically, the transfer of ownership by means of smart contracts which are governed by the laws of no jurisdiction and which therefore exist independently of any legal or regulatory enforcement mechanism – should be the subject of further study. Are, in their present state, international arrangements which determine the legal forum of any given transaction sufficient to encompass the blockchain?

## Recommendation 8

A detailed comparative study of what is meant by "ownership" in the world's three primary legal systems – the common law, civil law and Shariah law – should be undertaken, jurisdiction by jurisdiction. A good start would be to apply the principles of Kelsen and of Wittgenstein which are referred to in chapter 2. This study should include a critical analysis of the pragmatic ownership constructs being put forward by international regulators and the extent to which such artificiality may cause regulatory systems to fail or to underperform.

# Index

Printed in Great Britain
by Amazon